A Conqueri

Fire Ant Books

A Conquering Spirit

Fort Mims and the Redstick War of 1813–1814

GREGORY A. WASELKOV

THE UNIVERSITY OF ALABAMA PRESS
Tuscaloosa

A DAN JOSSELYN MEMORIAL PUBLICATION

Typeface: Minion and Stone Sans

∞

The paper on which this book is printed meets the minimum requirements of American
National Standard for Information Sciences-Permanence of Paper for Printed Library
Materials, ANSI Z39.48-1984.

Publication of this book is made possible in part by support from the College of Arts
and Sciences and the Center for Archaeological Studies, University of South Alabama.

Library of Congress Cataloging-in-Publication Data

Waselkov, Gregory A.
A conquering spirit : Fort Mims and the Redstick War of 1813–1814 / Gregory A. Waselkov.
p. cm.
Includes bibliographical references and index.
ISBN-13: 978-0-8173-1491-0 (cloth : alk. paper)
ISBN-10: 0-8173-1491-1
ISBN-13: 978-0-8173-5573-9 (pbk : alk. paper)
ISBN-10: 0-8173-5573-1
1. Creek War, 1813–1814. 2. Massacres—Alabama—Fort Mims—History. 3. Fort Mims
(Ala.)—History. I. Title.
E83.813.W37 2006
973.5′ 238—dc22
                                                                    2006003877

Contents

Illustrations

Figures

Plates (following p. 212)

Kinship Charts

Tables

Introduction

September 11, 2001 . . . December 7, 1941 . . . "Remember the *Lusitania!*" . . . "Remember the *Maine!*" . . . "Remember the Alamo!" Every generation of Americans, it seems, has collectively experienced an event of such palpable violence and manifest injustice that the very mention rallies the nation to a common purpose, a bloody-minded determination to destroy this new enemy and avenge the fallen. With the passage of years, however, earlier national traumas fade in emotional impact, each in turn replaced in the country's consciousness by more immediate, more horrific insults. Historical perspective can also lead to reevaluations of events thought patently evil at the time. The explosion that sank the U.S. battleship *Maine* in Havana harbor, directly precipitating an American declaration of war against Spain in 1898, may have been due to a shipboard accident rather than a bomb planted by either Cuban provocateurs or Spanish agents, as originally supposed.[1] The civilian cruise liner R.M.S. *Lusitania,* torpedoed by a German U-boat while bound for England with numerous neutral American passengers in 1915—an event that contributed to America's eventual entry into World War I—may have carried contraband munitions, British denials at the time notwithstanding.[2] And historians argue endlessly over the reasons some 200 Texan revolutionaries chose to defend the Alamo to the death in 1836 rather than withdraw in the face of Santa Anna's overwhelming Mexican force.[3] These epochal moments invite continuing intellectual scrutiny for their influence on the course of American history. Why and how did they pull us collectively in new national directions, ending in the acquisition of an overseas colonial empire, involvement in a European war, and American expansion at the expense of Mexico (still a contentious issue for our neighbors to the south)? But, of course, they appeal at another level: they kindle the imagination and excite emotions as tales of intense human interest.

The battle at Fort Mims was one such turning point in American history. At noon on August 30, 1813, a fiercely fought battle occurred on the southern frontier of the United States, at the fortified plantation home of Samuel Mims in the Tensaw district of Mississippi Territory (in modern-day Alabama). Amidst the War of 1812, America's second struggle against Great Britain, a large segment of the Creek Indian nation, the Redsticks, rose up to defend their lands and their traditional culture from U.S. encroachment and domination. The battle of Fort Mims is best known in that context, as a stunningly bloody Indian victory, but just one in a very long series of armed conflicts between American Indians and whites spanning four centuries. If that is the extent of our understanding of Fort Mims, then we do not grasp why that event came about or how it influenced the course of United States history in many important ways. One task here is to look closely at the battle, to cut through the legends and misinformation that have grown around this event almost from the moment the last embers died at the smoldering ruins of Fort Mims. At least as important as the details of battle, though, are the remarkable convergence of social forces that sparked that conflict and the repercussions of the battle, which echo still, nearly 200 years later.

The extreme violence that erupted at Fort Mims on that late summer day in 1813, the horror of 250 or more soldiers and refugees—men, women, and children—immolated in buildings set ablaze by the Redsticks, has long claimed the nation's attention for a permanent place in our collective historical memory. But memory registers more than emotional shock and anguish. Events such as this have great moment because peoples' thoughts and behaviors change in response. The prevailing attitude of white Americans toward Indians shifted significantly in the aftermath of the battle, away from the government's policy of cultural assimilation and toward a new style of American colonialism. We are not yet accustomed to that notion, despite a generation of consciousness-raising by American Indians and others in the popular media and scholarly literature. The expansion of the United States involved not just the purchase of vast land tracts from European and Mexican claimants but the imposition of American colonial rule on the indigenous Indian nations that occupied (and actually owned) those lands. A study of this battle and the ensuing Redstick War offers an opportunity to explore, from that still novel perspective, a stunning failure in American colonial policy toward the Creek Indians, well-meaning though its intentions surely were. This well-documented battle also permits a close examination of the Creeks themselves, a numerous and ethnically complex people who inhabited a large portion of the American Southeast at the turn of the nineteenth century. Historians are currently engaged in an important debate on the rise of the concept of race in Indian societies of that era, and the Redstick War figures prominently in that ongoing dialogue. The open gate at Fort Mims beckons us to confront these and other neglected facets of our common past.

~

This book's title, *A Conquering Spirit,* derives from correspondence written on September 30, 1813, precisely one month after the engagement at Fort Mims, by Benjamin Hawkins, since 1796 the federal government's Principal Agent for Indian Affairs South of the Ohio. Hawkins invoked Indian imagery recalling the ferocity of Gulf coast hurricanes, both surprising (before our era of satellite imagery) and devastating in their impact. To General John Floyd of the Georgia state militia he wrote, the "master of breath," supreme deity of the Creek Indians, "has permited a conquering spirit to arise among them like a storm and it shall ravage like a storm."[4] Hawkins alluded to Redstick warriors exhilarated by their success at Fort Mims. But "a conquering spirit" reveals equally well the psyche of General Andrew Jackson and other white Americans who saw in the tragedy of Fort Mims at once a national disaster and an opportunity to seize vast expanses of Indian lands by conquest. Thousands in Tennessee, the Carolinas, Georgia, and Mississippi Territory volunteered, in Jackson's words, to "carry a campaign into the heart of the Creek nation and exterminate them."[5]

Yet another conquering spirit arose in the battle's aftermath. As we shall see, the conflict that erupted at Fort Mims resulted from the colliding interests of four peoples: settlers of European descent, the Native American Creeks, African Americans (held in slavery by both whites and Indians), and the mixed-race offspring of the other three. Some thirty years earlier, former British loyalists had sought a haven at this southern limit of the Creek nation following the loss of their homes in the Carolinas, Georgia, and Florida during the American Revolution. In ensuing years, a few Creek Indians—nearly all of mixed European-Indian descent—settled nearby, where they might freely embrace the plantation economy of their white neighbors, far from the social controls of traditional Creek culture. Ultimately, rejection of American pressures (by a large segment of the Creek people) to assimilate and cede their lands to the expanding United States took violent form, in a five-hour battle between at least 700 Redstick warriors and a besieged garrison of 100 militiamen from

Mississippi Territory and the 300 white, Creek, and African civilians they were sent to protect. In its final stage, the fight at Fort Mims degenerated into a massacre of civilians by Redsticks.

In the ashes of Fort Mims we can read the failure of these groups to coexist. As they sought new ways forward in the wake of war's destructive fury, we can also appreciate the resilient spirits of these diverse peoples.

Creek Indians in a Changing Colonial World

The two decades preceding the battle at Fort Mims brought radical upheaval to the lives of Creek Indians. In the span of a single generation a populous, expansion-minded United States colonized the Creek country more intrusively and completely than the French, British, and Spaniards had ever imagined doing in the previous two centuries. To understand the traumatic events of 1813, one must grasp the nature of Creek culture and society in earlier days and the wrenching changes forced upon the Creeks by their powerful neighbor. Fortunately we can draw on a century of fine scholarship to outline and interpret this complex subject in brief.

By the end of the American Revolutionary War in 1783, the diverse peoples that composed the Creek nation had been in contact with Europeans for two and a half centuries. The first foray by Spaniards into the heart of the Southeast was Hernando de Soto's *entrada* of 1539. In the wake of that failed attempt at conquest, Spain established modest settlements and missions in Florida that maintained sporadic interaction with the native peoples of the interior Southeast throughout the late sixteenth and seventeenth centuries. These intermittent contacts introduced several Old World organisms into the region, most notably some disease pathogens that devastated previously unexposed Indian populations, along with benign cultigens like the peach and black-eyed pea.[6]

As interior southeasterners became familiar with the technologies and desires of the Spaniards to their south, a small-scale trade developed between the two peoples. Common forest products like deerskins, sassafras bark, and bezoar stones excited great interest among the Europeans, who willingly gave glass beads, brass ornaments, and iron tools in exchange. Each side thought they had the better of the deal, and each imbued the others' goods with mystical, even sacred powers. For their part, Europeans hoped sassafras would cure syphilis, and paranoid nobles deployed bezoar stones—spheroidal concretions, "gastric pearls" found in deer intestines—as antidotes to poisons. Southeastern Indians, on the other hand, imagined copper and brass to be sacred materials, long associated with the ruling elites of prehistoric chiefdoms. While the Indians welcomed easy access to hitherto scarce commodities, these imported objects did not immediately replace native counterparts. European ornaments and tools were integrated slowly into native technologies on native terms and with considerable deliberation, in ways that seemed most beneficial to the southeastern Indians.[7]

Far to the north, however, the Dutch and the English began trading firearms to the Iroquois and a few other native groups. Unequal access to those weapons sparked a seemingly endless series of wars between Indian peoples, wars that set into motion long-distance relocations of populations armed only with stone-tipped arrows desperate to escape the onslaughts of warriors with guns. Disease and warfare reworked the population map of the Southeast. By the late seventeenth century new "tribal" societies had formed from the dispersed remnants of late prehistoric chiefdoms that once occupied the region during Soto's time.[8]

The Creek people emerged from this demographic chaos of the seventeenth century. A century earlier, peoples speaking the Muskogee (*Mvskoke*) language are thought to have occupied two clusters of towns in the future Creek heartland.[9] One group lined the banks of the lower Tallapoosa River (in modern-day central Alabama, northeast of Montgomery), with a second along the central Chattahoochee River (the present Alabama-Georgia border, south from the vicinity of Columbus, Georgia). These core areas of stable settlement attracted refugees as surrounding peoples suffered epidemics and slave raids. Many of the newcomers, such as Abekas and Hitchitis from northern Georgia, Koasatis from eastern Tennessee, and Alabamas from eastern Mississippi and southern Alabama, spoke related Muskogean languages. Others, like the Yuchis, Tawasas, and elements of the Shawnees, came from greater distances and spoke unrelated languages. Entire towns of refugees were apparently welcomed if they respected the customs of the original towns and agreed to forgo warfare with other disparate members of this union of convenience.

By 1700, dozens of independent towns had become loosely allied in four geographical clusters—Abekas on the Coosa and upper Tallapoosa rivers; Alabama towns on the upper Alabama River; Tallapoosas on the lower Tallapoosa River; and Cowetas on the central Chattahoochee (Figure 1). The British gradually came to refer to all of these peoples collectively as Creeks (a name derived from a group of Muskogees living in Georgia along Ochese Creek, whom the British called "Ochese Creeks," or "Creeks" for short). The Cowetas became known as Lower Creeks and the others as Upper Creeks, "Upper" because their towns were farther "up" the trading path from Charleston. However, the British term "Creeks," or even the more specific "Upper Creeks" and "Lower Creeks," suggested political and social unities that barely existed in the early eighteenth century. Individuals self-identified first with a family—their mother's lineage and clan—then with a town, and finally with a regional division of towns (Tallapoosas, Alabamas, etc.).[10] A sense of common identity as "Creeks" developed very slowly in the course of the eighteenth century. Even today, among Creeks and Seminoles in Oklahoma, individuals often think of their relationships to others primarily in terms of town affiliation. With those disclaimers in mind, for the sake of simplified discussion I use the term "Creeks" when referring to all the native peoples of central Alabama and Georgia, without necessarily implying any particular degree of political cohesion.

Creek families of the eighteenth century were matrilineal. Such families differ in many ways from the bilineal families of modern America, in which we consider ourselves equally related to our father's family and our mother's family. Among the Creeks, a couple's children belonged to the mother's extended family or lineage, but not the father's. Perhaps most foreign to our way of thinking, a biological father had little to do with raising his sons, a responsibility that fell to the mother's brothers, and any of his property left as inheritance would have gone to his sister and her children, members of his matrilineage, not to his own children. This matrilineal system of kinship was common among the farming peoples of southeastern North America and may have arisen as families invested immense labor in clearing and maintaining agricultural fields. Nearly all farming tasks—planting, weeding, and harvesting—fell to women in the late prehistoric Southeast. Agricultural clearings were hard-won from the forest with stone axes and the judicious application of fire and strenuously maintained year after year with stone or shell hoes. A matrilineal system of descent and inheritance kept fields under the control of related, cooperating women and their children.

A clan consisted of matrilineages related to each other through a common ancestor, represented by a mythical clan spirit or totem. Centuries earlier each society probably had just a few clans, but adoption of so many refugee groups by the historic Creeks resulted in their proliferation. In fact, clans were so numerous that they, too, like Creek towns, were organized into larger groups, the Hathagalgi (*Hvthakvlke* or White clans, specifically the Beaver, Bear, Bird, and Wind clans) and the Tchilokogalgi (*Celokhokvlke*, literally "speakers of a different language," comprising all other clans). This division may reflect the separate origins of the core Muskogee groups and later immigrants. Clans

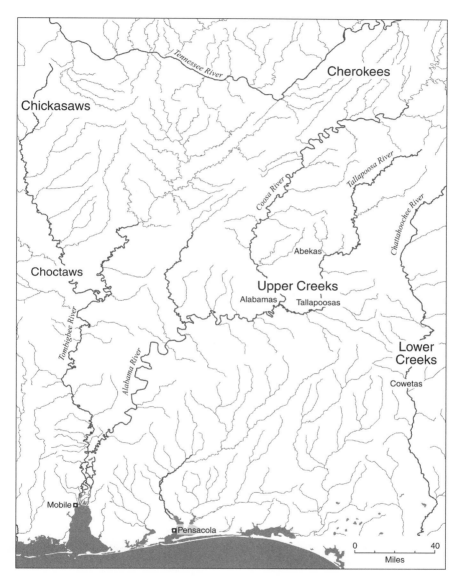

Fig. 1. The Creek Indians and their neighbors in the eighteenth century.

served many purposes in Creek social life. Most importantly, they were exoga-
mous; a person could not marry another from the same clan. Such a pairing
would have been incestuous, a marriage between relatives. Children, of course,
belonged to their mother's clan, not their father's. Because each clan's members were dispersed throughout Creek society (since men moved away from
their mothers' homes to take up residence with wives of different clans), a native traveler could usually find a clan relative no matter how far from home,
even when visiting other societies like the Choctaws and Cherokees.

Clan leaders organized the major social events of the year, such as the annual poskita (*posketv*) or "fast," known to whites as the Busk or Green Corn
ceremony, and other periodic dances and feasts. The eldest members of a clan
passed judgment and meted out punishment to wrongdoers within the clan, a
practice that controlled interclan conflicts and limited otherwise endless cycles
of blood revenge. Birth into particular clans also determined to some extent
the roles and options one could aspire to in life. For instance, women of the
Wind clan were shown great respect, with even the youngest called "grandmother" by all other Creeks. A man of the Wind clan could ascend to the second
tier of authority, to the roles of heniha (*henehv*) or councilor and isti atcagagi
(*estecakucvlke*) or Beloved Man, but seldom if ever became mico (*mēkko*) or
headman. On the other hand, men of the Bear clan achieved the status of mico
more often than others. Unfortunately, we know little about the histories and
internal functionings of the clans, but they clearly imposed a structure and
order on Creek social life and integrated a dispersed population.[11]

Each Creek family was affiliated with a talwa (*etvlwv*).[12] Usually translated
as "town," a talwa comprised the people of a community, distinguished from
its physical place and buildings, which were known collectively as a talofa
(*tvlofv*). Most talwas had populations of a few hundred. But more important
than size was social and political coherence and independence, represented by
several public structures: the choccothlucco (*cuko rakko*) or square ground,
consisting of four open-fronted buildings facing a plaza; the tcokofa (*cukofv*),
rotunda or council house, an enclosed circular or multisided building; and the
chunky yard or ball yard where games were played. A town's leading men met
regularly at the square ground (in the warm season) or the rotunda (in winter)
to discuss and reach consensus on important issues. For any number of reasons, a portion of a talwa might decide to break away from the rest. Such a
splinter group could either create a new, separate talwa (a daughter town to the
original mother town) or establish an outlying talofa, a smaller residential center lacking public structures and still associated with and subordinate to the

original talwa. In the late eighteenth century, as Creek residences became increasingly dispersed, widely separated talwa members maintained ties by attending town social events at public buildings and game yards that frequently stood alone, no longer surrounded by residences.[13]

This drift of residences away from the talwa square grounds coincided with changes in farming methods. Creek agriculture inherited much from the prehistoric Mississippian farmers of the Southeast who had developed corn (maize) into a staple crop hundreds of years earlier. They discovered that fields cleared alongside major streams and rivers could be planted year after year, because the silt deposited on riverbank levees by annual spring floods replenished nutrients drawn out of the soil by the corn plants.[14] Prehistoric southeastern farmers also knew to interplant beans among the corn; those clingy legumes would climb the corn stalks while their underground rhizomes fixed nitrogen in the soil. Many other plants—some domesticated, like sunflowers, others wild, like hickory nuts—supplemented the major crops. Apart from the dog, early southeasterners lacked domesticated animals, so hunting remained important until the nineteenth century. White-tailed deer provided the bulk of consumed meat, followed distantly by other mammals and wild turkeys.

That said, a simple itemization of species critical to Creek subsistence does not convey an accurate sense of Creek interconnectedness with the environment. Animals, plants, places, earth, water, fire—to the Creek people of the eighteenth century, all were manifestations of spirits. Principal among them was Hisagitamisi (*Hesaketvmesē*, literally "breath holder"), commonly translated as "Master of Breath" and represented on earth by the sacred fire, among other forms.

The Master of Breath gave the Creeks the Black Drink. One can make a pleasant-tasting caffeinated tea from the roasted leaves of yaupon holly, but the Creeks prepared it for ceremonial consumption as a frothy, bitter infusion that men consumed in volume, followed by self-induced vomiting. During a visit to the Creeks in 1790, Caleb Swan learned they thought the Black Drink efficacious; it "purifies them from all sin, and leaves them in a state of perfect innocence; that it inspires them with an invincible prowess in war; and that it is the only solid cement of friendship, benevolence, and hospitality."

The polluting activities of everyday life caused accumulation of bodily and spiritual impurities, which would in turn cause illness and eventually death unless treated by healers administering sweat baths or purifying plant medicines. Many diseases caused by animal spirits offended by hunters, for instance, could be counteracted by specific plants, such as red root (*mēkohoyvnēcv*, dwarf willow, *Salix tristis*) or button snake root (*passv, Eryngium yuccifolium*) or the white medicine (*heles-hvtke,* ginseng, *Panax quinquefolius*). Human witches could also inflict illness and injury on others, unless prevented by ritual countermeasures.[15]

Rituals of personal and community renewal were essential to maintaining individual health and group well-being. Daily baths in a running stream were considered beneficial, as were abstinence and fasting before important tasks and events. Menstruating women and wounded warriors lived apart from the town until they regained bodily purity. Every talwa celebrated an annual communal poskita or Green Corn ceremony in late summer to usher in a new year. In the course of this four- to eight-day ritual, the Creeks celebrated the ripening of the new corn crop, cleansed their homes and public places of the old year's accumulated filth and worn furnishings, set aside revenge feuds and punishments for minor crimes, and rekindled the sacred fire in the square ground.[16]

Life in a Creek talwa of the late eighteenth century was inextricably bound to the spirits, by clan and talwa origins and rights and matrilineal gender roles, and to the animal and plant spirits upon which health and subsistence depended. Human respect for spirits maintained a balance in the world, a world that had roots in antiquity, while the clans and matrilineages and talwas gave structure and purpose to individual lives. Even so, the Creeks had adapted to the changing colonial world on their borders. In response to changing economic and political circumstances—particularly the rise of the young United States—the Creeks repeatedly responded pragmatically and effectively by reworking their own economy and political organization, all the while remaining faithful to their core values and traditions. Those values and traditions, however, were going to be challenged directly in the coming years by the emergent American nation.

~

Native agricultural and hunting practices changed slowly during the eighteenth century, remarkably slowly considering the great pressures exerted on the Creeks to conform to the colonial economic system. European and Indian economic interests happened to coincide most closely in the realm of deer hunting. English and French demands for deerskins, highly valued in Europe for making fine leather gloves and bookbindings, sent hundreds of merchants deep into the Southeast. Native hunters responded by increasing their annual take far beyond the number of deer needed to feed and clothe their families. In exchange for flintlock muskets, steel axes and knives, colorfully dyed cloth, and rum and brandy, Indian hunters extracted deerskins by the hundreds of thousands from the region every year. In 1715, trader excesses—routinely cheating their native trading partners, assaulting Indian women, inciting wars between Indians to obtain captives to sell as slaves—led to a temporary expulsion of all South Carolinians from the interior Southeast during the Yamasee War. Upon their return two years later they found the French newly established at Fort Toulouse, a military and commercial entrepôt at the head of the Alabama River, and actively competing for Creek trade. Even by this early date, European-made goods had become essential to the southeastern Indian way of life. From that point on, the Creeks sought trade relations with multiple colonial partners to gain the benefits of economic competition.

The Creeks similarly maintained political independence by consciously avoiding unilateral alliances with any colonial government. As individual native leaders sought economic and political advantages from relationships cultivated with French or British officials, pro-French and pro-British factions naturally developed among the Creeks. A tolerance for opposing factions, and a general realization that European competition for the attentions of one faction or another benefited the Creeks in the form of lavish presents from both colonial powers, in effect persuaded the Creeks to remain neutral in the European contest for control of the region. With the abrupt departure of the French in 1763 (an outcome of the Seven Years' War), the Creeks had to readjust their collective approach to foreign interlopers. Renewed Spanish interest in the region, from their base in Louisiana, enabled the Creeks to continue playing one European power against the other. Perhaps more important, though, British colonial officials effectively restrained American immigration into the Creek country. With the outbreak of the Revolutionary War, American and British negotiators found, to their frustration, the Creeks once again divided by factions and unwilling to side decisively with one or the other.

Britain's reluctant acceptance of American independence and withdrawal from the Southeast in 1783 left the entire Gulf coast under Spanish control and the new United States struggling to remain united under the Articles of Confederation. To their east, the Creeks faced thousands of Georgians and Carolinians who began moving into long-coveted Indian lands. For the first time since Brims and other native leaders hit upon the neutrality policy in 1717, the Creeks could no longer effectively play one foreign neighbor against another. Under these difficult circumstances, the métis Alexander McGillivray rose to prominence as a Creek leader. Between 1783 and his death in 1793, McGillivray worked assiduously to weaken the political powers of individual Creek towns and the society's matrilineal clans. In their place he promoted a Creek national council that could impose decisions on all the disparate factions that previously had served Creek interests so well. McGillivray's fluency in written and spoken English (thanks to some formal colonial schooling and years spent in his father's employ in Charleston and Savannah) and his ability to negotiate effectively with both Anglo-American and Spanish officials earned him high status among the Creeks. At the height of his power, McGillivray parlayed political authority into economic advantage, acquiring great wealth in slaves and livestock for himself and his relatives. Development of a wealthy class of Creeks accelerated after McGillivray's death. Eventually, Creek society began to split along a new factional line dividing those aspiring to accumulate private wealth from those holding to the older norms that subsumed individual aspirations under responsibilities to lineage, clan, and talwa.[17]

In the years following 1783, the Creeks' obstreperous white neighbors to their east became increasingly threatening. At their most aggressive, landless white squatters and wealthy speculators attempted repeatedly to take Creek lands. Subtler American officials and missionaries began to urge the Creeks to adopt American ways, to abandon deer hunting and maize farming in favor of cattle raising and the spinning and weaving of cotton. Such change could not be accomplished easily and not without profound effects reaching every aspect of Creek culture. Finally, in 1813, some Creeks would draw inspiration from the spirits that animated their world to drive out the pollution and impurities originating with the Americans on their borders and in their midst.

Terms of Discussion, Terms of Debate

The language of race and ethnicity is treacherous terrain. In writing about the history of a socially diverse corner of the early United States, I have consciously decided to use certain terms and to eschew others, recognizing that by my choices I will undoubtedly (regrettably) offend some readers. Such an outcome is probably inevitable at a time when political correctness often seems more a matter of conforming to an approved lexicon than exercising sensitivity to words that have labeled and constrained elements of society in the past. Perhaps I can defuse a few verbal landmines by discussing the reasons behind my choices.

I use *Americans* to refer to citizens of the United States—nearly all white, nearly all of Western European descent—because that is the name they applied to themselves in the early nineteenth century, and that is what their Indian and European colonial contemporaries called them. Of course, the southeastern *In-*

dians were Americans too, Native Americans, with arguably a better right to the name than any of those U.S. citizens of relatively recent European descent. The Creeks and others, however, did not refer to themselves as Americans at that time, while they (at least on occasion) spoke of Indian peoples, as did Tecumseh so notably in the years prior to the Redstick War. It is my impression that the label "Native American" has not gained much popularity among southeastern Indians, most of whom refer to themselves officially and familiarly as Indians.[18] In this book, that is the term I use preferentially. *Creeks,* too, is a controversial label, first applied imprecisely by the English early in the eighteenth century to a group of loosely allied peoples who formed a Creek nation by the end of the eighteenth century. The term "Muskogee" (also spelled "Muscogee") is used now in Oklahoma by the descendents of many of the characters in this book and is applied by some historians to all the peoples of that early historical confederacy and nation.[19] But one of my purposes here is to explore the diversity of Creek society, particularly the role of the Alabamas in the history of the Tensaw. And the Alabamas were not, and are not today, Muskogees. While acknowledging the classificatory inadequacies of the terms "Creeks" and "confederacy" and "nation," I will use them here when they suit the historical context. When referring to the third major racial group in the early American South, I use *Africans* or *blacks,* of course eschewing the now archaic "Negro" of the period (unless quoting from period documents). One can reasonably argue that "African Americans" is more appropriate for persons of color born in the United States. However, many blacks living on the Tensaw frontier, circa 1813, were in fact born in Africa.

All of these terms are objectionable on a couple of scores. First, each term implies ethnic homogeneity, when in fact each subsumes an enormous amount of ethnic diversity. Although Americans, by my definition, were similar in terms of their common European background, they included French, Spanish, Germans, Dutch, Scots, and Welsh as well as the more numerous English. At least as misleading, though, is the implied coherence of any such group, as if *Americans* or *Creeks* or *English* or any ethnic descriptors define the social equivalent of separate species with immutable boundaries. So my second objection derives from the observation that biology trumps ethnicity in that one important way. Whenever people of two socially defined races or ethnic groups come together, some inevitably reproduce, creating offspring that challenge the very notions of definable, bounded races and ethnic groups. Among the Creeks of the early nineteenth century, offspring of Creek women and American or African men (the most common pairings) were considered ethnically Creek by the Indians, because they belonged to their mothers' matrilineages. Yet even the tolerant Creeks acknowledged their unusual descent, and the Creeks too were eventually drawn into thinking in racialist terms. Americans, in the early nineteenth century, generally viewed children of mixed race parents as ethnically ambiguous.[20] By then, many names were available to label these in-between people. Some, like "half breed," were overtly pejorative. All carried more or less disparaging connotations of racial impurity and social marginality, words such as "mixed blood," mestizo, mustee, métis, mulatto, zambo, and innumerable others like quadroon and octoroon developed in Spanish, French, and English to specify "blood quotient," the percentage of an individual's racial "content."

A few modern historians employ the phrase "mixed blood," but I consider that just too pre-Mendelian and unscientific, harkening back as it does to a folk biology (of animal breeding) which maintained that genetic inheritance was carried in the blood. Since some term is necessary, if only to discuss the issue, and all the available words come to us freighted to some degree with unfortunate etymological baggage, I have settled on *métis* (French for "mixed") as less objectionable in the context of the American Southeast. "Métis" (with a capital M) has long signified the indigenous people of the Red River valley of Manitoba, descendents of Cree Indians and French. In recent years, however, "métis" (with a lowercase *m*) has been applied more broadly to any person of Indian-white ancestry, and "métissage" has come to refer to the process of racial mixing, as well as the creation of a new culture from the intermingling of two peoples.[21] Since French colonists were among the first Europeans to intermarry with the Creeks, *métis* seems a reasonably appropriate term to designate the descendents of colonists and Creeks. It is important to note that métis ethnic identity is culturally constructed and distinct from genetic descent. Most of the individuals described in this volume as métis were labeled as such (actually, as "half breeds" and "mixed bloods") by European colonial and American writers on the basis of ancestry. But their sense of identity as ethnically métis, as a separate ethnic group distinct from Creek or American, is much more difficult to establish and in most cases remains problematic. To think ancestry determined ethnicity would be a serious error.

So these are the terms I have elected to use in this book. To compensate, in some degree, for the imprecision of such words—Americans, Indians, Africans, métis—I hope readers will look over the more specific information compiled in Appendix 1. In collaboration with colleagues James Parker and Sue Moore, I have endeavored to determine the racial and ethnic backgrounds of the persons involved in the events that transpired before, during, and after the battle at Fort Mims. The 224 individuals we have been able to identify at Fort Mims on the day of the battle—less than a quarter of all those present, but about double the number known previously—comprise a remarkably diverse cross section of early America's population, America in the broadest sense. The history that follows is a story of American origins.

1

The Tensaw

On the eve of the eighteenth century the area soon to be known as the Tensaw had no full-time occupants, although the Tomé Indians claimed those lands as a hunting ground. Their towns, Tomé and Naniaba, sat atop bluffs west of the lower Tombigbee and upper Mobile rivers, overlooking fields planted on the low natural levees lining the opposite banks. To the east lay the swampy expanses of the Mobile-Tensaw delta, an 80,000-acre bottomland forest of cypress and tupelo gum dissected by innumerable slow-moving streams, old river meander bayous, and marshes. For thousands of years the delta's abundant wild game and fish attracted Indians, who left traces of their lives in the hundreds of shell heaps still visible in eroding stream edges and riverbanks. Tensaw River, as the lower reaches of the Alabama River came to be called by the mid-eighteenth century, bounds the delta on the east, beyond which the land rises abruptly into dissected piney hills less suitable for agriculture.

During the era of French colonization, from 1699 until 1763, a few *habitants* established modest plantations on the margins of the delta, mostly on the west banks of the Mobile and Tombigbee rivers, insinuated between native fields and villages. About the year 1720 French officials persuaded the Tawasa Indians, refugees from Florida, to establish their town along the Tensaw River, where they could serve as a protective buffer, standing between the French, Tomés, and other allies west of the delta and the potentially hostile Creek Indians to the northeast. When the Tawasas, tiring of their assigned role of human shield, moved north to join the Creek confederacy a few years later, French officials found the Taensa (or Tensaw) Indians willing to fulfill the same function. The Taensas had originally lived along the lower Mississippi River. They relocated to the Mobile area in 1715, first making their home at Twenty-one Mile Bluff on the Mobile River, then moving by 1725 to the east bank of the river that would take their name. There they remained, tending fields on a large island in the delta west of their settlement, until they returned to the Mississippi River valley as the British took control of the region from France.[1]

The Taensas abandoned their village in 1764, part of a general emigration of French-allied Indians from the Mobile area (Figure 2). All of these small tribes, or *petites nations,* had fought alongside the French against the British and their Creek and Chickasaw allies. Some had even converted to Roman Catholicism. When King Louis XV turned his back on the French colonists of *La Louisiane* and the native peoples who had depended on French political, military, and economic support for six decades, the petites nations felt betrayed. Certainly they dreaded a transfer of allegiance to British rule, so most moved to Spanish-held lands west of the Mississippi River—all except the Tomés, who joined fellow Choctaw-speakers in the Chickasawhay towns of the Choctaw confederacy to their north. The Creek Indians viewed this abrupt departure of the petites nations as a victory and claimed, by right of conquest, the lands of their erstwhile native opponents in the Mobile area. Newly arrived British colonial officials disputed Creek claims, since they wished to offer these same recently vacated lands as grants to attract potential settlers. By 1765, after protracted negotiations, the Choctaws and the Creeks reached understandings with British officials that colonists might occupy all the high ground on the west banks of the lower Tombigbee and Mobile rivers but only as far north as the "Cut-off" on the east bank of the Alabama and Tensaw rivers. The Cut-off is a channel of the Alabama River that connects with the lower Tombigbee River some miles above their true confluence.[2] All lands north and east of the Cut-off were now mutually agreed to belong to the Creeks.

One of the first British colonists to settle the eastern border of the delta was Major Robert Farmar. In 1763 he had commanded the British military expedition that accepted Mobile from the departing French. After a brief, controversial tenure as commandant of Mobile's British garrison at Fort Charlotte, Farmar resigned his military commission and established a profitable plantation immediately south of the abandoned Tensaw Indian lands, called "Taensa Old Fields," west of present-day Stockton, Alabama.[3] He built his home, Farm Hall, amid a cluster of smaller tracts granted to ethnic French who had remained behind after the departure of French colonial officials and troops. These ten neighboring plantations came to be known collectively as the Tensaw (or Tassa) Settlement, immediately south of the 1765 Indian boundary line. Even then, however, at least two colonists (both probably French creoles) oc-

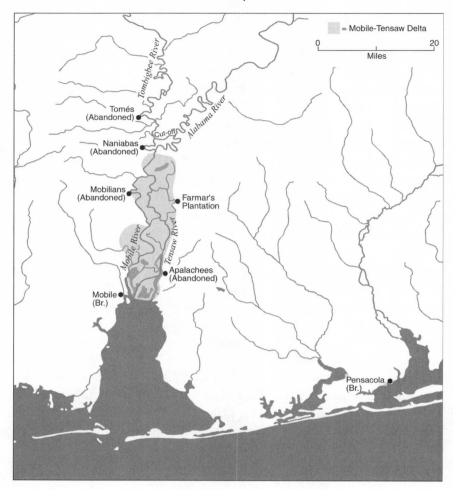

Fig. 2. The Mobile area, circa 1765.

cupied lands farther north, in the vicinity of Boatyard Lake east of the Alabama River. According to a map drafted by David Taitt in 1771, one of these
unidentified settlers built a home near the spot where Fort Mims would later
stand (Plate 1).[4]

In lengthy talks with the British, Creek micos explained that lands above
Tensaw occupied by colonists under the French regime "were never ceded to
them and that they had only allowed the French to settle them on sufferance."[5]
During the eighteenth century the Creeks—and especially the talwas of the
Alabama, Abeka, and Tallapoosa divisions of the Creek confederacy around the

junction of the Tallapoosa and Coosa rivers, near modern-day Montgomery, Alabama—hunted there and throughout the vast hinterland east of the Mobile-Tensaw delta and north of Pensacola. In talks held with British officials during the early 1770s, Emisteseguo, mico of the prominent Abeka town of Little Tallassee, repeatedly affirmed Creek intentions to settle the valleys of the Escambia and Conecuh rivers, north of Pensacola, "as soon as we have peace with the Choctaws."[6] They evidently did not do so, nor did the Creeks establish a settlement in the Tensaw, before the decade ended and the British colonial regime came to a close.

In an often overlooked campaign of the American Revolution, a Spanish army led by Bernardo de Gálvez conquered British-held Mobile in 1780 and Pensacola in 1781, bringing the entire Gulf coast under Spanish colonial rule. Many of the English-speaking colonists who settled along the Tombigbee and Tensaw rivers during the British colonial period fled in advance of Gálvez's troops or left soon thereafter rather than swear an oath of loyalty to the Spanish crown.[7] Within a few years, however, growing Spanish fears of the newly independent United States—particularly the threat that land-hungry American immigrants would overwhelm sparse Spanish colonial populations in La Luisiana and Las Floridas—led to Spain's reconciliation with its old enemy, Britain. At the center of this rapidly evolving, three-way colonial competition for southeastern North America lay the Creek nation, with a population approaching 15,000 and an undeniable right to possession of the bulk of the region that would become modern-day Alabama.[8]

In these years immediately following the American Revolution, Alexander McGillivray rose to leadership among the Creeks. Son of a prominent Creek woman, Sehoy of the Wind clan, and the loyalist Lachlan McGillivray, a Scot who had grown wealthy trading with the Creeks, Alexander achieved great influence among the Creeks for his ability to negotiate effectively with American and Spanish officials. In this he was aided by the Scottish partners behind the British commercial firm of Panton, Leslie and Co., which maintained a highly profitable trade with the Creeks through the Spanish ports of St. Augustine, Pensacola, and Mobile.[9] Until his death in 1793, McGillivray and other leaders of the nascent Creek national council enlisted Spanish support to counter growing American political and economic influence among the southeastern Indians and to restrain American aspirations for Creek lands.

∼

In the wake of Britain's recognition of an independent United States in 1783, thousands of loyalist families fled the thirteen former colonies to escape a pervasive climate of political intolerance and persecution. Many sailed to the British Isles (among them, Lachlan McGillivray), Canada, or the Bahamas. Loyalists from the Carolinas and Georgia, in particular, were tempted by a Spanish offer of lands near Mobile and Natchez. With Alexander McGillivray's encouragement, Spanish officials permitted some loyalist refugees, including retired British officers, to settle along the Tombigbee and Tensaw south of the vaguely defined U.S. border, in the colony of Spanish West Florida.[10] Not every *Americano* (as Spaniards called all English speakers in the region) arrived as a political refugee. Other immigrants were "Indian countrymen," Whigs and Tories alike, who had lived in the Creek Indian towns as traders and packhorse wranglers and in many instances had married Creek women. A substantial number of these men left the Creek country as profits from the deerskin trade declined after the Revolution. Many of these former traders congregated on the Tensaw; one was Samuel Mims.[11]

Decades later, an acquaintance of William Weatherford jotted down William's recollection that his father Charles Weatherford had come with Samuel Mims to the Upper Creek towns following the Revolution, after Mims had spent some time in the employ of George Galphin, a prominent trader operating out of Silver Bluff, South Carolina. During the war Galphin served as rebel agent to the Creeks, actively promoting the patriot cause until his death in 1780. Mims may have been a patriot sympathizer as well (although his later close association in the Tensaw with numerous unrepentant Tories raises doubts).[12] He first appears in Spanish records of the Mobile District on a census certified the first of January 1786, as an unmarried American, a *soltero Americano*.[13] An enumeration the following year reaffirmed his bachelor status, gave his age as forty-five years, and indicated his residence on a river near Mobile, without specifying whether the Tombigbee or Tensaw.[14] Soon afterwards Mims signed an oath of allegiance to the Spanish crown, adding his name to a list of "English established on the Tensaw" (*Ingleses establecidos en el Tinza*).[15] In January 1788 he married another Americano, Hannah Rains of St. Augustine, Florida, in a Catholic ceremony in Mobile.[16] Over the next decade Mims dabbled in land speculation, acquiring farmlands along the Tombigbee River and town lots on the north edge of Mobile, all the while maintaining a residence on the Tensaw.[17] When he discovered in 1797 that two prior British grants conflicted with one of his Spanish land claims, Mims obtained a new grant of 524 acres near Boatyard Lake, where he remained firmly ensconced for the next sixteen years, becoming wealthy from his slave plantations and by operating a ferry across the Alabama River at the "South margin of the Cut-off."[18]

Virtually all of the earliest American settlers on the Tombigbee and Tensaw depended on the labor of African slaves. In fact, colonial-era censuses reveal a population in Mobile and surrounding areas that was predominantly black during the Spanish regime.[19] Samuel Mims claimed ownership of eight male and eight female black slaves (*negros y negras*) in 1786 and fifteen the following year.[20] Few Americans owned slaves classified by Spanish officials as racially mixed *pardos,* although many pardos were held in ethnic French and Spanish households of the Mobile District. Several dozen more pardos and negros lived in town as free people of color. Since the American newcomers generally either purchased anew or brought with them recently enslaved African men and women, their treatment of slaves differed substantially from the relationships created over preceding decades between the pardos and negros and the ethnic French and Spaniards who together comprised a creole population with long ties to the region.[21]

With the benefit of an enslaved labor force, Mims and his neighbors exploited the diverse environment of the Mobile-Tensaw delta and surrounding uplands, adopting wholesale the plantation economy developed nearly a century earlier by French colonial farmers. The first European settlers planted in fields abandoned by Indians as introduced Old World diseases reduced the native population. Those maize fields were confined almost entirely to the banks of delta waterways, where slightly elevated natural levees had accumulated from silt deposited during annual spring floods.[22] Pine-covered hilly uplands on either side of the delta were far less productive of crops, though colonists found that cattle could forage well enough in the woods, a method of cattle raising employed for over a century by Spanish ranchers in northern Florida. According to the 1786 and 1787 Spanish censuses of the Mobile District, Samuel Mims' slaves harvested 150 barrels of maize the first year and raised 10 horses, 90 cattle, 100 pounds of tobacco, and 200 barrels of maize the next.[23] Most planters further diversified their personal economies by harvesting the forest products so abundantly at hand, setting their slaves to rendering pitch and tar from pine trees and riving barrel staves from oaks.[24] Some experimented with the cultivation of indigo, rice, tobacco, and cotton, but cattle raising proved most profitable. African drovers had introduced the idea of fenced cowpens to South Carolina in the late seventeenth century, and the concept spread across the South during the British colonial period.[25] The Americanos continued their use along with Spanish-style open-range grazing when they arrived in the Mobile District.

As this settlement of whites and blacks formed below the Cut-off, another was developing north of the Spanish boundary line on Creek Indian lands (which now, incidentally, fell entirely within the territorial claims of the State of Georgia). Centered on Little River at its confluence with the lower Alabama, this new Creek community consisted mostly of métis, the offspring of Creek women married to white men—Scots, French, English, Americans—who had lived among the Indians as traders. In the racist language of early America they were called "half breeds" or "mixed bloods." As has always been the case when populations collide, many of these métis found their ethnicity questioned and some had difficulty fitting into either native society or colonial society. A number sought a more comfortable middle ground by founding a new settlement at Little River where they hoped conflicts posed by competing cultures could be avoided.[26] Over the next quarter century, neighboring Creek métis and Americanos (both holding black Africans in bondage) would come to consider themselves halves of a single Tensaw community, still racially distinct and spatially separated by an international boundary, but routinely interacting and frequently cooperating in every conceivable way, socially, economically, militarily, and politically. Later references to this region usually call it simply "the Tensaw" without distinguishing Indian from white.

∼

The Little River métis began to coalesce in 1783 when Alexander McGillivray and his sister Sophia Durant established a plantation and cowpen near Little River to raise cattle and crops to sell to the residents and garrison of Spanish Pensacola.[27] In that era, anyone keeping cattle near traditional Creek towns, whether colonial trader or Creek innovator, risked offending the matrilineages that controlled each town's unfenced agricultural fields, mainstay of Creek subsistence. Those who wished to raise large herds of livestock were compelled to find grazing lands far from community fields. With the market for deerskins beginning a relentless decline that would continue for three decades, cattle raising increasingly appealed as an alternative to hunting. Where cattle could range freely in the woods, especially in forests depleted of wild game at the eastern periphery of the Creek nation, many hunters shifted their efforts from stalking deer to rounding up and shooting cattle to meet household subsistence and commercial needs.[28] Still, this transition met steady resistance from some Creek men who felt their gendered identity, their traditional masculine roles of hunter and warrior, undermined by pressures to tend livestock. During the long simmering border conflict with Georgia during the 1780s and 1790s, Creek warriors reaffirmed traditional gender roles in new ways by stealing horses and slaves and killing cattle belonging to American settlers on the frontier.[29] Nevertheless, Creek cattle herds did increase slowly in number and size, and Creek settlements gradually dispersed during the late eighteenth and early nineteenth centuries as nuclear families moved their households away from matrilineage-dominated towns and fields.[30]

The first individuals to raise livestock on a large scale were by and large métis—men and women, but mostly men, whose British fathers could provide the capital necessary to acquire large herds—and micos, town headmen who received presents annually from colonial and American officials and could afford expensive breeding stock.[31] Furthermore, those micos and other leaders who were also métis, such as Alexander McGillivray, could afford the numbers of African slaves that large-scale plantation-style agriculture required. When McGillivray situated his plantation at Little River, he apparently took into consideration the ready accessibility of colonial markets in Pensacola and Mobile for corn, cotton, beef and hides, as well as the political and economic benefits to be derived from strengthening ties with the region's Spanish colonial officials and the British trading firm of Panton, Leslie and Co. headquartered in those towns.

By 1787, McGillivray's thriving Little River plantation seemed to some European observers a harbinger of future prosperity and social stability not only for the Creeks but for the colony of Spanish West Florida as well. Writing in July of that year to the Marqués de Sonora, Governor Arturo O'Neill advised that marriages be encouraged between Creeks and colonists: "Through these alliances in due course I think that in a short time the most fertile lands from the head of the Escambia River to the Tensaw River . . . would be immediately cultivated by friendly Indians and mestizos." In his vision, O'Neill imagined this future Elysium would arise from the docility of the Indians, "swayed generally by what the Europeans or whites advise, letting themselves be governed entirely by those who have lived with some . . . of the English nation. . . . the mestizo sons of these are most inclined toward the whites. There is need that a good missionary should come promptly to make all the necessary arrangements to bring about marriages between the persons of these nations and some of our Europeans already distinguished for excessive fondness for the Indian women, and these equally enamored of the whites."[32]

O'Neill's sentiments coincided closely with an Indian policy then evolving among American political leaders influenced by European Enlightenment philosophers. Since the end of the Revolution, American refusal to acknowledge Indian sovereignty over native lands, along with the inability of the government under the Articles of Confederation to prevent intrusions by settlers on native lands, had caused nearly continuous warfare on the western frontiers. These wars were costly for a young, impoverished nation with a small standing army. They also raised moral concerns in the United States and in Europe, since calls from the border settlements for the destruction or forced expulsion of native peoples evoked images of sixteenth-century Spanish conquests of the Aztecs and Incas, historical precedents thoroughly vilified by British and American writers of the late eighteenth century. With adoption of the federal Constitution in 1789, executive officers of the new republic—President George Washington, Secretary of State Thomas Jefferson, and Secretary of War Henry Knox—sought to expand the limits of American settlement by means more consistent with the founding principles of the young republic. Knox, in particular, envisioned a new, benevolent American Indian policy. The United States (not individual states) would claim sole right to negotiate with independent Indian societies as foreign nations (Figure 3). The paramount goals of these negotiations would be the lawful establishment of boundaries and the peaceful acquisition of Indian lands, freely given to the United States by Indian leaders (empowered by the will of their people) in exchange for payments of cash and goods. Westward expansion could then proceed in an orderly way, with Indian populations retreating before the advancing American frontier or assimilating with American society. In either case, warfare would be averted and Indian lands made available to the nation's burgeoning population. For U.S. officials, the question was not whether Americans would occupy Indian lands but how the transition should occur.

Knox, Jefferson, and others advocated the process of "civilization" to speed this transition and, furthermore, considered it the only practical way to save Indians from extinction. To American policymakers, the few thousand Indians left in the wake of the previous two centuries' westward-moving frontier seemed impoverished and demoralized, with poor prospects for survival in a nation dominated by Euro-Americans. Accordingly, for their own long-term benefit, Indians would be encouraged to give up their ways of life; to accept American notions of education, justice, religion, and private property; and to adopt plow agriculture, livestock raising, and home production of clothes by spinning and weaving. By these means, Knox argued, Indians could be assimilated peacefully into American society and their vast lands, no longer needed by them for hunting, could be acquired by the federal government for redistribution to white settlers.[33]

Some, such as Jefferson and Spanish Governor O'Neill, initially considered intermarriage of whites and Indians an efficient and desirable mechanism to

Fig. 3. Silver U.S. peace medal, presented to Efa Hadjo in 1789 at the Rock Landing Conference in Georgia; 3 inches wide; Accession #85.14.118 (courtesy of the Alabama Department of Archives and History, Montgomery).

speed assimilation. The willingness of many Indian-white métis to adopt elements of American culture and their frequent success in western-style economic endeavors suggested how Indians might simply be absorbed into the larger American population. The rise of racialist thought in early nineteenth-century America would soon turn public discourse away from assimilation toward discussions of Indian removal. But that lay in the future when Alexander McGillivray led a delegation of Creek leaders to New York City in the summer of 1790 to negotiate and sign a "Treaty of Peace and Friendship" with the United States. This early implementation of the "plan of civilization" contained the following clause, Article XII: "That the Creek nation may be led to a greater degree of civilization, and to become herdsmen and cultivators, instead of remaining in a state of hunters, the United States will from time to time furnish gratuitously the said nation with useful domestic animals and implements of husbandry."[34] For nearly half a century, agents of the government and missionaries from several Protestant sects would labor tirelessly to lead all Indians living within the bounds of the United States, and most particularly the Creek Indians, toward "civilization."

Despite the undoubtedly benevolent intentions of its principal promoters, the federal "civilizing" policy proved to be deeply flawed. As Article 12 exemplifies, American officials routinely insisted upon the fiction that Indians hunted to the exclusion of farming. This intentional deceit shifted attention from the existing agricultural basis of Indian economies to a focus on the market-driven hunting for hides and furs supported by deer herds ranging over millions of acres—acreage the American government, and the vast majority of the American people, thought would be better used by American farmers. Numerous modern scholars have noted the fundamental ethnocentricity of this policy, with American cultural values and practices presumed superior to all others.[35] By implication, millennia of Indian cultural achievements (and land rights) shriveled to insignificance. Full acquiescence to the policy would have stripped Indians of their Indianness, their own languages and cultures, a terrible price to pay for physical survival. Certainly very few Indians considered their own ways inferior to those of white Americans. However, even those Americans most concerned for the survival of Indians in an expanding United States could not understand why so few Indians sought assimilation to American culture and society. Knox and others assumed that Indians, once exposed to the fundamental elements of American civilization by missionaries or government agents, would willingly abandon their old customs.

Nowhere would the "plan of civilization" find more enthusiastic advocates than among the followers and relatives of Alexander McGillivray settled around Little River. Yet, even there, proponents of civilization would proudly and steadfastly maintain Creek traditions as they selectively adopted elements of American culture. And, most tellingly, even among pro-American métis families, many came to believe the path to civilization would lead to the destruction of the Creek people. Founded as a haven for Creeks exploring novel modes of economic and political independence from native traditions, the Tensaw also fostered aspirations for a Creek future free of American influence among those disenchanted with the spiritual vacuum left in civilization's wake. The fissures in Creek society that appeared so dramatically in 1813 divided the people of the Tensaw as well. But this anticipates events unforeseen in 1790.

∼

During the last few years of his life, Alexander McGillivray spent winters with his Scottish and Spanish friends in Pensacola, "leaving his wife, servants, and horses at a plantation he has near Tensau."[36] Although McGillivray considered those considerable possessions to be his own property, after his death in 1793 his sisters ignored their brother's wishes that his son receive his estate and instead enforced traditional Creek rules of inheritance, claiming his plantations, livestock, and slaves for their own children, McGillivray's matrilineal nephews.[37] From his sisters' perspective, McGillivray's ambition to invoke European rules of patrilineal inheritance (an aim he shared with numerous European and métis men married to Creek women) would have transferred their rightful property to the control of his wife's (that is, his son's mother's) matrilineage. Even the most prominent métis families harbored deep divisions between those who favored retaining traditional customs, such as matrilineal rules of inheritance, and those preferring to adopt European modes of behavior. In the end, McGillivray's own matrilineage retained his Little River plantation, and many of his extended kin established new plantations in the area.

A steady trickle of American immigrants passed through the region in the 1790s. Most moved on to the Natchez District, but some stayed to claim lands along the Tombigbee and Tensaw, until by 1800 the 1,250 inhabitants there far outnumbered the creole population residing in Spanish-held Mobile. Equally distressing to Mobile's old French and Spanish families was the outcome of the Ellicott-Dunbar survey, a joint American-Spanish expedition that established the official boundary line separating the United States from the Spanish colonies of East and West Florida at 31° north latitude. In 1799 the Spaniards evacuated Fuerte San Esteban, at the upper limits of Americano settlement on the Tombigbee since 1789, when the fort was discovered to lie on the American side of the new dividing line. So too did the Tensaw settlement. U.S. troops established Fort Stoddert immediately north of the relocated international border. Residents of the Tensaw, including many who settled there after the Revolution precisely to escape American jurisdiction, found themselves once again living in the United States.[38]

With this change of legal authority, Tensaw became part of Mississippi Territory, created by Congress in 1798 for the benefit of several thousand inhabitants of the Natchez District occupying the far southwest corner of the United States (Figure 4). Samuel Mims and his neighbors who had obtained land grants from colonial governments (or had claimed to have done so) were suddenly required to show proof of those grants to U.S. officials. For most settlers,

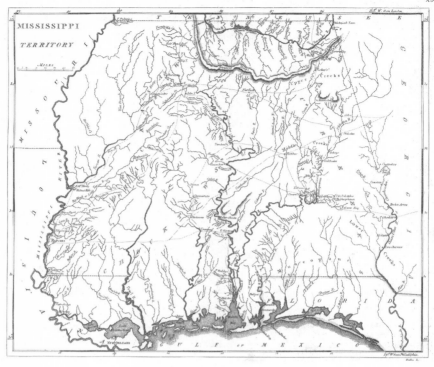

Fig. 4. Mississippi Territory, Plate 23 of *Carey's General Atlas, Improved and Enlarged: Being a Collection of Maps of the World and Quarters, Their Principal Empires, Kingdoms, &c.,* by Mathew Carey (Philadelphia: Mathew Carey, 1814).

this was the beginning of a long process, which for Mims concluded only in 1811 when Congress confirmed his principal grants near the Cut-off.[39]

A few years prior to the boundary revision, in 1796 or 1797, Samuel Mims and Adam Hollinger had cooperatively established two river ferries (Mims' across the Alabama River and Hollinger's across the Tombigbee) to carry the increasing flow of immigrants through the substantial impediment to travel posed by the Mobile-Tensaw delta. During the French and British colonial periods, a series of enterprising souls had ferried travelers across the upper part of Mobile Bay to Mobile. But more recent overland traffic from Georgia followed more northerly routes, bypassing Mobile altogether unless one made a special effort to visit the old colonial town. Mims and Hollinger hit upon the highly profitable ferry venture, and it made them wealthy. During dry spells, ferrymen carried travelers across the Alabama River to Naniaba (or Nannahubba) Island, in the center of the delta. A trail wound through fields cultivated by Mims' slaves to Hollinger's ferry on the opposite side. In times of high water, when the island trail submerged, ferrymen undertook the more arduous task of poling passenger- and baggage-laden "flats" the entire ten miles across the delta.[40] With the establishment of Fort Stoddert in 1799 just a few miles downstream from Hollinger's ferry, the Mims-Hollinger link across the delta became the favored route through the region. In his capacity as U.S. Principal Agent to the Creek Indians, Benjamin Hawkins controlled American traffic across Creek lands. In 1798 and 1799 he issued half a dozen passes a month to families immigrating to Mississippi Territory, a number that rose dramatically to 100 per month in 1802 and increased steadily every year thereafter. Upper Creeks, and the Alabama Indians in particular, began to worry that so many American travelers disturbed game in their best remaining hunting grounds.[41]

The Louisiana Purchase in 1803 brought New Orleans into American possession (along with an enormous territory stretching to the Rocky Mountains occupied by Indians who did not acknowledge U.S. ownership) (Plate 2). To provide a means of moving troops and mail quickly to New Orleans, U.S. officials began negotiating for permission to improve a road crossing Creek lands to the newly acquired city, a right the Creeks granted in the 1805 Treaty of Washington. In two years, parties of axemen transformed the old Lower Creek Trading Path and other trails into the Federal Horse Path (eventually known as the Federal Road, which Interstate 65 parallels today across southern Alabama). Express riders were contracted to carry the mail from Benjamin Hawkins' Creek Agency, in central Georgia, to Fort Stoddert in three days, a goal seldom achieved. Despite all efforts, postal service remained undependable, although the improved route did expedite immigrant traffic, to the consternation of the Creeks.[42]

To inform his administration of the "imperfectly known" settlements on the Tombigbee and Tensaw recently acquired by the United States, President Thomas Jefferson appointed Ephraim Kirby as commissioner of public lands and dispatched him to Fort Stoddert (Figure 5). Kirby would inspect recently organized Washington County, which encompassed all land in the territory north of 31° latitude from the Pearl River to the Chattahoochee and respond to the president's queries on the region's physical and human geography. Although his report of May 1, 1804, overlooks the métis component of the Tensaw population, Kirby's comments are otherwise insightful and provide a rare outsider's assessment of the region's American population.

This settlement may be computed at about two hundred families; fifty or sixty of which are on the east side of the Mobile, called the Tensaw

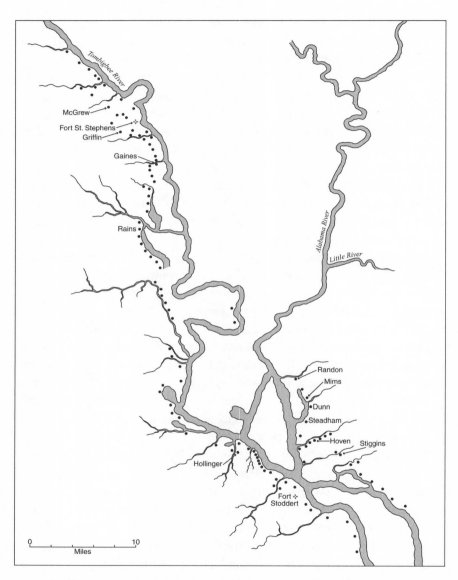

Fig. 5. American plantations in the Tombigbee and Tensaw districts, circa 1802 (based on "Settlements on the Tombeckby & Tensaw Rivers," Alabama 2, Old Map File, Records of the General Land Office, RG 49, NARA.

settlement, and extends upwards to a place called the cut off about eight miles above the confluence of the Alabama and the Tombigbie.—This is much the most opulent and respectable settlement in the country.— The remaining inhabitants are very equally distributed within the limits abovementioned, on the west side of the Mobile and Tombigbie, and on the Creeks which flow into them. . . .

This section of the United States has long afforded an assylum to those who prefer voluntary exile to the punishments ordained by law for heinous offences.—The present inhabitants (with few exceptions) are illiterate, wild and savage, of depraved morals, unworthy of public confidence or private esteem; litigious, disunited, and knowing each other, universally distrustful of each other. The magistrates without dignity, respect, probity, influence or authority.—The administration of justice, imbecile and corrupt. The militia, without discipline or competent officers.

The most antient inhabitants of the country, are French people who resided in it previous to the peace of 1763, and have continued under the several successions of government since that period.—These with their descendents are few in number, and generally peaceable honest, well disposed citizens.—The next most antient class is composed of emigrants from the Carolina's and Georgia, who were attainted and proscribed for treasonable practices during the revolution.—These not only hate the american government, but having long lived without any restraint, committing many enormities against society are now hostile to all law and to every government.—Another class who emigrated generally from the States last mentioned, at a later period, are almost universally fugitives from justice, and many of them felons of the first magnitude.—The last and most meretorious class are also generally emigrants from the States already named, since the organization of government here, and are mostly poor people who have come hither to avoid the demands of creditors, or to gain a precarious subsistence in a wilderness.[43]

Kirby died soon after writing this report, before he could receive Jefferson's offer of the territorial governorship. So he was spared the presumably outraged response of the Tombigbee settlers to his scathing assessment of their characters (and we must rest content with this one example of his devastating wit). Nevertheless, Kirby's description of the region's extraordinary social diversity effectively sets the scene for a close look at some of the individuals and families that found their way to Fort Mims a decade later.

2

Many Paths to the Tensaw

A common literary and cinematic conceit of authors and screenwriters brings together people with metaphorically opposed backgrounds and interests in a confined setting, a tight spot, where the intersection of their personalities reveals great strengths and great failings of character. Thornton Wilder's *The Bridge of San Luis Rey* and John Ford's *Stagecoach* famously employ this effective device, as has virtually every drama set in a spacecraft, submarine, prison, or jury deliberation room. Similarly, the pine log stockade of Fort Mims drew together, in real life, exemplars of the major social groups present on America's southwestern border in 1813. Remarkable personal histories intertwine through this account of the origins and implications of the battle at Fort Mims.

William Weatherford, the part-Creek, part-English métis who planned and helped lead the Redstick attack on Fort Mims, is undoubtedly the best known of the combatants. Later he famously regretted the massacre of civilians that ensued. Opposing him were two commanders of the forces defending the fort. Dixon Bailey led the local Tensaw militia. Like his adversary Weatherford, Bailey was métis, son of an English trader and a Creek woman of the Wind clan. He and his family had been highly vocal proponents of Creek assimilation to American culture and consequently drew the ire of the nativist Redstick faction of Creeks, so-called for the red-painted war clubs that came to stand as symbols of their opposition to the Americans.[1] Commanding the Mississippi Territorial Volunteers, which comprised most of the garrison at Fort Mims, was Major Daniel Beasley, a native of Virginia and for nearly a decade sheriff of Jefferson County, Mississippi Territory. Outbreak of war with the Creeks could have been his opportunity for political advancement, but he is principally remembered for losing Fort Mims through arrogance and lack of vigilance.

Alongside these principal figures were approximately 700 men in the attacking Redstick force and at least 400 people inside the fort. Among the defenders were roughly 100 enlisted men of the Volunteers, nearly all of English descent and lately immigrated to Mississippi Territory from Georgia, the Carolinas, and Virginia in search of opportunities on the American frontier. Most were young, like twenty-six-year-old Nehemiah Page, who would survive the battle at Fort Mims and eventually become a wealthy rancher in the Republic of Texas. Guarded by this garrison were over 200 free residents of the Tensaw, white and métis families, exemplified by Vicey McGirth (former wife of Alexander McGillivray), who, with her five daughters, would survive the battle and ensuing seven-month captivity to return to her home in the Tensaw. All were friends and neighbors of old Samuel Mims, who had come to the Creek country three decades before as a retired trader. Now they crowded into the pallisaded compound he had built around his home, where they hoped to protect their lives and their valuables during the impending attack. Among their highest-valued possessions were 100 or so enslaved humans, Africans owned by both whites and métis. Some, such as fifty-year-old Cyrus, held in bondage by the métis Sam Moniac, would take his chance at freedom during the Redstick assault.

Hidden in the forest near the fort on the morning of August 30, 1813, were hundreds of Creek warriors, many métis themselves, many of them acquaintances, friends, even relatives of the people inside the stockade. One was William Steadham, a métis who would fight as a Redstick and see many of his white and métis siblings die that day. The battle at Fort Mims, far from being a stereotypical clash between white Americans and red Indians, opens a window on the social and demographic complexity that truly characterized early America. What forces drew these diverse people to a cramped one-acre compound in a remote corner of the American frontier?

This and the next chapter trace the courses of several lives that ultimately converged at the Tensaw in 1813. These brief sketches show us how some individuals (those few who are reasonably well documented in contemporary records) attempted to cope with great changes beyond their control. The Creek Indians felt tremendous pressures—from the U.S. government, from white settlers on their borders, from many micos and others of their own nation—to abandon traditional ways and dearly held beliefs. Over the previous century the Creeks had proven an adaptable people, not only surviving but actually increasing in numbers while creatively reshaping their culture as a colonial world formed around them. Their collective grasp on native tradition was malleable and pragmatic, but no less valued for that. They had embraced change as they retained their sense of cultural worth and independence, the latter making the former possible. So this sudden push to abandon everything—almost to the point of losing their very identity as Creeks—engendered strong resistance, even among many métis, whose own upbringing in mixed households suggested how two very different cultural traditions could meld. One famous Creek métis who struggled with the dilemmas of cultural persistence and change at this most difficult of times was William Weatherford.

William Weatherford and the Sehoy Matrilineage

William Weatherford was born, probably in 1781, in or near Coosada, one of the Alabama towns of the Upper Creeks clustered near the head of the Alabama River (just north of present-day Montgomery, Alabama). During a visit in 1799, Benjamin Hawkins described Coosada as "a compact little town situated three miles below the confluence of Coosau and Tallapoosa, on the right bank of Alabama; they have fields on both sides of the river; but their chief dependence is a high, rich island, at the mouth of Coosau. They have some fences, good against cattle only, and some families have small patches fenced, near the town, for potatoes. These Indians are not Creeks, although they conform to their ceremonies; the men work with the women and make great plenty of corn. . . . The Coo-sau-dee generally go to market [in Mobile] by water, and some of them are good oarsmen."[2] Coosada was occupied by Koasatis, who spoke a language related to but distinct from the Muskogean languages of neighboring Alabamas and Creeks. Koasatis had migrated southward in the late seventeenth century from their ancestral homeland in the eastern Tennessee Valley.[3] Seeking refuge from slave raids by Indians armed with English muskets, they formed a close alliance with the Alabamas, whose towns were located nearby. Weatherford's mother, Sehoy of the Wind clan, had close ties to Coosada; in fact, there is a strong likelihood she considered herself ethnic Koasati, not Muskogee Creek as previous historians have assumed.[4]

To appreciate William Weatherford's role in the Creek nation and the social stature he enjoyed among both Americans and Creeks, one needs to know something of his background, particularly his relationship to his matrilineage, a topic best approached through genealogy.[5] Unless one happens to be a lineal descendant with an intense personal interest, genealogical charts and recitations of ancestors can be mind-numbing, like endless lists of biblical begats with little apparent relevance to larger historical issues. Consequently, historians have long left genealogy to amateurs, to those history aficionados often portrayed as family eccentrics who zealously search cemeteries and archival collections for the least traces of obscure, and sometimes dubious, ancestors. That is, historians largely disdained genealogy until recently, thinking this sort of indiscriminate fact-gathering an inefficient and inadequate way to plumb the historical essence of a life or an epoch. Lately, though, some historians are reexamining genealogical research methods and finding them particularly appropriate to the study of small-scale communities where people interacted face-to-face on a daily basis. Anthropologists, of course, discovered over a century ago that charting a village's kinship relations reveals much about underlying community structure, but that lesson has taken some time to filter into the field of American history. Now a convergence of ethnohistory, historical demography, and the increasingly professionalized field of local history is kindling renewed interest in genealogical data, which, it turns out, can address all manner of significant historical questions. In the case of the Tensaw, genealogy reveals the numerous ties that bound whites, blacks, Indians, and métis together and helps us understand where rifts developed in 1813. And Weatherford's matrilineage, the family of the Sehoy women, lay at the heart of the Tensaw.

∼

William's great-grandmother, Sehoy (referred to as Sehoy I, in the modern literature, to minimize confusion with like-named descendants), grew to adulthood in the vicinity of Fort Toulouse aux Alibamons, Fort Toulouse among the Alabamas (Chart 1). Early abuses by British traders based in South Carolina convinced the Creeks that they needed an alternative, competitive source of the cloth, muskets, steel knives, and other European manufactured commodities they exchanged for deerskins, furs, and peltries. In the aftermath of the Yamasee War of 1715, when all British traders were either killed or expelled from the Creek country, Alabama leaders invited the French to establish Fort Toulouse in their midst. This modest-sized, isolated military post served principally as a trade entrepôt for the many nearby Creek towns while thwarting British claims of sovereignty over the region. According to McGillivray family legend, Sehoy I had an affair with a fort commandant, Captain François Marchand de Courcelles, at about the time a mutiny of the French garrison occurred in August 1721. Sources are unclear on Sehoy's origins, but historians have generally concluded that she lived either at Coosada or at Taskigi, another Alabama town in the vicinity of Fort Toulouse. Perhaps significantly (if Sehoy I was indeed a Koasati), French officers are said to have turned to the warriors of Coosada for assistance in capturing the mutinous deserters.[6] We do not know whether the Creeks considered this relationship between Sehoy I and Marchand a marriage or a casual attachment, but a daughter, Sehoy II, was born from that brief union. Sehoy I soon afterwards married a Koasati headman, Red Shoes; they had a daughter and a son who likewise came to be called Red Shoes (II). Sehoy I evidently died after just a few years (around 1730), and Red Shoes I remarried, producing another son also called Red Shoes (III).[7]

The métis daughter of the Marchand liaison, Sehoy II (William Weatherford's grandmother), married Lachlan McGillivray, a Scot, who became one of the wealthiest traders in the Southeast (Chart 2).[8] By the 1750s Lachlan established a plantation and apple grove at Little Tallassee, on the Coosa River a few miles north of Fort Toulouse.[9] His marriage with Sehoy II lasted a dozen years, and they had five children, three of whom—Sophia, Alexander, and Jennet— lived to adulthood. With Lachlan's final departure from Creek country in 1757, Sehoy II married again, to another Scots trader named Malcolm McPherson. They had three children, Malcolm McPherson II, who became mico of Hickory Ground, and two daughters, Elizabeth and Sehoy III (who became William Weatherford's mother).[10] Little is known of the elder McPherson, but he evidently died or left the Creek towns within a few years. Sehoy II then (according to family history) married a leading man of either Tawasa or Tuckaubatchee, whose name is unknown.[11]

In 1764 or thereabout, Sehoy II acquiesced to Lachlan McGillivray's request that their son Alexander be permitted to live in Charleston, South Carolina, with him and his white family. There Alexander learned to speak English fluently, received a formal English colonial education, and apprenticed in the accounting end of the deerskin trade. The now-literate young man returned home to Little Tallassee in 1777, in the midst of the American Revolution, as assistant deputy to John Stuart, Britain's Indian superintendent in the South. Through adroit political and diplomatic maneuvering, Alexander ascended rapidly in authority among the Creeks. By 1783 he told British officials the Creeks had chosen him their "King and Head Warrior,"[12] although others might have characterized him more objectively as their chief spokesman during the following decade. No matter his title, there is no doubt his influence was immense among the Creeks as well as with American and colonial officials in this corner of the continent.

During the last years of his life, Alexander had two wives. Most Creeks of this era were serial monogamists, married to one partner at a time but free to remarry after losing a spouse through death, divorce, or abandonment.

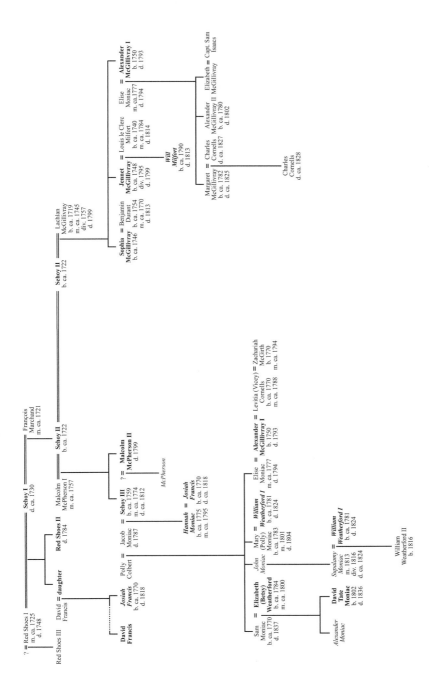

Kinship Chart 1. Sehoy I Lineage. Names of Sehoy matrilineage members in bold; names of Redsticks (1813–1814 era) in italics.

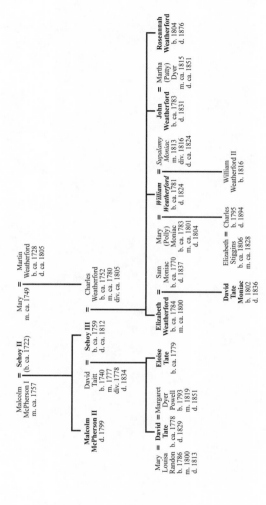

Kinship Chart 2. Sehoy II Lineage. Names of Sehoy matrilineage members in bold; names of Red-sticks, during the 1813–1814 war, in italics.

McGillivray's polygyny reflected his exceptional wealth and high status in Creek society. His first and principal wife was Elise Moniac, daughter of Jacob Moniac, a Dutch trader and interpreter at Little Tallassee during the Revolution, and Polly Colbert, a Chickasaw-French métis.[13] Elise resided on McGillivray's plantation at Little Tallassee with her son and two daughters; she died in 1794, within a year of Alexander's death. One daughter married the Coosada headman Captain Sam Isaacs.[14] Alexander's second wife was Levitia "Vicey" Cornells, daughter of a métis woman from Tuckaubatchee and Joseph Cornells, a white trader and interpreter at the Upper Creek town of Tallassee. Joseph and his daughters moved to the Tensaw as early as 1788, perhaps upon Vicey's marriage to Alexander. Maintaining widely separated households for his two wives may have been wise domestic strategy on Alexander's part. Although the Cornells returned to Tuckaubatchee upon Alexander's death, Vicey and her siblings Lucy and James reestablished residence in the Tensaw a decade later.[15]

In the 1770s Alexander's sister Sophia married Benjamin Durant (who would die inside Fort Mims), a French Huguenot from South Carolina (Chart 3). Together they oversaw operation of her father Lachlan McGillivray's Savannah plantation until the course of the Revolution prompted many loyalists, the Durants among them, to flee to the Creek country. Alexander and the Durants established the first Creek plantation in the Tensaw area in the fall of 1783 when they and forty slaves drove "a good herd of cattle" south from Little Tallassee. Three of Sophia's seven children would take up the Redstick cause, including daughter Betsy, who married the Redstick leader, Peter McQueen. Jennet McGillivray, Alexander's younger sister, married the French adventurer Louis LeClerc Milfort, a friend of Alexander's who had gained the position of tastanagi (*tvstvnvke,* war leader) among the Creeks. Milfort abandoned his Creek family in 1795 and returned to France, where he published an informative, albeit self-serving, volume on the Creeks intended to catch the eye of Napoleon, who was briefly considering a renewal of French colonization in La Louisiane. When Napoleon sold Louisiana to the United States in 1803, the opportunist Milfort lost his chance to return to the Creek country.[16]

Sehoy III, the daughter of Sehoy II and Malcolm McPherson and maternal half-sister of Alexander McGillivray, had a difficult childhood. At the age of eight, around the time her mother died, she moved into the household of Jacob Moniac, Alexander's trusted advisor. Jacob's daughter Elise may have been married to Alexander by then, perhaps explaining Sehoy's living arrangements, but the nature of the relationship between the young girl and the old Dutch trader remains murky. When she was about fifteen Sehoy had a child

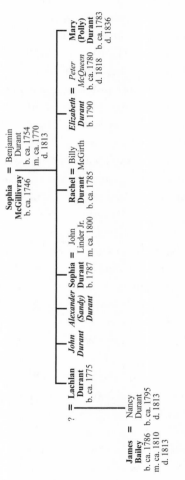

Kinship Chart 3. Durant Lineage. Names of Wind clan members in bold; names of Redsticks (1813–1814 era) in italics.

by Moniac, a daughter named Hannah. Modern writers have speculated that Jacob married Sehoy III, but he was already married to Polly Colbert and would remain so for another dozen years. An illegitimate birth (and Sehoy's possible rape) seems more likely.[17]

This is an appropriate place to interject a word on the nature of marriage in Creek society of the eighteenth century. Historical writings, from Pickett in 1851 up to today, have consistently assumed that southeastern women exercised absolute freedom of choice in decisions of marriage and divorce. That overly romantic view ought to be tempered with some awareness of the role of the lineage and particularly the role of clan uncles in arranging (and rearranging) marriage alliances. In the matrilineal society of the Creeks, relationships between men were established principally through women, while women could influence, shape, and dissolve old lineage alliances and form new ones. Many of the marriages of the Sehoy women, from Sehoy I's union with Marchand onward, benefited their clan and lineage politically and economically. Whether or not these marriages were arranged from the outset by male relatives, we can be sure those male relatives were consulted and their opinions considered before the alliances were finalized, particularly in the case of very young brides.[18]

When she reached the age of eighteen, Sehoy III married David Taitt, deputy to Britain's Indian superintendent, John Stuart. Taitt spent much of 1775 through 1778 at Little Tallassee, home of his friend and assistant Alexander McGillivray. Indeed, Taitt's marriage to Sehoy seems to correspond closely with McGillivray's arrival at Little Tallassee in 1777, and particularly with McGillivray's dramatic facedown of a war party intent on assassinating the young Scot on September 19 of that year. Their children, David and Eloise (who subsequently spelled their name "Tate," to the eternal confusion of later historians), soon lost their father to the Revolution in the South. By the summer of 1778, Taitt had been "obliged," as Governor Peter Chester put it, "to quit his residence in the Indian country through fear of being massacred by the disaffected part of the [Creek] nation." As American agents, led by George Galphin, maneuvered against Taitt and his British colleagues for influence among the Creeks, that society split into pro-American and pro-British factions. When Taitt found he could no longer remain safely in the Creek country, he redirected his energies to recruiting Creek warriors to assist British military operations elsewhere in the region. He participated in the sieges of Savannah and Mobile and was arrested by the Spanish at the latter city in mid-1780. At war's end—upon release from his Spanish cell—David Taitt sailed to England, where in 1782 he sought compensation from the Loyalist Claims Commission for back pay and for property abandoned in the American South. Immigrating to Nova Scotia in 1784, he surveyed the town of Sydney and resided on Cape Breton Island for the rest of his ninety-three years. There is no evidence that Taitt maintained any contact with his Creek wife or children after he left the South.[19]

Even before David Taitt lay languishing in a prison in Spanish Mobile, contemplating what must have seemed his poor prospects for a future, Sehoy III had remarried. Late in 1779 or early in 1780, Charles Weatherford, a loyalist, and Samuel Mims, a Virginian of uncertain political leanings, rode together into the Upper Creek country to escape the ravages of war in the East.[20] Both men had engaged in trade there for several years. Now they sought homes as well as livelihoods among the Creeks. Mims' activities for the next few years are unknown, but Weatherford must have gone almost immediately to the town of Coosada. He and Sehoy III married, and their son William was born in late 1780 or early 1781.

As husband of Alexander McGillivray's maternal half-sister, Charles Weatherford quickly discovered what mercantile advantages derived from his relationship to Sehoy's lineage. And, as a confidante of the increasingly powerful McGillivray, Charles accrued some political advantage as well by participating in Creek council deliberations and decisions. That a white trader, no matter how well married, should have been invited to participate so fully in Creek internal politics would be surprising. But, it turns out, historians have mistakenly assumed that Charles Weatherford, variously identified as Scottish or English in descent, was white. According to modern Weatherford family records, the patronymic derives from Witherford, which originated in Warwickshire, England. Charles' father, Martin (born in James City County, Virginia, around 1728), married a half-Indian métis, Mary (last name and ethnicity unspecified), around 1749, probably in Lunenburg County, Virginia. Son Charles grew up in Augusta, Georgia, on the principal road from the English colonies to the Creek nation, across the Savannah River from George Galphin's major trading establishment at Silver Bluff.[21] Unfortunately, nothing further is known about Charles' mother. The specifics of her Indian ethnicity would be especially interesting. But certainly his own métis status and his early exposure to Creeks and the Creek trade must have proven useful in later life, whether or not Charles was part Creek himself.

Charles Weatherford established a plantation on the east bank of the Alabama River, across and slightly downstream from his wife's residence at Coosada. There his workforce of enslaved Africans raised crops and cattle and cared for a large herd of horses, which he raced on the first horse track in the region. The origin of Weatherford's fine horses raised suspicion at the time. During the 1780s and 1790s Creek warriors stole hundreds, perhaps thousands, of horses from American frontier settlers during bloody border disputes with Georgia and Tennessee; some of the best of these probably ended up racing on the track near the prehistoric Indian mounds on Weatherford's plantation.[22]

Besides trafficking in stolen horses (and slaves), Charles Weatherford became entangled in numerous other controversies.[23] His first serious difficulty arose from his refusal to pay a sizeable debt he owed the trading firm of Panton, Leslie and Co. With McGillivray's acquiescence, Spanish officials imprisoned Weatherford in New Orleans for twelve months over this unpaid debt. Sehoy's entreaties belatedly persuaded McGillivray to intercede on behalf of his brother-in-law. "It had been my Intention," McGillivray wrote to Governor Miró, "in Consideration of the distresses of Weatherfords wife & children to have requested of Your Excellency the release of that Man that he might return back to his family. . . . probably the punishment he has received will make a favorable alteration in his manners & disposition." McGillivray could not have been more mistaken. From 1788 onward, a free but embittered Weatherford sought "revenge from the *Dons* [the Spaniards]," took every opportunity to undermine McGillivray's diplomatic relations with Spain, and furnished American officials with detailed information on Creek intentions toward their eastern neighbors in Georgia. After McGillivray's death in 1793, Weatherford continued working assiduously to undermine Spanish influence and strengthen relations between the Creeks and the United States.[24]

In 1798, a council of Creek leaders named Charles Weatherford as one of seven resident traders of "unworthy character and unfit" to remain in the Creek nation. The micos intended to banish these men, whom they castigated as "liars and medlars and rogues; they will meddle in public affairs, are constantly circulating reports injurious to our peace. . . . They disturb the peace of our land by making our young men uneasy by their false and foolish stories." Once again, however, Weatherford benefited by his connection to Sehoy's lineage and avoided exile in exchange for a promise of future good behavior.[25] This time he held true to his word. No further conflicts involving Charles Weatherford appear in the historical record, although his personal finances declined precipitously. By 1799 he no longer engaged in the deerskin trade, most of his horses had succumbed to "some unaccountable malady," and he had moved downriver to a smaller residence. In contrast, his wife Sehoy III, from whom he was probably estranged by this time, had been operating a trading establishment of her own for several years, living "in some taste, but expensively," according to Benjamin Hawkins. Sehoy, like her sisters and other clan relatives, vigorously defended Creek traditions by denying her husband any say in her matrilineage's wealth.[26]

In 1803 Charles Weatherford assisted Benjamin Hawkins, the American agent, by helping apprehend the English-American loyalist adventurer William Augustus Bowles. Beginning in 1783, Bowles tried repeatedly to organize and lead an autonomous Creek state, which he called the Muskogee Nation. He imagined Muskogee could, if allied to Britain, challenge Spanish and American claims to the interior Southeast. Although Bowles never achieved a large following among the Creeks, nor managed to create a Muskogee state, through personal force of will and sheer audacity he kept the Southeast in turmoil for two decades. At his most successful, his small band of warriors in 1800 briefly captured the Spanish fort at St. Marks, on Apalachicola Bay, which he grandiosely declared a free port of trade before a Spanish fleet arrived promptly to retake the outpost. When Bowles brazenly marched into the heart of the Creek country in May of 1803 to address the national council at Hickory Ground, William Weatherford and Sam Moniac, backed up by Charles Weatherford and others, seized Bowles and turned him over to Spanish authorities, finally bringing to an end his long-running filibustering antics. William Weatherford's prominent role in this affair won him broad recognition for the first time among the Creeks as a fearless and decisive young leader.[27] He had taken this bold action, however, at the behest of his pro-American father and the American agent Benjamin Hawkins. In subsequent years, William may have regretted helping to destroy this eccentric but potent (and, ironically, non-Creek) symbol of Creek resistance to the United States.

Charles Weatherford evidently left the Creek country soon afterwards to rejoin his father, Martin, who had emigrated to the Bahamas with his white family long before, at the end of the Revolution. Although he never returned to live with Sehoy and their Creek children, an event occurred near the end of Charles' life that suggests how thoroughly Creek he remained. In 1824, Charles (then well over seventy years old) conspired with a friend, John D. Smith, to cut the ears off of one Archibald Taylor, whom they caught in bed with Smith's wife. Known as cropping, this standard Creek punishment for adulterers must have come as a shock to the Bahamian, Taylor. Four years later, in one last historical glimpse of Charles, he still lived, having wielded a hatchet to fend off a wild boar that had invaded his home on Grand Bahama Island.[28]

By 1801, well before his father's departure, William Weatherford married Mary "Polly" Moniac, soon after his sister Elizabeth had married Polly's brother

Sam. They began developing their own plantation on the upper Alabama River, fifty-four miles downstream from Coosada. His brothers David Tate and John Weatherford had already taken charge of their maternal uncle Alexander McGillivray's plantations and cowpens at Little River. The McGillivray sisters had successfully defended those properties for their clan from John Panton's attempt to reserve them, under Spanish law, for Alexander's son. William spent much time in the Tensaw region, visiting his brothers' plantations frequently (although he would not establish a home of his own there until after the Redstick War). When Polly died in 1804, he maintained his plantation at "Point Thloly" on the upper Alabama River but thereafter took greater interest in Creek political affairs.[29]

Half-brothers William Weatherford and David Tate had much in common; besides sharing a mother (and, of course, a matrilineage), each continued to observe at least some of the cultural traditions of their Creek relatives. Both gained proficiency in English, interacted easily with Indians and whites, and accumulated great wealth from the labor of their plantation slaves. Despite these similarities, their upbringings had taken very different turns, as would the courses of their lives during the Redstick War.[30]

At the age of twelve, David Tate accompanied his uncle, Alexander McGillivray, to New York in 1790 to attend a conference between leaders of the Creek nation and officials of the United States. While the Creek delegation negotiated publicly with American officials, McGillivray and Secretary of War Henry Knox covertly drafted a private codicil to the treaty. One secret provision, Article 5, obligated the United States "to educate and clothe such of the creek youth as shall be agreed upon, not exceeding four in number at any one time."[31] When the Creek delegation headed home, David Tate and David Francis (another young McGillivray relation) went on to Philadelphia where they attended a Quaker school at government expense for the next five years.[32] After a brief visit home, Tate was again sent off to school, this time in Scotland as a companion for Alexander McGillivray, Jr., with all costs borne by John Panton, friend of the McGillivray boy's father and grandfather. In Banff, north of Aberdeen, the two Creek métis studied for a classical education until David offended the schoolmaster, ran away to London, and returned home within a year.[33]

Indoctrinated by formal schooling while absent from his Indian home for so many years, Tate may well have experienced difficulty returning to life as a Creek. Unlike many of his relatives, who moved easily between the towns of the Creek nation and plantations in the Tensaw, David Tate seems to have remained permanently on Little River. Nearly alone of the Tensaw Creeks, he participated in Mississippi Territorial court cases, as the defendant in three suits brought for debts in 1807 alone. In one exceptional case that occurred in 1810, the sheriff of Washington County, Mississippi Territory, rode to the Creek Agency on the Flint River in Georgia to serve a writ on Tate to recover payment for African slaves sold to Alexander McGillivray almost twenty years earlier. In that instance, Tate chose to affirm his Creek identity, successfully denying jurisdiction in the U.S. courts. With his ability to pose convincingly as American or Creek, as circumstances demanded, Tate effectively maneuvered between two very different legal and economic systems.[34]

William Weatherford, in contrast, had no formal American or European schooling and appears in no court records prior to the Redstick War. He may have had some reading ability, but no evidence exists that he could write.[35] Instead, Weatherford's boyhood education must have occurred mainly at the feet of the men of his mother's matrilineage, particularly his uncles Malcolm McPherson II and Alexander McGillivray, and by observing and participating in the ceremonies and councils of clan relatives and townspeople at Coosada and Hickory Ground. As he grew to adulthood, Weatherford would have gained valuable practical experiences by playing the Creek ball game—"the little brother to war"—with his age grade, hunting deer and bear with older men, and training horses for his father. By all accounts, he excelled in these strenuous activities and skills.[36] Although interviews with acquaintances in the mid- to late nineteenth century (which constitute our only information on his childhood) are certainly romanticized, they do offer plausible testimony for Weatherford's fearlessness, fine horsemanship, love of hunting, and eloquence in square ground deliberations.[37]

William Weatherford's notoriety for his role in the massacre at Fort Mims and his later recasting by American writers as a tragic "white Indian" complicate efforts to understand how he and other métis Creeks dealt with the challenges to their identities posed by mixed ancestry. Few elements of Weatherford's life are certain, primarily because the authors of our sources used him for their own ends, to villify or excuse or ennoble, almost from the moment the last embers expired at Fort Mims. Consequently, even his Muskogee name remains in doubt. Weatherford is best known to Americans as Red Eagle, *Lamochattee* (*Lvmhe catē*). That attribution, however, first appeared in print in a poem published in 1855, nearly three decades after Weatherford's death, which raises certain doubts on its authenticity. In the 1880s a descendant acknowledged as much when he characterized his ancestor as "The 'Red Eagle' of the poet." On the other hand, according to Thomas Woodward, an acquaintance of Weatherford's, he had two Creek names: one, a noble-sounding war name, "Hoponicafutsahia [*Hvponeka fvccetv*], or Truth Maker or Teller," the other a nickname—and, just possibly, a racial reference to his skin color—"Billy Larney [*lane*], or Yellow Billy." Distinguishing the authentic Weatherford, Truth Teller, from his fictionalized alter ego, Red Eagle, is not easily accomplished.[38]

~

The foregoing summary of William Weatherford's origins introduces many of the families that coalesced to form the Creek community at the Tensaw. Cornells, Durant, Francis, McPherson, Milfort, Moniac, Tate, Weatherford (and others still to come, such as Bailey, McGirth, and Stiggins)—all were linked in some way to the lineage of the Sehoy women, either by birth as members of the matrilineage or as in-laws by a complex web of intermarriage. Genealogical diagrams (which outline these complex relationships in simplified form) reveal several interesting facts (see Charts 1–3).

For one, the métis of Sehoy's Wind clan tended to marry other métis. Apart from Sehoy I, few non-métis Creeks appear on these charts, even though Creeks without European ancestry comprised the majority of the nation's population throughout the eighteenth century. These families stood apart from other Creeks. Creek métis preferentially married other Creek métis, a behavior probably favored for several reasons. Economic considerations surely played a role, as individuals, backed by their families, tried to improve their lot or protect existing sources of wealth. Yet, significantly, no wealthy non-métis Creeks appear on these charts after the first couple of generations. One must wonder whether an emerging racial consciousness contributed to this pattern of métis marrying métis.

Second, Sehoy's lineage members sought out multiple links by marriage with the Durants, Dyers, Moniacs, Randons, and Stiggins, thereby forging increasingly strong relationships with other métis families. Numerous social ties bound together the families of the Tensaw. This close network of intermarriage enhanced the ability of the Tensaw métis to consolidate wealth, which accumulated at an astounding rate, disproportionate to their small numbers in the Creek nation. In a landmark study of federal claims submitted by Creeks who lost property during the Redstick War, historian Claudio Saunt discovered that claimants from the Tensaw (just 4 percent of all Creek claimants) documented losses amounting to 21 percent of the property owned by pro-American Creeks that was destroyed in the war. The median of the twenty-six Tensaw claims (at $1,050) amounted to more than fourteen times the median value of claims emanating from elsewhere in the Creek nation.[39] In the Tensaw's thirty-year existence, from its founding in 1783 until its destruction in 1813, that community of McGillivray kin acquired great wealth by reorienting traditional Creek involvement with colonial markets from deerskins to cattle and field crops. They simultaneously learned to maintain control over their rapidly compounding wealth by preferentially intermarrying within a narrowly delimited social sphere. As a result, the Tensaw grew increasingly apart from the Alabama talwas from which it arose.

With a steady influx of Creek métis seeking economic and social alternatives to the talwa, Creek settlement in the Tensaw evolved rapidly away from the traditional plan of nucleated village with adjacent communal fields. Here plantations were dispersed very widely, with plenty of room for livestock to forage in the expansive canebrakes of the Alabama River bottomlands. That same habitat was gradually being cleared by the labor of African slaves for fields cultivated by horse- and oxen-drawn plows. The resultant landscape of widely spaced plantations, separated by the still heavily forested banks of the river and its major tributary streams, bore little resemblance to the compact town plans and expansive field clearings of long-established contemporary talwas in the Upper Creek country.

While information on the internal social workings of the Tensaw is very sparse, here too the Tensaw seems to have differed from its parent talwas to the north. In fact, available evidence supports the notion that the Tensaw was not organized as a talwa—an independent Creek town with a mico and an advisory council that conducted community business in a square ground. Instead, the Tensaw seems to have remained a talofa, a daughter community to the Alabama talwas. No individual is known to have held the title of mico in Tensaw; nor is there any evidence for community council meetings, or indeed of the existence of either a summer square ground or a winter council house in the Tensaw. One might infer from this apparent absence of talwa institutions that the Tensaw métis considered their own status subsidiary to the parent talwas. In fact, the leading men of Coosada and Taskigi sought repeatedly to project their influence and to exercise control over the affairs of the Tensaw. But a stubborn, steadfast resistance to talwa-level authority by many Tensaw métis suggests they held a very different perception of the Creek community at Little River—as a part of the Creek nation, yet willfully disengaged from the traditional social controls of clan and talwa. At the forefront of Tensaw métis resistance to Alabama authority were Dixon Bailey and his family.

Dixon Bailey

Dixon's father, Richard Bailey, appears in the historical record in 1772 as "a hireling trading for Mr Mackay in the Ottesey [Atasi] town." David Taitt noted, with disapproval, that Bailey had taken skins purchased on behalf of his employer, Robert McKay & Co. of Augusta, to Pensacola where he had traded them for rum. Bailey intended to give the rum to his Creek wife, who would use it to purchase more skins "as her own property, thereby depriving the merchant [McKay] of his just right." He had already drawn the ire of Creek leaders one year before for "driving Cattle and Settling Cowpens on our Land without our Consent."[40]

Bailey, an Englishman, had come to the Creek country around 1766, after ten years' apprenticeship as a carpenter and joiner in Savannah. He soon married a woman of the Wind clan, known to us only as Mary, with whom he lived at the town of Atasi for more than thirty years. His name—along with those of Charles and Martin Weatherford and William Panton—appears on a list of loyalists banished from Georgia in 1783, though by then he had long since given up any thought of returning to that state. By 1796 the former "hireling" had become one of the wealthiest traders in the Creek nation.[41]

In that year, Benjamin Hawkins visited Bailey's plantation west of Atasi. There the newly appointed U.S. agent wrote a series of lengthy journal entries, cumulatively the most detailed account available on a late-eighteenth-century trader's Creek family and their plantation. Hawkins thought Bailey "a good farmer" and noted with approval his ownership of seven enslaved Africans as well as "lands fenced, stable, garden, lots for his stock, some thriving trees, and a small nursery to plant out. His stock of horses, cattle and hogs numerous." However, Bailey's success in animal husbandry made the Creeks "uneasy" because his livestock damaged their crops, "so much so, that Mr. Bailey finds his [cattle] not safe, but as the property of his wife and children." Just as he had done a quarter of a century earlier, Bailey sheltered his assets by converting them to matrilineage ownership, in the process thereby gaining the political support of his wife's clan relatives (who undoubtedly considered those livestock to be clan property, in any case).

"He has an Indian woman," the U.S. agent observed, "and 5 children and as many grand children. His wife is of the Otalla (wind) family. She is neat, cleanly, prudent and economical, as careful of her family concerns as a white woman." That last condescension, "as a white woman," might be expected from the chief promoter of Creek Indian conversion to an American vision of civilization (Plate 3). But his further comments reveal more. Hawkins thought he found, in Mary Bailey, the means by which Creek women could aid his cause. "I have been much pleased in my visit here as well as at Mr. Grierson's [at Hillabee town]. It being demonstrated to me that the Indian women from these two [families], are capable of and willing to become instrumental in civilising the men. Mrs. Bailey shares in all the toils of her husband when there was a necessity for it. She attended the pack horses to market, swam rivers to facilitate the transportation of their goods, is careful of the interest of her family and resolute in support of it."

Hawkins, who was clearly taken with the Bailey women, also commented upon the two daughters (Chart 4); "married to white men, they both spin cotton and the youngest, Elizabeth Fletcher, can read and write and is very industrious. This whole family are remarkable for being healthy and cleanly. This may be owing to a custom continued by Mrs. Bailey, she and her family every morning winter or summer bathe in cold water." The fortitude of this family— an Englishman, a Creek woman, and their métis children—surely impressed Hawkins during his mid-December visit, when morning temperatures hovered around freezing.[42]

After a brief stop at Charles Weatherford's plantation near Coosada, Hawkins returned a week later to spend Christmas with the Baileys at Atasi. Once again, he felt compelled to compliment this "good woman[,] as cleanly as any of her sex." After dinner, "I applied particularly to Mrs. Bailey for her opinion of the practicability of carrying the benevolent views of the government into effect, explaining them fully to her. She replied it was uncertain; her daughters had learnt to spin among the white women, at Tensaw, were cleanly, neat and industrious. That many of the Indian women were industrious, but not cleanly, nor so provident and careful as the white women." "This," Hawkins replied, "might be owing to want of information, and the means of helping themselves." Mary Bailey "said she did not know whether it was so or not, but of one thing she was certain, they all had water enough, and yet they never kept their husbands clean, even the white men, that this was really a source of vexation to her, and put her under the necessity of scolding the men whenever she saw them, for not making their wives wash their linen; and the women for their want of cleanliness."

Despite their apparent agreement on (and obsession with) this subject, Benjamin Hawkins and Mary Bailey almost certainly held very different opinions on the purpose of a daily dip in the chilly Tallapoosa River. What Hawkins viewed primarily as a physical cleansing, Bailey understood as internally puri-

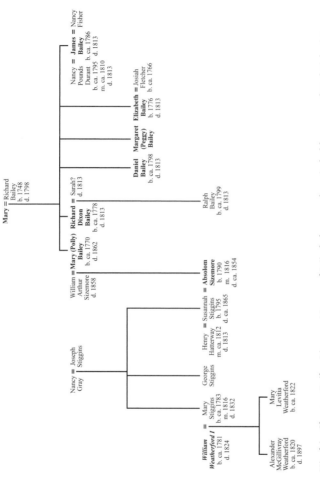

Kinship Chart 4. Bailey Lineage. Names of Wind clan members in bold; names of Redsticks (1813–1814 era) in italics.

fying, too. This daily invocation of household ritual mirrored a community's
annual poskita purification ceremony, which included periodic group plunges
into a river to achieve spiritual renewal. Mary Bailey's insistence that her family
respect and maintain this custom suggests a commitment to traditional Creek
religious beliefs that contrasts with her willingness to adopt new modes of
household economy, such as spinning, weaving, cattle raising, and a dependence on the labor of slaves. But cleanliness for her also entailed washing her
family's clothes. Before European traders introduced woolens, linens, and cot-
tons to the region, southeastern Indians had not washed their clothing, treatment that would have damaged leggings and flaps of leather and skirts made
from fragile plant bast fibers. Once imported woven cloth became available,
they treated those new forms of clothing as they had done the earlier kinds,
by wearing a few changes of clothes all year and discarding them at the annual poskita ceremony, when new garb was donned for the coming year. Mary
Bailey's inclusive advocacy of Creek bathing *and* American laundry demon-
strates an open-mindedness not shared by many of her Creek or American contemporaries.[43]

In the course of their after-dinner conversation, Hawkins' hosts confided
that their pursuit of stock raising had strained relations with the townspeople
of Atasi. "Some few years past they were under the necessity to move to Tensaw,
on account of their stock, and the ill nature of the Indians, who always have
had fences are in the habit of distroying hogs or cattle whenever they tress-
pass on the fields under cultivation. By this removal the town was three years
without a trader and the Indians sent several messages to them to return, but
Mrs. Bailey said she would not unless their stock could be secure, and it should
be left to Mr. Bailey to choose his place of residence near the town. The Indians sent their king to confirm this agreement, which they adhere to with some
little murmuring at the largeness and increase of his stock."[44] Notwithstanding
Hawkins' claim to the contrary, the Creeks had fenced their community fields
and household gardens only recently, and then only to protect their crops from
domestic livestock. The deer, bears, raccoons, and turkeys that raided cornfields
had always been (literally) fair game, so injunctions against killing cattle that
ruined crops seemed unjust, particularly to those who saw no general benefit
to the private ownership of livestock. Rising discontent with Bailey kept pace
with the "increase of his stock." In May 1798 he was banished again, by the
Creek national council meeting at Tuckaubatchee, as "an unfit character" who
treated "some of his town people with contempt." Permitted to return to Atasi
a few months later, he died from a fall from his horse soon afterwards.[45]

The trader's widow retained possession of his plantation, which their son Richard Dixon Bailey thereafter managed. Dixon had been educated in Philadelphia in the mid-1790s at U.S. government expense, another beneficiary of McGillivray's secret treaty article. So, too, were his younger brother James and another Creek métis youth, McGillivray's nephew Alexander (Sandy) Durant, who were placed with the Philadelphia Quakers in 1796 to learn "such mechanical professions as they shall fix upon, and as the boys may show an aptitude to learn," to have them bound to "the turner's, carpenter's, or blacksmith's trade." Dixon, however, had been schooled "under the care of the Secretary of War," Henry Knox, not by the Society of Friends.[46] By the time Hawkins met him in 1799, upon his return to Atasi, Dixon had "brought with him into the nation so much contempt for the Indian mode of life that he has got himself into discredit with them." By 1801, the American agent thought Dixon "neither an Indian or white man," adding hopefully, "yet he promises to mend."[47] Dixon wrestled with the classic métis dilemma: could he find acceptance among Indians or whites, and, if not, was there a middle ground for people like him?

Hawkins presumably wished Dixon Bailey would "mend" not only by acting like a white man but by hewing to the path of civilization and leading his countrymen along that same course by his example. Whether or not the Baileys considered themselves harbingers of civilization, role models for "the new order of things," they evidently found they could coexist no longer with the old order at Atasi. Sometime after 1802, Mary Bailey, her children and their families returned to the Tensaw, where they had spent their three-year exile a decade earlier and where their lifestyle—a combination of conservative native religion and liberal American-style economics—found acceptance among a majority Creek métis population.[48]

Even here, at the southern edge of their nation, innovative métis like the Baileys could not escape the forces slowly pulling apart the Creek people. Part of the tension was certainly due to economic competition, and nowhere was rivalry more evident than between the Tensaw plantations and the Alabama towns and plantations near the forks of the Coosa and Tallapoosa rivers. The fields of the Alabama Indians were, according to Hawkins, "the granary of the upper [Creek] towns and furnished considerable supplies by water to Mobile."[49] The Alabamas watched their income from the American markets in Mobile and Pensacola (and, ultimately, New Orleans via Mobile) dwindle in competition with the increasingly productive Tensaw plantations.[50] Repeated efforts by American agents at Fort Stoddert to impose duties on Alabama canoe shipments to Mobile, although twice forbidden by presidential order, further outraged the Creeks in the nation. Captain Sam Isaacs, a Coosada headman (and husband of Alexander McGillivray's daughter Elizabeth), threatened war with the United States in 1807 when custom duties were demanded of him at Fort Stoddert. In the end, he contented himself with "insulting and plundering some travellers and attempting to injure the post rider," but relations between the Upper Creeks and their American neighbors to the south continued to deteriorate.[51] Since the Tensaw métis enjoyed unfettered, and untaxed, access to American and Spanish markets, this became an additional point of irritation to Creeks upriver.

In March 1809, Captain Isaacs, backed up by a dozen Coosada warriors, arrived in the Tensaw to levy taxes on the properties of "half breeds." According to Tensaw resident Dr. Thomas G. Holmes (as revealed in an interview with historian Albert James Pickett nearly four decades later), Isaacs "called upon Dixon Baily . . . & demanded $100 as the rent of Bailey's [Alabama River] ferry, for the privilege." Bailey rejected the implication that he and the other Tensaw métis were foreigners, subject to fees, and "refused to give it to him, for he thought he was entitled to all the privileges of any other of the [Creek] nation." Threatening to "cut his flat [boat] up & drive him off" if Bailey did not pay the tax, Isaacs proceeded downriver collecting payments from other métis. "He charged stock keepers $2.00 per Hundred . . . & told them if they did not pay him he would drive their cattle off to the nation." Upon returning to Bailey's ferry, Isaacs confronted Linn McGee, Bailey's ferry operator, and "demanded of him if he had the $100 for him in his hands." "No," replied McGee; "Bailey did not intend to pay him a cent."

At that, Isaacs and "his party fell abord of McGee & beat him almost unto death & then began to cut up his flat." On Isaacs' approach, McGee had sent an enslaved African boy to find Bailey, who was hunting in the woods. Hearing that Isaacs' men "were cuting his Flat up," Bailey ran to the ferry, picked up a handspike and charged at Isaacs, who brandished a tomahawk and warned him off. Bailey, "fearless of all men, rushed upon him, knocked him down." Soon surrounded "by Isaacs warriors with their tomahawks one after another he laid them out. one fellow getting behind him, about striking him with a tomahawk," Dixon's sixty-year-old mother suddenly appeared on the scene and "seized the fellow round the middle & with a fortunate exertion threw him into the river. the indian carry the woman with him—one trying to drown the other. They both got to shore & crawled out. By this time Bailey had concured Isaac & his men   they were glad to retire."[52]

Mary and Dixon Bailey's victorious skirmish at the ferry landing reflected the weakened power of the talwas. Ethnohistorians have rightly identified a widening economic rift in early-nineteenth-century Creek society between those unable or unwilling to adopt Western economic values and the increasingly wealthy—exemplified most starkly by the market-driven plantation owners on the Tensaw but represented also by individuals, particularly headmen, throughout the nation with access to capital.[53] The conflict that arose between the Alabamas and Tensaw métis families like the Baileys, however, was of a different sort.

A few years earlier the Atasi headmen and leaders on the Creek national council had opposed Richard Bailey's independent efforts to accumulate wealth outside the normal channels permissible for a foreign resident deerskin trader. Now, however, Coosada métis leaders attempted to enforce their talwa's authority over Tensaw métis families operating precisely the same sort of businesses and plantations on the lower Alabama River as the Coosada métis operated on the upper Alabama River. That they tried to do so implies that the Coosada leadership considered Tensaw a talofa or daughter settlement of the Coosada talwa—which it seems to have been, given the documented ties between Coosada and the Sehoy women, whose lineage founded the Tensaw. Not simply a struggle between haves and have-nots (although economic disparity must have exacerbated the discord), this conflict pitted proponents of the Creek talwa against individuals who recognized allegiance only to their own lineage and to Creek national authority. Captain Isaacs' involvement in this affair perhaps misleadingly suggests that inspiration for this conflict with the Tensaw métis came primarily from the Creek leadership, particularly the micos. But later events demonstrated that defense of the talwa as a political institution drew broad support from the majority of Upper Creeks.[54]

3

Americanization of Mississippi Territory

William Weatherford and Dixon Bailey, both Creek métis, are two principal protagonists in this story of Fort Mims. But the presence of several hundred Americans and Africans inside the stockade on August 30, 1813, widened immensely the impact of that battle well beyond the scope of a Creek civil war. Who were these other "inmates" of Fort Mims, and what brought them to this southwestern frontier of the United States? One was Zachariah McGirth, a liminal figure who bridged (or, rather, tried to cross) the racial divide between whites and Indians.

Zachariah McGirth

Like Samuel Mims and Charles Weatherford, Zachariah McGirth took up residence among the Creeks in the chaotic aftermath of the American Revolution. His father, James, and uncle Daniel McGirth had been infamous Tory "banditti," equally feared by patriots and loyalists on either side of the St. Marys River border between Georgia and East Florida. According to McGirth family tradition, Daniel scouted for the Americans early in the war but switched loyalties when unjustly whipped and imprisoned by a patriot officer who coveted his horse. In fact, he was an active Tory as early as 1775. The two brothers organized a band of mounted volunteers—often accompanied by Creek warriors—who rode with the King's Rangers in East Florida and quickly gained notoriety for indiscriminate pillaging. After the war, when Florida reverted to Spanish jurisdiction, Daniel continued his depredations—kidnapping slaves, stealing horses—until landing finally in the dungeons of the Castillo de San Marcos in St. Augustine. James, on the other hand, adjusted to civilian life and settled quietly with his family on a plantation near that town. A census of St. Augustine residents taken late in 1786 lists "Jayme [James] McGirt," native of Carolina, a farmer and a Lutheran, age fifty; his wife "Ysabela [Elizabeth] Sanders," also a native of Carolina and a Lutheran, age forty-three; six unbaptized "Negro slaves"; and six unmarried children, including "Esacarias [Zachariah]," a native of Carolina, farmer, age sixteen.[1]

Within a few years Zachariah took up residence on Little River. In 1793 he and his cousin Billy moved from there to Tuckaubatchee, on the lower Tallapoosa River, where he soon married Alexander McGillivray's widow, Vicey Cornells, who had herself recently returned from the Tensaw to her family home (Chart 5.) McGirth presumably engaged initially in the deerskin trade, although this is uncertain. In 1797 he became embroiled in a dispute with a Tensaw resident, Joseph Thompson, over ownership of two enslaved Africans, Monday and Nancy, that McGirth claimed had belonged to his father and who he now maintained were his wife's property. Thompson called upon Benjamin Hawkins to settle the matter. Whatever the outcome (and the record does not inform us), Hawkins seems to have been impressed by the young Carolinian. A year later, when the Creek Agency's blacksmith shop, at the public establishment several miles downstream from Tuckaubatchee, closed for lack of fuel for the forge, the agent "applied to Zachy McGirth, and in five days had twenty cords of [char]coal wood cut." In his journal of travels in 1799 through the Creek country, Hawkins described McGirth as "a careful, snug farmer, has good fences, a fine young orchard, and a stock of horses, hogs, and cattle. His wife," he added, with characteristic condescension, "has the neatness and economy of a white woman" and was spinning wool from sheep raised by her cousin Alexander Cornells, mico of Tuckaubatchee. Did Hawkins think Zachariah, this "careful, snug farmer," was Creek? Why else would he include him in his litany of accomplished Creeks without otherwise specifying that he was white? Hawkins' ambiguity suggests McGirth had already begun his transformation from loyalist refugee to "métis."[2]

Despite his evident success as a planter, Zachariah (along with cousin Billy) temporarily abandoned his Tuckaubatchee farm and joined William Augustus Bowles, self-styled Director General of the Muskogee Nation, at the adventurer's port on the Apalachicola River. Upon release from prison, Daniel McGirth had evaded Spanish authorities in 1792 by joining Bowles and his Seminole allies. A decade later, Daniel's son (now assuming the more formal name William) donned the robes of Muskogee's judge advocate, while Zachariah apparently engaged in trade under the Muskogee flag, temporarily free of the import

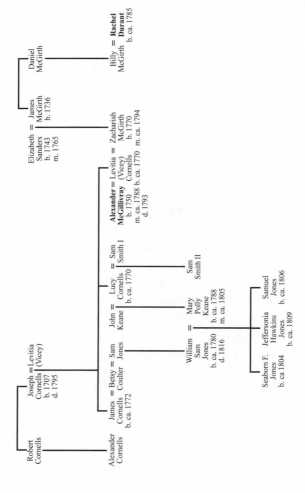

Kinship Chart 5. Cornells and McGirth Lineages. Names of Wind clan members in bold.

duties levied by Spanish and American authorities at nearby ports. Whether or not the McGirths accompanied Bowles on his ill-advised march north to confront Benjamin Hawkins at Hickory Ground in 1803, they certainly abandoned the Muskogee enterprise upon learning of Bowles' capture and imprisonment and returned to their families in the Creek nation.[3]

McGirth's next appearance in the historical record occurs in correspondence regarding the horse path (precursor to the Federal Road) from Georgia to Fort Stoddert designed to speed delivery of the U.S. mail between Washington, D.C., and New Orleans. The route through the Creek nation largely followed existing Indian paths. Parties of axemen were dispatched from either end to widen the trail to at least four feet and to fell logs for simple bridges over the narrowest streams. Indian paths as a rule followed ridges between stream drainages, dropping off the high ground only for the most essential river and creek crossings and thereby avoiding most of the extensive bottomland swamps so prevalent in the coastal plain. Even so, traversing the horse path posed formidable physical challenges; finding dependable riders, fit horses, and adequate forage along the mail route also proved difficult.

Joseph Wheaton contracted with the Postal Department in mid-August 1806 to complete the horse path in three months and put the mails on a dependable schedule. On October 1, Wheaton subcontracted "with one McGirth, a man of some property, and industry" to carry the mail 249 miles in three days, from Coweta (on the Chattahoochee River) to Fort Stoddert. It took McGirth less time than that to realize his mistake. According to Wheaton, "he became alarmed at the magnitude of the object, and before he commenced abandoned it." McGirth's second thought proved sensible. Problems plagued the mail riders, from rain-swollen streams and unusual snow and ice storms to worn-out horses to missed connections with other riders. Wheaton's riders never covered the route in less than seven days.[4] That McGirth even considered the task suggests he knew the route well. He would ride it many times, under conditions unimagined by Wheaton's mail carriers, during the Redstick War.

The McGirths left their Tuckaubatchee plantation sometime after 1807 and moved once again to Little River.[5] Zachariah henceforward apparently focused his considerable energies entirely on farming with his large labor force of slaves.

⁓

The personal histories of the men of the Mississippi Territorial Volunteers who mobilized to protect the Tensaw during July and August 1813 set them apart from most of the refugees flocking to the makeshift fort hurriedly erected on

Samuel Mims' plantation. In contrast to the Creek métis, former loyalists, families of old "Indian countrymen" (like Mims himself), and enslaved Africans who made up the bulk of the Tensaw population, the Volunteers were all white (mostly of English descent), all males, and, by and large, recent immigrants to Mississippi Territory. Nearly all of General Ferdinand L. Claiborne's regiment of 600 men hailed from the Natchez District, seven counties in the southwest corner of the territory—Adams, Amite, Claiborne, Franklin, Jefferson, Warren, and Wilkinson (Figure 6). The district's population of about 40,000 was divided roughly half white, half black. Separated from the Tombigbee settlements by 200 miles of Choctaw country and sparsely occupied coastal lands, Natchez had originally been settled by a succession of French, British, and Spanish colonists and their slaves. Surrendered to the United States in 1798, the district's rich soils and access to the port of New Orleans via the Mississippi River immediately attracted American settlers. They arrived initially by water, on flatboats down the Ohio and Mississippi rivers from Kentucky, Tennessee, and western Pennsylvania. Overland migration accelerated with improvement of the Natchez Trace from Nashville, and creation of Gaines Trace from the Tennessee Valley to the Tombigbee River north of Fort Stoddert. Once the horse path through the Creek nation was widened in 1811 into a wagon road, the Federal Road, that direct route from Georgia to Fort Stoddert enticed more than 10,000 émigrés to the Natchez District in the short interval between the U.S. Census of 1810 and the beginning of the Redstick War in 1813.[6]

Such a rapid influx of Americans and American-owned slaves, drawn largely from Virginia, the Carolinas, and Georgia, quickly swamped the small creole population of native-born whites, blacks, and métis that had developed during a century of European colonization. The old Natchez colonial frontier, characterized by diverse interacting cultures, was transformed in less than a decade to an American-dominated society supported by a labor force comprised no longer primarily of enslaved black creoles but of slaves imported recently from Africa.[7] While many elements of creole culture would seep into the dominant culture—through architecture, foodways, language, and land use—the new political and economic elite was intent on imposing an American legal system and American social standards on the Natchez District.

The Americans chose a location six miles east of old Natchez for the territorial capital, a place they named Washington. Early territorial politics at first reflected the national contest between Federalists and Republicans, until the Federalist Party self-destructed a few years later. By 1813, virtually all voting white males in the district considered themselves Republicans, although that

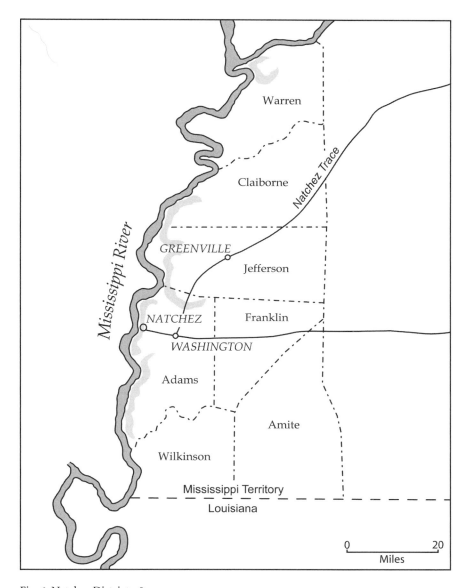

Warren

Claiborne

Natchez Trace

Mississippi River

GREENVILLE

Jefferson

NATCHEZ

Franklin

WASHINGTON

Adams

Amite

Wilkinson

Mississippi Territory

Louisiana

0   20

Miles

Fig. 6. Natchez District, 1813

party's numerous factions, as well as differences over strictly local issues, insured a continuous stream of political attacks and counterattacks in the territory's partisan newspapers. Yet the geography of Natchez District (and the Tombigbee and Tensaw settlements north of Mobile) focused political concern on issues of broader national interest. From their perspective, wedged between populous Indian nations to the north and Spanish colonies to the south, virtually all American settlers in the district considered acquisition of neighboring lands vital to their security and future prosperity. To that end the U.S. government negotiated treaties in 1805 with the Chickasaws, Choctaws, and Creeks, although the pace of land cessions never satisfied the insatiable demands of frontier Americans and their political representatives. President Jefferson's 1803 purchase of Louisiana placed the entire course of the Mississippi River in American hands but left the Gulf coast east of New Orleans, including Mobile, under Spanish control. Extortionate Spanish duties on American goods transiting their colony of West Florida, and general impatience with slow-paced federal negotiations to acquire Spanish lands peacefully and legally, inspired a series of controversial, and mostly ill-fated, filibustering efforts.

Undoubtedly the best known of these attempts to implement American Manifest Destiny on the southwestern frontier was Aaron Burr's infamous conspiracy—still mystery-shrouded after two centuries—to enlist followers for a conquest of Texas (or Mexico) from among the discontents of Louisiana and Mississippi Territory. That scheme ended with Burr's arrest by U.S. troops on the road north of Fort Stoddert in 1807. Dissatisfaction was widespread in the territory because the Louisiana Purchase treaty had ambiguously delimited the purchase's eastern limit. Congress passed the Mobile Act early in 1804 to clarify U.S. intent that the treaty should include West Florida, but the government made no move to push that claim with Spain and resolve the matter. Consequently, many settlers, led by a rabble-rouser named Reuben Kemper, felt emboldened to organize private raids aimed at undermining Spanish control. These culminated in a small-scale revolution in 1810 by Americans settlers living in the Baton Rouge area, who successfully expelled Spanish troops from the Florida parishes (the area of Louisiana east of New Orleans). President Madison applauded this development, and the United States immediately annexed the territory. However, the federal government's reluctance to further antagonize Spain—and Great Britain, Spain's ally in the Napoleonic Wars—tempered official enthusiasm for other unsanctioned forays into West Florida. When Kemper joined forces with Tombigbee militia commanders John Caller, James

Caller, and Joseph P. Kennedy to plot the seizure of Mobile, federal judge Harry Toulmin and territorial governor David Holmes assured Spanish governor Juan Vincente Folch that official U.S. policy now prohibited filibustering. In the event, Spanish troops easily deflected an attack by a hundred of Kemper's drunken followers on December 10, 1810. Mobile and the coast west of the Perdido River (the modern border between Alabama and Florida) remained in Spanish hands until the War of 1812 gave the U.S. military an opportunity to seize the region, which General James Wilkinson did in April 1813.[8]

Americans immigrating to Mississippi Territory between 1798 and 1813 understood this as a region in transition. In the decades after the American Revolution, white Americans had come to believe that North American lands claimed by European nations or possessed by Indian nations would inevitably become available to them, absorbed as part of their own country. This national goal provoked disagreement only as to the means and the speed by which it could be accomplished. Foreign colonial officials and troops should be persuaded to withdraw, by popular uprisings and force of arms or by the slower diplomatic process. Native peoples should accept the steady reduction of their lands, abandon their ancestral homes and seek new lands to the west, or else adopt American cultural ways and values and let their separate status and identity as Indians fade away. Few white Americans on the frontier disagreed with the objective of Americanizing the region, most hoped by the quickest means possible. The majority, in fact, already dreamed of ways national expansion might better their personal situations by freeing the lands of others for American farmers, by creating prospects for new towns and businesses, and by expanding markets for crops, commodities, and slaves.

The men of the Mississippi Territorial Volunteers must have had such thoughts in mind during their midsummer march toward the Tensaw in 1813. They worried, of course, over the well-being of their own families and for the lives and property of fellow American settlers they hoped to defend, and perhaps about their own chances of surviving the impending war with the Redstick Creeks. Beyond those immediate concerns, though, lay prospects for final resolutions of longstanding disputes with the Creek nation, Spain, and Great Britain, as well as expectations that opportunities might arise for personal glory, social recognition, and financial gain. Among those seeking a step up in life—assisted by a timely appointment to the rank of major in the Volunteers by his friend General Claiborne—was a forty-seven-year-old Virginian, former sheriff of Jefferson County, Daniel Beasley.

Daniel Beasley

In 1803, Daniel Beasley moved to the Natchez District from Chesterfield County, Virginia, south of Richmond.[9] His parents, Benjamin Beasley and Obedience Cheatham (who were cousins), had married in Chesterfield in 1750. Marriage of Benjamin's brother Thomas to Obedience's sister Tabitha a few years later further strengthened the union of families. Both Beasley brothers inherited sizeable estates. Benjamin and Obedience established their principal plantation in Chesterfield County, where Daniel, the second oldest son, was born around 1766. Benjamin held onto lands he inherited in Amelia County, farther west across the Appomattox River, while continuing to acquire more properties in Chesterfield County, probably with the intention of leaving land to each of his four sons. Upon both parents' deaths, in 1781 and 1782, the surviving children inherited properties totaling more than a thousand acres, some urban lots, and ownership of at least ten slaves of African descent.[10]

The elder Beasleys evidently succumbed to the great epidemic of smallpox that swept across North America during the American Revolution. According to historian Elizabeth Fenn's recent chronicle of the contagion's spread, smallpox first appeared in Massachusetts early in 1774. Marching armies carried the disease throughout Britain's rebellious colonies in the coming years, reaching the Creek nation by 1779 and ravaging Charleston soon afterwards. General Cornwallis' surrender at Yorktown in 1781 ended major armed conflict, but capture of his infected troops, and the slaves who had sought freedom under their protection, hastened the spread of smallpox to Virginia's civilian population, including the Beasley family of Chesterfield County. In 1782 the executor of Benjamin Beasley's estate paid a neighbor, Elizabeth Morgan, for "attendance on the family when they had smallpox." Obedience had died shortly after Benjamin, as did three of their children: Samuel, Tabitha, and Betsy. Daniel and his surviving siblings may have been disfigured physically and traumatized psychologically by this loss, bodily and emotional scars they likely carried for the rest of their lives.[11]

Upon Benjamin Beasley's death, one of his Amelia County tracts devolved to Daniel, although the sixteen-year-old would not gain legal control of that property before his twenty-first birthday. Executors' accounts filed in the interim document the scope and routine of Beasley plantation operations, which included managing family-owned properties in Chesterfield and Amelia counties. Disbursements appear for cooperage and blacksmithing, repair of a set of cart wheels, tobacco inspections, oat and wheat purchases, stud service, ferriage, and payments to a doctor and a midwife for attention to the enslaved African workers. Income derived from sales of tobacco, oats, wheat, beef, hogs, two lambs, and the trade of a horse, as well as the services of two sawyers. This last account entry suggests the estate gained important supplemental income from hiring out those slaves with marketable skills. The older Beasley children benefited from several years of formal education, reflected by payments to tutors and boarding schools. In December 1787, Samuel Jeter was paid an entrance fee "for teaching Daniel Beasley," probably reading in the law, which later qualified Daniel for his role as sheriff and justice of the peace in Mississippi Territory.[12]

By 1790, Daniel had taken legal possession of his inheritance: a 240-acre tract in Nottoway County (formed from a portion of Amelia County in 1788), two slaves age twelve or older, and two horses. By 1794, he had disposed of 180 acres and a horse. Within two more years, Daniel sold the remainder of his land and the other horse, retaining a single slave from his father's estate. He seems to have moved in 1796 from Nottoway to Chesterfield County, where he paid taxes on a horse, ass, or mule, but no slaves. In a remarkably short time, due to bad luck or his own financial mismanagement, Daniel Beasley saw his inheritance evaporate. His father's acquisitions of land and slaves had gained the Beasleys a place among Virginia's Revolutionary War–era upper middle class. However, uneven division of the estate among the three surviving sons (with Peter, the eldest, receiving the most) left Daniel with too few enslaved workers and draft animals to make his land productive. His taxable assets rank him among the lower middle class of Chesterfield County's white households, where 62 percent owned slaves (the majority between one and five) and 79 percent had horses, asses, or mules for farming. In his descent to "one-horse farmer" status, Daniel was not alone. The postwar decades were a time of economic crisis in Virginia. Wartime debts, loss of export markets, depleted soil fertility from long-term cultivation of tobacco, and the tendency for large plantations to be subdivided into small farms all contributed to the general economic decline. When Daniel set out in 1803 for a new start in Mississippi Territory, he joined an exodus that included many of his neighbors. Fully one-third of white residents abandoned Chesterfield County between 1800 and 1810, seeking better economic opportunities in the young republic's urban centers and rural frontiers. As later events would demonstrate, Daniel Beasley went west to reclaim the upper-middle-class status of his youth.[13]

Why Beasley chose to leave Virginia, the nation's most populous state, for Mississippi Territory remains an unanswered question. Several of his maternal uncles and cousins fought for independence in the Revolutionary War, so he certainly did not harbor the sort of loyalist sentiments that had propelled so many Tories to the Tensaw in previous decades. Neither was his move part of a migration of the entire Beasley family, although many other extended families did move westward together for mutual assistance in their new homes. Instead, Daniel apparently set off alone for the Natchez District, as did numerous other unmarried men, many of them second sons like him, in search of better economic prospects on the frontier. Perhaps he knew Thomas Hinds, Ferdinand Claiborne, or other former Virginians who had emigrated earlier and whose successes now beckoned to their eastern friends.[14]

Beasley's westward trek ended at Greenville, described by Governor W.C.C. Claiborne as "a flourishing little village about 28 miles distant from Natchez and immediately on the post road [the Natchez Trace] to Tennessee, . . . the county seat for Jefferson County, and the place for holding Superior Court." Early in 1805, acting territorial governor Cato West appointed Daniel Beasley sheriff and jailor of Jefferson County. In that office, which he held until February 1813, Beasley's duties involved arresting suspected felons, apprehending escaped slaves, meting out punishments, auctioning property for unpaid taxes, and serving warrants, writs, and summonses for the court.[15] In such a sparsely settled county, however, the intermittent duties of sheriff afforded considerable leisure time. Beasley soon found ways to expand his public role. In January 1806 he and a dozen other prominent Jefferson County citizens created the Franklin Society to promote the establishment of Franklin Academy. Their desire to found a school in Greenville, the county seat, evidently arose in response to the territorial legislature's 1802 decision establishing Jefferson College in Washington, the territorial capital in neighboring Adams County. The ensuing competition between Greenville and Washington factions left both schools inadequately financed. After years of rivalry, Jefferson College finally opened in 1810; Franklin Academy never achieved much success. Daniel Beasley's foray into philanthropy well exemplifies the infighting—so often parochial, spiteful, and self-defeating—that typified territorial politics in the Natchez District.[16]

Beasley quickly garnered the esteem of his fellow citizens by election as captain of the Jefferson County militia. On January 14, 1807, Lieutenant Colonel Ferdinand L. Claiborne, commander of the Mississippi Territorial militia, enlisted his aid in apprehending Aaron Burr, then descending the Mississippi River on his filibustering expedition to the Spanish colonial frontier. Joining Beasley's little command of thirty men at Claiborne's camp near the mouth of Coles Creek was Captain Thomas Hinds' Jefferson County Troop of Horse, a militia company of mounted riflemen that included many of the wealthiest young men of the district. Claiborne's little army of 300 persuaded Burr and his handful of followers to surrender to acting governor Cowles Mead two days later. Their participation in this easy victory created a bond among the three Virginians—Claiborne, Hinds, and Beasley—who would remain close friends, political allies, and fellow militia officers until Beasley's death in 1813.[17]

A duel, however, not partisan patronage or part-time soldiering, would earn Daniel Beasley the renown he sought. Throughout the summer of 1810, subscribers to the Natchez *Weekly Chronicle* followed a spiraling succession of insults, charges, and challenges that passed between Sheriff Beasley and four other citizens of the district, compiled and distributed on successive Mondays for the amusement of an eager readership.[18] The feud began with a minor, even trivial, incident, which Beasley perceived as a slight to his honor.

On May 18, four Greenville businessmen decided to host a ball in town on the evening of May 25, the following Friday. As was customary, the group—which included one William Elliott, agent for Trigg, King & Co., a household merchandise retailer in Natchez—chose four managers for the dance, individuals of sufficient social standing to insure a certain level of propriety, gentility, and exclusivity to the affair. Those elected to manage the night's entertainment included Sheriff Daniel Beasley, Major Thomas Hinds (militia dragoon commander and Jefferson County tax collector), Dr. J. A. Maxwell, and agent Elliott. The following morning, Elliott called on Beasley, who consented to manage the ball (so said Elliott) if his friend Major Hinds was agreeable. The two then discussed which ladies would receive tickets (invitations), and Elliott rode off to deliver them.

During the ball Beasley realized, apparently for the first time, that he and Hinds were not the only managers and reacted angrily, engaging in some unspecified conduct that Elliott felt "was calculated to both wound my feelings and injure my standing." Thus began the highly ritualized exchange of taunts and declarations of injury that characterized the code of honor for upper class and upwardly aspiring white men in the early United States. Confronting Elliott several days later, Beasley accused him of associating "my name with yours and others as managers without my consent." By letter Elliott demanded a retraction. His note was delivered the following morning by his second, James Wood, another agent for Trigg, King & Co.[19] Beasley clearly considered Elliott his social inferior, an opinion he reinforced by refusing to receive Elliott's challenge but offering to meet Wood on the field. In a note carried to Beasley by John Doherty, yet another associate of Trigg, King & Co., Wood refused, "in justice to my friend, who will not relinquish the right of receiving satisfaction in his own proper person," and insisted "that my friend's standing is equal to your own." Beasley countered that "duty to my own character" forbade him from condescending to meet Elliott. He now considered Wood his principal adversary and offered to meet at suppertime at Winn's tavern in Natchez on June 4 to make "the necessary arrangements." He further accused Samuel Frye, an attorney who had arrived in the district two years earlier from Maine and now acted as one of Wood's intermediaries, of altering correspondence on the affair, which was beginning to appear in the *Weekly Chronicle*.[20]

Wood's continuing refusal to accept a challenge on behalf of Elliott prompted Beasley to declare, in a handbill circulated on June 11, "the said James Wood, of Port Gibson, esquire, a poltroon and a coward," and to proclaim William Elliott "villainous." That evening, Beasley understood, "it took two or three gentlemen who were with Elliott," who had by then seen the handbill, "to keep him from coming to my own house to kill or to beat me. . . . that I was to be cow-hided [whipped]." The next day, while Beasley sat in the gallery of Searcy's tavern,

> I saw the *young hero* [Elliott] approaching with a tremendously large cudgel; but he called in at Smith's tavern and seated himself in the gallery; I rose and strolled on homewards having to pass Smith's tavern; I had a small hickory cane, a small dirk, and a stone of about a pound in weight in my pocket. As I got nearly opposite to Smith's the *hero* sallied out and took from under his coat a pistol—cocked it, and pointed it towards me, and spoke to me something about my having a pistol, (I had put my hand into my coat pocket by this time) that if I would say that I had not he would throw his away. I answered "fire away;" but the young hero was thrown into a state of such violent trepidation that he lost his priming, therefore was deterred from putting his threats into execution, tho' there was no person except a woman nearer than eighty or an hundred yards, and what is more extraordinary there was no body holding him.[21]

On June 13, Elliott and Beasley were each compelled to post bonds of recognizance in the amount of $2,000, half themselves and half from friends as security, and ordered to appear before the Superior Court at the September term and "keep the peace in the mean time." Whether Sheriff Beasley or attorney Frye petitioned for the bonds is unknown, but the maneuver effectively forestalled a duel for a time, though the public bickering and intimidation continued unabated. On one occasion, Wood, Frye, Elliott, and Doherty rode around the outskirts of Greenville for two hours, firing pistols "about eighty times." A few days later, Wood issued a statement, branding Beasley a "pompous braggadotia, this supercilious puff of empty air," and "an Egregious Coward." Beasley retaliated by calling Doherty "an eye servant" who does "pretty well while the whip is in sight; but leave him to himself, make him free, and he is worthless." Delving deeply into gossip, the sheriff alleged that Elliott had whipped a mulatto prostitute, Miss Maria, who was Doherty's mistress, and that Doherty had done nothing to protect her.[22]

Extant issues of the *Weekly Chronicle* end abruptly at this point, but we know a duel did eventually occur, perhaps after court convened in September and the bonds were revoked. According to Frye family legend, Samuel Frye bore yet another challenge from Elliott to Beasley, who once again refused Elliott and instead challenged Frye. The young attorney accepted "and fell in mortal combat." The duel took place on a sandbar in the Mississippi River, in Concordia Parish, Louisiana, beyond Mississippi Territorial jurisdiction. Frye belonged to a prominent New England family and had been engaged to a daughter of Isaac Ross, one of the wealthiest planters in Jefferson County.[23] Mid-nineteenth-century historian J.F.H. Claiborne mistakenly thought the duel had taken place early in 1813 and surmised on that basis that Beasley resigned from the office of sheriff as a consequence and enlisted in the Volunteers filled with remorse over Frye's tragic death.[24] In fact, no link exists between the duel and his resignation two and a half years later, nor did Beasley's career suffer. To the contrary, his evident willingness to fight to defend his honor confirmed his stature as a gentleman in the eyes of the territory's elite and undoubtedly contributed to his appointment as major in the Volunteers when the war provided an opportunity for advancement. That Beasley regretted the outcome of the affair seems equally unlikely, given the role of aggrieved party he assumed throughout the public dispute.

The Beasley-Frye duel, and its lengthy prologue, offers a unique perspective on the man who would command at Fort Mims. In several ways, he epitomized a romantic ideal of the era. Many who knew him considered Daniel Beasley to be "brave, chivalrous, frank . . . the soul of honor," an impression undoubtedly enhanced by his duel-related conduct. On the other hand, the apparent willingness of Beasley and his adversaries to kill one another because they imagined someone "had been inconsistent, and had denied facts," as Beasley put it, defies modern standards of logic. Their archaic terms of defamation—

"poltroon," "supercilious puff of empty air," "addlepated fool"—may strike us as ludicrous, until we recall the farce's deadly outcome. Challenges to a man's honor were an unavoidable fact of public life in early America, although the notoriety of some duels (the 1804 affair between Alexander Hamilton and Aaron Burr being the most infamous) misleads us into thinking they were unavoidable and nearly always fatal. In fact, most challengers reconciled (often through intervention of their seconds); for those who did not, few became fatalities.[25] Lethal outcomes required at least one party be inflexible to the point of obstinacy and with murderous intent. In the case of Beasley versus Wood and friends, both sides were determined to fight and both rejected numerous opportunities to settle their perceived grievances peacefully. But Daniel Beasley's attitude seems the less defensible. He was a county sheriff, after all, and repeatedly violated an 1803 territorial statute that made the sending, receiving, or bearing of a challenge to fight a duel a felony. Punishment included a fine of $1,000 and imprisonment for twelve months, as well as disqualification from "holding any office of honour, profit, or trust under the government of this territory, for and during the term of five years from the time of such conviction." Beasley ought to have lost his job for even issuing challenges, let alone killing his opponent, which was considered "wilful murder" under the territorial statute, punishable by death. Further, he was nearly twice the age of any of his adversaries and should have known better, by the standards of his own day as well as ours. While there is no denying Beasley's courage and unwavering adherence to a principle, once committed, his judgment seems highly questionable. We may also deduce, from his arguments by innuendo and his willingness to demean others on the basis of their racial and social status, that Daniel Beasley was deeply racist and arrogant. Those character flaws would not serve him or his command well in the multi-ethnic Tensaw.[26]

Several other facts about Daniel Beasley's life in the Natchez District have come to light. The ambitious Virginian ran successfully for the territorial legislature in 1809 and served in that body through 1812.[27] Governor Holmes appointed Sheriff Beasley U.S. census taker in Jefferson County for the 1810 enumeration, during which he listed himself as head of a household that included two other adult white males and nine slaves. On March 23, 1812, Beasley stood security for a bond for Asa Searcy's tavern in Greenville, suggesting a financial interest in that establishment. Finally, in December of that year, he was first signatory on the "Beasley Petition," which appealed to Congress to delay statehood for Mississippi until the war with Britain ended and planters could once again sell cotton to pay their debts.[28]

All of these activities reflected Beasley's absolute dedication, shared by virtually all of his white neighbors, to see American political and economic systems transplanted to the Natchez District (just as the duel manifested his adherence to a social code transferred wholesale from the East). Daniel Beasley's values were formed in Virginia, and he carried that worldview with him as he traversed the Creek nation on his journey west. Tellingly, as sheriff he apparently had little or no contact with Indians, though this would have been unimaginable for any white resident of the lower Mississippi Valley just a decade earlier. Mississippi Territorial legislators like Beasley measured their collective success by the inexorable increases they witnessed in white and black populations, pounds of harvested cotton, heads of livestock raised—and in the construction of new homes, capitalization of new businesses, attendance by the thousands at religious revivals, filings at land offices transferring government lands to individuals for farms and plantations, and the platting of towns where forests had stood for centuries. American expansion happened with breathtaking speed in the Natchez District and almost as rapidly elsewhere in the territory. The old economics of the Southeast—hunting for deerskins to barter for cloth, guns, and beads—suddenly struck nearly everyone, Indians and whites alike, as outmoded and irrelevant. Which new course to follow proved less obvious to the Creeks.

4

Red Path to War

U.S. government efforts throughout the late eighteenth and early nineteenth centuries to encourage the Creeks and other eastern Indians to adopt the lifestyle of white Americans and relinquish sovereignty over their lands created deep discontent. For the Creeks, American insistence on replacement of hoe cultivation and deerskin hunting by intensive plow agriculture, livestock raising, and household cloth production called for a radical reorientation of native society—the abandonment of traditional Creek concepts of property ownership, economic motivation, division of labor, and gender roles. Certain elements of Creek society, especially the métis of the Tensaw and others who benefited from U.S. political and economic paternalism, did begin this difficult transition. In his eagerness to achieve results, Benjamin Hawkins, U.S. agent to the Creeks, pointed to these economically assimilated Indians as proof that the "plan of civilization" could succeed.[1]

Among white Americans of the era, this was the liberal position. Indians must adopt American lifestyle and give up their "waste ground" if they hoped to remain within the boundaries of an expanding United States. Opposed to this assimilationist stance was the preference, generally held in the western states and territories, to take Indian lands and push the native peoples westward, beyond the limits of current white settlement. Very few white Americans advocated the status quo. In fact, only slight differences in approach separated these two prevailing American philosophies for resolving the future of the southeastern Indians. An exchange of correspondence in 1803 between two principal proponents of these alternative "solutions" reveals their common ground. In response to criticism that Hawkins was too sympathetic toward the Creeks to effectively negotiate land away from them, President Thomas Jefferson reassured Andrew Jackson that the bedrock elements of U.S. policy toward the Indians—"1. The preservation of peace; 2. The obtaining [of their] lands."—remained unchanged.[2]

Although American government officials considered assimilation or removal the only options available to Indians occupying lands between the Appalachian Mountains and the Mississippi River, the majority of Creeks resisted both. In the years before the War of 1812, few Creeks even considered leaving the eastern woodlands. Most members of that heterogeneous nation evidently thought they could adapt to American economic and demographic challenges and still retain their homelands and essential components of their diverse cultures. Some moved south to join relatives among the Seminoles, who had become politically autonomous from the Creeks several decades earlier, and a small number moved west to Arkansas. But, in general, Creeks responded to the growing crisis of American colonization much as they had during the preceding two centuries of conflict with Europeans, by selectively adopting and refashioning elements borrowed from the cultures of their neighbors—the Americans and other Indian societies—that suited their needs while holding fast to their own core beliefs, languages, and customs. Indeed, a steadily dwindling market for deerskins persuaded hundreds to experiment with American modes of production and to accept the plows, spinning wheels, and looms offered by the U.S. agent. Distribution of those implements, however, was controlled by the micos. Instead of dispersing these new tools—and symbols of Americanization—fairly and indiscriminately to their people, the micos looked to their own narrow self-interests (as chiefs throughout the world typically have done when co-opted by colonizers), parceling them out primarily to factional supporters and matrilineal relatives.[3]

Consequently, in the three decades following the American Revolution, the economic status of most Creeks fell from comfortable affluence to poverty and indebtedness, with little prospect for betterment. Only certain métis and the political elite (largely also métis) retained sufficient capital to acquire slaves and breeding livestock, the principal avenues to prosperity under the new economic order. Increasing centralization of power in the hands of the Creek national council, a trend that began under Alexander McGillivray's leadership and accelerated with Hawkins' encouragement, marginalized factions opposed to the micos and further limited options for the majority of Creeks.[4] Benjamin Hawkins' plan of civilization offered little hope for thousands struggling to subsist, for Creek women still tilling their plots of maize by hand, and for Creek men still hunting for deerskins now worth next to nothing.

The Prophets

In these bleak times, many Creeks grew increasingly receptive to alternative paths. They all recognized American encroachment on Creek lands, meddling by the U.S. agent, and enticement to indebtedness by unscrupulous white traders as menacing contributors to the growing economic disparity. But they simultaneously accepted their predicament as partly of their own making. Instead of redistributing talwa wealth to needy families, headmen had signed away vast tracts of Creek land and kept federal annuity payments intended for their people. Too many hunters were accumulating debts to merchants they could never repay. Consumption of liquor—at first rum, the "tafia" of British traders, and more recently the whiskey of the Americans—was wrecking lives through alcohol addiction and impoverishment of the addicts' families. Too many Creeks were abandoning traditional ways in favor of foreign lifestyles. These sorts of improper, non-Creek conduct were as much spiritual as behavioral failings. A sacred renewal, a *poskita* for the Creek soul, was needed to guide the people from this destructive path toward a brighter future.

One persuasive advocate of a new way was Tenskwatawa, the Shawnee Prophet, who promised a return to earlier, happier conditions for those Indians who rejected most tools and customs of the whites. Tenskwatawa's teachings have long been recognized as a classic example of a nativistic revitalization movement.[5] The Prophet's religion addressed both evils oppressing the eastern Indians: military and cultural domination by the Americans and the Indian peoples' own loss of spirituality. Influenced directly by the Shawnee Prophet's admonitions, a large segment of Creek society attempted in a dramatic and violent fashion to reorder, to revitalize a world so altered by the presence of whites that traditional Indian methods of coping no longer worked. The Prophet offered mystical powers, summoned by prescribed proper behaviors, that would enable his followers to rid the world of this threat to their very existence.[6]

The Shawnee Prophet's militant religious doctrine was inspired by earlier nativistic movements, particularly the revitalistic teachings of Neolin, a Delaware living in what is now eastern Ohio during the early 1760s. Neolin's visions enabled him to overcome his own deep depression and alcoholism and to animate a pan-Indian effort, known today as Pontiac's War, to drive the British from the trans-Appalachian West at the end of the French and Indian War. Historians once considered Pontiac and Tecumseh, Tenskwatawa's elder brother, to be charismatic but essentially pragmatic political leaders who cynically used revitalistic religious enthusiasm to attract followers from disparate Indian peoples normally divided by faction and ethnicity. However, modern scholars now understand the central role of revitalistic religious beliefs in the recurrent attempts—some peaceful, some belligerent—by eastern Indians from the mid-eighteenth century onward to express their underlying antipathy toward imperialist expansion, whether British or American. A firm conviction in the possibility of religious renewal motivated the impressive political and military achievements of Pontiac and his numerous allies in the 1760s, the determined resistance to American domination by the Chickamaugas under Dragging Canoe in the 1790s, and the drive for pan-Indian unification under Tecumseh at the onset of the War of 1812. They all hoped to accomplish, by successes on the battlefield, a diplomatic outcome that did not consign their peoples to a landless, alcohol-addicted, spiritually diminished existence. For the Creeks and other Indian nations on the American frontier of 1810, many found the teachings of the Shawnee Prophet a plausible alternative to the increasingly apparent inevitability of that grim fate.[7]

Not a great deal is known about Tenskwatawa's specific teachings. Those, of course, were directed at Indians, not the literate white missionaries and officials who might have left a more detailed record except for their general indifference to native religion. Eventually, a belated recognition that his beliefs had sparked widespread frontier warfare prompted a few firsthand observers to jot down their imperfect recollections of the knowledge revealed to Tenskwatawa by the Master of Life, the Shawnees' creator. In a series of visions beginning in 1805, two spirits dispatched by the creator took Tenskwatawa to a fork in a road. The right fork led to an Indian paradise, "a rich, fertile country, abounding in game, fish, pleasant hunting grounds and fine corn fields." Those who violated the Master of Life's instructions followed the left fork, beside which were three large lodges. In two of the lodges, multitudes of lesser sinners endured fiery tortures of atonement; drunkards, for instance, were forced repeatedly to imbibe molten lead until they repented. The unredeemable suffered eternal torment. Tenskwatawa "heard them scream, cry pitiful, and roar like the falls of a river."[8]

The Shawnee Prophet emerged from these visions freed from the hopelessness of his previously dissolute life. He urged followers to abstain from liquor or "any provisions raised by white people, as bread, beef, pork, fowls, etc." and "to endeavour to do without buying any merchandise" from the whites. Because sexual promiscuity offended the Master of Life, men should take no more than one wife, and all single men should marry. Indian women married to white men should be brought home, although not their children (considered, in patrilineal societies like the Shawnees', to be white), "so that the nations might become genuine Indians." All medicine bags of the ancient religion must be destroyed, and former dances and songs were to be abandoned; continued adherence to those corrupt old ways was evidence of witchcraft. Transgressions of these and many other proscribed behaviors must be confessed, and crying and trembling would signify the sincerity of confessions.[9]

Despite his numerous prohibitions, Tenskwatawa's visions carried an uplifting message. If Indians would conform their behavior to the will of the Master of Life, earth's natural abundance would once again feed and clothe them. Game would again be plentiful. In place of now-banned religious rituals and social ceremonies, Tenskwatawa initiated prayers morning and evening to the earth, the water, and to the fire and sun. Old fires were to be extinguished and new ones kindled by friction (not flint and steel) and not allowed to go out. New dances were learned. In the "Dance of the Lakes"—a variation on the traditional Shawnee War Dance—men stripped to breechclouts and painted red and black, several carrying pipes and war clubs, danced before women to drumming and singing. This and other elements of the new religion were explicitly militaristic, with hostility directed toward the Americans, not other Indians. It also incorporated some elements of racialist thinking borrowed from the whites. The races would be separated, as the Indians reclaimed their lands by force. In the spirit of earlier Indian revitalistic movements, the Shawnee Prophet sought converts among other native peoples and trained lesser prophets to carry his innovations to distant nations. Indian peoples would fight each other no longer. Their animosity was reserved for the Americans and for those individual accommodationist Indians who followed them. A clear path lay ahead for all who accepted the teachings of the Shawnee Prophet, a path away from the evil influences of the Americans.[10]

⌒

Tenskwatawa's first spiritual disciples came from among the Delawares, Wyandots, Kickapoos, Odawas, and other northern peoples. Over the next five years his religion spread, gaining broad acceptance throughout the Great Lakes region, although not without resistance. All of those native societies—even the Shawnees—split into anti-American and pro-American factions, the latter frequently led by traditional headmen tied economically and politically to American agents, missionaries, and traders. The proclivity of Tenskwatawa's converts and subsidiary prophets to expose, and in several cases execute, native shamans, healers, and Christian Indians as witches also split villages and families apart.

By 1810 a new leader had arisen among the Shawnee Prophet's followers. Incessant American demands for Indian lands throughout the prior decade had resulted in a number of treaties signed by headmen of the northern nations. At a meeting in August 1810 with William Henry Harrison, governor of Indiana Territory, the Shawnee war leader Tecumseh seized control of his brother's movement and, in the name of all Indians, threatened any Indian leader who signed away native lands with death.[11]

From this point forward, Tecumseh, the Shawnee Prophet, and their followers overtly opposed the Americans. In a bold move to strengthen their cause, Tecumseh and a small band of Shawnees set off across the Ohio River in August of 1811 to impart the new pan-Indian religion, and his own conception of Indian political and military unity, to the southern nations. Late in the month the party slipped through the Chickasaw nation without attempting to enlist those inveterate enemies of the northern Indians. A tour of the three districts of the Choctaw nation, which had not yet felt intense pressure from white settlement, elicited some anti-American sympathy from the overall population but outright opposition from their most influential leader, Pushmataha. No more than a few dozen Choctaw warriors would side with the Redstick Creeks two years later, opposed by hundreds who fought with the Americans.[12]

Tecumseh's undoubted disappointment with the Choctaws may have been tempered by optimism as he and his companions crossed the Tombigbee River into the Creek nation. His mother, Methoataaskee, and his father, Pukeshinwau, had grown to adulthood at two expatriate Shawnee towns that had found a haven in the Upper Creek country early in the eighteenth century. One or both parents may have been Creek as well as Shawnee (as offspring of patrilineal Shawnee fathers and possibly of Creek mothers, who would have been matrilineal). About 1759 the family moved north to join Shawnee towns on the Scioto River in the Ohio country, where Tecumseh and Tenskwatawa were born. Riding east toward Tuckaubatchee in mid-September, Tecumseh may well have anticipated a receptive hearing among his southern kinsmen.[13]

Tecumseh's arrival among the Creeks coincided with the annual meeting of the Creek national council. At Tuckaubatchee there gathered several thousand Indians—members of the Creeks' diverse confederacy and delegations from other great nations like the Cherokees—as well as American officials (including, most prominently, Benjamin Hawkins), all interested in hearing the words of the Shawnee emissary. In public Tecumseh diplomatically urged all Indians to "unite in peace and friendship among themselves and cultivate the same with their white neighbours." Only when Hawkins tired of waiting, closed the official conference, and departed Tuckaubatchee did Tecumseh at last address the Indian assembly on the last day of the month. Hawkins had been pressing for Creek acquiescence to a planned widening of the mail path through the Creek country into a wagon way, the Federal Road (Figure 7). When his proposal met near unanimous disapproval, the American agent informed the council he did not require their consent and was simply informing them that the road would be built. Hawkins could hardly have chosen a worse time to antagonize the Creeks.[14]

Addressing an enormous crowd assembled in the square ground at Tuckau-batchee, with whites barred from the daylong proceedings, Tecumseh advocated a revival of old Indian ways and rejection of all things American. Seeka-boo, a Shawnee with Creek kin ties and a skilled translator and relative of Tecumseh's, relayed the content of his speech in fluent Muskogee. Unfortunately, no trustworthy contemporary accounts exist of this momentous speech. At the conclusion of the Redstick War, Benjamin Hawkins offered this interpretation based on recollections of his Creek friends. Tecumseh had incited the Creeks to

> Kill the old Chiefs, friends to peace; kill the cattle, the hogs, and fowls; do not work, destroy the wheels and looms, throw away your ploughs, and every thing used by the Americans. Sing "the song of the Indians of the northern lakes, and dance their dance." Shake your war clubs, shake yourselves: you will frighten the Americans, their [fire]arms will drop from their hands, the ground will become a bog, and mire them, and you may knock them on the head with your war clubs. I will be with you with my Shawnees, as soon as our friends the British are ready for us. Lift up your war club with your right hand, be strong, and I will come and show you how to use it.[15]

Later events almost certainly colored Hawkins' 1814 recitation. In 1811, Tecumseh and his British allies were not yet ready for war with the Americans. In fact, Tenskwatawa's premature attack on U.S. troops at Tippecanoe, during Tecumseh's absence in the South, surprised and chagrined the Shawnee war leader. He does seem to have urged the Creeks to prepare to fight but to bide their time until a unified Indian uprising could be organized with British support. Ap-

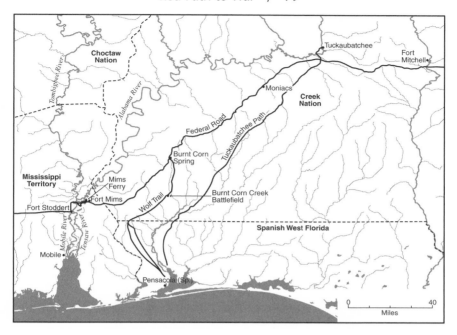

Fig. 7. The Federal Road through the Creek nation, 1811

parently Tecumseh offered to smoke a war pipe with the Creeks, and some may have done so; he claimed one year later that the Creeks had pledged to join his war against the Americans.[16]

Tecumseh's party busied themselves throughout October visiting the towns of the Upper Creek country and explaining Tenskwatawa's sacred visions. Seekaboo, who had become one of Tenskwatawa's prophets, now translated the Shawnee religious doctrine for believers in the Creek Master of Breath, Hisagitamisi. By the time Tecumseh and his entourage departed the Creek nation in November, he left assured that they had found fertile ground for their spiritual message and potential allies in the coming war with the Americans.

Two extraordinary natural events occurred at about this time that suggested, by their coincidence with Tecumseh's southern tour, what great supernatural powers the Shawnee Prophet's religion could summon. A great comet had appeared and grown brilliant in the night sky as Tecumseh (whose Shawnee name means "Shooting Star") entered the Creek nation in September, then faded as he returned north in November. Before his departure he had promised the Creeks a further sign of his power. According to Tensaw métis George Stiggins, Tecumseh told them he "would assend to the top of a high mountain. . . . And there he would whoop three unbounded loud whoops slap his hands together three times and raise up his foot and stamp it on the earth three times and by these actions call forth his power and there-by make the whole earth tremble." That prophecy seemingly was confirmed by the destructive New Madrid earthquakes of 1811–12, a three-month-long series of some 2,000 tremors and aftershocks felt across a vast portion of the midcontinent.[17]

The intensity and scope of these quakes, the greatest in magnitude to strike eastern North America for centuries, traumatized the region's inhabitants. Both the Shawnee leader and his brother's religious movement suddenly gained credibility among Indian populations and particularly among the Upper Creeks, witnesses to Tecumseh's apparent prediction. But the psychological impact of the quakes extended beyond the native population. Whites, Africans, and Indians alike turned to revelatory religions for explanation and solace in the face of such troubling events.[18]

∼

When the Master of Life sent his vision spirits to enlighten the Shawnee Prophet in 1805, another spiritual revival was already under way among the white and black populations of the trans-Appalachian West. Sometimes referred to as the Second Great Awakening, this Protestant "revitalization movement" spread across America beginning around 1795. In the eastern cities, a wave of pietism among Congregationalists and Presbyterians helped propel the federal government's civilization policy as a sort of organized benevolence aimed at the Indians. On the frontier, itinerant preachers roamed the vast western territories of the young United States, ministering daily to the spiritual needs of isolated families and staging open-air services periodically in the larger population centers. At these camp-meeting revivals, they regaled participants with emotional, spellbinding oratory suffused with cries for mercy and extemporaneous exhortations to accept the gospel and repent of sins. As good theater and rare displays of religious ritual and public piety in the sparsely settled frontier, revivals naturally drew huge crowds. But itinerant preachers (like the eccentric, charismatic Methodist minister Lorenzo Dow and his wife, Peggy, who passed through the Tombigbee and Tensaw settlements several times between 1803 and 1811) made slow headway with conversions in the rowdy Southwest—slow, that is, until the first of the New Madrid quakes in December 1811.[19]

In Mississippi Territory, white Americans and enslaved Africans alike took the tremors to be admonitions from the Almighty to seek salvation, maybe the last such warnings they could expect to receive. Thousands responded by conversion at Baptist, Methodist, and Presbyterian revivals. Methodist membership alone jumped from 789 to 1,307 in a single year, a greater increase for the territory than occurred in the next five years combined; comparable numbers flocked to other Protestant denominations.[20] Indians, Americans, and Africans all turned to spirituality for an explanation of this evident sign of divine displeasure, and many promised to mend behaviors considered offensive to their own supreme spirit. Comparable responses of peoples so culturally diverse beg the question: Why did they react so similarly?

A century ago, anthropologists and historians might have sought answers to this kind of question in a psychic unity of humanity based on innate self-interests that were thought to bind together all peoples. But such universals remain elusive, and modern scholars instead try to compare the cultures involved, to understand what particular behaviors might mean in their own cultural contexts. In this case, the cultural contexts had become partially intertwined after centuries of intense interaction. Specifically, evidence points toward sustained influences of Christian religions that had substantially altered the religions of many American Indians (and essentially replaced, through extreme coercion, the religious expressions of enslaved Africans) over the previous two centuries. Archaeologists are still piecing together a coherent picture of religion in America prior to the arrival of Europeans and Africans.[21] Ethnohistorians are likewise working back from historic-era observations and more modern Indian explanations of native religions to understand how native peoples responded spiritually to the invasion of their continent. These tentative efforts have identified several historical changes in the religions of the Shawnees, Creeks, and other Indian nations that are exemplified in Tenskwatawa's visions.

By way of example, consider first the preeminent nature of the Master of Breath (Creek counterpart to the Shawnee Master of Life) for early-nineteenth-century Creeks. Some anthropologists and modern-day Muskogees suspect this manifestation of a supreme spirit developed in the seventeenth or early eighteenth centuries after Christian missionaries introduced the concept of a single deity to the native peoples of eastern North America.[22] In addition, Tenskwatawa's description of fiery tortures reserved for the spirits of the unrepentant unquestionably resembles contemporaneous revivalist Christian imagery of purgatory and hell. In 1807 the Prophet told three visiting Shaker brethren that observations of Roman Catholic missionary priests insisting on confession of sins by converts had influenced the practices of some of his own followers.

Of course, despite these and many other apparent convergences (such as the Prophet's strong recommendation to set aside traditional polygyny in favor of monogamy), very significant differences still divided Indian and Christian religions. Strong nativist elements—from the primacy of a sacred fire to the consumption of the purifying Black Drink and the ritual significance of war dances—suffused the Shawnee and Creek prophetic movements. Most revivalist Protestant preachers were strict evangelicals, promising salvation only by absolute acceptance of faith in Christ, not by good deeds or reformed behavior (although those, too, were generally encouraged). Both the Prophet's co-religionists and evangelical Protestants were intolerant of unbelievers. While revivalist preachers frequently offered up fervent prayers "that the Indians might also share in the blessed hope and joyful anticipation of the future state [of God's grace]," the Shakers alone among Protestant sects believed God "was mightily at work" among the Prophet's followers. Nevertheless, after two centuries of interaction in the forests of eastern North America, native and Christian religions had converged enough for all to see the hand of a creator spirit behind the enormous forces unleashed by the New Madrid earthquakes. Thus forewarned (of God's or the Master of Breath's wrath), how should the diverse people of the frontier respond?[23]

Tecumseh's impressive performance at Tuckaubatchee notwithstanding, the Shawnee Prophet's influence among the Creeks grew slowly at first. Despite deep undercurrents of discontent in Creek society, most Creeks did not advocate immediate overthrow of their micos, their healers, and their ties to the Americans. To Seekaboo, who stayed in the South, must be attributed the eventual conversion of a majority of the Upper Creeks. His proselytizing inspired an indigenous prophetic movement, especially among the Alabamas.[24] In 1812 several Alabamas from Coosada, home of the Sehoy matrilineage, made the long trek north to confer directly with Tenskwatawa, to "imbibe his notions of the whitemans oppressive and domineering encroachments on indian rights . . . contrary to order purposed by the creator and [to learn how] he in his wrath would assist the Indians in the recovery of their lands and country, which he had made on purpose for their special use."[25] These Creek neophytes inspirationally combined native elements of traditional Creek religion with Shawnee innovations.

This new kind of prophet seems to have shared many characteristics with the traditional Creek *kithlas* (*kērrv*) or "knowers," a small number of men who diagnosed diseases, practiced clairvoyance and sleight of hand, and could control rain and hail.[26] Some enlightening parallels can be drawn between a rare eighteenth-century description (by Jean-Bernard Bossu, written in 1759) of Alabama kithlas and the behavior of Redstick prophets. According to Bossu, "The Indians have a great deal of confidence in their medicine men, whose hut is covered with skins which he uses for clothing and blankets. He enters the hut completely naked and utters words, understood by no one, in order to invoke the spirit. After that, apparently in a complete trance, he gets up, shouts, and moves about as the sweat pours from every part of his body. The hut shakes, and the spectators think that this is evidence of the presence of the spirit."[27]

Compare this with a description by George Stiggins of an early revitalization prophet, Captain Isaacs (the same Coosada headman who, a few years earlier, had challenged métis Dixon Bailey's status as a member of the Creek nation). Isaacs employed traditional Creek methods to acquire supernatural power. "Capt Isaacs bore a very conspicuous part, in the catalogue of inspired men . . . he began as a conjuror first, . . . diving down to the bottom of the river and laying there and traveling about for many days and nights receiving instruction and information from an enormous and friendly serpent that dwels there and was acquainted with future events and all other things necessary for a man to know in his life."[28] The self-induced trance, spirit visions, and shaking tent employed by the earlier kithlas are similar in many respects to the repertoire of the revitalization prophets. Tecumseh called for the earth to shake, a recurrent theme of the prophets, and to "shake yourselves," a remonstrance which the Creeks also interpreted according to their own traditions.[29]

One disconcerted nonbeliever—the Tensaw métis Sam Moniac—described an encounter with the Creek prophet High-head Jim (Kasita Hadjo), who "shook hands with me, and immediately began to tremble and jerk in every part of his frame, and the very calves of his legs would be convulsed, and he would get entirely out of breath with the agitation."[30] To the initiated, the prophet's shaking was a clear indication of ritual pollution, the presence of a nonbeliever, "for they could tell a man who was opposed to their measures, so quick as they touchd any part of him, or a man that eat salt victuals, for on shakeing hands with any man of the description aforesaid the prophet instantly commenced trembling and the defilement subsided by a gradual jerking and working of all his muscles, not excepting his face, which jerking of his muscles concluded in a tremble of all his flesh."[31]

Salt had long been a special substance to the southeastern Indians. For a thousand years they had processed the mineral from saline springs in the forks of the Tombigbee and Alabama rivers for export throughout the region (Figure 8.) Because of its rarity, and its necessity as a dietary supplement for people dependent upon agriculture, salt distribution must have been a prerogative of chiefs during the prehistoric era and remained a valued trade commodity in early historic times. As a material obtained from the underworld, the realm of Captain Isaacs' spirit serpent, salt also would have been considered a potentially dangerous substance. This may explain why the Creeks abstained from consuming salt during the poskita renewal ceremony and accompanying initiation rites.[32] As the Creeks, and particularly the Tensaw métis, acquired increasing numbers of domestic livestock in the early nineteenth century, however, many adopted the American method of preserving meat by salting. For the Redsticks, followers of the Creek prophets, salt victuals symbolized American influence, and consequently the polluting touch of a salt-using nonbeliever was doubly offensive to a prophet.

During the poskita, town members annually cleansed their spirits and redefined their places in Creek social order. The prophets' movement had similar goals, though clearly the traditional methods of achieving renewal had proven ineffective and new, more powerful means were sought. That the prophets perceived their movement as similar in intent to the poskita ceremony can be inferred from a description of the siege of Tuckaubatchee, one of the initial battles of the Creek civil war. Redstick warriors of the prophets' faction attacked the town, according to Benjamin Hawkins, "for seven days and nights. . . . The eighth day was the day the town was to be sunk by the prophets." Eight days, the traditional time required to perform the poskita ceremony at Tuckaubatchee and other large towns, was considered an appropriate period in which to cleanse the town of white influence.[33]

Although the prophets retained many traditional Creek religious beliefs, the movement also demanded an explicit rejection of most cultural elements derived from the whites. Redsticks were to destroy all their cattle, hogs, and chickens, throw their iron hoes and axes into the rivers, even abandon their cornfields, in a comprehensive rejection of the U.S. agent's program to encourage domestic husbandry by Creek males.[34] This sort of behavior, which completely baffled Hawkins, is a typical element of revitalization movements. The prophets sought to remake their world, cleansing Creek households, towns, and nation of pollutants introduced by the Americans, even to the foods on which they had come to depend. In turn, the Master of Breath "in his wrath would

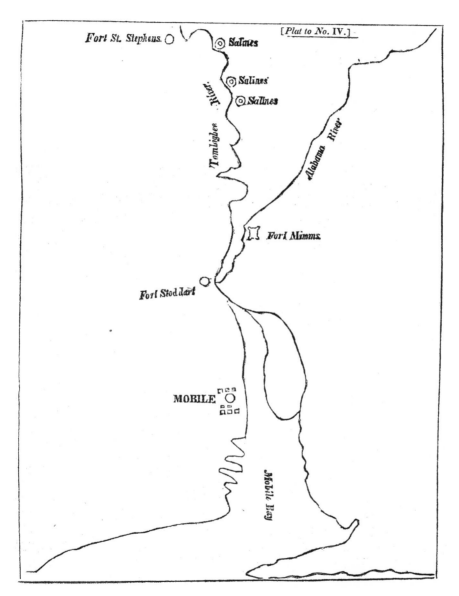

Fig. 8. Saltworks north of the Mobile-Tensaw delta, from Walter Lowrie, ed., *American State Papers*, vol. 3, *Public Lands*, 237.

assist the Indians in the recovery of their lands and country, which he had made on purpose for their special use and suited it for 'em in fruits of all kinds acorn trees &c spontaneously bearing eatables for their subsistance of nature and comfort of life." Instead of beef and bacon they would again feast on venison and turkey; instead of corn and sweet potatoes, acorn meal and hickory nuts would nourish Creek children.[35]

Such a subsistence base had been adequate for Archaic-era hunters and gatherers thousands of years earlier, when wild animals and wild plants supported a smaller human population. But the new regimen soon imposed great hardships on the Redsticks, who had derived the bulk of their sustenance from farming before the war.[36] Yet they accepted this instruction with implicit faith and little or no concern that the prophecies might fail. Only when the Americans entered the war, in the aftermath of the battle at Fort Mims, did the Redsticks change their subsistence tactics. Even then, they maintained their resolve not to keep livestock, and instead slaughtered almost 8,000 head of cattle and hogs belonging to whites and métis living in the Tombigbee and Tensaw settlements, carrying only the dried meat back to their own country. By these actions they hoped to redress the serious imbalance that had appeared between the roles of men and women in Creek society, even as they recognized the impossibility of a simple return to the old dependable reliance on hunting for the deerskin trade. This shift in subsistence was accompanied by a movement of the Redstick population out of their old towns and villages into camps in the woods and new towns protected with invisible holy barriers to their enemies. Other changes in lifestyle advocated by the prophets included a return to bows, arrows, and war clubs for warfare, though firearms continued in use as long as weapons functioned and ammunition could be obtained.[37]

~

Although the origin of the term "Redstick" aroused much erroneous speculation by American writers in the early nineteenth century, there is no doubt it referred to the red-painted, wooden war club, the atássa (*vtvssv*), of the Creeks. An early form of Creek atássa is known from the eighteenth century—a long, straight wooden club notched along one edge. Four of these clubs adorn an Alabama council house sketched by a French officer in 1732. A gunstock-shaped variety of club had replaced the earlier form in popularity among the Creeks and other eastern Indians by the turn of the nineteenth century (Figure 9). As a weapon of distinctively native origin (albeit reconfigured with attributes of a European weapon), the Redstick atássa was an appropriately militaristic symbol of opposition to the Americans.[38]

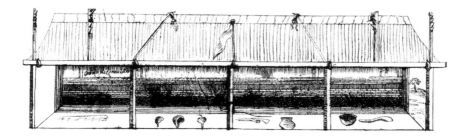

Fig. 9. Creek war clubs (*atássa*), prototypes of the Redstick war clubs. *Top,* a 1732 sketch of an Alabama council house, with a notched club on floor at the left and symbolic "war club" poles and scalp hoops atop the building (courtesy of the Département des cartes et des plans, GE DD 2987 (8816) B, Bibliothèque nationale de France, Paris). *Bottom,* a 1757 sketch by William Bonar of Creek weapons, showing a ball head club and a gunstock club at lower right (courtesy of The National Archives, Kew, U.K.).

George Stiggins described the war club of the Redsticks as "shaped like a small gun about two feet long and at the curve near where the lock would be is a three square piece of iron or steele with a sharp edge drove in to leave a projection of about two inches." Lewis Sewall similarly defined "Red-sticks," in his epic poem of the Redstick War published in 1833, as "a kind of war club, about two feet long, thick and heavy at one end, in which was fixed a piece of sharp iron or bone; with which they struck their captives with great violence on the head and speedily put an end to their existence. They were painted red, hence the term 'Red-sticks.'"[39]

Benjamin Hawkins (who surely knew the term's derivation but failed to leave us an explanation) referred to the prophets' adherents as "Red Sticks" or "Red Clubs" but preferred the latter, a clear reference to the war club. His frequent employment of quotes around these phrases reflects his disparaging usage, suggesting the terms were alternate translations of the anti-American faction's own name for themselves. This is confirmed by one of the very few documents written by Hawkins' opponents during the war, a letter that begins, "We the Chiefs of the red Stick Nation." Writing in 1895, Henry Halbert agreed the term had been "considered an honorable appellation" and testified that "Red Stick War" was "the name by which the War of 1813 is still known among the Creeks of the Indian Territory." That seems reason enough to retain the name for the people and the war.[40]

～

The rise of the prophets' movement caused immense disruption in Creek society, since their message was by no means universally accepted. But a spiraling cycle of violence steadily eroded confidence in the U.S. agent and the micos. Beginning in the spring of 1812, Redstick militants began targeting white Americans traveling the Federal Road from Georgia to Mississippi Territory. Thomas Meredith was murdered near Sam Moniac's stand in late March, followed in April by the murders of William Lott at Warriors Stand in the nation and two white families settled on the Duck River in Tennessee. Having labored years to reorganize Creek political structure by reinforcing the centralized authority of the national council, Benjamin Hawkins perceived these peacetime atrocities as a direct challenge to the council. He demanded that the micos order the execution of those responsible. Exercising their considerable police power, the national council had the murderers pursued. Four who would not surrender were killed, including one shot by métis William McIntosh while claiming sanctuary in the micos' bed of the square ground in the "white/peace" town of Tallassee. Hillabee Haya, leader of the attack on the Duck River settlement, was "decoyed to the old council house at the Hickory Ground, put to death . . . and thrown into the Coosah river." Those exercises in peremptory justice violated a basic precept of traditional Creek law, which had always depended on clan leaders to enforce order and, in exceptional circumstances, execute miscreants. By usurping the authority of the clans, the Creek national council created immense political discontent, which convinced many (who otherwise might not have joined the Redstick movement for religious reasons alone) to oppose Hawkins and the micos. While overt violence abated for a time, simmering outrage over these incidents among the prophets' adherents led directly to civil war among the Creeks.[41]

In the spring of 1813, a party of Upper Creeks led by Little Warrior of Hickory Ground journeyed to the Ohio country to confer with Tenskwatawa. On their return, aroused by false rumors of open warfare between the Creek nation and the Americans, they attacked and wiped out seven white immigrant families near the mouth of the Ohio River. Once again Hawkins pressured the micos to take decisive action through the Creek national council. The execution of Little Warrior and seven of his men in April by a council-sanctioned war party commanded by Captain Isaacs, with James Cornells and David Tate participating as witnesses, overtly defied the clans and directly precipitated the long-feared civil war among the Creeks.

The prophets now urged their followers to do as Tenskwatawa and Tecumseh had instructed: "Kill the old Chiefs, friends to peace." Although most of the micos stood by the U.S. agent and the head of the council, Tastanagi Thlucco (*Tvstvnvke Rakko*, Big Warrior) of Tuckaubatchee, a few leading men turned against them. Most notable among the latter were Peter McQueen and Hopoithle Mico of Tallassee, who accepted the prophets' message and became ardent, articulate spokesmen for the Redsticks. By June 1813, full-scale war had broken out. Hundreds of Upper Creeks opposed to the prophets' movement abandoned their homes and fled for protection to Hawkins' agency in Georgia, to the Lower Creek towns along the Chattahoochee River, and to the white settlement in the Tensaw, across the boundary of the Creek nation near Little River. Others retreated behind a makeshift stockade erected around the square ground at Tuckaubatchee—the same square ground where Tecumseh and Seekaboo first conveyed the Prophet's doctrine to the Creek people less than two years earlier. Captain Isaacs barely escaped assassination and joined the other besieged refugees there. After wielding great influence as a prophet, his willingness to lead the council's police force against Little Warrior led to his abrupt political decline and condemnation as a witch. And the participation

of Cornells and Tate in the executions of Little Warrior and his men emphasized to the enraged Redsticks the central role of the Tensaw métis in their
opposition.[42]

The seams along which the fabric of Creek society parted have proven difficult to identify. Geography played a role but not in the way one might expect.
Direct pressure from white neighbors poaching on Creek hunting grounds or
grazing livestock across the boundary line apparently influenced the outcome
little, if at all. The Alabamas agitated most strenuously for war yet were barely
impacted by white encroachment (apart from the Federal Road crossing their
hunting territories). On the other hand, the Lower Creeks (on the front line of
American expansion) and Abeka towns of the middle Coosa Valley (among the
farthest removed from white settlement) sided overwhelmingly with the Americans. Perhaps proximity to the U.S. Agency contributed to the Lower Creeks'
general disinterest in the Redstick movement, which found its greatest expres-
sion among the Upper Creeks. But, as implied above, the split did not occur
precisely between Upper Creeks and Lower Creeks. Although most Redsticks
inhabited Upper Creek talwas, some support for the prophets also appeared
among the Lower Creeks and more than a few Yuchis (in the Lower Creek
country) took up arms against the Americans. Even among the Upper Creeks
there were important exceptions. Tuckaubatchee, Aubecooche, and Nauchee
sided with the "peace" faction, and at least nine other towns (Coosa, Coosada,
Eufalee, Hatchechubba, Immookfau, Okfuskee, Tallassee, Thlothlegulgau, and
Taskigi) fissioned. Some divided towns struggled to remain neutral, but un-
compromising extremists on both sides polarized the situation, with Redstick
leaders threatening to tomahawk the uncommitted and Hawkins ordering the
Indians to "take sides."[43]

Modern analysts of Redstick social cleavage reject the notion, popular among
American officials during the War of 1812, that the Creeks split along pro-
American and pro-British lines.[44] Ross Hassig argued convincingly many years
ago that an individual's decision to adopt or reject the Redstick cause was influenced less by the major structural divisions within prewar Creek society (such
as clan, white/Tchiloki moiety, and white/red town affiliations) than by age
grade and talwa association.[45] Claudio Saunt has more recently revealed the
important positive correlation between Redstick converts and those individuals who received few economic and political benefits of the "plan of civilization."[46] These factors do explain a great deal. But the narrow choice open to
individual Creeks—stand alongside either the Americans or the Redsticks, and
in either case accept a radical redefinition of what it meant to be Creek, with

each course possibly leading to widespread death and destruction—suggests just how wrenching and intensely personal a decision each of them faced.

Weatherford's Dilemma

For most Creek métis living near Little River, the decision was a simple one, made all the clearer by the Redsticks' determination to expel from the nation (or kill) any Indians who defied the will of the prophets and refused to abandon their accumulated wealth and property. David Tate, John Weatherford, Dixon and James Bailey, and Sam Moniac had each determined years before to compete and succeed according to American standards. Their holdings in slaves, plantations, cotton gins, taverns, and other properties secured their highest rank among the Creek economic elite. Redstick doctrine held no allure for these men. Similar reactions prevailed north of the American boundary line in mixed-race households of white men married to Creek métis women. For the Dunns, Fletchers, Hatterways, Joneses, McGirths, and Randons, the Redstick revolution threatened dissolution of their families. Tenskwatawa had called on his people to repatriate only Indian women from mixed marriages; children of white men were considered white, not Indian, by the patrilineal Shawnees. The Creek prophets, logically enough, reinterpreted that Shawnee dictum in matrilineal terms appropriate to their own society, and Redstick warriors soon began abducting métis women *and* their children from the households of white and "unreformed" métis men. When the Creek civil war swept southward, threatening to overtake the Little River métis by mid-summer 1813, these families abandoned their homes in the Creek nation and took up temporary residence at the crude frontier forts hastily constructed by their American neighbors, from the Tensaw to the Tombigbee, on the presumably safer side of the border, in Mississippi Territory.

This prejudice against interracial marriage—deemed necessary by the Shawnee Prophet "so that the nations might become genuine Indians" again—had arisen relatively recently among the native societies of eastern North America. Its appearance reflects (ironically, considering the Prophet's intent to rid the native world of American influences) an insidious acceptance of early-nineteenth-century white America's own brand of racialist bigotry. The incipient racism directed toward intermarried couples and their métis offspring was just one manifestation of this new social order. For more than one hundred years, Creeks had adopted Africans taken on raids, intermarried freely with Africans who had run away from slavery, and considered the offspring of those marriages fully Creek. In more recent decades, however, the Creeks had been selling Africans—those taken in raids from white frontier plantations as well as captured runaways—back to white slavers, and they had been holding others enslaved on Creek plantations. An insidious effect of this commodification of Africans, transforming people into property, was an acceptance of the underlying color-based precept of American-style racism. By 1813 most Creeks had come to believe dark-skinned Africans to be inherently inferior. When internecine warfare began breaking up Creek plantations, the Redsticks treated captured Africans first and foremost as property. Some African men evidently considered their lot improved under the Redsticks and fought desperately against their common enemies, the Americans, when the conflict broadened to include the whites.[47] But there was no mass defection of Africans to the Redsticks, as American officials feared would happen and as did occur a few years later when British agents in Florida working in concert with the Redsticks promised freedom to runaway slaves. Most Africans living in the Creek nation and in Mississippi Territory apparently thought Redstick ownership not greatly preferable to white domination, an impression that inevitably weakened the Redsticks' military position.

Although the Tensaw Creek community at Little River—including métis, intermarried whites, and most of their enslaved Africans—stood impressively unified in their defiance of the Redsticks, two famous Creeks with close ties to the Tensaw, William Weatherford and Josiah Francis, chose the opposite path. Why did these two influential men turn away from their Americanized lifestyles of economic privilege to lead forces in battle against friends and relatives? In both cases, religion played a key role.

Josiah Francis, Hillis Hadjo (*Heles Haco,* or "crazy-brave medicine") is a shadowy historical figure. Born in the Alabama town of Autauga where he made his home as an adult, he spent some of his youth in the Tensaw. We know he spoke fluent English, but his inability to write indicates he lacked the formal education afforded a relative (perhaps his brother), David Francis, under the secret article of the 1790 Treaty of New York. Our most informative source on Francis is the fiercely anti-Redstick chronicler George Stiggins, a Natchez métis and resident of the Tensaw who knew Francis before his conversion and emergence as the Alabama Prophet. Stiggins despised all prophets and especially Francis, whom he considered a coward and a religious charlatan. Given the highly biased nature of the historical record on Francis, ascertaining the sincerity of his religious beliefs is probably beyond our grasp. But his prominence as a Redstick prophet and his effectiveness as a proselytizer for the Creek prophets' movement are beyond doubt. His converts numbered in the hundreds, including virtually every member of his brother-in-law Sam Moniac's family. Despite the numerous military defeats suffered by Redstick forces after Fort Mims, including an attack Francis himself led (ineffectually) against Fort Sinquefield early in September 1813, his influence as a religious leader waned only well after he and his remaining followers retreated south into Spanish Florida (Plate 4).[48]

Historical sources about William Weatherford are a good deal more abundant, although their contradictory nature leaves his motivations for joining the Redsticks open to divergent interpretations. He seems to have shared many of the interests and values of his plantation-owning relatives—brother John Weatherford, half-brother David Tate, and brother-in-law Sam Moniac—all of whom opposed the Redsticks. Yet not only did he join the Redsticks, he helped lead them to a stunning victory, one of the greatest successes of Indian warfare.

After the war Weatherford tried on several occasions to explain why he had joined the Redstick cause. In every instance he emphasized his reluctance, based on fears that war with Americans would end in the destruction of the Creek people. Weatherford "was as much opposed to that war as any one living," recalled one admirer, "but when it became necessary to take sides, he went with his countrymen." In essence, he chose to follow the Redsticks because no other choice was possible for him; "they were his people—he was raised with them, and he would share their fate."[49] But why, we may well ask, did he think himself more like the Creeks who espoused the prophets' religion? Were not the Tensaw métis also his countrymen? From every indication they considered themselves Creeks, too, albeit a new order of Creeks. The question stands: What separated William Weatherford from his Tensaw kin?

While he visited the Tensaw frequently before the Redstick uprising, staying often with his brothers at their Little River plantations, Weatherford was not (at the outbreak of war) a Tensaw métis, an important point missed by nearly every modern writer. After the Redstick War, he did establish a plantation near Little River, but his prewar residence was situated 150 miles to the north, on the upper Alabama River. The physical distance separating him from his downriver kin measures the strength of other ties that bound him close to the place of his birth, close to the peoples of Coosada, Taskigi, and Hickory Ground.

As historian Karl Davis has cogently argued in his recent dissertation, Weatherford held conservative Creek religious beliefs throughout his life, and because of his strong faith he "struggled with his feelings" about the revitalistic message delivered by Tecumseh. Our most revealing insight to Weatherford's deepest convictions comes from J. D. Dreisbach, David Tate's son-in-law, who wrote in 1883 about Weatherford's final days in 1824. "A short time before the death of Weatherford, he was one of a party of hunters who were engaged in a deer and bear hunt on Lovet's Creek, in Monroe county, Ala. Whilst on this hunt a white deer was killed, which seemed to make a marked impression on Weatherford, who withdrew from the hunt and went home, remarking that some one of the party engaged in the hunt would soon be called to the hunting ground in the spirit land; that the white deer was a 'token.' And the next day he was taken suddenly ill, and died three days thereafter, and during his illness imagined that Sofoth Kaney (his former wife) was standing by his bed waiting for him to go with her to the hunting grounds of the spirit land."[50]

Weatherford's lifelong adherence to traditionalist beliefs suggests the prophets' nativist religious doctrine may indeed have attracted him, despite his later disavowal. In the wake of their crushing military defeat in 1814, most former Redsticks who surrendered to the Americans undoubtedly felt misled by the prophets. But the movement's initial promise of a better world probably appealed greatly to Weatherford, an appeal apparently reinforced by a developing relationship with an early convert to the prophet's religion, "Sofoth Kaney" or Supalamy Moniac.[51]

Weatherford remained single for nine years after the death of his first wife, Polly Moniac, Sam's sister. In the summer or fall of 1813, though, Weatherford married Polly's niece, Supalamy, in the Creek nation. They took up residence at a refugee town (known to us only as "Weatherford's town," probably located around his former plantation) near Holy Ground on the upper Alabama River. Supalamy and her father, John Moniac, had joined the Redsticks, presumably at the persuasion of Josiah Francis, husband to Hannah Moniac (half-sister of John as well as William Weatherford). These fragmentary bits of evidence—multiple familial ties and the coincidence of his marriage just when prospects for success of the prophets' movement seemed brightest—suggest emotional as well as intellectual motives for Weatherford's attachment to the Redstick cause, an attachment earlier studies have left essentially unexplained. On the other hand, the historical record abundantly documents how Weatherford committed himself entirely to that cause and "participated in a conspicuous manner in their war measures."[52]

There was considerable speculation during and after the war that the Redsticks had coerced Weatherford with threats against his first wife's children, held at the Hoithlewaulee camps on the Tallapoosa River to insure his good behavior. Others conjectured that Weatherford and his family were hedging their bets on the outcome of the war, William and his female relatives siding with the Redsticks and his brothers with the Americans. No matter who prevailed, the family might still emerge with at least a portion of their substantial wealth intact. Such arguments, however, hardly explain Weatherford's wholehearted efforts on behalf of the Redsticks. One barely noted event indicates his active participation well before the attack on Fort Mims. Early in the summer of 1813, he and Sam Moniac drove a herd of beef cattle to sell at Chickasawhay, the southernmost Choctaw town. While there, Weatherford held a "secret interview" with the Choctaw leader, Mingo Mushulatubbee, to enlist Choctaw assistance in the coming war. Mushulatubbee rejected the overture, and Weatherford soon afterwards openly sided with the Redsticks. He had made his choice.[53]

5

Creek Civil War to Redstick War

As civil strife split the Creek nation in the late spring and summer of 1813, neighboring populations grew increasingly concerned about the prospects of a broader war between the Redsticks and the United States. By this time the United States had already been at war with Great Britain for a full year, a struggle so far confined to the northern states, Canada, and the high seas. But Tecumseh's 1811 tour of the southern tribes had always been understood by Benjamin Hawkins and other U.S. officials as an attempt to align Indian nations against American expansion in anticipation of military support from Britain. In the South, only the Creeks responded in numbers to Tecumseh's call for pan-Indian unity, and British aid was slow in coming. But a coalescence of the two conflicts seemed inevitable to most observers, Creek as well as American. The governors of Tennessee, Georgia, and Mississippi Territory stood ready to respond to attacks against American citizens and called up militia armies (commanded by Generals Andrew Jackson, John Floyd, and Ferdinand L. Claiborne, respectively) prepared to invade the Creek nation. On either side of the Creek country were sizeable populations of Cherokees and Choctaws, each with large factions discontented with their own leadership and their relationship with the United States. In the end, both nations sent warriors to fight alongside the Americans and against their erstwhile enemies, but that outcome seemed far from certain in mid-1813.[1] To the south, the Spanish colonies of East and West Florida maintained a neutral posture, although their royal governors looked to the Redsticks and to Britain for support in the seemingly imminent confrontation with U.S. forces. Just months earlier, on April 13, General James Wilkinson had seized Mobile, leaving isolated Spanish garrisons at Pensacola and St. Augustine the only European colonial outposts on the U.S. southern border.

Some Americans had been lobbying for war with the Creeks since the outbreak of the War of 1812. Among the most vocal was Andrew Jackson; he or a like-minded supporter wrote the following commentary for the Nashville *Clarion* in the summer of 1812.

> Loading his vessel at the head of Mobile bay, [a merchant] will proceed up the Mobile river ninety miles, to McGilvrey's town [that is, the Tensaw] in the Creek nation. Here he will find the Mobile divided into two streams, one the Alabama, coming down from the North-East, the other the Tombigbee coming down from the North. . . . Imagination looks forward to the moment when all the southern indians shall be pushed across the Mississippi: when the delightful countries now occupied by them shall be covered with a numerous and industrious population; and when a city, the emporium of a vast commerce, shall be seen to flourish on the spot where some huts, inhabited by lawless savages, now mark the junction of the Alabama and Tombigbee rivers. The present is a favorable moment of accomplishing a part of this great design. The Floridas will soon be occupied by the American troops. Our settlements on the bay and river of Mobile will require to be strengthened, and to strengthen them a part of the country inhabited by the Creeks will be indispensable to us. Fortunately the crimes of this nation have supplied us with a pretext for the dismemberment of their country.[2]

With such sentiments so openly expressed, the Redsticks may have felt they had nothing to lose in a war with the United States. On the other hand, we may well ask why the Tensaw métis, whose plantations this correspondent characterized as "some huts, inhabited by lawless savages," remained so steadfast in their support of the United States. In fact, as we have seen, Creek opposition to the Redstick movement derived from many causes, but complex motivations and subtle differences of philosophy meant little in the face of increasing violence.

In mid-July 1813, Redstick warriors destroyed some outlying plantations and other properties owned by Tensaw métis Sam Moniac, James Cornells, and Leonard McGee.[3] A Pensacola-bound Redstick delegation led by High-head Jim of Atasi accosted Moniac near his home on the Federal Road. When pressed by Jim to join their movement, Moniac feigned agreement, saying he would sell his property "and buy ammunition, and join them. He [Jim] then told me that they were going down to Pensacola to get ammunition, and that they had got a letter from a British General which would enable them to receive ammunition from the Governor. That it had been given to the Little Warrior, and saved by his Nephew when he was killed, and sent down to Francis. High-Head told me that when they went back with their supply, another body of men would go down for another supply of ammunition, and that ten men would go out of each Town, and that they calculated on five horse loads for every Town." The Redsticks also planned, according to Moniac, "to make a general attack on the American Settlements—that the Indians on the waters of the Coosa and Tallapoosa and on the Black Warrior, were to attack the Settlements on the Tombigby and Alabama, particularly the Tensaw and Fork Settlements. . . . I found, from the talk of High-Head, that the war was to be against the whites and not between Indians themselves,—that all they wanted was to kill those who had taken the talk of the whites."[4]

Moniac and Cornells evaded the Redstick force (which then lay waste to the outlying métis plantations) and rode hard toward the Tombigbee and Tensaw settlements to report this threat of imminent attack. Earlier rumors now seemed confirmed. The Redsticks did intend to fight the Americans.[5] Without waiting for instructions or assistance from General Claiborne's Territorial Volunteer troops, Colonel James Caller commanding the 15th Regiment of Mississippi Territorial militia promptly sent out a call, to gather a force to intercept the Redstick pack trains.

Burnt Corn Creek

Burning and pillaging of a few métis plantations caused little immediate alarm in the Tensaw and Tombigbee settlements. This was standard punishment meted out for decades by Creek talwas to enforce order and encourage obedience among recalcitrants.[6] American militia officers became very concerned, however, at Moniac's report of Redstick efforts to obtain ammunition from the Spaniards for a general assault on those settlements. The Americans might have construed warnings by Moniac, Cornells, and other Tensaw métis as attempts to maneuver the United States into interceding on their behalf in what had been, to this point, a civil war between Creeks. Instead they interpreted Redstick moves to acquire large supplies of ammunition (just as the civil war was ending and the last of their opposition fled the Creek nation) as reflecting

Redstick intentions to broaden the war. While the Redsticks contemplated attacks against the white, black, and métis peoples living immediately north of Mobile, they sought to replenish supplies of gunpowder and shot depleted in their successful battles to cleanse the Upper Creek country of enemies to the prophets' movement. During this civil war, Benjamin Hawkins had supplied his Creek allies sparingly with arms and ammunition, fearing that captured weapons would be turned against white settlers. By mid-July he considered the Redsticks "badly armed [with] much reliance placed by the opposition on their bows, arrows, war clubs and magic." With American sources of munitions closed to them, and British naval forces not yet active in the Gulf, their only hope for resupply rested on military and traders' stockpiles in Pensacola. Several parties of Redsticks now converged on that small colonial port, home to Governor Mateo González Manrique, a Spanish military presidio, and warehouses full of goods belonging to the British trading firm of Panton, Leslie & Co.

In Pensacola, the Redsticks led by Peter McQueen, a Scots-Muskogee métis and head warrior (tastanagi) of Tallassee, intimidated the Spanish garrison of that isolated post for several days. McQueen demanded ammunition from newly arrived Governor González Manrique and threatened to burn down the town if sufficient powder and lead were not forthcoming. González Manrique relayed to his superiors the Redsticks' intention to broaden the war because of incessant American incursions on Creek lands, especially along the Federal Road. McQueen now presented González Manrique with an ultimatum— openly support the Redsticks and break relations with the Americans.[7] With the seizure of Mobile by U.S. forces a recent memory, the governor considered the Redsticks important potential allies against any American attempt on Pensacola. But McQueen's warriors proved difficult to control; at one point, Governor González Manrique called out his troops to face down the impatient Creeks. In the meantime, one townswoman ransomed a captive taken by the Redsticks, James Cornells' wife Betsy Coulter, abducted from his plantation at Burnt Corn Springs. Zachariah McGirth happened to be visiting Pensacola at the time and was threatened by Redsticks until a Creek intervened to save his life. And David Tate and an American friend, William Peirce, both from the Tensaw, slipped secretly into Pensacola at the request of the U.S. commander at Fort Stoddert, to gather intelligence on Redstick negotiations with the Spaniards.[8]

Despite the presence in Pensacola of at least three spies for the Americans, precisely how González Manrique responded to McQueen's demands remains uncertain, since the documentary record contains many contradictions. According to James Innerarity, agent for Panton, Leslie & Co. and one of the more objective observers on the scene, González Manrique presented McQueen and his warriors with twenty barrels of flour and twenty-five of corn, "about 50 Blankets, a quantity of Scissors, Knives, Rasors [razors], Ribbons &c 4 or 5 Steers about 1000 lb Gunpowder" and a proportionate quantity of lead balls and small shot.[9] The Redstick Creeks' need for flour and corn at a time of year when they normally celebrated the ripening of their first corn crops reveals the deprivation they already suffered from the prophets' injunction against planting. On the other hand, Innerarity commented upon the remarkable deportment of the Redsticks. To his amazement "not a single one would taste a drop of liquor, or any thing else but water," while near the taverns and grog-shops of Pensacola, a salubrious result of prophetic exhortations to abstain from polluting rum.[10]

With their requests partially satisfied and their packhorses loaded, the Redsticks returned northward in several groups along different paths to safeguard their valuable supplies. When reports on the transfer of Spanish goods to the Redsticks arrived in Mississippi Territory from the American spies, Colonel Caller's mounted force set out to intercept the "contraband." Accompanying approximately 150 white militiamen was a small contingent of perhaps thirty Tensaw métis led by Dixon Bailey. Caller's six militia companies of mounted riflemen rendezvoused in the Creek nation at David Tate's cowpens, rode northeast on the Federal Road to the ruins of James Cornells' plantation at Burnt Corn Spring, then turned south toward Pensacola on the Wolf Trail. On July 27 they ambushed McQueen's pack train at the Wolf Trail crossing on Burnt Corn Creek, as the unsuspecting Redsticks were encamped, preparing and eating their midday meal (Figure 10).[11] The dismounted American/métis militia initially surprised and chased their enemies into a canebrake, killing a Creek woman and an enslaved African and capturing some packhorses. However, the Redsticks soon regrouped and counterattacked the undisciplined militiamen, most of whom had begun plundering the packs, immediately routing all but a handful led by Captains Bailey, Smoot, and Dale. Fighting continued for about three hours before the rest of the militia withdrew. Colonel Caller lost his horse and wandered in the woods for fifteen days before rescue by the Tensaw métis. Losses were small, as battles go, with two killed and about fifteen wounded on the American side and the Redsticks losing ten or twelve.[12] But the low casualties belied the battle's significance.

The Redsticks, for their part, were at once elated at their defeat of a much larger American force (which seemed to confirm Tecumseh's prophecy of an

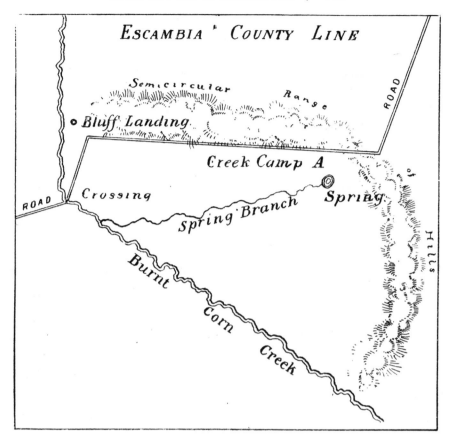

Fig. 10. Burnt Corn Creek battlefield, according to Halbert and Ball, *The Creek War of 1813–1814*, 133.

easy Indian victory over the whites) and infuriated at the prominent role of Bailey and the other Tensaw métis, who led the American militia into the Creek nation, were responsible for most of the Redstick losses, and had covered the militia's retreat.[13] On the other hand, the militia's overall poor performance disgraced and humiliated the Tensaw and Tombigbee settlements. Although militiamen did manage to capture some ammunition, cloth, and "Liverpool Salt" bound for the Upper Creek towns, the Redsticks' other pack trains had eluded them, despite boasts to the contrary.[14] As news of the failed preemptive strike swept across the frontier, whites, blacks, and métis alike concluded that Burnt Corn Creek had certainly emboldened and provoked the Redsticks; attacks against the settlements were now inevitable.[15] In the Forks, between the Tombigbee and Alabama rivers, isolated farmsteads were abandoned. Hundreds of refugees fled to the towns of Mobile and St. Stephens and the two federal stockades at Fort Stoddert, while those who remained near their farms assembled at fifteen to twenty strongly built houses. Those Little River métis and African slaves who still remained at their plantations in the Creek nation gathered up what valued possessions they could carry, boarded flatboats, and floated down the Alabama. Near the Cut-off they found whites and blacks of the Tensaw already gathering for mutual protection at Samuel Mims' house and at a nearby saw and grist mill owned by William and John Peirce.[16]

Volunteers to the Tensaw

One month earlier, Governor Holmes had anticipated trouble. In late June he ordered 550 men of General Claiborne's Mississippi Territorial Volunteers to march east from their base at Baton Rouge and assist with the protection of the Tombigbee and Tensaw settlements. Drawn largely from the populous Natchez district, these six companies of infantry and two troops of cavalry had been federalized by the secretary of war for defense against potential British invasion from the Gulf of Mexico. Despite their new status as U.S. volunteers, they remained militia, with little training and no uniforms, and suffering from shortages of even the most basic equipment, including blankets and weapons. Claiborne had to rely on his personal credit to cover the cost of moving his troops and baggage 300 miles to the frontier over the next several weeks, so impoverished were the federal coffers at this point in the War of 1812.[17]

Inhabitants of the Tombigbee and Tensaw, however, did not wait for help from Claiborne, Holmes, or the secretary of war. Several weeks before the battle at Burnt Corn Creek, as concerns rose in the settlements, civilians began fortifying private homes (Figure 11). At Carney's Bluff on the Tombigbee one young refugee, Margaret Eades, then about ten years old, watched her father help build a fort. "It was a busy scene," she recalled late in her long life, with "all hands, negroes and whites . . . hard at work chopping and clearing a place for the fort. Women and children crying; no place to sit down, nothing to eat, all confusion and dismay, expecting every moment to be scalped and tomahawked. . . . With superhuman exertion, the Fort was finished in one week. The tents all comfortable, and streets full of soldiers, boys drilling, drums beating, pipes playing, but no Indians yet." In the ensuing days, young observant Margaret noticed how "Time passed on with fear and trembling with the grown folks, but we children enjoyed every moment."[18]

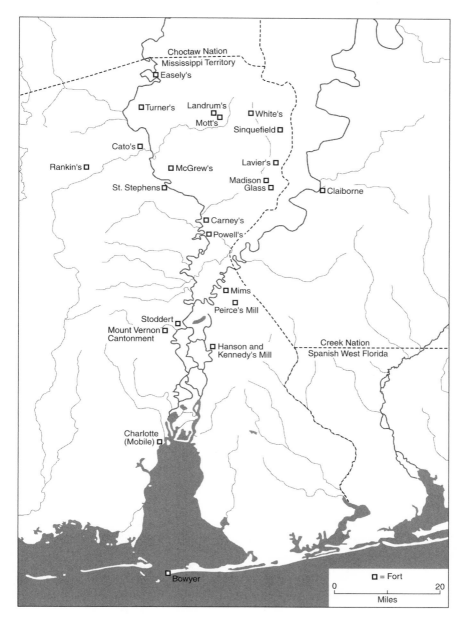

Fig. 11. American forts in the Mobile, Tombigbee, and Tensaw districts, 1813–1814; locations very approximate (based largely on Halbert and Ball, *The Creek War of 1813–1814*, 105–15).

In mid-July, while McQueen negotiated with González Manrique in Pensa-cola, the Peirce brothers in the Tensaw wrote Judge Toulmin, "All is confusion here. We are encompassing one [saw] mill with Pickets, in order to try to de-fend ourselves if the Spaniards should supply the Indians, we shall be in a dan-gerous situation here without assistance. . . . Nearly half the people here are destitute of arms or ammunition, and some of both."[19] Near the end of July the commander of Claiborne's advance troops at Fort Stoddert, Colonel Joseph Carson, informed the general that "About twenty families have forted at Mims' house, on Tensaw, and I have sent Lieutenant Osborn, with sixteen men—all I could spare—to assist in erecting the stockade." Colonel Carson no doubt hoped that Lieutenant Spruce Osborne, one of the few Volunteer officers with formal military training (at West Point, no less), would be able to improve the defensibility of this vulnerable post (Figure 12). Events a month later would prove any such hope misplaced.[20]

When General Claiborne finally arrived at Fort Stoddert on July 30, he found "the inhabitants on Tombigby and Alabama in the state of the utmost confusion and alarm . . . flying from all quarters."[21] Governor Holmes had al-ready determined it would be "impracticable for any army that we can possibly bring into the field to protect completely the settlements on the frontier against sculking parties of Indians who can attack them at defficient points and retire to the wilderness when pressed by a superior force. Block Houses and places inclosed by pickets form the safest defence for the inhabitants against this mode of warfare and can be speedily erected   a sufficient number should be constructed at convenient distances to contain all the families who may be ex-posed to the incursions of the savages."[22]

Claiborne soon learned that most settlers had indeed "forted up" in far more small, makeshift stockades than his Volunteers could hope to defend. With ad-vice from Judge Toulmin and other prominent citizens of the district, the gen-eral developed a plan to concentrate his forces at five critical strongpoints. Clai-borne ordered the two largest contingents of 156 men each to Fort Mims and Fort Madison (a stockade in the Forks). Three smaller detachments would keep an eye on the Choctaws to the north, and protect the U.S. Indian factory at St. Stephens and the federal cantonment near Fort Stoddert. Three additional companies of Volunteers arrived a few days later, but territorial forces still re-mained inadequate to garrison so many widely separated posts, a criticism Claiborne would hear from many quarters in the aftermath of the battle at Fort Mims.[23]

As Territorial Volunteers dispersed throughout the settlements, preparing

Fig. 12. Lieutenant Spruce McKay Osborne, Mississippi Territorial Volunteers (courtesy of the Alabama Department of Archives and History, Montgomery).

for the onslaught most felt sure would come, the commander of regular troops in this 7th U.S. Military District, Brigadier General Thomas Flournoy, refused to deploy his professionally trained forces on the Creek frontier. Instead he kept the 3rd and 7th Regiments of U.S. Infantry in camps and forts along the Gulf coast, where they might react swiftly to an anticipated British invasion aimed at either Mobile or New Orleans. While clearly considering the Redsticks a lesser threat than the British, he did furnish Claiborne with "a quantity of ammunition, swords, pistols &c," but ordered him to assume a defensive posture, adding "I can scarcely think that the Creek Indians will hazard a war against the United States. . . . They do know their exposed situation will subject them to a forfeiture of their Country and lives." Nearly everyone in the Tombigbee and Tensaw settlements thought otherwise. General Claiborne had hoped to march, in conjunction with federal troops, into the Creek nation and confront the Redsticks "in the land of their fathers." Now he and his Volunteers were reduced to garrison duty, "skulking behind pickets and ramparts."[24]

Major Daniel Beasley's detachment of 1st Regiment, Mississippi Territorial Volunteers, set out from Mount Vernon cantonment near Fort Stoddert on August 2. Crossing the Tombigbee at Carson's ferry, the force of 102 infantry and 10 mounted dragoons camped for the night on Naniaba Island in the Mobile-Tensaw delta, along the path that had recently become the Federal Road. They proceeded across the Tensaw River at Mims' ferry the following morning and bivouacked at the newly fortified house already known as Mims' Stockade. There they found Lt. Spruce Osborne and his sixteen men, who had been working on the fort's defenses for the last five or six days.[25]

The fortuitous survival of a portion of Major Beasley's official correspondence to General Claiborne over the succeeding four weeks documents the steps he took to protect the local population, offers some remarkable insights into the major's perceptions of the threat posed by the Redsticks, and reveals much about daily life at Fort Mims. Beasley typically drew up reports early in the day for dispatch about midmorning by mounted courier to Fort Stoddert. His byline on the first report, from "Mims' Block House," indicates how the fort had already evolved by August 6. The simple perimeter wall of sharpened upright posts—a stockade—had been strengthened by the addition of a two-story blockhouse at the southwest corner, from which enfilading fire could be directed down the length of the two adjacent walls (Plate 5).

Once he had an opportunity to view "the country around," Beasley "determined to continue at this place. Upon my arrival here we found upwards of twenty" local militia to augment his Volunteer force. The major "issued an order that they would be allowed to draw rations, and ordered an election for them to choose their officers; they voted unanimously for Mr. [Dixon] Bailey for Capt. . . . We have had no hostile indians about as yet but it is believed by the Inhabitants here that they will come."[26]

As a longtime resident of Jefferson County, at the other end of the territory from the Tensaw, Beasley may not have known previously any of the militiamen he would now command. With a precisely worded "no hostile indians about as yet," the major tacitly acknowledged the presence of many Tensaw Creeks in his charge. The following day Major Beasley began appending his rank to his signature, perhaps a sign he was mentally adjusting to his new role as post commander.

"We have a number of men on fatigue now and will have for some time; Could we be furnished with Whisky to give them an extra gill in such a case as has been usual, they expect it; and I allowed it to them yesterday, out of the Whiskey Composing a part of the rations drawn and brought here, in expectation that it may be replaced. If you think it right to allow the extra gill to fatigue men an opportunity offers to send it up by Doctor Osborne."[27] Lieutenant Osborne had trained in medicine at the University of North Carolina and consequently was named surgeon of the garrison. A standard practice of military surgeons of the era was to prescribe extra rations of whiskey for soldiers on sick call. As Beasley notes, enlisted men routinely received a ration (one gill, ¼ pint) of whiskey a day, and those on heavy work details ("fatigue" duty) customarily expected a second ration. Officers were permitted their own private stocks of wine and spirits.

Osborne's comings and goings (in this case, back and forth to Fort Stoddert) hint at the constant movement of people to and from Fort Mims throughout the month prior to the battle. Express riders traveled between posts, and troops on furlough usually opted to spend their free time in Mobile. Beasley's initial detachment had consisted of men from many companies; once the bulk of the regiment reached Fort Stoddert, Claiborne attempted to consolidate Captain Jack and Captain Middleton's men at Fort Mims and rotate out those from other companies, a process still incomplete by the end of August. Civilians came and went as they pleased. For various reasons, some large families were split up among various forts, prompting visits with relatives at nearby posts to pass the time, find food, prepare meals, and wash laundry. Enslaved Africans moved about more frequently and ventured farther when dispatched on potentially hazardous duties, such as harvesting crops left in fields and tending livestock roaming the abandoned landscape. And immigrants continued to filter into the Tensaw, despite the obvious dangers of traveling at this time. One such bold band of immigrants was the Rigdon family from Georgia.[28]

Beasley's dispatch of August 7 requested a drum "to be used by one of the Militia who beats exceedingly well having been in the regular Service for five years." This militia drummer must have been Martin Rigdon. He and his brother John both had served as musicians in the U.S. Infantry, specifically as drummers. John first joined the army in 1803 at the age of nine years, ten months and served two five-year enlistments. Martin signed up in 1808 at the age of twelve. Their stationing at Fort Stoddert in 1811 prompted their entire family's move to Mississippi Territory (just as their earlier postings had carried the family progressively southwestward, from North Carolina to South Carolina to Georgia, in the previous decade). Both men mustered out of the service on May 8, 1813, after General Wilkinson's seizure of Mobile, at a fort established briefly on the Perdido River, the new international boundary. The family settled in the Tensaw, leaving a third brother, Corporal Enoch Rigdon, still serving at Fort Stoddert. One of these young men, probably Martin, rode the dangerous Federal Road as a courier in the early summer of 1813, carrying mail through the Creek nation until waylaid by Peter McQueen's warriors in mid-July. Initial reports of the murder of "Rigdon the Post Rider" proved erroneous, but the Redsticks had shot at him, killed his horse, and stolen the U.S. mail. After that narrow escape, Martin (and possibly John) joined Dixon Bailey's militia company and he, along with his family (probably consisting of his parents and unmarried sisters), moved into the compound under construction at Samuel Mims' plantation.[29]

Beasley's arrival on August 3 had caused severe overcrowding within the original stockade. Volunteers competed for space with the ever-increasing numbers of civilian refugees. So soldiers on fatigue duty were set to work erecting an additional outer stockade on the fort's east side, effectively creating a separate compound in which some of the Volunteers could billet in tents. Officers were provided separate quarters, either cabins or tents, to reinforce their social distinction from common soldiers. Such privileges of rank were thought important, even in this minimally trained volunteer militia force, to instill a sense of hierarchical order reflecting the chain of military command. For instance, some months later Lieutenant John Sojourner of the Volunteers would face charges of "unofficerlike conduct" after "puting himself on an equality with his men in playing ball & runing foot races," "for taking the dam lye from a private without punishing him," and "for escorting a woman of bad repute by the arm . . . in presence of his men." From Major Beasley's earlier insistence on social distinctions in civilian life, and from his long stint as county sheriff, we might guess that he disapproved of such fraternization and lax discipline. But events in the days to come would demonstrate how little soldierly discipline the major himself exhibited.[30]

General Claiborne arrived at Fort Mims on August 7. After a personal inspection of the fortifications, he instructed Beasley to correct some deficiencies but seemed largely content with the progress made so far. "I am pleased," Claiborne wrote, "after taking into view all the advantages incident to this place, at your continuance at it with your command, & recommend to you to strengthen the picketing & to build at least two other block Houses." He then added, "I am not fully satisfied that a Block House may not be necessary at four places." Perhaps sensing in the inexperienced major some overconfidence and disdain for Indian adversaries, Claiborne urged his protégé to "respect the Enimy," "to prepare in the best possible way to meet him," and to "frequently send out some scouts."[31]

Only local militia had, to this point, manned the nearby stockade arising around Peirces' Mill, not quite two miles to the south on Pine Log Creek. Claiborne now encouraged Beasley to dispatch elements of his command to guard that smaller post and another at Hinson and Kennedy's mill fifteen miles farther south. The mills' owners, as well as local residents gathered around each, had been lobbying military and civil officials for weeks for protection. The general finally agreed to furnish troops on the basis of both sawmills' strategic value. Hinson and Kennedy's was already supplying boards for repairs to the forts in Mobile and at Mobile Point (Fort Bowyer, at the mouth of Mobile Bay), thought to be prime targets of the impending British invasion of the U.S. Gulf coast. Finally, the general permitted Beasley to feed "Friendly Indians & families really in distress," though sparingly since provisions for the troops were barely adequate for the coming weeks.[32]

Major Beasley's correspondence to General Claiborne resumed on August 12. "The men belonging to Capt. Dent's Company here, will be sent on to morrow but it is with regret that I send them as it weakens my command very much and Lieut Bowman having enlisted the most of the men, and having also been at a deal of pains and trouble in disciplining of them, he thinks hard of their being taken from him. One of our Soldiers died the night before last and from the report enclosed you will see that we have a good many on the Sick report; but none of them dangerous   We are perfectly tranquil here, and are progressing in our works as well as can be expected considering the want of tools, we shall probably finish the Stockade to morrow." Beasley noted, in a postscript, the arrival of Ensign Robert Swan, with "two barrels of flour and a bbl Whisky, instead of one of flour, pork and Whisky each as you wrote me."[33]

General Claiborne's determination to defend the mills with Volunteers—and the outbreak of disease that always accompanied military camp life in the early nineteenth century—substantially weakened the garrison at Fort Mims, largest of the refugee compounds east of Fort Stoddert. Major Beasley compensated to a degree by encouraging enrollment of civilians in Captain Bailey's militia company, which by mid-August numbered at least 45 men.[34] As the American defense of the Tensaw and Tombigbee settlements took final form, to the north the Redstick Creeks debated how and when to carry their war to the Tensaw métis and their white allies.

~

Their unexpected encounter with American and Tensaw métis militia on the Wolf Trail at Burnt Corn Creek—and particularly, the Tensaw métis' outright betrayal of the Redstick resupply expedition—by all accounts infuriated the Redsticks. From his vantage point in western Georgia, Benjamin Hawkins heard rumors that Redstick leaders, immediately upon return of the pack trains to the nation from Pensacola, had decided to strike Coweta in twenty days. Coweta, the largest Lower Creek town on the Chattahoochee, had welcomed those Upper Creeks who had opposed the Redsticks. But, according to Hawkins, "the families of the killed and wounded [at Burnt Corn Creek] and those who were plundered of the [Spanish] Governor's present forced the leaders," in general council, "to change the attack." Instead of Coweta, "the half breeds and their assistants" to the south would suffer the brunt of their retaliation. Writing many years later, George Stiggins recalled the Redsticks' "whole wish and aim was to humble and destroy fort mimbs as they knew that there was a great many men in there that they had devoted to destruction to revenge the burnt corn fight."[35]

For weeks before the battle at Burnt Corn Creek, Judge Toulmin at Fort Stoddert had been hearing rumors and reports from Creek and Choctaw informants of an attack on his region planned for "the full moon of August." When that celestial event passed on the twelfth without incident, "our citizens began to grow careless and confident," according to Toulmin, "and several families who had removed from Tensaw to Fort Stoddert, returned again."[36]

Heavy rains throughout early August compounded delays caused by disagreement over their next target, but around the middle of August a day was set for Redstick war parties to assemble. The expedition's leaders, Far-off Warrior (Hopoie Tastanagi) of Taskigi and the prophet Paddy Walsh, an Alabama métis, "sent the broken days to all the towns." As Stiggins explained, in his labored English, "the broken days is a bundle of broken parts of twigs about four inches long every piece for one day tied carefully in a bundle   one of the sticks is thrown away at sun rise every day to the last which is the day appointed." In anticipation of battle, Redstick warriors "were drinking their war physic," a purifying emetic tea made from willow bark and button snake root, and "making their war food," parched corn meal to be consumed on the march. By Stiggins' account, "the leaders of different towns on an appointed day collected their warriors at every town separately and held a war dance, and after it was over they started on different routs" for the rendezvous point at the mouth of Flat Creek on the lower Alabama River (now known as Big Flat Creek, west of Monroeville). Nearly 1,000 warriors from 13 towns of the Alabamas, Talla-poosas, and lower Abekas converged on Flat Creek with the objective of destroying the Tensaw métis who had rejected the prophets and fought alongside their enemies, the Americans. In a display of traditional Creek justice, the combined power of the talwas would punish their wayward daughter talofa in the Tensaw.[37]

∿

On August 13, the Fort Mims garrison experienced the first of many Redstick sightings that would become almost routine over the next two and a half weeks.

There was an alarm here yesterday, but I believe entirely a false one; a boy of Mr. Manac's lost his horse in the Swamp, and said that he saw Indians. The Swamp was Scoured, but no Indians found; there were appearances of a canoe having been put over the river, which was thought to have been done by Indians; but it was all, I believe, a mistake. The Horse has been found to day.

As many as 8 or 10 of Capt Baily's company are without arms; and there are some Citizens at Mr. Pierce's Mill without also. If you could furnish from 20 to 30 Muskets for the purpose of arming of them I should be glad. Also Mr. Tate requested me to endeavor to procure two rifles if Possible for him and Mr. Manac, he said he had Spoken to you on the Subject.[38]

Beasley and his garrison reacted well to this initial scare. Poorly armed though the militia may have been, they and the Volunteers seemed in high spirits, ready to confront the Redsticks and zealous in their watch. That spirit would wane steadily in the coming days, a casualty to the tedium of confinement and enforced inaction even as a steady stream of warnings should have kept them on alert. Claiborne was unable to furnish sufficient muskets, and some militiamen apparently still lacked firearms at the time of the battle.

On August 21, Colonel Carson received a credible report from a Choctaw named Baker's Hunter of Redstick plans to attack within a week at three specific points: "Mims' Fort, in the Tensaw settlement, . . . Easely's [Easley's] fort, near the Choctaw line on the Tombigby," and the fort and U.S. trading house at St. Stephens. Considering the other two adequately defended, General Claiborne gathered reinforcements and proceeded to Easley's fort in the Forks, the northernmost and most isolated of the presumed targets—but not before he had summoned Major Beasley to Fort Stoddert for a conference to impress upon his eastern commander the merits of vigilance.[39]

As Lieutenant Osborne penned a letter, on August 24, to General Claiborne requesting transfer from Fort Mims to a place more likely to see action, the Redsticks assembled at Flat Creek, where they finalized their plans for a two-pronged assault. After performing a "great war dance," the Redstick army divided. A large force of about 750 men (Stiggins thought 726) would march against the Tensaw. The Alabama Prophet, Josiah Francis, would lead a smaller war party of perhaps 200 men against white settlements in the Forks. William Weatherford accompanied the larger force. Through the strength of his personality, and because he knew the area intimately, Weatherford rose rapidly in influence to a position of leadership as the Redstick army approached the Tensaw.[40]

Moving cautiously toward Fort Mims, traveling mainly at night under a waxing crescent moon and using the cover of swamps and canebrakes, the Redstick Creeks took four days to cover the fifty miles overland between Flat Creek and the limits of white settlement. They lived off crops left in the fields and provisions stored at the plantations abandoned by the fleeing Tensaw métis and their slaves. However, the Little River plantations were not entirely devoid of inhabitants. All of those poorly supplied, hungry people forted up in the Tensaw thought longingly about their corn crops going to waste in unattended fields, sure to be eaten by deer, not to mention the cattle and pigs they had turned loose in the woods. Seizing an opportunity to help his neighbors (or perhaps of profiting from their distress), Zachariah McGirth sent several of his enslaved Africans upriver by flatboat to harvest corn from his plantation fields for the hungry inmates of Fort Mims. The Redsticks captured three, but one escaped (Weatherford later claimed "it was made convenient" to let him escape, so the garrison would be warned) and he carried word to the fort. Major Beasley, however, began to suppose slaves were falsely reporting Redstick sightings, just to see the reaction of the garrison. To this latest warning, Beasley "gave but little credit."[41]

Each day of that last week of August 1813 brought a new report, always by Africans or Creek métis, of Redsticks in the Tensaw. Each time Major Beasley responded with growing incredulity. On the twenty-seventh, James Cornells "discovered the trail of a considerable body of Indians going towards Mr. McGirt's," and another told of seeing "a great many Indians of mounted and a foot . . . on the road that led directly to the fort that their number appeared immense as they could only see one end of them in single file." Since these witnesses (Cornells included) generally hailed from Peirces' Mill, Beasley suspected they meant to incite panic among the Fort Mims occupants for the amusement and diversion of their friends at the neighboring stockade. One might further surmise that racism influenced Beasley's unwillingness to accept the word of social inferiors, as he surely considered slaves or other people of color. Perhaps most important, neither he nor many of his fellow officers in the Volunteers seriously expected Indians to attack a strongly built, well-manned fortification.[42]

General Claiborne did not hold such a view. Indeed, as warnings came in from all quarters, he grew more firmly convinced of the certainty of a Redstick attack on Forts Easley, Madison, or Mims and urged Major Beasley, in messages conveyed by express riders, to remain vigilant. The major did encourage his Volunteers to "greater exertions," essentially completing on August 28–29 construction of the blockhouse begun nearly a month before (although no progress had been made on the other two blockhouses ordered by the general). On the evening of Sunday, the twenty-ninth, at least one member of the garrison, Nehemiah Page, a private in Cornet Rankin's dragoons, celebrated that accomplishment with "a drunken frolic."[43]

Plan of Attack

A dragoon patrol had come close to discovering the Redstick army that afternoon. As more than 700 warriors stopped to enjoy a brief respite from the intense heat of late August in the cooling waters of a stream, two mounted men rode past at a distance of 300 yards to another ford and back, seemingly "careless and in deep conversation," without noticing any sign of the enemy army hidden nearby. After some hurried discussion, Redstick leaders decided not to pursue and kill the dragoons, since, it was hoped, a safely returning, uninformed patrol "would ensure security and carelessness at the Fort." Historical sources differ on what next transpired. The war party may have camped near Little River, about six miles north of Fort Mims. But, more plausibly, they seem to have followed the oblivious dragoons down the Federal Road, camping for the night only three-quarters of a mile from the fort.[44]

Family legend maintains that William Weatherford addressed the warriors that evening "and proposed to them, that in the event they took the fort, not to kill the women and children, [he] said that they had come to fight warriors, and not squaws." The assembled warriors then supposedly accused him of having a "white heart" and of wanting "to spare his relations (several of whom were in the fort)." Outright conflict between Weatherford and the other Redsticks at this juncture seems doubtful, however, since he otherwise played a critical role in planning the next day's battle. Over the previous weeks the war party had been accumulating intelligence, from "a few Indians and several Indian negros that had run away from Fort Pierce," about the defenses and garrisons of the Tensaw forts. Now Weatherford determined to have a look for himself. With two companions, he reconnoitered Fort Mims after dark, first at a safe distance, then (with one of the warriors) up to the very pickets of the fort stockade. Without challenge from the fort's sentries, the two men were able, unexpectedly, to "look through the port holes which was easily done for they were four foot high and about four foot apart all around without ditch or bank." Inside they could make out "a few glimmering lights scattered about," but "all looked so obscure and gloomy" that they could see little of the fort's interior layout. But the ease with which they approached the fort unnoticed convinced Weatherford of the garrison's carelessness. When he overheard those inside "conversing on common topics of life," without an inkling that an army hovered nearby, Weatherford realized the Redstick warriors might yet surprise the unsuspecting fort.[45]

At dawn Redstick leaders met to finalize the plan of attack as warriors stripped to breechclouts and painted themselves red and black. Based on Weatherford's nighttime assessment of the fort's poorly designed stockade, they determined to "run up to the wall without firing a gun, and take possession of the port holes." To ensure victory, the prophet Paddy Walsh selected four men, made invulnerable to bullets, to "enter the fort and fight inside as long as they thought fit." Walsh explained, "their safe retreat out of the Fort again, was to be an omen" that the Redsticks would take the fort. As an additional precaution, he planned to run around the fort three times, after which the Redsticks could handily slay all within with their knives and war clubs, "as all the men would be in a state of torpitude and paralised."[46]

Walsh's stratagems were, of course, inspired by the Shawnee Prophet's teachings, that nonbelieving Indians and their white accomplices could be rendered powerless by magical injunction. However, one element of Walsh's plan—the tactic of rushing into a military encampment—was militarily sound in a real world sense, quite apart from its spiritual efficacy. The Shawnees and associated tribes had employed similar gambits effectively (though not always decisively) in several crucial battles with Americans: against Virginians at Point

Pleasant during Lord Dunmore's War in 1774; by Blue Jacket when he crushed General St. Clair's U.S. army in the Ohio country in 1791; and at Tippecanoe against General William Henry Harrison in 1811. Weatherford would advise making a desperate charge into encamped Georgia troops at Caleebee Creek later in the Redstick War.[47] All of those attacks occurred at dawn. For the treacherous Tensaw métis and their white allies cooped up inside Fort Mims, Redstick revenge would be served at noon, in pointed remembrance of their friends and relatives cut down at the midday meal on the Wolf Trail at Burnt Corn Creek.

6

The Battle of Fort Mims

As the sun rose at 5:27 A.M. above the hills east of the Tensaw, August 30, 1813, began as just another in the seemingly endless procession of steamy days of a Gulf coast summer. Regimental and militia drummers beat reveille to rouse 400-some troops and refugees crowded within the picketed walls of Fort Mims.[1] Voluntarily penned up for over four weeks, these "inmates," as they came to think of themselves, had placed their own and their families' safety and the security of their possessions above the many inconveniences of life circumscribed by wooden palisades. Outside, their livestock (beef cattle, milk cows, hogs, even some sheep) foraged freely in nearby woods, and tethered horses grazed in the fallow fields of the Mims plantation. Inside, though, neighbors and strangers thrown together by fear of a common enemy had fit dozens of makeshift living quarters into every available corner of the 1¼-acre compound. The Mims family shared their plantation buildings enclosed by the stockade—their house, kitchen, smokehouse, loom house, and blacksmith's shop. Hastily erected log cabins sheltered about twenty white and Creek métis families—including the Baileys, Steadhams, Dyers, Randons—and the 100 or so Africans held by them as slaves. Most of the Mississippi Territorial Volunteers and Tensaw militiamen were billeted in tents lining the northern and eastern (double) walls of the fort (Plate 6).[2]

An Acre of Ground

Imagine an early morning stroll through Fort Mims, visiting with soldiers, civilians, and slaves as they dressed, prepared breakfast, and planned the coming day. Apart from the undoubtedly fascinating sights, sounds, and smells emanating from that throng of humanity, what kind of fortification would we have seen? What sort of built environment had these hundreds of souls created for their self-imposed confinement? Major Daniel Beasley might be our guide as he inspected his post that Monday—something he surely must have done. At this historical distance, however, with so many details out of focus to us, maybe bleary-eyed Private Page would be a more appropriate medium. Fortunately, we need not rely too heavily on imagination, since two important primary sources reveal the general appearance of the fort and associated buildings of Samuel Mims' plantation immediately prior to their destruction. The first is a detailed sketch of the fort drawn by one of General Claiborne's officers less than a month after the battle. While this map provides much information otherwise unavailable on the layout of the fort, we should keep in mind it postdates the fort's fall. Our unnamed cartographer (probably a senior member of the burial detail) drew this sketch hastily, without surveying instruments, based on whatever charred remnants existed weeks after the battle and tempered with input from survivors. Lacking a signature or other attribution, the sketch has come to be known (inaccurately) as the Claiborne Map.[3]

Our second key source is a compensation claim filed late in 1815 by Samuel Mims' son Joseph and other Tensaw survivors to accompany a petition to the U.S. Congress seeking federal recompense for property lost during "Indian depredations." According to that document, the estate of Samuel Mims, Senr., "who was killed at his own house, called Fort Mims," included:

1 Framed dwelling House with two Piares [Piasars] burnt	1000—
1 Spining House made of hewed timber	150—
1 Kitchen and Smoke House	150—
3 Horse Stable 2 of hewed timber & 1 of round logs	150—
2 Corn Houses	100—
1 Weaving Do. [Ditto]	50—
1 Blacksmith shop & tools	100—
[other property, such as a feather bed, livestock, two slaves, mill stones, and 3 saddles]	[5520—]
Doll[ar]s	7220.00[4]

The Mims plantation, one of the largest in the Tensaw, consisted of at least ten buildings. Samuel Mims and his family occupied an expensive frame structure made of sawn boards, a form of construction unusual at that time in the region. Along the Gulf coast, ethnic French families still preferred traditional half-timber buildings plastered with bousillage, a mixture of mud and Spanish moss. Spanish colonists had previously employed tabby (cement made from burned oyster shells), but that method of construction seems to have fallen out of use by the early nineteenth century, replaced by French-style architecture. American immigrants from the East generally built log cabins (from round logs) or log houses (from hewn timbers), using the corner-notch construction technique long popular on the American frontier. Only the wealthiest inhabitants of the Tombigbee-Tensaw could afford to build frame houses.[5]

The Claiborne map shows the Mims house to have been a one-story building with galleries (porches) on two sides and an internal off-center chimney. A contemporary account describes the house as "old," with "an upper room."[6] Since our unskilled draftsman made no attempt at perspective, we cannot determine whether the high roof was hipped or gable-end. During the battle, James and Daniel Bailey, "with other men, ascended to the roof of Mims' dwelling, [and] knocked off some shingles, for port-holes."[7] Other major structures within the fort presumably had wood shingle roofs as well. The puzzling term "Piares" in the compensation claim refers to the house's two galleries or "piasars" (the writer garbled the spelling by transposing "s" and "r," perhaps just as he mispronounced the word). Piasar was an early American English form of the word "piazza," commonly used in the Mobile area at that time to mean a veranda. Judging particularly from the building's galleries and interior chimney placement, Samuel Mims' house was a Creole cottage, a vernacular style of building derived from French colonial Gulf coast architecture. Frame versions of this style had evolved from earlier half-timber forms during the British and Spanish colonial periods. By the early nineteenth century, Creole cottages could be found from Pensacola in the east to the Natchez District in the west, with frame examples mainly in urban settings.

Apart from the Mims home, just two (or perhaps three) other structures listed in the claim are identifiable on the Claiborne map. One, labeled on the map as "Kitchin," immediately southwest of the main house, seems to equate with "1 Kitchen and Smoke House" listed in the claim, where the wording suggests a single building serving both functions. Thomas Woodward, however, related in his reminiscences how the attackers shot fire arrows "into the roof of Mims' smokehouse, which was an old building, and formed a part of one line of the Fort." Unfortunately, it is not clear whether Woodward (who was not an eyewitness to the battle) meant the smokehouse stood apart from the kitchen. If these were in fact two separate buildings, then the one (labeled "first-house fired," on the Claiborne map) located in the offset of the fort's southern perimeter wall must be the smokehouse.[8]

On the north perimeter, in another offset of the palisade, was a building referred to alternatively by fort survivors as Patrick Mahoney's "loom-house" or "the bastion."[9] This might logically be equated with the "Weaving" house listed in the claim, except for the low evaluation of that structure at $50, equivalent to a "Corn House" used for grain storage or to one of the stables. Since the term "bastion" suggests a substantial building, a more likely candidate may be the spinning House "made of hewed timber," valued at $150.

Although none of the three horse stables are shown on the Claiborne map, the location of one is mentioned in Henry S. Halbert's 1884 article on Private Nehemiah Page. In his assignment as hostler, that Mississippi Territorial Volunteer groomed and fed the horses of the garrison's dragoons and officers. On the morning of August 30, "he went outside of the pickets into a stable, situated some eighty yards southeasterly of the eastern gate, and threw himself down on some fodder" to sleep off a night of dissipation.[10]

None of the other outbuildings mentioned in the claim correlate with structures shown on the Claiborne map, although one can be placed using archaeological evidence. Discovery, during excavations in 1981, of abundant coal slag from a forge located the "Blacksmith shop" in the southeast corner of the fort. On the other hand, the map depicts numerous small buildings inside the stockade not described in the claim, presumably representing the "cabins and board shelters, recently erected by the settlers" (as described by Pickett), as well as cabins and guardhouses used by the Volunteers and militia. South of the fort, the three "Negro Cabbins" drawn next to the "Potatoe patch" (on the Claiborne Map, both surrounded by symbols representing rail fences) may have survived the battle, since they are not listed in the compensation claim. Two wells found during archaeological excavations in the 1960s near the western gate are neither mentioned in the claim nor shown on the Claiborne map.[11]

The nature of the fortifications erected around Mims' house between late July and the end of August 1813 was a matter of considerable dispute for nearly 200 years, until resolved recently by archaeology. From extensive interviews conducted in the late 1840s with battle survivors and acquaintances of survivors, historian Albert James Pickett concluded Fort Mims was built in the following manner: "Around it [the Mims house] pickets were driven, between which fence rails were placed. Five hundred port-holes were made, three and a half feet only from the ground. The stockading enclosed an acre of ground, in a square form, and was entered by two ponderous but rude gates, one on the east and the other on the west. Within the enclosure, besides the main building, were various out-houses, rows of bee-gums, together with cabins and board shelters, recently erected by the settlers, wherever a vacant spot appeared. At the south-west corner a block-house was begun, but never finished."[12]

In appearance, the blockhouse presumably resembled others of the era—built of horizontal logs, round or hewn and notched at the corners, with a projecting second story and a shingle roof. The upper story must have had windows or gun ports for use by defenders using small arms; the blockhouse (and fort) contained no cannons, despite their menacing appearance in a widely reproduced, highly romanticized 1858 engraving of Fort Mims by Alonzo Chappel. The blockhouse and adjacent sections of pickets were the only elements of the fort left unburned at the end of the battle, perhaps because the Redsticks thought the blockhouse contained the fort's gunpowder supply. Aside from that conjecture, the blockhouse engenders little controversy.[13]

Pickett's interpretation of the fort's outer wall, however, raises many suspicions. Pickett's "pickets" were "driven" into the ground at wide intervals, with fence rails stacked between the intermittent uprights. This matches no documented method of American frontier fort construction. Erection of a stockade —consisting of logs, whole or split, placed upright side-by-side in a narrow trench—had been a standard method of fortifying American frontier homes and villages (or "stations") since before the Revolutionary War. Other methods of enclosure were sometimes used, ranging from various types of paling to rectangular arrangements of closely spaced or abutting structures. For instance, picketing erected around Hinson and Kennedy's Mill, which was garrisoned by Mississippi Territorial Volunteers protecting lumber being cut under government contract, consisted of 4-inch-thick planks with cut portholes. But every historic account of Fort Mims' encircling wall describes it as a "stockade" or specifies its construction of "pickets" or "picketing," all terms implying upright posts. None mention horizontal rails, and Pickett's source for this notion is unknown. Archaeological excavations in 2004–2005 revealed a portion of the fort's western wall—a foundation trench containing the charred bases of some upright, split pine posts from a palisade—finally resolving the uncertainty created by historian Pickett's imaginative description.[14]

Contemporary sources agree that the Fort Mims pickets had gun portholes or loopholes cut at a height of 3½ to 4 feet from the ground. Albert James Pickett's estimate of 500 portholes seems excessive for the fort's approximately 1,100-foot perimeter. His own suggestion of 4-foot spacing implies about half that number.[15] One oddity of the fort was a double wall on the east end, which resulted from an expansion of the original picketed compound to accommodate the tent and cabin quarters of the Mississippi Territorial Volunteers. Early in August, Beasley ordered the picketing extended 50 or 60 feet on that side of the fort, "forming a separate apartment, for the accommodation of the officers and their baggage," but leaving the old east wall in place.[16] Fort Mims' many structural deficiencies—too few blockhouses, low musket ports, flimsy picketing—would soon became evident to all.

~

With 50 or more small children and dozens of dogs roaming a compound of 1¼ acres, living conditions in this corral of cramped humanity grew increasingly unhealthy as the days wore on. Even under normal conditions, August in the Deep South of the early nineteenth century was a time of fevers, malarial and yellow. Swamps had long been implicated in their spread, although an understanding of mosquitoes (which bred by the millions in adjacent swampy habitats) as disease vectors lay in the future. A few years earlier, the cantonment at Mount Vernon had been established in the hills west of Fort Stoddert precisely to cut mortality from disease at that poorly situated, low-lying post. Every summer most of the federal garrison bivouacked at the higher, healthier cantonment four miles away, leaving the swamp-infested fort to the care of a sergeant's guard. With its similar situation next to an extensive swamp, Fort Mims must have been recognized widely as a sickly place.[17]

Some Tensaw métis carried on the beneficial Creek tradition of bathing every morning in a stream, no matter the season. Indeed, years earlier Benjamin Hawkins had praised the Baileys for just such behavior and for the extraordinarily fastidious housekeeping of Dixon Bailey's mother. In contrast, many settlers on the American frontier cared little for cleanliness or hygiene. Lieutenant Spruce Osborne and Private Thomas Golphin Holmes, the garrison's surgeons, treated troops reporting to sick call principally by bleeding and prescribing an extra gill of whiskey or a bottle of wine; such therapies offered patients little beyond a placebo effect for most maladies. At least one Volunteer died in mid-August of an unspecified illness. An apparent absence of latrines inside the fort—none are mentioned in historical sources, nor have any been found by archaeologists, although Pickett speculated there were "out-houses"—suggests a likelihood of dysentery. Little wonder then that Fort Mims and the other refuge stockades soon became noisome places, "filthy pens" from which inmates sought respite whenever threat of attack subsided.[18]

Feeding the assembled multitude posed challenges, too. Volunteers and militia drew rations, replenished sporadically by flatboat deliveries from Fort Stoddert, and consequently fared rather better than the residents of Tensaw, who had abandoned their plantations before the corn crop could be harvested. As weeks passed and their original supplies dwindled, refugees scoured the vicinity for wild edibles, purchased food from those with surplus, or ventured back to their farms to pick corn, despite the possible danger. After a month inside Fort Mims without any confirmed Redstick sightings, though, garrison and assembled refugees alike had grown complacent.

Thus, as the morning of the thirtieth wore on, many "inmates" walked out the gates of Fort Mims intent on various mundane activities, much as they had done throughout the preceding month. Once morning roll had been called, Private Nehemiah Page trudged out the eastern gate to his post in one of the Mims stables and bedded down with the horses to sleep off his hangover. Dixon Bailey's sister Peggy led a band of women, some with infants, to the banks of Boatyard Lake a third of a mile southwest of the fort, where they would bathe, wash bundles of laundry, and hopefully find good fishing. And two adolescent Tensaw métis, Peter Durant and Lavinia "Viney" Randon, crossed the Alabama River to pick grapes (so they said) on Nannahubba Island.[19]

Although few realized at the time, 1813 fell amid one of the coolest decades of the modern era. During the period known as the Little Ice Age, from A.D. 1550 to 1850, worldwide average annual temperatures were markedly cooler than today's (which, we are slowly realizing, are abnormally high). How this overall cooling affected day-to-day weather in the Tensaw during the late summer of 1813 is difficult to say. We have few basic meteorological data from this region (though information such as daily temperature highs and lows were being recorded at several spots in the United States by that date). But historical research does provide a few clues.[20]

For instance, Peter Durant and Viney Randon's foray from Fort Mims to pick muscadines, wild grapes, is just the sort of information sought by historians of climate change. Grape harvest dates are highly subject to yearly fluctuations in weather. They correlate particularly closely with several interrelated factors: severity of winter temperature, rate of spring warming, and date of first new growth on perennial grape vines. Climatic historians consider dates of harvest to be "proxy" data for otherwise unrecorded mean annual temperatures, with a later harvest reflecting a cooler spring (but not necessarily a cooler summer) and, hence, a later start to the growing season. Today wild muscadines in the Mobile-Tensaw delta ripen early in August; by month's end, few if any can be found. This historical note of late ripening muscadines in the Tensaw of 1813 reflects the cooler overall temperature regime typifying the first decades of the nineteenth century. And there is additional anecdotal manuscript evidence. In 1807 the postmaster at Fort Stoddert, Edmund P. Gaines, wrote of weather "nearly as cold at this place, as I ever recollect to have found it in Virginia," a 6-inch snowfall on January 19 that lingered "for several days," and ice on the Tombigbee River extending "20 to 25 perches [110 to 137 yards] from shore"—the sort of events that simply do not occur in our day.[21]

As we are experiencing in the current round of climate change, overall warming or cooling trends do not necessarily result in noticeably warmer or cooler average temperatures for any specific day of the year or in correspondingly simple trends in daily highs or lows. Even though the Earth's average temperatures were cooler in 1813, that August 30 in the Tensaw may well have equaled in heat and mugginess a typical southern Alabama late summer day of our own era. A rare record of daily highs and lows kept at Fort Stoddert in 1807 and 1808 suggests summer temperatures much like today's, reaching the upper 80s to mid-90s, a heat portrayed in one upbeat promotional tract as "seldom oppressive within doors." Written descriptions of early-nineteenth-century southern summers prominently feature vivid descriptions of the stifling humidity and violent afternoon storms that likewise characterize today's weather patterns. On that long day in August 1813, thunderstorms would not bring cooling relief. As the sun rose slowly higher in the sky, the temperature rose apace, combining with a daunting humidity that could sap the strength from even the fittest.[22]

"False Alarm"

Following procedures that had proven adequate over many days, Major Beasley did not post advanced pickets or send out mounted patrols that morning. Of the fort's two double gateways, centered on the east and west palisade walls, only the inner west gate was barred shut. About 10:00 A.M., Major Beasley dispatched an express rider from "Mim's Block House" to Fort Stoddert with the previous day's (Sunday's) "Morning Report," a tabulation of officers and men under his immediate command and their fitness for duty. The original of this report has not survived, but several descriptions of the document's contents exist among the papers of General Claiborne. On August 29, the Fort Mims garrison consisted of 106 soldiers of the 1st Regiment, Mississippi Territorial Volunteers (one major, two captains, one lieutenant, five ensigns, eleven sergeants, six corporals, five musicians, and seventy-five privates; eleven unfit for duty)—including six on leave in Mobile—and forty-one or forty-two militia-men from the Tensaw. To this tabular report Beasley appended a letter addressed to General Claiborne, written a few hours prior to the Redstick assault.

Mims' Block House 30th Augt. 1813
Sir

I Send You inclosed the morning report of yesterday of my command; from which you will perceive from having ordered from this place a good many of those who came up with me; and also in having Scattered my command in so many places that you render me unable, if the Indians should appear in any force, to do any thing more than to defend the several forts; that I should be utterly unable to leave the fort, and meet any number of the enemy, more especially when you know that but a few of the volunteer militia can be relied on. I Have improved the fort at this place and have it much Stronger than when you were here. Messrs. Pierces' Stockade is not very Strong, but he has erected three Strong Block Houses & I received from Ensign Davis who commands at Major Hanson's Mills, a letter of the 27th Inst. in which he States "We shall be by to morrow in so great a State of defence that I should not be afraid any number of Indians that would come against us." I went down at the time I sent the men from this place, and concerted with Mr. Kennedy; (Maj. Hanson being absent) the plan of defence. I received of Mr. Kennedy the plank the QrMaster gave an order for but the boat could carry only a part of it, and I directed Mr. Davis to Send the balance when he should send over for provisions, which will be in a few days as the men who went over from the Cantonment took with them only twenty days' Provisions which will now be soon out. I wrote to you Yesterday requesting that the Messr. Pierce's might be furnished with Some of the Muskets in the hands of the QrMaster unfit for use; they will have them repaired at their own expense having a Smith at their Service and a Shop of their own; also for 15 or 20 good Muskets if you have them and can possible Spare them.

The major's letter betrays no glimmer of suspicion that a Redstick army lay hidden within a few hundred yards of his post or that the hostile Creeks posed any real threat to the three improvised forts in his charge. Knowing what fate awaited the hapless major and his troops, we can appreciate the irony of

Beasley's only expressed regret over the unfeasibility of offensive action against the Redsticks, should they appear. Following Claiborne's orders, he had scattered his command, dispatching eighteen men under Ensign Isaac Davis to Hinson and Kennedy's Mill and twenty under Lieutenant Andrew Montgomery to Peirces' Mill, where, after a month of unanswered requests for spare weapons, many auxiliary militiamen still lacked firearms.[23]

Beasley's letter continues, in a more disturbing vein:

> There was a false alarm here yesterday; two negro boys belonging to Mr. Randon were out Some distance from the Fort minding some beef cattle and told that they Saw a great number of Indians Painted, running and hallooing, on towards Messrs. Pierces' Mill. The Conclusion was that they knew the Mill Fort to be more vulnerable than this and that they had determined to make their attack there first. I dispatched Capt. Middleton with 8 or 10 men all mounted to reconnitre & ascertain the strength of the enemy, that if they were not too powerful we would turn out the most of the men here and pursue on to Pierces Mill; but the alarm has proved to be a false one. What gave some plausibility to the report of the negro boys at first was some of Mr. Randon's negroes who had been Sent up to his plantation for corn and had reported his plantation to be full of Indians committing every Kind of Havoc; but I now doubt the truth of that report; I was much pleased at the appearance of the Soldiers here at the time of the Alarm yesterday   When it was expected every moment that the Indians would appear in Sight, the Soldiers very generally appeared anxious to see them.

Faced with this rising crescendo of alarms, Major Beasley's unshakable skepticism must have caused some unease among those métis in Fort Mims with firsthand knowledge of Redstick threats made against them. But the ever-complacent Beasley concluded his letter with mundane supply requests and noted in passing how the other forts of the Tombigbee district lay "more exposed" to Redstick attack than his own.

> I expect the Liberty detachment of Volunteers [from the southern part of the Natchez district] must have arrived at the [Mount Vernon] Cantonment by this time; if so I hope you will let me have the remainder of Jack's and Middleton's men; and any others that the more exposed situation of other posts taken into view you may think it convenient to Spare.

Among our Sick there is but one man in any way dangerous, and he Suffers for Such nourishment as Suits his case; particularly wine, and I have directed Doctor Osborne to avail himself of the opportunity that now offers, to Send to Dr. Kerr for some of that article. It is probable that a few bottles of it would Save his life.

The Command which now go down to Mount Vernon, are sent for Provisions; I have Wrote Mr. Henry Particularly on that Subject.

> I am with the highest esteem
> Your Obt Servt.
> Daniel Beasley Majr.
> Commg. Station[24]

As the post rider trotted down the road to Mims' ferry, scouts of the Redstick army hidden in the woods several hundred yards north and east of Fort Mims moved ahead to discern whether the garrison seemed to anticipate an attack. They soon reported welcome news to the war party's collective leadership. Both east gates had been left open, as was the outer western one, and there were no particular signs of readiness among the garrison. Two columns of warriors silently took up their positions, with the strongest wing hidden in a shallow ravine of tupelo gum and cypress southeast of the fort.[25]

As Major Beasley suggested in his final letter to General Claiborne, Africans sent out for provisions to the métis plantations upriver from the fort had spotted Redstick warriors several times over the preceding two days. On Saturday the three slaves belonging to Zachariah McGirth had been captured by the Redsticks at his plantation and interrogated about white/métis defenses in the Tensaw. Most slaves living on this multiethnic frontier spoke English and Muskogee; these three may have divulged much about the number and disposition of troops and the whereabouts of specific métis leaders. One of them, a man named Jo, escaped and carried the alarm to Fort Mims, where Major Beasley (as we have seen) gave him no credence.

When Captain Hatton Middleton's mounted patrol on August 29 found no sign of Redsticks—after the afternoon alarm raised by the two boys tending Randon's cattle near Peirces' Mill and the earlier report of "Indians committing every kind of Havoc" on Randon's plantation—Beasley declared all such tales baseless. To discourage future rumormongering, the major ordered one of the Randon slave boys whipped. During his eight-year term as sheriff of Jefferson County, Beasley routinely imposed punishments of 39 lashes on recalcitrant or rebellious slaves to maintain order by reminding the enslaved workforce of their subservient role in this white-ruled society. Now he undoubtedly hoped a public whipping would dispel any concerns among the fort's residents that an attack was imminent and bolster the resolve of his jumpy troops. He probably also suspected the presence of Redstick sympathizers among the 100 slaves assembled in his midst, particularly those from Creek métis plantations, slaves aware that a battle might offer a chance at freedom.[26]

The same young African who had suffered the lash on Sunday set out to tend John Randon's cattle again the next morning, Monday the thirtieth, along with a boy owned by Josiah Fletcher. They immediately spotted Redsticks within a mile of the fort. Keen to avoid a second whipping, Randon's slave ran to Peirces' Mill, while the other returned to Fort Mims and related his story to an incredulous Major Beasley. Fletcher believed the boy and initially deflected Beasley's demands to give him up for punishment but finally relented. As some Volunteers tied the boy to a stake for whipping, Zach McGirth and two of his enslaved men left the fort for Mims' ferry landing on the Alabama River to ready a flatboat with the intention of gathering corn and pumpkins for the fort's hungry families. James Cornells, Vicey McGirth's brother, rode up to the fort's east gate and shouted to Major Beasley that he had just seen thirteen Redsticks in the woods, proof enough, he felt, that the long-anticipated attack on Fort Mims was bound to occur this day. Cornells recalled years later how Beasley (who appeared drunk) thought he must have "only seen a gang of red cattle," to which Cornells replied, "that gang of red cattle would give him a hell of a kick before night." As Cornells rode off, inside the fort men sat "in two circles in the yard talking what they would do if Indians should come." Someone played a fiddle, and the second public flogging in as many days began.[27]

The Assault and Massacre

William Weatherford crouched in the thickly vegetated ravine 400 yards east of Fort Mims, close enough to recognize James Cornells gallop up to the fort's open main gate and leave just as hurriedly. As 700 or more Redstick warriors awaited their signal to attack, they heard a drum beat—whether to announce the noon meal or to accompany the flogging is uncertain—and feared it meant their presence had at last been discovered.[28] Hopoie Tastanagi, Far-off Warrior, principal leader of the war party, gave the word. The men in the eastern column rose and started running, silently, at full speed for the fort. Halfway across an open field 150 yards wide, they passed the Mims stable where Nehemiah Page slept. Awakened by rhythmic tramping, he peered through a gap between the hewn logs and glimpsed a sobering sight—hundreds of men, each stripped to a loincloth, some painted red, some black, "rushing past him towards the fort." Moments passed as the Redsticks closed the distance, still unseen by the fort garrison. The gate sentry, who had been "looking over the shoulders of a couple playing cards," at last noticed the lead runners a mere "thirty steps of the gate," gave a shout, "Indians," fired his musket, and ran inside the fort. His cry was echoed throughout the compound, "the Indians, the indians," amid great confusion.[29]

With surprise achieved, the Redsticks "set up a most terrible war-whoop" and poured in the east gate. Others dashed across a sweet potato patch near the Mims' slave cabins, grabbed fence rails, and stopped up many of the gun loopholes in the southern perimeter wall. The northern column made for the other fort entrance, immediately took possession of a guardhouse inside the western outer gate, but found their progress blocked by the fort's single barred inner gate (Figure 13). Warriors also managed to scale the wall and occupy the blockhouse, completely undefended at that moment, on the fort's southwest corner. Back on the east side, Major Beasley rushed out of his cabin and was shot (or struck with a spiked war club) in the belly while struggling to shut the heavy gate himself.[30]

Leading the eastern Redstick column were four men selected for that dangerous task by the Alabama prophet Paddy Walsh and made invulnerable to bullets by his magic. These four reached the center of the fort, where three were killed immediately; the fourth, who managed to retreat unscathed, gained the war name Nahomahteeathle Hopoie, "foremost man in danger in time of battle." From his vantage point outside a loophole on the east wall, a mico of Wewocau, whose men led the attack, could hear American officers killing one of the prophet's chosen men, "cuting him to pieces with their swords." A general melee then ensued in the area between the inner and outer east gates, where troops from intermingled companies of Mississippi Territorial Volunteers had set their tents. Upwards of half the Volunteers were killed here in the first minutes of battle. Survivors fled through the inner gate, where Captains Jack and Middleton, both wounded in the initial onslaught, organized a defense of the main compound (Figure 14). Only the northern fort wall remained firmly in the hands of the defenders, where Captain Dixon Bailey's white and métis militia—well armed with rifles and extra muskets, mostly double-barreled shotguns—retained control of the loopholes. The Redsticks (following Weatherford's plan) had quickly taken possession of loopholes in the western, southern, and inner eastern walls, as the fort's defenders real-

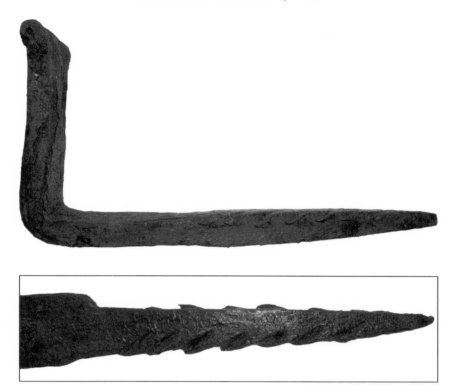

Fig. 13. Wrought iron gate catch from one of the western gates of Fort Mims; 12.6 inches long. Detail shows barbed end. Found during archaeological excavation of a fort well in 1968 (courtesy of the Alabama Historical Commission, Montgomery).

ized too late how those ill-designed gun ports, placed just 3½ to 4 feet above the ground, could be used from either side of the wall. Placed at a normal height of 6 to 7 feet, they should have been accessible only to defenders standing on a raised earthen firing step constructed inside the walls of a properly designed fort. With gunfire now entering the fort from three sides, the roughly 100 armed defenders and approximately 250 civilians caught inside the one-acre inner compound desperately sought cover, crowding into the fort's dozen interior structures.[31]

The prophets had predicted no more than three Redstick warriors would be lost in this battle. Undeterred by heavy initial losses, Paddy Walsh began sprinting around the fort, intending to lap it three times to deaden the force of bullets fired from the fort or cause them to fly upwards, hitting no one. His men could

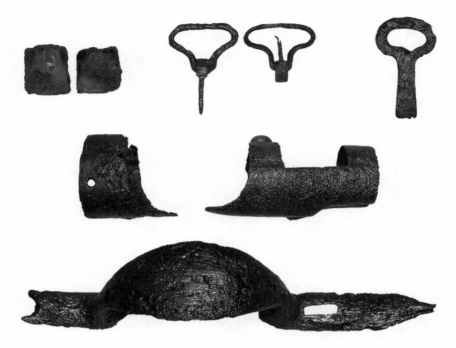

Fig. 14. U.S. Infantry musket parts, 1795 model, used by the Mississippi Territorial Volunteers at Fort Mims, all from archaeological excavations. *Top row, left to right:* two flints, two sling buckles, screwdriver (2¼ inches tall). *Middle row:* end barrel band, front barrel band. *Bottom:* trigger guard (all courtesy of the Alabama Historical Commission, Montgomery).

then enter the fort and slay all inside with their knives and red-painted war clubs. On his third circuit, he was wounded by a shot fired by a militiaman from the loom-house bastion, on the fort's north side. Disabled as he was, he continued to urge his followers to throw aside their firearms and "enter the fort with war clubs and scalping knife in hand," to which the Muskogee-speaking Tensaw métis in the fort responded that they wished they would try.[32]

On the west, the Redsticks found an "abundance of Carpenters tools" on the ground of the captured guardhouse bastion and set to work with axes chopping a hole through the shut inner gate and cutting away wall pickets adjacent to the blockhouse (Figure 15). In this effort they were assisted by an African called Siras (or Cyrus), one of Sam Moniac's slaves. Captain William Jack and surviving members of his company, armed with rifles, regrouped along the south wall and dislodged some Redstick warriors who had been firing into the central

Fig. 15. Zachariah McGirth's broad axe (9 inches tall), with his initials in the poll end (*detail*), found during archaeological excavation of a fort well in 1968 (courtesy of the Alabama Historical Commission, Montgomery).

compound from the elevated corner blockhouse. A few of the Tensaw militia, which had retained control of the loom house bastion and loopholes in the north wall, now climbed into the attic of the Mims house, the tallest structure in the fort. James and Daniel Bailey, with assistance from other civilian men and women, removed some shingles and began firing very effectively with rifles at Redstick warriors in the fields north and south of the fort. By about 2:00 in the afternoon, the fort's defenders had halted the momentum of the Redstick attack. As survivors told Judge Toulmin a few days later, they had so far withstood the ordeal "with undaunted spirit."[33]

The Redsticks, on the other hand, "found themselves so roughly handled" they withdrew from the battlefield and convened an impromptu council around a cabin of a Mrs. O'Neal, on the Federal Road northeast of the fort. For nearly an hour they debated whether to continue the fight. Their force had suffered many casualties, far more than the prophets had foreseen. Weatherford purportedly "advised them to draw off entirely," according to a later account, since they had already inflicted great damage and "sufficiently humbled" their enemies. But eventually a consensus developed to renew the attack. Modern scholars generally agree on the reason: the Tensaw métis led by Dixon Bailey had so far suffered few losses. These were the Creeks who stood against Peter McQueen's force at Burnt Corn Creek. These wayward Creeks had, from the Redstick perspective, willfully abandoned so many traditions, rejected the new religion, and now fought their own people alongside the whites. These Creeks of the Tensaw evaded their punishment still, contrary to talwa law and the prophets' teachings. George Stiggins, the Tensaw métis who fought later in the war as a U.S. militiaman, recalled in his memoirs what he had heard about this critical moment in the battle for Fort Mims. Africans in the Redstick army, it was said, had most vehemently urged the destruction of the fort and its inhabitants. Perhaps they realized more keenly than their Creek brethren the retribution their assault on an American post had already ensured. Better to destroy their hated Tensaw opponents and accept some additional battlefield losses than let them escape, leaving the Redstick dead unavenged. With a decision reached, Weatherford rode north toward the plantation of his brother, David Tate, to hide his family's slaves in nearby canebrakes. Those slaves would neither gain their freedom nor fall captive to Redsticks that day. He later told his sister-in-law, "as soon as he was satisfied . . . the Fort would fall, . . . he rode off, as he had not the heart to witness what he knew would follow, to wit, the indiscriminate slaughter of the inmates of the Fort."[34]

About 3:00 P.M. the battle resumed when the Redsticks (specifically, "Seekaboo, and some of the McGillivray negroes," according to Thomas Woodward) set ablaze one of the fort's interior structures, either the smokehouse or the blacksmith's shop, "with cotton matches fixed to arrows." Death by fire had been a traditional method of dispatching non-Creek captives. Now the purifying blaze of the poskita would rid the nation of the apostate Creeks of the Tensaw. Flames quickly spread to the palisade and other buildings in the fort, all constructed of longleaf pine, "heart pine," which burns with tremendous intensity once alight. As each building ignited in turn, those sheltering inside had to choose, to flee and risk the gunfire, arrows, and war clubs of the Redsticks or accept death in the inferno (Figure 16). Seventy-six-year-old David Mims was shot down while running from his brother's house toward the north bastion, as was the garrison's chief surgeon, Lieutenant Osborne. Others perished by fire (Plate 7). Hours of desperate fighting under an August sun, combined with the heat of the burning fort, gave an unbearable thirst to all involved. But those inside could no longer reach the fort's wells, now exposed to the guns of their enemies, while Redstick warriors could slip away to rest and cool off in the nearby swamps.[35]

With resistance diminishing, Redstick warriors searched the fort for cap-

Fig. 16. (*Top*) Brass arrowpoints used by Redstick warriors; point on left, 1½ inches tall. (*Bottom*) Lead balls: .69 caliber musket (*left*) and .53 caliber rifle balls. All from Fort Mims (point at upper right from Frances Cleverdon Collection, courtesy of the Weeks Bay National Estuarine Research Reserve, Fairhope, Alabama; remainder courtesy of the Alabama Historical Commission, Montgomery).

tives and booty.[36] One African (his name is not mentioned in the historical records), taken captive in the Mims house, escaped several weeks later and made his way to the Lower Creek town of Coweta where he told his story. "An Indian seeing him in the corner said come out, the Master of Breath has ordered us not to kill any but white people and half breeds. An Indian woman, who was in the house, was ordered out and to go home. Dixon Bailey's sister was asked what family she was of. She answered pointing to her brother [James], I am the sister of that great man you have murdered there, upon which they knocked her down, cut her open, strewed her entrails around. They threw several dead bodies into the fire and some who were wounded." A white militiaman who survived the battle, Samuel Jones, afterwards told Benjamin Hawkins, "One of our Indians, Jahomobtee, in his presence shot three Indians in the act of tomahawking white women." The historical evidence is unequivocal on this point; Redsticks warriors killed many civilians in this final stage of the battle.[37]

Remaining fort defenders crowded into the north bastion, sheltered somewhat from Redstick gunfire by Patrick Mahoney's loom house and another unidentified building, "surrounded by columns of smoke and fire . . . and the unceasing echo of the war whoop." With the fort largely in the hands of their enemies, the survivors, in the words of Judge Toulmin, "began to despond." According to Albert James Pickett, "The women now animated the men to defend them, by assisting in loading the guns," and the fighting continued some time longer. They gathered up as many guns as they could from the dead and threw the weapons, along with the remaining gunpowder, into the flames so these would not fall into the hands of their opponents. Thomas Golphin Holmes, the garrison's assistant surgeon, had earlier as a precaution chopped nearly through two wall pickets. Now, with many Redsticks distracted elsewhere on the battlefield—tending to their own wounded, scalping enemy dead, arguing over prisoners, plundering the smoldering ruins for booty—he broke away those stockade pickets, opening a hole through which those able to run might make for the swampy woods over a hundred yards northwest of the fort. As best as can be determined, ten Mississippi Territorial Volunteers, sixteen men from the Tensaw, two women (one white, one black), and one African girl managed to escape.[38]

The first to flee were Holmes, Hester (a slave of Benjamin Steadham), militia Captain Dixon Bailey, and his slave Tom carrying Bailey's invalid son Ralph. As Dr. Holmes related to Pickett many years later, "soon after passing the north west corner of the fort 150 indians attempted to cut off their retreat when by the by as they ran Capt B gave them a fire from his rifle and Dr Holmes from both barrels of his gun." As Holmes explained, "Bailey had boiled his bullets in oil with the buck skin patch sewed over them to make them go down easy," allowing him to reload on the run. All five reached the cover of the woods, but Hester and Dixon Bailey had been shot, Bailey mortally. Tom carried Bailey's son "out of danger far in the woods, but afterwards carried the Boy back" to the Redsticks who dispatched him with a war club. Holmes supposed Tom had gone back to the fort to appease the Indians and gain his freedom, "but had no idea they would kill the Boy which Tom regretted afterwards."[39]

In the previous hour, métis Peter Randon had witnessed the brutal deaths of his parents, sisters, and brothers; now he scrambled atop the crowd struggling to escape through the hole Holmes had cut, scaled the top of the palisade, leapt off, and raced to the treeline. A wounded Ensign Chambliss fought his way through the hole, dashed for the woods, and was hit with two barbed, metal-tipped arrows. Bleeding now from four wounds, he hobbled away and hid under a pile of brush, where he lost consciousness from loss of blood. A group of thirteen men—militiamen James Beale, Aaron Bradley, John Hoven, Joseph Perry, Martin Rigdon (probably the drummer whose long roll had inadvertently set off the Redstick attack), Samuel Smith, Jesse Steadham, and

William Stubblefield (also wounded by an arrow); Privates Elemuel Bradford, Joseph Cook, A. J. Morris, Corporal Abner Daniels, and Sergeant John Mountjoy of the Volunteers—intended to make a stand in the open and enable more civilians to escape. But their resolve withered under heavy Redstick fire, and they scattered for the woods. Steadham received a gunshot in the thigh while Smith helped the stricken Stubblefield flee, and all reached the safety of the swamp.[40]

When Betsy Hoven, John's sister, emerged from the fort, she spotted an officer's horse loose in the field, caught it, and rode off. Two of the last to leave the north bastion, Tensaw militiamen Samuel Jones and Ned Steadham, were both wounded by gunfire, Jones in the leg and Steadham losing a finger. Josiah Fletcher now felt the northern escape route too dangerous and slipped into the mud with the fort's hogs, remaining there until the Redsticks departed at nightfall. Of the whites and métis remaining in the fort, all the men and many of the women and children were killed. Substantial numbers of Africans gave themselves up as prisoners, as did three métis women—Susannah Hatterway, Vicey McGirth, and Vicey's niece Polly Jones, all Creek wives of white Americans. When Hatterway saw all was lost, "she took hold of a little white girl, Elizabeth Randon [Peter's four-year-old sister], with one hand, and a negro girl named Lizzie, with the other, and said to them, 'Let us go out and be killed together.'" To their surprise, Efa Tastanagi, Dog Warrior of Atasi, claimed them as captives. Redstick warriors killed Vicey McGirth's son James but spared her five daughters and Polly Jones' three children—nine-year-old Seaborn, seven-year-old Samuel, and little Jeffersonia Hawkins Jones, age four—making prisoners of them all. Just before 5:00 P.M., an hour and a half before sunset, the killing ended.[41]

Zach McGirth and his two African companions, aboard their provisions flatboat a few miles up the Alabama River, had listened to the fighting for hours. When gunfire ceased for a time, they threw the supplies out of the boat and rowed rapidly toward Mims' landing. At the resumption of firing, however, they ran the boat into a thick canebrake and "there lay untill only one gun could be occasionly heard at intervals   presently all firing ceased." They then saw "immense volumes of smoke rise up . . . succeeded by light flames of fire" and knew "all was lost." Lieutenant Montgomery, at Peirces' mill less than two miles to the south, heard "firing and yells of the Indians" all afternoon but could render no assistance with his small force. He would keep every man under arms through the night, as "Indians were continually seen, passing the fort, at a distance."[42]

It was but this morning that Major Beasley wrote down that he believed
that the indications of the approach of Indians, of which he had recvd. an
account, was unfounded and at noon he was vigorously assailed at Fort
Mims on Tensaw by a considerable body of them. What the result is we do
not know, but the smoke of burning houses in that quarter are now seen
on the river bank at Fort Stoddert.

—Judge Harry Toulmin, August 30, 1813[43]

On Monday evening, Territorial District Judge Harry Toulmin regretfully
informed General Flournoy, commander of U.S. military forces in the South,
of the long-awaited Redstick attack on the Tensaw settlement, ten miles to his
northeast across the Mobile-Tensaw delta. As he watched the frontier literally
erupt in flames, with his own family among the hundreds of women and children crowded into nearby Mount Vernon stockade, Toulmin could "anticipate
nothing but a dreadful blow upon our Settlements, and a melancholy destruction of our population."[44] He did not know the worst had already occurred. In
the coming days the assiduous Toulmin, as ranking federal official in the region, would interrogate eyewitnesses to the battle who made their way across
two rivers and through swamps to the haven of Fort Stoddert. Among the first
were Hester and some who had been outside Fort Mims, by chance, when the
attack occurred (probably including Private Page, Peter Durant, and Viney
Randon). They offered their impressions of the size of the Redstick army—
one thought 200 warriors, but he had seen only the eastern column; another
guessed 400 or 500. None knew the fate of the garrison or of the families sheltered inside Fort Mims.[45]

McGirth and his two slaves were the first to inspect the scene after the
battle, at twilight, within sight of Redstick campfires to the east. As relayed
many years later to historian Pickett by Robert James, a McGirth relative who
had heard these stories numerous times, "Dogs in great numbers were running
about all over the woods, alarmed & making no noise." The three men searched
for their friends and kin among the dead, "some still bleeding, all scalped &
mutilated, and smoked with fire," while "the shouts of the murderers could be
distinctly heard & their camp fires seen" to the east. Hundreds of painted war
clubs littered the battlefield, each signifying a Redstick enemy slain. When
darkness overtook them and McGirth still had not found the bodies of his

wife and children, the melancholy trio set out across the delta toward Fort Stoddert.[46]

When Ensign Chambliss regained consciousness, he realized two Redstick men, smoking their tobacco pipes, stood next to the pile of brush that was his hiding place "and had actually kindled a fire at one end of it. Just as the heat became intolerable they went off." Despite his wounds, he staggered to the riverbank where he found a boat, then managed somehow to steer it down the Alabama Cut-off and floated to Fort Stoddert. Southwest of the smoldering ruins, Samuel Jones hid under the bank of Boatyard Lake. He had killed a Red-stick on his run from the fort. Now a party of warriors made camp near him for the night. Before leaving next morning, he saw them throw three of their people into the lake, "and they left a boy 12 years old dead on a hide at camp."[47]

Dr. Holmes lay under a brush heap until about 9:00 P.M., watching as the Redsticks set fire to the Randon and Peirce homes and the Peirces' gin house, containing 100,000 pounds of cotton, next to Boatyard Lake. With "the homes at the fort still burning—all was light." Overcome by exhaustion, he slept until awakened by a light rain an hour before dawn. Because he did not know how to swim, Holmes decided against crossing the Alabama River and set his course east for the piney uplands. In less than a mile, "to his astonishment he came upon the whole Indian encampment" on the hills east of the smoldering fort ruins, within "ten steps of them . . . all asleep with small fires." Regaining his composure, he skirted the camp, which was three-quarters of a mile long, and hid in a canebrake, where he remained for the next five days. (After a two-week odyssey, Holmes was rescued by a Tensaw resident, John Buford, and carried by flatboat to Fort Stoddert.)[48]

That evening the victors counted their own losses. George Stiggins claimed, years later, that "of all their men that went into action fully half was killed and disabled and wounded. . . . they rose in fury at night against the prophet and leading man Paddy Walsh for their losing so many men by death and wounds, tho' he was shot through the body himself in three places, it did not excuse him." To save Walsh from "the infuriated populace," Stiggins wrote, the Ala-bamas retrieved their canoes hidden at the mouth of Flat Creek and "trans-ported him and themselves up the river to the towassee town as he was of their clan."[49]

A considerable consolation to the Redstick survivors must have been the great numbers of captives (about 100), scalps (200 or more, cut apart to make many times that number of trophies), horses, and other property they had taken at Fort Mims. What more did the Redsticks now expect to accomplish in coming days as terrified Americans abandoned their settlements in the wake of this devastation? Not since the expulsion of British traders from the interior Southeast during the Yamasee War of 1715 had Creeks warriors achieved such a success. And how often had garrisoned forts fallen to an Indian army? None since the conquests of Pontiac's allies nearly fifty years earlier, at the end of the French and Indian war. True, the Redsticks had paid a very high price. Yet they must have exulted in their victory, one of the greatest in the history of Native American warfare.

7

A Country Given Up

The hostile party got a vast number of horses and a great deal of other effects in their pillage of fort Mimbs and country, from which they concluded that the time had arrived that was spoken of by Tecumseh, and repeatedly confirmed after that by the prediction of their own prophets, that there was to come and be a time, when the Indians would have the lone possession and undisturbed range of all their lands and country, and no white man dare to put his foot thereon without their permission.

—George Stiggins[1]

All the next morning fresh columns of smoke arose from ransacked and torched Tensaw plantations as parties of Redstick warriors roamed across the district, "hunting negros, horses, and cattle" missed during the prior day's carnage. Around noon the main body of warriors abandoned their temporary camp east of the smoldering fort and began the long trek north on the Federal Road. The severely wounded were left at Burnt Corn Spring, where they might recuperate (or die) without delaying the others' return to the Upper Creek towns. Even so, the victorious warriors made slow progress, taking eight days to cover those 150 miles, encumbered as they were with captives and plunder. As the bound, desolated prisoners trudged away from their ruined homes and their unburied loved ones, moving ever deeper into the Creek nation, Vicey McGirth grew "excessively distressed." When a warrior threatened to club her, she "cried out aloud," one of her fellow captives recalled, and "urged them to do it as in the situation of her family she wished to die." McGirth, Polly Jones, and their children all survived the journey north; they were taken to Wewocau, where they would spend the next seven months among the Redsticks.[2]

With the departure of the main Redstick force, an officer and three men ventured out of Peirces' Mill "on horseback, to reconnoitre." They reported back to Lieutenant Andrew Montgomery that Fort Mims was destroyed and any survivors likely taken captive. At this news, Montgomery "determined on a retreat by land" after his scouts found the rivers and swamps "full of Indians." They set off at dark; three hours later an orange glow appeared on the horizon in the direction of Peirces' Mill. Three nights of forced marches, through the unsettled pine barrens east of Tensaw River, then across the delta, brought Montgomery's party of 40 men (including John Weatherford, James Cornells, and David Tate, who lost his wife at Fort Mims) and 164 women and children safely to Mobile.[3]

Fifteen miles to the south, Ensign Isaac Davis and his command of eighteen Volunteers stood watch throughout the night as Redstick warriors passed by their post at Hinson and Kennedy's Mill. In the previous weeks, Davis and his men had made their small fort nearly impregnable by raising the height of the mill dam, which flooded the area surrounding the palisade except for a narrow entrance path along the millrace. Late that night, from across their "moat," sentries heard the cries of women from Fort Mims. At the first sounds of gunfire, Peggy Bailey and others doing laundry at Boatyard Lake ran to the banks of the Alabama River, two miles to the southwest. Bailey swam across the river to a flatboat tied to the opposite bank, "took it across, and the women got upon it" and floated downstream to the mill. "Ensign Davis went out and brought them in. After a few days, being short of provisions and receiving no orders from any quarters, he took his command with the fugitives on board of a sloop lying at the mill" and reached Mobile soon afterwards.[4]

With the fall of Fort Mims, Redstick war parties raided abandoned settlements at will, burning houses, killing livestock, and carrying off property throughout the Forks, between the Alabama and Tombigbee rivers, and as far south as Fish River east of Mobile Bay. For much of late August, stories had been circulating among the settlers of a second war party, nearly 200 men from the Black Warrior towns, expected to strike Easley's station in the Forks. Easley's, however, was not their target.[5] Benjamin Hawkins, Judge Toulmin, and other Americans on the frontier heard rumors this smaller war party was led by the Alabama Prophet Josiah Francis (Hillis Hadjo). On September 1, Redstick warriors killed twelve white women and children at a cabin near Bassett's Creek, in the Forks a mile from Sinquefield's stockade, a palisaded farmhouse sheltering about fifteen American men with their families. Sarah Merrill and her infant son survived, though she was scalped and both badly wounded. Colonel Carson, commanding the Volunteers at Fort Madison, the next morning dispatched Lieutenant James Bailey (a white man, no relation to the Tensaw Baileys) and eleven mounted riflemen to bury the dead. Bailey's troops escorted the bodies transported by oxcart to Fort Sinquefield, where the soldiers assisted with interment in a mass grave. As the burial service concluded, the

Redsticks reappeared and rushed the fort's open gate, a tactic that had worked so well at Fort Mims. Some women doing laundry at a spring were nearly cut off, except for the quick thinking of Isaac Heaton (or Hayden), a cowherd and reputed horse thief, who rallied the fort's pack of hunting dogs and charged the attacking warriors. "The Indians had to take their war clubs to the dogs & it took sometime before the dogs could be beaten off," just long enough for most of the settlers and dragoons to reach the fort. They eventually repelled the attack with muskets, rifles, and fowling pieces during a two-hour siege. The Redsticks lost five dead, killed one man and one woman from the fort, and took seven dragoon horses.[6]

The métis chronicler George Stiggins, no admirer of the Alabama Prophet, attributed these actions around Fort Sinquefield to "the dog warrior called by the alabamas Coo le jer," not to Josiah Francis. Stiggins portrayed Francis as a coward who envied the great wealth taken by the Redsticks at Fort Mims but waited for an opportunity to loot abandoned settlements once there was "no formidable enemy" left to oppose him. Resolving Francis' role in these attacks is probably impossible, but all sources agree that his men engaged in widespread raiding after the Sinquefield fight. They "gathered all the horses that were overlooked and left by the others and burned all the dwelling houses saw mills &c." on the Tombigbee and Tensaw frontiers. And they even visited the devastated site of Fort Mims, where they "dug up got and destroyed an immense quantity of household furniture being shewn by the negro prisoners where such had been buried by their former owners on their going to the unfortunate fortress."[7]

Apart from the aborted assault on Sinquefield's stockade, the Redsticks never launched another major offensive strike against the southern settlements. Raiding, however, continued for months and resulted in enormous cumulative damage. After the war, heirs and survivors of burned-out white and métis settlers filed seventy-six claims for compensation against the U.S. government for "depredations by the Creek Indians." Tensaw and Tombigbee property owners swore they lost over 5,400 cattle, some 300 horses, almost 2,500 hogs, 8,000 bushels of corn, and 55 slaves, along with their homes and household goods, altogether valued at $121,000. Among the most severely hurt economically were the Tensaw métis; John Randon and Dixon Bailey's families alone lost 560 cattle and 22,000 pounds of seed cotton. The abandoned fields of the Tensaw now became a granary for the Redsticks, who had largely neglected their own crops at the urgings of the prophets. For the next three months, bands of Upper Creeks would methodically glean the fields of their enemies, first of corn and then sweet potatoes, for their own immediate needs and for transport by dug-out canoe to their settlements upriver.[8]

Panic

Survivors of the battle at Fort Mims straggled into Fort Stoddert all day Tues-day. As rumors of a massacre spread to adjacent Mount Vernon cantonment, "like the fort on Tensaw, wonderfully encumbered by helpless families, . . . there was no longer any hesitation." Concerned for the safety of his own family, Judge Toulmin joined the exodus. Such "was the hurry of a flight conducted almost at midnight, that few took any thing with them, even to support them-selves on their way to Mobile. Some pushed off by water, others fled by land in the darkness of the night, and the whole face of the country exhibited a scene of consternation and distress. . . . The river was strewed with boats from fort Stoddert to Mobile; and here many have no shelter and no means of support."[9] For the unsuspecting residents and military garrison at Mobile, their first re-alization of unsettling events to the north came at dawn Wednesday with the arrival of a bedraggled fleet of refugee-laden dugouts, bateaux, and flatboats. Over the coming weeks, Mobile's population of fewer than 500 would struggle to accommodate several thousand displaced persons, nearly half the entire population of the Tensaw and Tombigbee districts. Soon they were joined by still more evacuees from the coastal region westward, now homeless in a coun-try at war. Some settlers on the southern fringe of Choctaw territory drew on hard lessons learned from the mistakes of Samuel Mims and Daniel Beasley and erected new, improved forts. The builders of Fort James, for instance, on the Pearl River, "availed ourselves of the defects in that [fort] already taken by the Indians. Our Fort is a square of sixty yards with two Block houses at right angles, the port holes seven feet high & the pickets nearly one foot thick." Similarly, in the Creek nation Redstick leaders fortified strong points and pre-pared their own people for the American armies everyone knew would come, while the prophets invoked spiritual powers to protect their homeland from invasion.[10]

News of the Fort Mims debacle filtered slowly to the more remote settle-ments and posts. Reliable details of the disaster finally reached the commander of Mississippi Territorial Volunteers when General Claiborne rode into St. Ste-phens on September 3. He had spent the previous week at Easley's station, awaiting the Redstick menace at the Americans' northernmost fortified plan-tation in the Forks and had hurried down to St. Stephens upon hearing the first astonishing report. Persistent Choctaw warnings identifying Easley's as the most likely primary target of the Redsticks had proven incorrect. With the fall of Fort Mims, it now looked as though the Choctaws had been duped by Red-stick misinformation—or, more ominously, perhaps the Americans had fallen for Choctaw subterfuge, signifying a general Indian uprising.[11]

With strong support from his senior officers, Claiborne contemplated an immediate march into the Creek nation. Two of his mounted scouts had en-countered a Redstick force at Randon's plantation, on the lower Alabama, where a substantial number had evidently gone after the battle at Fort Mims "to provision themselves & to prepare for another enterprize." The panic spread-ing through the American settlements, however, and Claiborne's growing rec-ognition of his own troops' ineffectiveness soon forced him to put aside any thought of offensive action. Within two days the upper Tombigbee district had become depopulated, "except the places occupied by my troops and one or two small stations that will brake immediately." From his days on the Ohio fron-tier with General Anthony Wayne, Claiborne remembered a tougher breed of settler, who "taking their guns in their hands would go to their fields plant cultivate & gather in their crops." The general felt ashamed of his fellow Ameri-cans. "Never in my life did I see a Country given up without a struggle for it before. . . . Here are the finest crops my eyes ever beheld made mostly fit to be cribed & immence stocks, negros and other property, abandoned by their own-ers almost on the first alarm."[12]

Jesse Griffin, who settled in the Forks in 1805 with his twin brother David and their families, left a rare, first-hand account of this wholesale retreat from the Tombigbee.

> St. Stephens, 5th Septr 1813
>
> Belovd Parents in great confusion I Drop you a line   The Indians has Murdered at the lowest calculation Four hundred souls within five days on our frontiers and a frontier of one hundred miles have been visited by them at the same time   I am at this time fifty miles from home with my family   I have lost my crop of corn   horses and Every part of stock and a good part of my household furniture   our country is compleatly destroyed . . . no more time Fairwell   your affectionate son[13]

At Carney's Fort on the Tombigbee, little Margaret Eades watched with ris-ing apprehension (as she recalled many years later) while "Every heart nearly became paralyzed with fear and our men that had been so brave, became panic stricken, and their families pleading to be taken to Fort St. Stephens. . . . they stampeded, some families took to the canebrakes, some to St. Stephens, some down the river to Ft. Stoddard."[14] With an enormous refugee population to protect and his forces spread thin, Claiborne withdrew the Volunteer companies posted at Forts Easley and Madison, leaving a garrison only at St. Stephens and forty convalescent soldiers at Mount Vernon cantonment, near Fort Stoddert, who were reinforced on September 3 by one hundred troops of the 7th Regiment U.S. Infantry under Captain Uriah Blue.[15]

Claiborne had immediately forwarded the "melancholy intelligence" on Fort Mims to Governor David Holmes, who received his official report on the tenth in Washington, Mississippi Territory. Two days earlier, the first (erroneous) accounts of events to the east appeared in the territory's principal newspaper, the *Washington Republican*—Peirces' Mill had been "carried by storm," the garrison at St. Stephens fired cannons to repel an attack, 500 British and Spanish troops had landed at Pensacola. Panic, nursed by rumors of massacres perpetrated by combined forces of Creeks and Choctaws, swept through Jefferson and Claiborne counties, nearly 300 miles west of the Tensaw. Many of the Volunteers who fell at Fort Mims, including Jefferson County's former sheriff, Major Daniel Beasley, came from this cluster of towns and plantations north of Natchez. Suddenly their shocked, grief-stricken relatives and neighbors feared the Redsticks were unstoppable. Seventy-seven years later, John Watkins, half-brother of Captain William Jack who died at Fort Mims, recalled that day: "I was then a small boy and remember well the alarm and consternation that nearly all suffered when it was announced at the door of the school house the 'Indians are upon us,' and ordering us all to go home in 'double quick,' and by the shortest route. Some were overcome by fear, wept and raved." Eventually, when no hostile Indians materialized, those who had fled reclaimed their abandoned farms, erected palisades and blockhouses, and reflected with some embarrassment on their precipitate flight.[16]

~

Contrary to rumor, for the time being the Choctaw nation remained neutral at the urging of medal chief Pushmataha. Many of his warriors burned war clubs to symbolize their rejection of the red path of war. Even so, a prophets' faction arose at Nanifalia town, which moved north, away from the Americans, for the security of their women and children in the event they were drawn into the war. The Redstick Creeks had, likewise, created havens for their families at a number of locations chosen for their defensible terrain—the Black Warrior towns at the western edge of the Creek nation; the Hoithlewaulee and Atasi camps on the lower Tallapoosa River; inside the Horseshoe Bend of the upper Tallapoosa; and at a place on the upper Alabama River decreed by the Alabama Prophet as Ikanachaki (*ēkvn vcakē*), Holy Ground.[17]

Once again we must depend largely on George Stiggins for information on Redstick actions and motivations. Stiggins attributed creation of the Holy Ground settlement entirely to Josiah Francis, who had been inspired to create a separate town for the Alabamas, apart from the rest of the Creeks who had congregated at the Hoithlewaulee camps, which had "turned to a Babel" from the "inviollable confusion of Languages" spoken there. On a great bend of the upper Alabama, Francis erected his town at "a spot made sacred by the great spirit . . . never to be sullied by the footsteps of the real white man." At the instruction of the Master of Breath, Francis encircled the site with a "destructive barrier . . . which a white man could not pass over alive." After the great victory at Fort Mims, many Alabama families left their old towns and took up residence at this refuge and around Moniac and Weatherford's plantations a few miles upstream, where Supalamy Moniac joined Weatherford. Holy Ground also became, in Stiggins' words, a "receptakle of every runaway negro." Together Redsticks and escaped former slaves awaited an American army, bolstered by confidence acquired in battle and by their belief in the power of the prophets' religion. For a brief two months, the Redstick nation would be free of the polluting presence of Americans and their apostate Creek accomplices. The entire Upper Creek country of the Alabamas, Tallapoosas, and Abekas lay uncontested in Redstick hands, some 30 talwas with at least 8,000 inhabitants, a quarter of whom would die in the coming conflict.[18]

As they awaited the expected American counterattack, small parties of Redsticks skirmished with their enemies at the three avenues into their country: the upper Coosa, the lower Alabama, and the central Chattahoochee valleys. To the east, small-scale fights had been occurring intermittently since early August between Peter McQueen's warriors and the Lower Creeks in and around Coweta. All the while, ammunition supplies had been dwindling; now the major fighting at Fort Mims had made resupply essential.[19]

The Redsticks turned once again to Governor González Manrique at Spanish Pensacola. Although Spain and Britain were allied against Napoleon's France, Spanish Florida remained officially neutral in the ongoing war between Britain and the United States. Nevertheless, the American seizure of Spanish Mobile earlier in the year had violated the spirit of neutrality and contributed to González Manrique's decision to supply McQueen's warriors with ammunition prior to the battle at Burnt Corn Creek. With few options, Josiah Francis urged the governor to furnish badly needed aid, promptly. His appeal is remarkable on many levels but principally for the unique glimpse it offers of a Redstick point of view within days of their greatest victory.

The letter was penned for Francis, "the old king" (of Tallassee?), and Mougceweihche (otherwise unknown) by "the old intepreter." This mysterious figure must have been James Walsh, stepfather of the prophet Paddy Walsh and "a despisable Murdering Swamp Tory" from South Carolina (according to George Stiggins), who had been living in the Creek country since the Revolution. The first voice in this complex document seems to be that of the Alabama Prophet and his fellow Redstick leaders. The letter begins with an introduction, "Three person in number that has been informed from the spirit above to take the war club in hand." Francis, the old king, and Mougceweihche then explained how they had carried the Shawnee Prophet's message to their people; "we have give our talk out to the nations and have taken the talk and whole creek nation is united and taken up the red stick." Without offering further details, they broke their astonishing news to the governor; "as the power we recived was to fight the americans the intepreter son heded an army and went against a garrison at tennisau and he put the garrison in flames." The interpreter's involvement suddenly becomes clear. This father of the prophet Paddy Walsh, as one of the few literate Redsticks, was an invaluable interlocutor in negotiations with the strategically situated Spaniards at Pensacola.

Their remarkable feat in the Tensaw had been accomplished with old and primitive weapons and inadequate supplies of ammunition. Now they pleaded for new weapons and the lead and gunpowder needed to carry on the fight and protect their nation: "our guns is all rusted up in a manner and we are poor for every thing   our old gun lock is tumble to pecies   want of gun locks and blankits to cover our naked bodys   we want powder and led   we hope that you will furnish us with these article before cold weather comes on   even knife we are poor for as mean to rout our enemes on all acations . . . you saw when we was in Pencola how poor we was for arm   you saw that we had nothig but the bow and arrows and the red stick   we petitioned to you to supply us with arms   not only us but the choctor two and semiles [Seminoles] two   as we have no white people to supply we look to you for a supply of arms."

The old interpreter, apparently, then turned to a topic of interest to the Spaniards: "I hope that you will make hast to take posesion of mobeale . . . you lent mobeale to the american   they have held that town two long   if you have really given it up to the american you will give us an answer   for if you have we will fire the town." He added, "we will allow all the corn as far as up to the cutoff as we call that conquered property from the cutoff up will geather and eat," seemingly offering to share abandoned American crops with the colonists of Pensacola. The letter concludes, largely in the voice of the old interpreter, with some specifics of recent victories: "I send you a small talk   my son commanded the army that defeted the fort and I was in battle   old a man as am I help to cut the fort down and the young men they desroy the enemes . . . 499 of the enemeas was slain   243 negro's taken prisoner   330 horses taken   30 men was kill by the enemes   seven out the 30 was kill by our own people by bad condock." Looking back at the civil war battles of July, "our great head men was forted at the Tobachis [Tuckaubatchee] but they had to run to the cowwiter [Coweta] and have forted themself there." Soon "the whole nation is going to hold a talk with them   the broken days is 15 days to march   they will demand the principal hed men   if not given up they will destroy the hole." To Governor González Manrique, Francis and his allies offered their friendship: "we hole you fast by the hand   we tell you no lie   the true statement of things"[20]

This correspondence clearly conveys a sense of Redstick confidence in their vision, in their force of arms, and in their resolve to carry the fight to their enemies at Coweta and Mobile.

Redstick war parties posed a tangible and unambiguous threat to American lives and property in the Tombigbee and Tensaw districts. But the thought that Redstick success on the battlefield might spark a regionwide slave revolt truly frightened federal, state, and territorial officials throughout the South. They constantly bickered about many issues, often dividing along political party lines, but a hint of slave insurrection could immediately dispel faction and party interests in this part of the country. A decade earlier the successes of black revolutionaries in Haiti displaced thousands of Creole elites who sought a slave-owning, francophone haven in Louisiana. Enslaved Africans in the South and abolitionists throughout the United States found encouragement in that greatest of all slave uprisings, but southern slave owners saw only the need to redouble efforts to defend and strengthen the institution of slavery. In the Southwest, federal land policies encouraged plantation development with enslaved labor. U.S. census takers had counted 40,352 persons in Mississippi Territory in 1810, 42 percent enslaved people of color. With such a large proportion of the population in bondage, everyone—black, white, Indian, métis—recognized the opportunities, in the midst of war, for slaves to seek their freedom.[21]

During the American Revolution, the British had encouraged enslaved Africans to run away from the plantations of southern Patriots. Now that Britain seemed about to open a southern theater in its current war with the United States, rumors circulated in the South that British agents on the Gulf coast would entice slaves into free Spanish Florida. Some imagined the Redsticks would welcome and arm escaped slaves as allies in a campaign against the Americans. But all remained speculation until the battle at Fort Mims unleashed war in the South. Within days of the battle, General Claiborne expressed apprehension that slaves on the frontier would immediately run off to the Creek nation. His brother, Governor W. C. C. Claiborne of Louisiana, relayed rumors a week later of slaves who had, indeed, escaped to join the Redsticks, leading him to urge all his militia colonels to "maintain proper discipline" among the slaves in their own state. General Flournoy, for one, never doubted the duplicity of slaves in Redstick hands. His orders to General Claiborne ominously stated, "All negroes, horses, cattles, corn & other property that cannot be conveniently brot in [from the frontier], must be destroyed." Despite official American concern, however, no widespread slave uprising occurred, even in the chaos of the war zone. Most enslaved Africans shared whites' fear of the Redsticks and fled with the rest of the evacuees. Some slaves abandoned in the panic were held as captives by the Redsticks and redeemed (and re-enslaved) by the whites at war's end.[22]

The numerous Africans held as slaves by the Creeks and métis most concerned Benjamin Hawkins. He knew many of them spoke the Muskogee language, yet not one of the hundreds living in the Creek nation had alerted him or the pro-American chiefs to the movements of the large Redstick force that destroyed Fort Mims. His initial suspicions of a slave conspiracy to aid the Redsticks—based on reports that "Siras [Cyrus], a negro man, cut down the pickets" early in that assault—were shaken when he discovered in early October that the Redsticks had killed several African men taken at Fort Mims. Months later, as defeated Redsticks surrendered African captives to U.S. troops, those "women and Children who were taken at Fort Mims" confirmed that the "Negroe fellows taken at same time were all put to death by the Indians, after that affair." The prophets seem not to have trusted every surrendering former slave, and word of their distrust surely dampened the enthusiasm of other slaves considering flight to the Creek nation. Some, like Cyrus, leapt at this brief chance at freedom, while those more dubious of Redstick success were offered the same terms as the métis before them—a choice between taking arms against the Americans or death. A few, such as Jo, Zachariah McGirth's slave, did join Redstick war parties and fought against their former owners. William Weatherford apparently persuaded his family's enslaved Africans to fight alongside him at the Holy Ground. But the number of Africans who joined the Redsticks remained small until the British military finally did appear along the Gulf coast late in 1814, well after the war in the Creek nation had ended.[23]

Last Rites

For the officers and men of the Mississippi Territorial Volunteers at St. Stephens and the Mount Vernon cantonment, enforced garrison duty grew increasingly unbearable with each passing day. Nearly a hundred Volunteers had died in a humiliating defeat, yet here their army sat with no prospects of combat, no opportunity to avenge the deaths of their fellow soldiers who lay still unburied on the field of battle. Only after Brigade Major Joseph P. Kennedy held a "funeral" service at Mount Vernon honoring the fallen did General Claiborne at last order a ten-man detachment by flatboat to Fort Mims, to "number the Dead" that could not yet be buried. On September 9, Major Kennedy and Captain Blue reported, in florid prose, what they observed the day before on their brief visit to the battle site.[24]

Agreeable to your Order of the 8th inst. we proceeded with all possible dispatch to Mims' Fort on Tensaw to examine the fatal field of Battle and the situation of the Country. We found the whole of the rich Tensaw Settlements a perfect desert: the hand of Desolation has passed over it; the remains of Major Beasley our fellow Citizens and Brother Soldiers still unburied next called our attention. You expect a faithful detail and correct picture of the scene. Language cannot convey it nor the pencil of the painter delineate it. Suffice it to say, that the small command of eight men who only accompanied us, touched by the affecting circumstances, we resolved to see the remains of our slaughtered fellow Citizens and Brother Soldiers—perhaps the last human office that ever we could render to the unfortunate and Brave Major Beasley, his slaughtered Citizens and Soldiers. Some felt the touch of nature for their relations, others for their friends, and all lamented the disasters of war, and the wretched lot of human nature. Our little band marched from the landing in gloomy solitude to the Fort. The place presented an awful spectacle, and the tragical fate of our friends increased the horror of the scene. Our business was to find our friends and number the Dead. An awful and melancholy duty. At the East gate of the Stockade lay Indians, Negroes, men, women and children in one promiscuous ruin; within the Gate lay the Brave unfortunate Beasley, he was behind the same, and was killed, as was said, in attempting to shut it. On the left within the Stockade we found forty five men, women and children in one heap, they were stripped of their clothes without distinction of Age or sex, all were scalped, and the females of every age were most barbarously and Savage like butchered, in a manner which neither decency nor language can convey. Women pregnant were cut open and their childrens heads Tomahawked. This was supposed to be the fatal Spot where the few, who escaped the general Massacre, made their last efforts and perished in the attempt.

The large house within the Fort was burnt to ashes, and the ruins Covered with human bones. the number and the persons who there perished could not be ascertained. The plains and the woods around were covered with dead bodies, in some places thinly scattered, in others lying in heaps as the men happened to fall in flight, or in a body resisted to the last. The result of the awful duty assigned us was that we found twenty Indians and two Chiefs, nine negroes, thirty children, ten infants, seventy one men and twenty nine women. The Indians were dressed in soldiers clothes no doubt for the purpose of disguise. we distinguished them from the Whites by their ears and the cut of their hair, the two Chiefs were carried from the fort and buried by covering them with rails, and from what we could discover considerable more Indians were carried off and buried by their friends. All the houses within the Fort were consumed by fire—except the Block House and part of the picketts yet unburnt. While employed in the Duty, our hearts were torn with contending passions, by turns oppressed with grief and burning with revenge. The Soldier and Officer with one voice called on Divine Providence to revenge the death of our murdered friends, and despaired of this unhappy Country, deserted by its inhabitants, seeking an asylum in some more happy clime, where the Peace Songs and Civil War stories will not delude the people and deceive those who are appointed to govern and protect them.

Yr. Sert.

U. Blue Capt. 7th Regt. Inft.

J. P. Kennedy Captain & Brigade Major[25]

Reconnaissance in the Tensaw after Fort Mims was hazardous duty, and Blue and Kennedy did not linger. Moreover, nine days of late summer heat and humidity must have turned the corpses black and bloated and scarcely recognizable. Although they endeavored to count the dead—"twenty Indians and two Chiefs, nine negroes, thirty children, ten infants, seventy one men and twenty nine women"—their total of 171 souls falls well short of the more than 400 Redsticks, Americans, Africans, and Tensaw métis who are thought to have perished. The two officers candidly admitted the impossibility of accurately numbering those burned in the Mims house.

Kennedy and Blue's implication that the "Indians . . . dressed in soldiers clothes" were Redsticks, based on "their ears and the cut of their hair," raises doubts. Many Creek men of this era wore multiple silver dangles and rings in their ears. A few may have had the outer cartilage of their ears severed and wrapped in silver coils, forming large hoops, although this style had nearly gone out of fashion by the early 1800s. Creek men's hairstyles would have included roaches along with the short to long cuts typically worn by white men on the frontier. While odd ear features and hairstyles may have been most common among the Redsticks, they would not have been unknown among the Tensaw métis. Abundant evidence indicates the métis retained other traditional elements of Creek culture, such as facility with the Muskogee, Alabama, and Koasati languages and participation in the Creek ball game. Kennedy and Blue's deduction that "The Indians were dressed in soldiers clothes no doubt for the purpose of disguise" is similarly suspect. None of the Volunteers or militia had been issued military uniforms; all dressed in civilian garb, except for officers who might have managed to acquire martial braid and buttons at their own expense. The Redsticks probably did not remove the bodies of those twenty Indians from the battlefield (as they did the two "Chiefs," hidden outside the fort beneath fence rails) because they were, in fact, Tensaw métis.[26]

Apart from this single, cautious venture into the Tensaw and occasional forays by small scouting parties monitoring Redstick movements, the Mississippi Territorial Volunteers kept to their forts awaiting reinforcement. To Holmes and Claiborne's surprise, General Flournoy had responded promptly to the governor's appeal for assistance. The rapidly deteriorating situation north of Mobile had compelled Flournoy to modify his strategic plan that tied down his best troops protecting the coast, between Mobile and New Orleans, from seaborne British invasion. Now he ordered the entire 3rd Regiment U.S. Infantry, about 600 soldiers commanded by Lieutenant Colonel Gilbert Russell at their base on the Gulf coast at Bay St. Louis, to proceed to Fort Stoddert. For his part, Holmes dispatched four troops of mounted Volunteers, forming a battalion of Cavalry (about 200 men) under Major Thomas Hinds, to augment the few dragoons in Claiborne's command. Despite this show of cooperation, relations remained strained between federal and territorial commanders. To the governor's chagrin, Flournoy refused to accept fiscal responsibility for his additional call-up of Volunteers; Holmes reluctantly paid for muskets, ammunition, camp equipage, and forage from meager territorial coffers.[27]

With these strong reinforcements en route by mid-September and an offensive likely to occur before long, Claiborne at last felt confident enough to order Major Kennedy and Captain Blue back to Fort Mims with 300 select men to "bury the bodies of our worthy and ever lamented Volunteer Soldiers, Officers & Citizens." Claiborne instructed Kennedy, upon arriving at the battlefield, to dismantle the fort's remnants and build a defensive work from unburned palisade pickets and blockhouse logs. The general would not brook another humiliation; "the first Regiment of the Mississippi Territory Volunteers must not be vanquished without loss of blood, and that on terms that will impress on our country & on our enemy the worth of our Corps."[28]

On the morning of September 22, more than three weeks after the battle at Fort Mims, Kennedy and Blue crossed the Mobile-Tensaw delta in strength, prepared to defend themselves as they buried the dead.

Agreable to your order of the 21st Inst. we proceeded to Mim's Fort, to collect the Bones of our countrymen that fell in the late attack on that place and to bury their remains—the last human office that we could perform to the obsequies of our fellow citizens, and brother Soldiers.

We collected, and consignd to the earth, Two hundred and forty seven, including men, women, and children—The adjacent woods were strickly search'd for our countrymen, and in that pursuit, we discovered at least, one hundred slaughtered Indians,—They were cover'd with rails, brush &c.,—we could not be mistaken as to their being Indians, as they were inter'd with their war dress, and implements,—and although they have massacred a number of our helpless women and children, it is beyond doubt to them, a dear bought victory. The adjacent country, we have strickly examined, and no sign of Indians could be discovered.

The object of our command being Compleated, we have return'd to this post, without an opportunity of losing our scalps, or getting those of the enemy.[29]

Dr. Thomas G. Holmes, who so recently had made his escape from the burning fort, accompanied the burial detail. Interviewed three decades later by historian Albert James Pickett, Holmes described the nature of the graves. The troops dug "two large vaults about 20 feet square, one in front of the Bastion on the North side where most of the bodies lay   they were rooled in & covered up. . . . [the burial party] saw many ravens devouring the Bodies—they were never seen before & have not been seen since—over four hundred persons were deposited in the vaults[30]—shockingly mangled. There were many women in the family way & all such the infants were cut out of their bellies, and fence rails run up their privates. Some families had 12 or 14 children all butchered. . . . They were striped of every article of apparel, not satisfied with this, they inhumanely scalped every solitary one—not satisfied with scalping in the ordinary maner but took from the skin of the whole head so as to make many scalps."[31]

On this visit, their second to the ruins of Fort Mims, Kennedy and Blue reported burying 247 men, women, and children—a precise and seemingly definitive count of the whites, blacks, and métis who died there on August 30—along with a less precise estimate of Redstick dead, "at least, one hundred." The discrepancy between this number and the counts of September 8, particularly the apparent inflation of Redstick dead in the interim, became a point of controversy in ensuing political debates between supporters and enemies of General Claiborne over his handling of the Volunteer corps during the Redstick War.[32]

Word of the disaster at Fort Mims gradually spread across the country. By September 24 express riders had carried reports to Nashville and had reached the nation's capital by mid-October.[33] Everywhere in the United States the immediate reaction was outrage mixed with astonishment. How could a well-garrisoned American fort have fallen to Indians? Experience in many wars, from well back in colonial times, had demonstrated how effectively even a few well-armed and determined American settlers fighting behind a simple stockade could defend themselves almost indefinitely against an Indian siege. Since the Redstick Creeks had not been aided by European troops with artillery, such an unusual outcome could only be attributable to gross carelessness. Because survivors' accounts invariably drew attention to the fort's open gates, Major Beasley, the fort's commander, drew criticism from the first for his apparent negligence and underestimation of his opponents. But the benighted Beasley had been the first to fall, thereby redeeming himself to an extent according to early nineteenth-century sensibilities that ranked personal honor and courage above all other virtues, at least for white American males. In any case, castigating a dead man seemed churlish. Must not others higher up the chain of command have been equally culpable?

General Ferdinand Leigh Claiborne, of course, instantly recognized his vulnerability. Upon learning of the "misfortunes attending the garrison of Fort Mims," Governor W. C. C. Claiborne of Louisiana commiserated with his brother over the potential harm to the general's good name from this debacle. Still, since the defeat was "not attributable to any neglect or inattention on his part," and the garrison's "gallant defence" had inflicted great losses on the enemy, he thought his brother's fame would not suffer.[34] Nonetheless, from his headquarters at St. Stephens, General Claiborne and his friend Judge Toulmin opened a literary offensive attributing responsibility for the war to Benjamin Hawkins, Principal Agent to the Southern Indians. Both men thought Hawkins had intentionally misled Secretary of War Armstrong and General Flournoy regarding the true nature of the Redstick movement. By persistently labeling their violence a civil war between pro- and anti-American factions of the Creek nation, Hawkins failed to alert others to the threat this internal conflict posed for U.S. citizens in the Southwest. To be fair to Hawkins, his correspondence from July onward (in contrast to earlier communications) does reflect his growing concern that the imminent defeat of the pro-American faction would require American military intervention. In fact, due primarily to his warnings, Governors Holmes, Claiborne, Blount (of Tennessee), and Mitchell (of Georgia) had raised territorial and state Volunteers and positioned them on the borders of the Creek nation.

General Claiborne, however, thought otherwise. To General Flournoy he wrote, "Col. Hawkins' communications for some time past, have unfortunately had a tendency to lessen our apprehensions, and to beget a belief of our almost perfect security. My little, but inestimable corps, have felt the effect begotten by the doubts. . . . It probably prevented yourself, and certainly Gov. Holmes, from sending troops to this exposed part of the country." Holmes denied the charge, pointing out that he had, in consultation with Flournoy, provided Claiborne with a force of 550 men, which should have been "sufficient to protect the frontier." Judge Toulmin joined the fray with a letter to the editor of the *Raleigh Register,* published in Hawkins' home state of North Carolina. Toulmin insisted he had only discovered the real object of the Redsticks, "to make immediate war on the white people," from some Tensaw métis (in particular, Sam Moniac and James Cornells) who had alerted him to the supply of ammunition entering the Creek nation from Pensacola. Hawkins foolishly believed war with

the United States "only a secondary and remote object," information fed him
by the duplicitous Creeks, Toulmin surmised, "for the purpose of putting us
off our guard." Hawkins' blunder, "his Civil War story," led directly to the loss
of Fort Mims and depopulation of the Tombigbee and Tensaw districts. In
late September, Peter Isler, publisher of the *Mississippi Messenger* in Natchez,
broadened the attack. In handbills "painting in sanguine colours, the horrors
and calamities of our Volunteers and citizens at Mim's on Tensaw," he heaped
blame on Governor Holmes for that sad affair.[35]

This barrage of calumnies aimed at Hawkins and Holmes did not long delay
scrutiny of Claiborne's role in the Fort Mims catastrophe by his political opponents. In mid-October his critics began a sustained campaign intended to
embarrass the general in the territorial capital's principal newspaper, the *Washington Republican,* published by Andrew Marschalk and Thomas Eastin. An
article lampooning Generals Hull, Dearborn, and other ill-starred U.S. military
leaders of the War of 1812 singled out General Claiborne for ridicule.

> "To give a good account of the enemy" it is sometimes necessary to con-
> struct a garrison upon the principles of a butchers' pen which the enemy
> are more safe in approaching than you can be in defending. As such a
> fortification is intended for the protection of women and children, the
> gates must be left open day and night in order to let the enemy come in.
> No sentinels, no guards, no spies are necessary around such a work. No
> discipline is to be observed within it, and all negroes or Indians who
> officially inform you of the approach of the enemy are to be tied up and
> flogged, as disturbers of the peace. After two or three hundred men,
> women, and children are cut to pieces in such a garrison, the command-
> ing general is to send two captains and eight men to aid the carrion crows
> to bury the dead, while he and his whole army exhibit the pomp of a
> funeral within the walls of his own fort. . . . *Brig. Gen. Claiborne of Vol-
> unteers*[36]

One week later an article, signed "Tacitus," bitterly berated the general and described, for the better understanding of readers, the layout of Fort Mims based
on his viewing of the sketch now known as the Claiborne Map.

> The rude attempts of Barbarians to defend themselves from their ene-
> mies, always displays some of the simple principles upon which the art
> of fortification is founded, but Fort Mims was not the work of a man who

had raised himself to power and office by the display of martial genius or of native sagacity, which elevates the savage chief. The fawning sycophant, who, by flattering and hollow pretensions creeps up the ladder of preferment, is too insensible to perceive the enormity of his own blunders, or to blush at the fatal consequences of his profound ignorance. If this were not the case, a bare description of Fort Mims and a simple account of the conduct of the Brigadier Genl. Volunteers previous and since the massacre, would overwhelm him with penitence and humiliation. The blood of our brethren in arms would cry out against him and visions of mangled women and children would banish his repose, and haunt him to despair. . . . "the still small voice of conscience" which would continually whisper to him, *"Fort Mims might have been saved."*. . . . By your unpardonable negligence or incapacity Two hundred and twenty seven of your fellow citizens are cut off in the "midst of their days."

Captain Joseph Kennedy, too, received his share of scorn for the "visit paid by him and Capt. Blue, with eight men, who, with admirable sagacity discovered *'by the cut of the hair'* the difference between Americans, who were all scalped, and Indians who were not." "Tacitus" further derided Kennedy (who also held a field rank of Brigade Major) for that officer's two very different counts of dead Redsticks on the battlefield: "to let these savage monsters despairing of concealing themselves *'by the cut of their hair'* from the inquisitive eye of the Brigade Major determined manfully to put on 'their *war dress and implements'* and mustered to the number of 'at least one hundred *slaughtered Indians'*—But I leave this Bone Picker his *filthy* occupation, and his wonderful power of *multiplication* . . . a man capable of mistaking *obsequies* for *dead bodies* and *rails* for *earth,* and mistaking 10 for 100 when the temptation to error was strong."[37]

"T." (Tacitus, again) renewed his newspaper attacks against Claiborne on December 1 (with the aid of a printed version of the Claiborne Map (Figure 17); claiming the general acknowledged "the loss of Fort Mims was attributable to ignorance, inattention and want of military discipline, and not to the Governor of the Territory, nor to Col. Hawkins, as he had formerly stated." Claiborne's severest critic wondered why he still made no move to retaliate against the Redsticks, two months after the Mims massacre, once federal troops and a corps of dragoons had reinforced the Volunteer brigade.[38]

General Claiborne would not directly address his handling of Fort Mims until late March 1814, as the Redstick War drew to a close. Referring to his

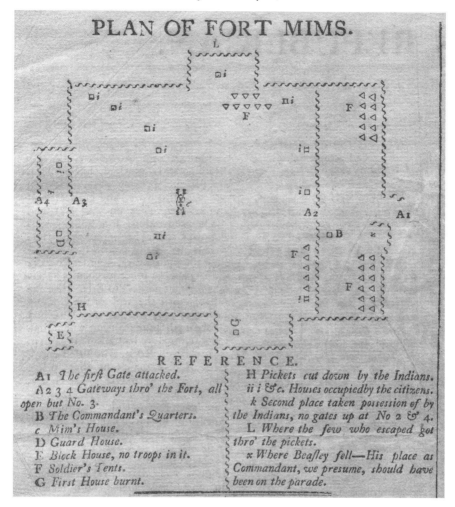

Fig. 17. Depiction of Fort Mims from the *Washington Republican* [Mississippi Territory], October 20, 1813 (courtesy of the Museum of Mobile, Mobile, Alabama).

August 7 inspection of the fort, Claiborne noted he had ordered Major Beasley to strengthen the pickets and build two additional blockhouses; he had dispatched Cornet Rankin and six dragoons to act as Beasley's scouts; and he had repeatedly warned the major to expect an attack and be vigilant. By now in failing health, Claiborne spent the last year of his life writing rebuttals to the continuing press attacks. His final, unpublished defense (written in the third person) endeavored to "vindicate Brigadier General Claiborne from the aspersions which have been cast at him." Despite his "sincere personal friendship" for "the brave and lamented Beasley," the general would not "throw a mantle over his errors." "But as my orders had not been obeyed relative to the additional works of the post, and as that vigilance had not been exercised which my orders required, and which the duty of the commanding officer would have imposed, my conscience acquits me of being the cause of the disasters of that lamentable day." Claiborne died confident he had done his best to protect the frontier but deeply hurt at the attacks on his own character and reputation.[39]

8
Trying Times, 1813–1814

General Claiborne struggled to retaliate militarily against the Redsticks, while defending his honor in the press. He and his counterparts in Tennessee and Georgia, Andrew Jackson and John Floyd, had long planned a three-pronged invasion of the Creek nation if a provocation should occur. This bold, surprise attack into U.S. territory against federalized militia ending in a massacre of civilians more than qualified as a legal basis for war against the Redstick Creeks. But major practical problems faced these three state and territorial Volunteer generals. Volunteers were called up for varying terms of service. Some served for twelve months, but militia enlistment often lasted just three months (and in some cases only 60 days), which left little time for equipping, training, and bringing force to bear against the enemy before an army dissolved with the expiration of enlistment. Service-grade weapons, equipment, and supplies were hard to come by everywhere in a United States ill-prepared for war on multiple fronts. And coordinating plans between American armies on opposite sides of the Creek nation proved extremely difficult. Limited communications were maintained across that hostile terrain by a few daring express riders who risked their lives to carry dispatches and orders on the Federal Road and the many less-traveled paths crisscrossing an interior Southeast hostile to Americans.

Among the first to carry the terrible news of Fort Mims to Benjamin Hawkins in Georgia was Barney O'Riley, an Irish-Creek métis, who rode into the Creek Agency on September 16, more than two weeks after the battle. Word had somehow reached O'Riley in the Lower Creek towns along the Chattahoochee, perhaps by way of a coastal ship calling near the mouth of the Apalachicola River. A second express delivered a packet of letters overland from Judge

Toulmin and General Claiborne on the twenty-first, followed by the arrival of a third rider, Zachariah McGirth, on September 26.[1]

For two decades McGirth had led a liminal existence, straddling two worlds before finding a comfortable niche with his métis wife and their children in the Tensaw. Witnessing firsthand the destruction wrought by the Redsticks at Fort Mims confirmed in him the belief that all his family had died. As he steered his flatboat that night through the Spanish moss–festooned waterways of the delta, leaving in his wake the emotional ruins of a life lived with Indians, McGirth must have committed his entire being to the destruction of his enemies. At Fort Stoddert he signed up for this most hazardous of duties, although he did not intend to commit suicide. As a longtime resident of the Creek nation, an "Indian countryman," McGirth knew well how to survive in this treacherous landscape. "To preserve his life & fulfill his office," McGirth's relative Robert James recalled, "he painted himself like a hostile warrior & shaved his head. Mounted upon a good horse with 3 pecks of shelled corn for his animal & 2 quarts of cold flour for himself, this fearless man   solitary & alone   persued his journey." McGirth successfully completed the ride to Georgia and back at least four times, carrying communications in late September and late October 1813 and again in January and May 1814. On his first mission he learned from Hawkins that his wife and daughters still lived, as captives of the Redsticks. He would survive to free his family and see his enemies vanquished.[2]

Guerrilla Warfare in the Forks

As American leaders gathered forces for an invasion and Redstick leaders fortified defensive strongholds, skirmishing continued in the contested lands on either side of the lower Alabama River. This ground formerly farmed by the Tensaw métis and their American neighbors still held tempting fields of unharvested corn and sweet potatoes needed desperately by refugees on both sides of the conflict. Several hundred Redstick warriors and their families (led at least nominally by William Weatherford) occupied this region in late September and early October, systematically gleaning abandoned fields and dispatching canoe loads of victuals to towns upriver. This force intermittently clashed with white farmers and their African slaves intent on the same task, with losses to both sides. As Claiborne prepared to move north, the pace and scale of conflict abruptly rose.

Redstick tactics involved harassment of American militia units in the Forks. When a party of 25 mounted militiamen commanded by Colonel William McGrew rode out of St. Stephens to intercept a band of 50 warriors spotted in the vicinity of long-abandoned Easley's fort, they were ambushed at Bashi Creek on October 12. McGrew and privates Edmund Miles, David Griffin, and Jesse Griffin (author of the simple, eloquent letter to his parents a month earlier) were killed. When Jesse fell, shot through the thigh, his twin brother David stayed by his side as the rest of the militia retreated. General Claiborne responded by marching a strong force of militia and dragoons in a circuit of the Forks on October 16–20 only to suffer more casualties, five men severely wounded in skirmishes without being able to force a battle. Their "Spies lay near our lines during the whole march," Claiborne complained to General Flournoy, but their main encampment remained hidden "in an almost impenetrable swamp," beyond his reach.[3]

A few days later, Major Thomas Hinds and his battalion of dragoons rode out of St. Stephens on an "Indian hunt." This elite troop of horse included many friends of Major Beasley, most notably Hinds himself, who along with Beasley had felt victimized by social inferiors during the notorious Greenville ball that led ultimately to the Beasley-Frye duel of 1810. Not content with the slow progress of Claiborne's advance into the Creek nation, Hinds and his officers—who counted themselves among the aristocracy of Jefferson County—had recently requested assignment to offensive operations instead of routine garrison duties and patrols. General Flournoy considered them undisciplined and insubordinate and dismissed the force over Claiborne's strenuous objections. Before returning to the Natchez District, and on their own initiative, Hinds and the bulk of his battalion (minus a few who objected to hunting Indians) set off toward Lower Peach Tree Landing on the Alabama River. Seemingly intent on proving Flournoy correct in his assessment, this rogue Volunteer unit proceeded to avenge Daniel Beasley's death in their own way. At an abandoned plantation they found easy prey. The horsemen swept down on several families of Creeks—eight or ten men, women and children (accounts disagree on the number) preoccupied with shelling corn—and killed all, along with two captive slaves, taking two slaves prisoner. According to an article published in the *Washington Republican*, "another Indian, in attempting to make his escape, plunged into the river, and . . . the Major in person pursued and killed him." Hinds and his "heroic band" were lionized in Natchez for their retaliatory massacre.[4]

In November, Claiborne shifted his base to Pine Level, ten miles from St. Stephens, from which he supported more guerrilla-style raids by partisan militia on Redstick foraging parties. One of these forays resulted in the famous Canoe Fight of November 12. A force of seventy Volunteers and militia including Sam Dale set out from Fort Madison (since reoccupied by the Volunteers) and crossed the Alabama River, "intending to reconnoiter the farms" of the Tensaw métis for signs of their enemies. Starting at Dixon Bailey's plantation and moving north, the dispersed militia began encountering small groups of Redstick warriors, some in canoes on the river and others in canebrakes along the riverbank. The two disorganized forces carried on a running skirmish that culminated in a hand-to-hand fight in the middle of the Alabama River, near the mouth of Randon's Creek. According to Jeremiah Austill, one of the participants, the militia spotted "a large flat Bottomed Canoe with 11 Indians in it decending the river and nearly within gun shot. They looked imposing all painted and naked except their flaps. and a Panther Skin round the head of the chief extending down his back in a round robe   they were sitting down with their guns erect before them." Two jumped out of the canoe, when fired upon, and swam to shore. Captain Dale, Privates Austill and James Smith, and Caesar, a free black living among the Tensaw métis, climbed into a small, square-bottomed dugout canoe and gave chase. Gunfire proved ineffective because of wet priming powder and the unsteadiness of the canoes, so the combatants wrestled, stabbed at each other with knives and a bayonet, and beat one another with canoe paddles, war clubs, and gun stocks and barrels. All of the Indians were killed in this vicious melee, a remarkable outcome that buoyed the spirits of the beleaguered militia and dismayed the Redsticks (including William Weatherford) watching from the riverbank.[5]

On the following day, November 13, General Claiborne risked another tentative step northward. His small army of 500 Volunteers and militia, accompanied by 51 Choctaws under Pushmataha, moved forward slowly, crossing the Alabama River on rafts four days later. On a 150-foot-high limestone promontory, Weatherford's Bluff (named for William's brother, John), the Mississippians erected a "strong stockade, two hundred feet square, defended by three block houses and a half-moon battery, which commanded the river." General Flournoy intended this advanced post, Fort Claiborne, as a provisions depot for General Jackson, who had contemplated a march the length of the Creek nation, down the valleys of the Coosa and Alabama, to link up with Claiborne's force. By then, however, Jackson's first campaign against the Redsticks had already stalled with the general personally facing down his mutinous short-term militia.[6]

Invasion

"Brave Tennesseans! Your frontier is threatened with invasion of the savage foe! Already do they advance towards your frontier with their scalping knifes unsheathed, to butcher your wives, your children, and your helpless babes. Time is not to be lost. We must hasten to the frontier, or we will find it drenched in the blood of our fellow-citizens."[7]

With his stirring proclamation of late September, Andrew Jackson rallied and recruited thousands of fellow frontiersmen for a retaliatory invasion of the Creek nation. He and Governor Willie Blount (whose elder half-brother, Governor William Blount of the Southwest Territory, the Creeks had called "The Dirt King [*Fakke Mēkko*] . . . [for] his insatiable avidity to acquire Indian lands") had long anticipated this war. Once the Redsticks provided the provocation at Fort Mims, these two ambitious Tennesseans mobilized the largest force available to confront them. Of all the American generals facing the Redsticks, Andrew Jackson proved to be the most tenacious and most effective. Even a recently acquired dueling wound did not prevent him from joining his army of Volunteers for the march south.[8]

In the first weeks of November, elements of Jackson's Tennessee army destroyed a number of Creek towns on the upper Coosa and defeated Redstick forces at Tallusahatchee and Talladega. In the battle at Tallusahatchee, General John Coffee's troops slaughtered all of the 200 Redstick warriors opposing them, as well as many women and children, presumably feeling justified by the massacre of civilians at Fort Mims. Another 300 Redsticks died when Jackson's army broke their siege of a small pro-American Creek force trapped inside Leslie's fort at Talladega. In both instances the Tennesseans faced a poorly armed enemy; for lack of gunpowder, many warriors fought with bow and arrow, an antiquated weapon that had been no more than a Creek child's plaything for nearly a century. With these first major victories for the United States against the Redsticks, Jackson's dispatch proclaimed, "We have retaliated for the destruction of Fort Mims." However, a misguided attack two weeks later by General Hugh White's east Tennessee troops on the Hillabee towns—Upper Creeks who had been negotiating surrender terms with Jackson—gave the Redsticks their own betrayal and a rallying cry for revenge. Embittered Hillabee survivors put aside any thought of submission and fought the Americans for the rest of the war. Meanwhile, inadequate provisions and dispersal of his three-month militia units put an end to Jackson's 1813 campaign on the Redsticks' northern front.[9]

To the east, the Redsticks faced General John Floyd and his army of 950 Georgia Volunteers and militia. Benjamin Hawkins worked strenuously throughout November to enroll Creek warriors disaffected with the Redsticks in an auxiliary force to assist the Georgians. When Floyd launched a foray against those Redsticks closest to his own forward base, Fort Mitchell, near the falls of the Chattahoochee, 300 to 400 allied Creek warriors marched with him.[10]

Before daylight on November 29, "a man who had camped out that night for an early Turkey hunt" found the Georgians and Lower Creeks poised to attack the paired towns of Atasi (Dixon Bailey's birthplace). A bayonet charge supported by cannons firing grapeshot soon overwhelmed the outnumbered defenders, who lost perhaps 200 dead to the Americans' 11 killed and 54 wounded (including General Floyd). According to Lieutenant Edmund Shackelford of the Georgia Militia, "the Indians loss was considerable   they pieled in the river until the water near the bank was bloody   they had caves under the bank for the women and children & where they took shelter." In reporting his victory, Floyd invoked (as had Jackson) the memory of those slain in the Tensaw. "There is no doubt, from the scalps of the whites, and many other articles which we found at Autossee, that they were the murderers of the Garrison at Mimms' Fort." Lack of provisions for his army and his own severe wound made a sustained campaign impossible, so Floyd returned immediately to Fort Mitchell.[11]

Flournoy and Claiborne proceeded (with considerable bickering) to carry out their portion of the three-pronged invasion plan, unaware of course that a juncture with Jackson and Floyd could no longer be accomplished. Colonel Gilbert Russell and the 3rd Regiment U.S. Infantry joined Claiborne's force by late November, having crossed the Tensaw at Mims' ferry and marched up the east side of the Alabama River. Despite poor support from General Flournoy, and largely at personal expense, Claiborne managed to furnish his troops with barely enough food and munitions for a quick advance on the Holy Ground. The majority of officers in his Volunteer regiment considered these preparations still insufficient and submitted their objections to their commander. "Considering that winter and the wet season have set in; the untrodden wilderness to be traversed; the impossibility of transporting supplies for the want of roads; that most of our men are without winter clothing, shoes or blankets; that a large majority of those ordered to march will be entitled to their discharge before the expedition can be accomplished; for these and other considerations, we trust that the enterprise may be reconsidered and abandoned, declaring at the same time that be your decision what it may, we shall cheerfully obey your orders and carry out your plans." Claiborne, nevertheless, decided this was his best, maybe his last, opportunity to punish the people who had humiliated him and his regiment at Fort Mims. He had already invested his personal fortune to equip this army, however inadequately. And he now had with him the 3rd U.S. Infantry, although those professional soldiers might be withdrawn at any time. Supported by a resolute Colonel Russell, the general decided to strike, and his Volunteer officers complied "with cheerful alacrity."[12]

Claiborne's army of nearly 1,000 men began the difficult march on December 13 as the weather turned cold. Sam Moniac guided the punitive expedition across 125 miles of trackless piney uplands, avoiding trails, and delivered them within 30 miles of the Redstick settlement on December 21. Leaving their baggage at a fortified camp named Fort Deposit, the army pressed on to within 10 miles of the Holy Ground by the following afternoon. Claiborne attacked about 11:00 A.M. on the twenty-third. His force was organized in three columns to encircle the large town, with the 3rd Infantry in the center, Volunteers on the right, and militia and Choctaw auxiliaries on the left. But the Redsticks had detected their enemies' proximity early that morning when a man out fire-hunting (driving deer by burning underbrush) had crossed their path. William Weatherford and the other Redstick leaders evacuated most noncombatants to the thick forest across the river, to the north, and quickly organized a defense.

The Alabama Prophet, Josiah Francis, had protected his sacred refuge with a magical barrier to repel enemies. When the Americans approached the town unhindered, however, most of the Redsticks fled. Nevertheless, the battle lasted nearly an hour, until Weatherford's heavily outnumbered band of ten dozen men, Creeks (including his cousin McPherson) and Africans fighting behind log breastworks, fell back to the river. Weatherford, mounted on his gray pony, Arrow, made a fabled leap under fire off a 15-foot-high bluff into the river and escaped to the opposite bank. Claiborne reported 20 wounded and one dead (the unfortunate Ensign James Luckett, a signatory of the petition to abandon the expedition). Redstick losses came to about 30 killed, including 12 Africans. Claiborne's left column had failed to encircle the town, allowing most of the Redstick warriors to escape.[13]

With the vaunted prophets' stronghold of the Holy Ground at last in their hands, the famished Americans appropriated 1,200 barrels of corn from Redstick storehouses before the Choctaws plundered and set ablaze the town's 200 buildings. "In the midst of the publick square as an ornament to their new town," wrote the militia's surgeon, Dr. Neal Smith, "was histed a great number of white scalps of every description from the infant to the grey head." Most of the 300 scalps presumably came from Fort Mims. (The Creek practice of cutting a single scalp into multiple trophies led to the cumulative recovery of more scalps than there had been victims at that unfortunate post.) On Christmas Eve the army moved upriver a short distance, found and killed three Shawnee "prophets," and spent the night "shivering in our old blankets in Weatherford's corn-field." Inside Weatherford's house Claiborne's men found a letter from Governor González Manrique, sent to the Redsticks on September 29 from Pensacola, expressing his "great satisfaction" at their recent victory. The Spanish official cagily declined their offer to retake Mobile from the Americans and warned his rambunctious allies not to burn that town since the buildings, he claimed, still belonged to Spaniards. After "parching corn for breakfast, which was the only thing left to eat," the American army burned the refugee camps at Weatherford and Moniac's plantations (the latter a sizeable settlement of 60 structures) and marched back to Fort Claiborne, where the Volunteers and militia mustered out of service.[14]

Claiborne's troops had suffered greatly from hunger and exposure on this expedition. From his headquarters at Mount Vernon cantonment on January 14, 1814, he wrote: "My volunteers are returning to their homes with eight months' pay due them and almost literally naked. They have served the last three months of inclement winter weather without shoe or blankets, almost without shirts, but are still devoted to their country and properly impressed with the justice and the necessity of the war." The same could be said of their general. Claiborne had shared his men's hardships, to the detriment of his own health. But he must have been deeply disappointed in the results of his hard-won campaign; a few dozen Redstick dead hardly atoned for the hundreds killed at Fort Mims. A debilitated and depressed Ferdinand Claiborne left the frontier's defense to Colonel Russell and rode west into retirement at Soldier's Retreat, his plantation home near Natchez, to ponder how the headstrong decisions of the lamented but foolish Daniel Beasley had brought him to this pass.[15]

～

Among the documents found by Claiborne's soldiers at Weatherford's home near the Holy Ground was a letter written by John Durant, son of Sophia McGillivray and Benjamin Durant (who died inside Fort Mims), to his formally educated brother Alexander (Sandy). This exchange between two of the very few literate Redsticks gives us another rare glimpse of the anti-American Creek perspective unfiltered by our usual source, George Stiggins. The letter opens with a reference to their sister Elizabeth, wife of Peter McQueen, who probably persuaded those three Durant siblings to adopt the prophets' cause and fight the rest of their family. That extended family may have included (until the battle at Fort Mims) brother-in-law James Bailey, who attended Quaker school in Philadelphia together with Sandy Durant in an earlier, more peaceful age. John Durant wrote:

> I imbrace this oppertunity of informing that we are all well what is yet alive   your mothere is liveing yet and your Sister betsy is very desiours to go and live with you if she nowed how to get there   it is trubsome time here now in this part of world but all we lack is powder and led   we have had two powerful armes in our country this winter but they had to run back faster then they came   the Creek has been counted cowards the[y] turne out to be brave soldere   they meet enemes and put them to flight   the spanards do not seem incline to supply us   they and the inglish is one and the inglish has rote on to them to supply us but we see no supply   we cant tell the reason   no more at present but remain your
> Brother John Durant

> Postscript   if this letter should find you in Pensacola you Please to send me powder and led   6 pound of Powder and of led[16]

Those two powerful armies of Generals Jackson and Floyd had inflicted severe losses on the Redsticks. Nevertheless, this confidential communication from the heart of Creek country suggests no sense of inevitable defeat at the hands of the Americans. Durant's letter, instead, conveys a grim determination to defend his own family and considerable collective pride in having done so well to this point. Conspicuously missing from this letter, or other later Redstick accounts of the war, is any mention of disillusionment with the prophets' magical defenses, which provoked much ridicule from their American opponents. While the influence of prophets did gradually fade among the Redsticks, commitment to Creek religion and militant opposition to American domination did not diminish. They would fight their own battles, but clearly expected Spain and Britain to provide the ammunition they so badly needed. In fact, from his station at the mouth of the Apalachicola River, Sandy Durant probably hoped to intercept British supply ships cruising along the Gulf coast.[17]

Redstick leaders pleaded repeatedly with Governor González Manrique for ammunition. In early December, William Weatherford and High-head Jim reportedly "demanded to have an audience and a Tete a tete with his Excellency," which yielded "three horse loads of powder and lead." Those meager supplies, and additional small quantities of gunpowder and shot smuggled from Spanish Florida, enabled Weatherford's outnumbered warriors to put up their brief defense of Holy Ground later that month, and for Redstick forces elsewhere in the Creek nation to launch three bold attacks against invading American armies (Figure 18).[18]

~

Claiborne's withdrawal from the Holy Ground gave the Redsticks less than a month's respite. General Jackson raised another army of west Tennessee Volunteers, which marched from their base at Fort Strother on the Coosa River in mid-January toward the confluence of Emuckfau Creek and the upper Tallapoosa River, where the Redsticks were building breastworks across a neck of land called Cholocco Litabixee (*corakko letvpekse,* literally "horse foot"), Horseshoe Bend. The Tennessee encampment three miles from Emuckfau was attacked at dawn on January 22, 1814, but high casualties soon forced the Redsticks to break off the fight. When General Coffee moved forward to destroy the enemy town, the Redsticks reappeared and drove the poorly trained American force back to their camp. Jackson decided to withdraw to Fort Strother but was again assaulted by Hillabees and other Redsticks two days later while his army crossed Enitachopco Creek. This time most of the militia panicked and broke, and a complete rout was only narrowly averted. Jackson portrayed both battles as victories in reports to superiors, claiming 189 Redsticks dead compared to his 20 killed and 75 wounded. Years later Redstick veterans of the fight at Enitachopco told historian Albert James Pickett "they whipped *Captain* Jackson, and run him to the Coosa river."[19]

In coordination with Jackson's second invasion from the north, General Floyd began his second advance from the east with 1,100 militia and about 600 Creek allies. The Georgians quickly reached the burned ruins of Atasi and began to fortify an encampment nearby, on the west side of Calebee Creek. To repulse this threat the Redsticks gathered at least 1,300 men, their largest force of the war, led by Paddy Walsh, High-head Jim, William Weatherford, and Billy McGillivray. Weatherford proposed to infiltrate the American camp with a few hundred warriors before dawn and kill the white officers, followed by a general attack on the ill-trained militia—a modified version of the nearly successful Shawnee plan of attack on General Harrison's camp at Tippecanoe in 1811. Instead, the Redsticks adopted Walsh's alternative to attack the encampment on all sides, and an affronted Weatherford apparently did not participate in the

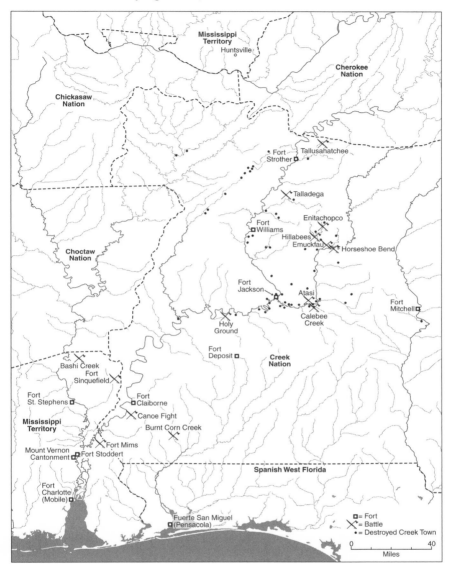

Fig. 18. Battlefields, forts, and Creek settlements destroyed in the Redstick War, 1813–1814.

battle. In any case, the Redsticks nearly prevailed, since night fighting less-ened the Americans' advantage in firearms and cannons. The early morning assault on January 27 completely surprised the sleeping Georgians, who de-fended themselves with bayonets against tomahawks and war clubs. At dawn, Floyd's two-gun artillery battery came into play and drove the Redsticks off.

His official report claimed 49 Redstick dead (including the prophet High-head Jim) to 26 American and Creek auxiliaries killed and 147 wounded.[20]

James A. Tait, a soldier in General Floyd's army (and no relation, apparently, to either David Taitt or David Tate), jotted down his impressions of the allied Creeks fighting alongside the Americans. When battle seemed imminent, the "friendly Indians," as he called them, blackened their faces "at some burnt lightwood stumps and logs . . . to exhibit to their enemies as ugly an appearance as possible." At the battle's conclusion, they "exercised great barbarity upon the bodies of our enemies slain, . . . riped them open, cut their heads to pieces, took out the heart of one, which was borne along in savage triumph by the perpetrators; and strange to tell, cut off the private parts of others. What bestial conduct," Tait exclaimed in his journal.[21]

Despite the bravado of his Creek auxiliaries, Floyd's army had been badly mauled and he fell back quickly to Fort Mitchell, leaving the Redstick homeland once again uncontested. In February, Colonel Russell briefly led his 3rd U.S. Infantry and a contingent of Chickasaws and Choctaws up the Alabama River toward refugee camps on the Cahaba River. He succeeded in burning several abandoned Redstick towns, but supply lines again proved inadequate and his men suffered greatly from hunger. Only by eating their horses were they able to reach their base at Fort Claiborne. During this lull between major American campaigns, partisan warfare continued in the South where followers of Josiah Francis, the Alabama Prophet, harassed any settlers bold enough to reestablish their homes in that region.[22]

By mid-March, General Jackson had solved his provisioning problem (by transporting supplies by water rather than overland) and had acquired the 39th U.S. Infantry regiment and thousands of new Tennessee Volunteers for his third campaign into the Creek nation. With about 500 Creek and Cherokee auxiliaries, his army totaled over 3,000 men, the largest force to confront the Redsticks. Once more his objective was the stronghold near Emuckfau Creek, which Jackson had since learned was called Tohopeka, a refugee town protected by strong fortifications across the Horseshoe Bend where the Okfuskee war leader Menawa had assembled about 1,000 Upper Creek warriors and their families. The American army followed the road blazed in January from the Coosa River and arrived opposite the Redstick barricades on March 27. Jackson deployed General Coffee's mounted troops and Indian allies to surround the bend so the Redsticks could not escape as they had at the Holy Ground and Atasi. After an ineffectual artillery bombardment of several hours failed to do much damage to the Redsticks' fortification, the 39th U.S. Infantry and Tennessee Volunteer troops stormed the barricade and killed most of its defenders. Jackson's army lost 49 killed and 153 wounded. His officers counted 557 dead Redsticks on the battlefield (and supposedly directed their troops to "cut off the tip of each dead Indian's nose," to assure an accurate tally), while Coffee estimated another 250 to 300 shot trying to swim the Tallapoosa. As many as 200 escaped, most badly wounded, and 350 were taken prisoner, all but three being women and children. Just as the battle at Fort Mims had degenerated into a massacre, so too did the battle at the Horseshoe.[23]

In July 1813 the Redsticks had boasted of perhaps 3,000 warriors; by April 1814 at least 1,600 had fallen in battle and uncounted others had been severely wounded. Avenging American armies had wrought a terrible retribution on the prophets' followers. Yet the suffering did not end with the fall of Tohopeka. Remembering the Hillabees' betrayal, few Redsticks surrendered immediately. Instead thousands hid in the swamps and canebrakes of their devastated homeland, awaiting discovery by the American armies that now scoured the Creek nation, while hundreds more slipped south into Spanish Florida where they would join their relatives the Seminoles and continue the war against Americans intermittently for decades, through two generations.[24]

Redstick Surrender

To quash remaining Redstick resistance in the Creek nation, Jackson marched his victorious army down the right bank of the Tallapoosa, in limited coordination with Colonel Homer Milton, who swept the left bank of the lower river with his South Carolina militia (which had replaced Floyd's exhausted Georgians). They met at the head of the Alabama River on April 17 and built Fort Jackson on a high peninsula between the Coosa and Tallapoosa, near the rivers' confluence. From this earthen citadel detachments of Americans and allied Indians fanned out to contact and encourage surviving Redsticks to surrender. All of the Upper Creek towns—nearly 60 in number—had been destroyed in the course of the war, depriving 8,000 Redsticks of their homes, as well as their stores of food and clothing (Figure 19). Starvation now threatened those who had evaded foreign armies and endured the sickly damp of an especially cold southern winter. Forlorn refugees, mostly noncombatant women and children, streamed into camps established by the Carolina troops—522 by early May at Fort Jackson alone, 1,700 more at two other locations—lured by rations shipped up the Alabama River by Colonel Russell's 3rd U.S. Infantry.

Near the end of April, William Weatherford walked into General Jackson's

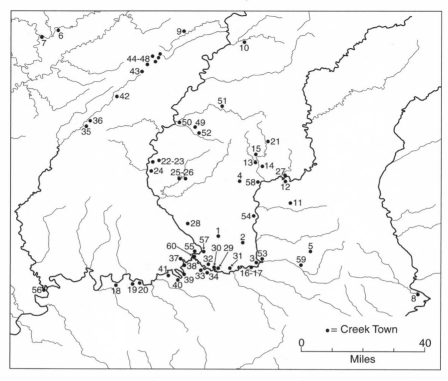

Fig. 19. Creek settlements destroyed or abandoned in the Redstick War, 1813–1814 (locations approximate).

Destroyed:

1. Hatchechubba, July 1813
2. Kialigee, July 1813
3. Tuckaubatchee, July 1813
4. Thlothlegulgau (Fish Ponds), July 1813
5. Chattucchufaulee (Peter McQueen's town), August 1813
6. Small village above Black Warrior towns, October 1813
7. Black Warrior town, 50 houses, October 1813
8. Yuchi town, October 3, 1813
9. Littafuches, October 28, 1813
10. Tallusahatchee, November 3, 1813
11. Mad Warrior's village, 11 houses, November 16, 1813
12. Nuyaka, 85 houses, November 17, 1813
13. Okfuscooche (Little Okfuskee), 30 houses, November 1813
14. Auchenaulgau (Genalga), 93 houses, November 1813
15. Hillabee towns, November 18, 1813

16. Atasi, 200 houses, November 29, 1813
17. Town adjoining Atasi, 200 houses, November 29, 1813
18. Ikanachaki (Holy Ground), 200 houses, December 23, 1813
19. Town at Weatherford's plantation, December 24, 1813
20. Town at Moniac's plantation, 60 houses, December 24, 1813
21. Enitachopco, 25 houses, January 20, 1814
22. Woccoccoie (1), March 21, 1814
23. Woccoccoie (2), March 21, 1814
24. Unchaula, March 22, 1814
25. Wehoofka (1, Muddy Creek town), March 23, 1814
26. Wehoofka (2), March 23, 1814
27. Tohopeka (Horseshoe Bend), 50 houses, March 27, 1814
28. Wewocau (Falling Creek), April 11, 1814
29. Fusihatchee (Bird Creek town), April 13, 1814

30. Columi, April 13, 1814
31. Hoithlewaulee (Cluwallee), April 14, 1814
32. Ecunhatke (White Ground), April 15, 1814
33. Mucklassa, April 15, 1814
34. Sausanogee (Shawnee town), April 15, 1814
35. Lower Penoolau, 28 houses, April 29, 1814
36. Upper Penoolau, 12 houses, April 29, 1814
37. Coosada, April–May 1814

38. Ecunchata, April–May 1814
39. Tawasa, April–May 1814
40. Pauwacta, April–May 1814
41. Autauga, April–May 1814
42. Occhooco, May 1, 1814
43. Tullavaligau (Mad town), May 1, 1814
44–48. Five unnamed towns, May 3, 1814

Abandoned:
49. Aubecooche, August 1813
50. Coosa, August 1813
51. Eufaula, August 1813
52. Nauchee, August 1813
53. Tallassee, August 1813
54. Hookchoi, July 1814

55. Hookchoioochee, July 1814
56. Kahaubah, July 1814
57. Ocheobofau, July 1814
58. Okfuskee, July 1814
59. Opilthlucco, July 1814
60. Taskigi, July 1814

References: Bassett, ed., *Correspondence of Andrew Jackson*, 1:334–35, 341, 457, 500; Eleazer Early, *Map of Georgia*; Grant, *Letters, Journals and Writings*, 654–55, 659; Christian Limbaugh, Fort Mitchell, July 6, 1814, "Consolidated Return of the distressed Indians," Andrew Jackson Papers (roll 66, series 5, 3:1291–92), Library of Congress; Lowrie and Clarke, *ASP, Indian Affairs*, 1:847, 850, 854, 858; Mauelshagen and Davis, eds., "Partners in the Lord's Work," 11–13; John Melish, *Map of Alabama*; Nuñez, ed., "Creek Nativism," 150; Palmer, *Historical Register*, 2:339, 341, 344–46; Sanders, *History of the Indian Wars*, 193–95; [Tatum], General Jackson's campaign against the Creek Indians, 1813 & 1814, RG 77, NARA; Samuel P. Waldo, *Memoirs of Andrew Jackson*, 69–70, 85–86, 102. Map and captions based on Waselkov and Wood, "The Creek War of 1813–1814," 11–14.

camp to surrender himself and his people, who were sheltering on Moniac's Island not far downstream. Weatherford knew his name had become irrevocably connected with the Fort Mims massacre in the minds of Americans. As he approached Jackson's marquee, the likelihood that this general who had fought hardest to crush the Redsticks would order his execution must have seemed a near certainty. The numerous accounts of his surrender agree on little, but this much seems certain. He arrived alone and evidently unafraid; he said he tried to prevent the massacre of women and children at Fort Mims; now that his warriors were all dead, he would fight no more; and he pleaded for the safe conduct of the Redstick women and children in his care. After a brief private conversation, Jackson spared Weatherford's life. The general must have taken an immediate liking to his opponent, presumably (although he never documented his reasons in writing) because he admired Weatherford's forthrightness and bravery. Here was a principled soldier, defeated but not humbled, who deserved honorable treatment at the hands of his conqueror. There is no doubt Jackson could have responded very differently. Four years later he ordered two unrepentant Redstick leaders, Josiah Francis and Neamarthla Mico, unceremoniously hanged as agents of the British when they stumbled unexpectedly into his control. Jackson must have seen characteristics he admired in the plainspoken Weatherford, who portrayed himself as a patriot fighting for his people. And, in the end, magnanimity toward a noble enemy brought low always reflects well on the victor.[25]

Weatherford's actions and whereabouts for the next several months have remained unclear to the present day. Historian Albert James Pickett stated, "He took no further part in the war, except to influence his warriors to surrender," then left the territory until animosity toward him subsided. Thomas Woodward recollected Weatherford had borrowed a horse from Barney O'Riley, the express rider, and assisted with a hunt for stray cattle to feed the native civilians collected around Fort Jackson. His romantic (and unreliable) biographers A. B. Meek and George Cary Eggleston both thought Weatherford remained at Fort Jackson until the ratification of a new treaty with the Creeks in August, then accompanied Jackson to his Nashville home, the Hermitage, where he remained as the general's guest "for nearly a year." This last anecdote seems baseless, but abundant evidence documents Weatherford's cooperation with the Americans to end the Redstick war in the Creek nation.[26]

In late May, Colonel John A. Pearson and his command of 300 men from the North Carolina and South Carolina Militias swept the central Alabama River Valley south of the Cahaba for Redsticks. Before setting out, Pearson enlisted "about seventy" former Redsticks, "out of the emmense number at Fort Jackson," who agreed to follow his orders and not plunder or kill prisoners "or those who might voluntarily surrender." Among them was "Bill Weatherford," who so impressed the colonel that he placed him "at the head of the Red Warriors." This mixed force persuaded nearly 300 Redsticks to surrender, including the "Cun-sa-da [Coosada] King, and 23 warriors, and 52 Women & Children." Pearson's men chased but could not catch one forlorn family, which abandoned their canoe containing the half-consumed legs and thigh of a colt.

Pearson demanded his refugees give up "the Negroes which they had taken at Fort Mims." Within a few days they retrieved 35 African women and children from the woods, including Milley who had seen her owner, Reuben Dyer, killed at Fort Mims. According to the colonel, "The Negro fellows taken at same time were all put to death by the Indians, shortly after that affair." About his métis lieutenant, Pearson concluded the "evil report" about Weatherford "has said more than he deserves. He does not deny that he fought, and that he fought desperately too, but he solemnly avers that he never, knowingly, or intentionally, hurt still less killed a woman or child during the War. He says that at Fort Mims he killed, he believes, as many *Men* as any other man there but that he never entered the part of the Fort where the women were."[27]

Thus began the American rehabilitation of William Weatherford—and his vilification by the remaining Redsticks and their British supporters. Weatherford's concern that Pearson not think him responsible for the massacre at Fort Mims tends to confirm that element of his surrender speech, for which there exists no definitive record.[28]

His name turns up again in an anonymous spy's mid-July report from Pensacola to the commander of a British naval squadron, which had at last arrived in the Gulf. A detachment of dragoons "headed by Colonel Carson, and joined by Wm Weatherford an Indian Chief, are pursuing the Creek Indians and are Killing them wherever they meet them. . . . they have also attackd a new Indian settlement called Coneta, and Killed all the Indians they could lay hands on, have taken what Women & Children could be found."[29] These little-known accounts indicate how thoroughly Weatherford threw himself into the task of bringing the Redstick War to a close. Carson and Weatherford's foray into Spanish territory undoubtedly colored the British spy's interpretation of events. Americans killing resisting Redsticks in Spanish West Florida might well strike impartial observers as a violation of international law. Pearson's report of his search for Redsticks in Mississippi Territory, on the other hand, describes how the Americans urged enemy men to surrender (as 64 did to his force), only resorting to fighting those who would not do so. These accounts do not necessarily conflict; they may merely reflect drastically different viewpoints. In either case, there can be no doubt that William Weatherford exercised his considerable skills and influence on behalf of the Americans during the last months of the war.

$\sim$

With the collapse of Redstick resistance to the American armies that converged on the Creek heartland, the numerous captives taken at Fort Mims—métis and African women and children, by and large—awaited opportunities for redemption or escape. Simple survival during a harsh winter had been a struggle. Now, with the remaining Redsticks dispersed in small bands in the woods, with little to eat, the captives found freedom still elusive. As the Americans advanced on the Redsticks' last major stronghold at Horseshoe Bend, Vicey McGirth, Polly Jones, and their eight children had been moved from Wewocau to Hickory Ground. When their captor and protector Sanota died fighting Andrew Jackson's soldiers, the women slipped away with their children to seek their own way home.[30]

Mrs. McGirth and her five girls walked home, 150 miles to the Tensaw. Her family's remembrance of their ordeal concludes the story.

Arriving here with her children she found all the country deserted. she placed her children in a rude hut constructed by two hands and one day while grubbing [sweet] potatoes, was discovered by Capt Blues spy company & captured   Telling the soldiers her name they informed her that her husband was alive & in Mobile. They placed her & her children all of whom were naked & nearly starved to death, upon pack Horses & reaching Blakely embarked them in canoes & it was on this occasion that [Zachariah] McGirth saw them at Mobile. . . . a friend accosted him one day in the streets of Mobile & told him there were people at the wharf who wished to see him. going down there, he saw in a canoe a woman & seven [more likely, five] children . . . he was asked if he knew them. He replied no. He again examined them without recognition. The woman now threw off her blanket & exposed her face & person.[31]

Having survived "the smoking ruins of Fort Mims," half a year's captivity, and an epic trek across a war-ravaged landscape, the McGirths were reunited by Captain Uriah Blue's company of mounted Choctaws. They had endured trying times, tragic times. The future of the Creeks, métis or not, would be no less difficult.

After nearly nine months of misery, Americans settlers and slaves emerged from frontier forts and refugee camps to reclaim their farms and a sense of normalcy. All the same, some would miss the intensity of life experienced in the little forts in wartime. Young Margaret Eades had celebrated her fifteen-year-old sister's wedding inside Carney's stockade. All the while, "the young folks" had been "courting and making love" (in adolescent defiance of mortality itself, as youth has done in all wars). Now, with the Redstick threat receding, old and young alike "returned joyfully to their houses." As an aged widow of Jeremiah Austill, Eades thought back to those remarkable days of her childhood, to "the last of [Eighteen] Fourteen," when "all the people were gay, money was plenty, and the people were pouring in by thousands."[32] Although a conquering spirit had momentarily reclaimed this land for the Indians, those countless new immigrants, Americans and Africans, could no longer be restrained by war clubs and a Prophet's visions.

9

Remembering Fort Mims

For most Americans living through the War of 1812, our country's second struggle for independence from Britain must have seemed one long string of military setbacks punctuated by outright disasters: Fort Dearborn, Detroit, River Raisin, Fort Mims, Chrysler's Farm, Lewiston, Lundy's Lane, Bladensburg, Washington, D.C. A few inspiring victories—the USS *Constitution* vs. HMS *Guerrière,* Put-in-Bay on Lake Erie, Horseshoe Bend, Plattsburg, Fort McHenry, and, most spectacular of all, New Orleans—retrieved the nation's honor and brought the war to a close as a virtual stalemate. Today most of those American successes continue to resonate in the popular conscience, while the failures, apart from the burning of the White House, are largely forgotten. Yet the destruction of Fort Mims, together with other events characterized at the time as Indian massacres (Fort Dearborn, River Raisin), arguably had a greater impact on the course of American history than any success of American arms in that conflict. Even though well-educated modern Americans may remember a fact or two about the Redstick War, after two centuries the emotional shock inflicted on the national psyche by the Redstick Creeks at Fort Mims has long dissipated. We have forgotten the astonishment and outrage—equivalent in intensity to our own anguish on December 7, 1941, or September 11, 2001—elicited by the first reports from Fort Mims. The long-lasting effect of this distant memory, however, was for Fort Mims to become one of our foundational myths (much as the Alamo did in Texas). That memory of the massacre of innocents on the Tensaw forever served to cast Indians in the role of savages, and to justify the removal of the Creeks and other Indians from the Southeast and the appropriation of their lands by white Americans.

⁓

Considering the impediments to communication typical of that era, and the near isolation of wartime Mobile (separated from most of the United States by the intervening Creek nation), news of the disaster at Fort Mims naturally took some time to cross the country. Word reached New Orleans relatively rapidly, by September 6 via coastal packet. An extra edition of the *Richmond Inquirer* carried the story in Virginia's capital on October 9. Officials and newspaper editors in New York City and Washington only learned in mid-October of the crisis on the southwestern frontier. All of these initial published accounts, and innumerable variations printed elsewhere, derived from letters and reports written by a few American officials—Judge Harry Toulmin, Indian agent Benjamin Hawkins, and Generals Thomas Flournoy and Ferdinand Claiborne, four men who usually disagreed vehemently with each other about virtually everything. But their public assertions on the nature of the Fort Mims catastrophe could hardly have been more similar. In every case, articles read by the American public beyond the borders of sparsely populated Mississippi Territory emphasized two critical "facts": (1) the Creek Indians committed a massacre at Fort Mims, and (2) white Americans, civilians as well as soldiers, had been the principal victims.[1]

Among the most influential early reports was Judge Toulmin's letter to the editor of the *Raleigh Register,* which numerous papers across the country copied or excerpted. Toulmin skillfully crafted his account to elicit unequivocal support from the American public by downplaying the key role of the Creek métis, whose involvement in the preceding Creek civil war had, of course, precipitated the Redstick attack on Fort Mims. Explaining to distant readers the ethnic complexity of the Tensaw frontier, Toulmin certainly realized, would have diluted his essential message to white America. Instead, he dispensed with nuance and characterized the attackers simply as "Indians." When he did mention the Tensaw métis (for their heroic efforts during the battle and for the assistance they might provide in the coming conflict), he referred to them as "half breeds" living in the Creek nation, not as the Creek Indians they and the Redsticks both knew them to be. In the immediate aftermath of the Fort Mims debacle, Toulmin and other American leaders on the scene still feared a more general war. Would the Choctaws and Cherokees join the Redsticks? Did this attack signal a slave uprising? Were the British about to invade the Gulf coast in coordination with Indian and African allies? In such a climate of fear and uncertainty, Toulmin concluded his epistle to the *Raleigh Register* with this plea to white American men: "our only hope for aid, or rather for revenge at some distant day, rests on the energy of our fellow citizens of the United States."[2]

This simplified message resonated across the nation, but especially in the western states and territories where large Indian populations still confronted American expansion. For instance, when news of "the late horrible massacre on the Mobile" reached Tennessee, the legislature spontaneously passed an act "To repel the invasion of the state of Tennessee by the Creek Indians" (an expansive interpretation of the attack on Fort Mims!) "and to afford relief to the citizens of the Mississippi territory."[3] The battle at Fort Mims had become instantly mythologized as an exemplar of Indian perfidy. That myth, distilled to the rallying cry "Remember Fort Mims," would become a staple of American public education for generations. Stripped of all its fascinating complexity, that myth also became ingrained in history texts as an antecedent to (and, implicitly, an excuse and rationale for) the eventual forced removal of Indians from the eastern United States.

Historical and Literary Frontiers

Notes on the War in the South, one of the first histories of the Redstick War, appeared in print in 1819 (though written before the larger War of 1812 had ended). Hardly a dispassionate chronicle of events, Nathaniel Claiborne penned this slim volume primarily to vindicate his much-maligned late uncle, General Ferdinand Claiborne. But, secondarily, he hoped to influence the ongoing debate about one of the country's great political challenges. What to do about the Indians occupying lands within the bounds of the United States? From his vantage point in Virginia (a state which, a century earlier, had relegated the Native Americans within its borders to a few inconspicuous reservations), Claiborne had long supported the federal government's program "to reclaim" the Indians "from the savage to the civilized state." He admitted a few of his fellow Americans "had always maintained the opinion that the idea of civilizing the savages was wild and chymerical," but he had opposed such talk until the "fall of Fort Mimms resounded through the Union." Now he and other like-minded easterners were "constrained reluctantly to acknowledge, that facts seem to countenance this opinion" opposite to their own. Yet, Claiborne argued, the Creeks' possession of so much land "was a principal reason why the efforts of thirty years to civilize them had failed." Suddenly stripped of half their country, the Creeks must now necessarily adopt American ways, if only they were given the resources to do so. Claiborne concluded with an appeal to reject calls for Indian removal. "What! remove them beyond the Mississippi to become extinct in the wars that will follow between them and their neighbors, and the tribes of savages by whom they will be environed! No, let them occupy the land of their fathers, but let them do it in peace. While we provide for our own safety, let us not overlook theirs. Our fathers bequeathed us a reputation clouded by no act of dishonor. The people of the present day, have demonstrated to the world, that they merited the legacy, and they will never stain it by an act of injustice."[4]

Claiborne's little tract neatly summarized the essential arguments of a complex debate that would rage with increasing passion over the next two decades. Meanwhile, migration shifted the demographic center of the United States steadily westward, and with that population redistribution came a rise in support for Indian removal as national policy, represented in the political arena by the evolution of Andrew Jackson's Democratic party from the Republican party of Thomas Jefferson. In the debate over Indian removal, American public attention focused most intently upon the Cherokees and their battles in the press, in Congress, and in the courts for the right to remain in their eastern homeland. But the legacy of Fort Mims and the Redstick War continued to be invoked by proponents of removal, until removal was accomplished (essentially) in the 1830s.[5]

Once the majority of Indians had been forcibly relocated to western territories, they became more abstraction than reality to most white Americans. With few opportunities any longer to meet and know Indians resident in the East, white American novelists and historians idealized their former neighbors and sometime-opponents as noble but tragic failures destined from the first to lose the struggle for North America and now fated for extinction. The tendency to romanticize defeated or marginalized peoples arose in part from a racialized view of humanity (privileging whites over all others) that dominated American literature and history throughout the nineteenth century and much of the twentieth. Since Asians were initially excluded from the United States, and Indians had been rendered "invisible," eulogies read over a "lost" race served to divert attention from the Indians who remained and avoided discussion of the other great racial issue in America. In the nation's literary treatment of Indians, one can detect much displacement of guilt over the enslavement of blacks.[6]

The sequential re-creation of the "American Indian"—from military adversary to political conundrum to romantic racialized paragon—is exemplified in a series of popular literary works set in the Redstick War. The first published imprint known from the region now called Alabama is a pamphlet-long satire, in verse, by Lewis Sewall about Colonel James Caller's 1813 skirmish with the Redstick Creeks at Burnt Corn Creek. Printed in St. Stephens in 1815, *The Last Campaign of Sir John Falstaff the II; or, The Hero of the Burnt-Corn Battle, A Heroi-Comic Poem,* lampoons the militia officer blamed by many in Mississippi Territory for provoking the Redstick attack on Fort Mims. Sewall mercilessly ridiculed his political enemy by portraying the quixotic Caller as "Sir John Falstaff the II," who imagines the trees of the forest to be "Savage foes" haunting his ignominious battlefield retreat.

But, muse, adhere to fact, not speculation;
And tell how JOHN in his great tribulation,
With pores chinck'd up, and courage pent within,
Stoutly resolv'd a combat to begin
With a young *pawpaw,* bold *Muscogee scout*
Which near his cavern had been *posted out:*
Doubtless a *Mingo* of the enemy;
Or, if a *private,* still a *warrior tree.*
This with drawn sword, in haste he did assail,
Nor could its spongy-texture ought avail.
Beneath his blows, which loudly did resound,
It groans, and bends, and tumbles on the ground—
"Lie there, fell monster!" manfully he said,
"Your *carcass* there, and here your sever'd *head?*"

Only at the end of Sir John II's indignities in the woods do actual Indians appear, rendered in serious tone to emphasize, by contrast, the tragic consequences of the anti-hero's bumblings.

Mean time the foe collected all his force,
And for the Fort at Mimm's bent his course;
Where women, children, hapless aged men,
Unfortunately coop'd up in a pen;
Were deem'd fit subjects to allay the rage
Engender'd by the *war* which JOHN *did* wage.
Impell'd by fury, they the Fort assail;
Nor could the best resistance ought avail.

Tho' all was done that valor could perform,
The Fort was carried by a *furious* storm.

There hoary age lay *mangled* on the ground,
And pregnant women, RIPP'd UP, there were found.
Here bleeding infants dash'd against the stones,
Their forms disfigur'd, broken all their bones:
Then thrown in heaps, with yells, a fire they raise,
And slaughtered bodies *disappear in blaze*!

Sewall wrote for readers who may well have known persons who died at Fort Mims. For friends and acquaintances of victims of Indian warfare, Redstick warriors were no hypothetical abstraction. Sewall's perspective is entirely that of an American settler; he betrays no indication he knew any Indians personally, and we see no hint of an Indian voice or perspective in his work. They remain two-dimensional images, handy for ridiculing political opponents but unlikely candidates for assimilation into American society. Even so, from Sewall onward the Redstick War would loom, in the words of literary critic Philip Beidler, "as the dominant, even obsessive theme of antebellum writing, both historical and literary," in Alabama.[7]

By the 1830s, with Indian removal imminent, the first novel appeared with a Redstick War theme, inspired by the wildly popular books of James Fenimore Cooper, whose *The Pioneers* (1823) and *The Last of the Mohicans* (1826) established the new genre of American historical novel. Professor Beidler identifies *The Lost Virgin of the South* (1832) as the first romantic novel set in the Redstick War. The author of this obscure fictional work remains uncertain; possibilities include an itinerant Baptist preacher, Rev. Michael Smith, or the publisher Wiley Conner. The book's heroine, Calista Ward, is rescued from a shipwreck by the Seminole warrior Ropaugh and his family, who find their way to Tallusahatchee in time for the attack on that Redstick town by General Jackson's army of Tennesseans. Ropaugh dies and Calista is swept up in a plot of gothic complexity, including several life- and virtue-threatening perils at the hands of white soldiers. She disappears in the confusion of battle at Horseshoe Bend, after which William Weatherford delivers his surrender speech to Jackson in one of several cameo appearances. The heroine reappears in (and perseveres through) a second volume involving pirates in a European setting. But the more important American volume introduces some elements of characterization that become standard in many later novels of the Old Southwest. Most important, according to Beidler, is the inclusion "of an actual mixed-blood hero of romantic stature," in this case William Weatherford, and other sympathetic Indian protagonists (Ropaugh and Calista's Creek mother Camera)—not authentic Indians, but characters socially and politically challenging to American readers nonetheless. By the 1830s, "mixed blood" leaders of the Cherokees and other Indian nations were increasingly denigrated as "Indian" poseurs out for political gain, so literary recognition of a métis as Creek is particularly significant.[8]

Perhaps inspired by popular interest in *The Lost Virgin of the South,* Lewis Sewall published a revised and expanded version of his Caller satire in 1833. Appended to that epic poem in the volume, *The Miscellaneous Poems of Lewis Sewall,* is a short work entitled "The Canoe Fight," the first published version of what must already have become a staple of Alabama oral history.[9]

American Lyrics, by Charles L. S. Jones, appeared the following year in Mobile, containing several tales of the War of 1812. In contrast to the humorous, vituperative satire of Sewall, Jones specialized in melancholy verse. Some had patriotic local themes, such as his Sapphic odes to the defenders of Fort Bowyer and to the state of Alabama. He evidently wrote most of *American Lyrics* during the 1820s while teaching at St. Stephens Academy, where Jones undoubtedly had many opportunities to absorb Redstick War lore from his neighbors. A brief extract from "A Souvenir of Fort Mimms" will suffice.

And, sudden, the loud sounding war-whoop, on the ear,
    With the rifle's dread dissonance blending,
Mark'd destruction's fell agents, of scowling aspect, near,
    And their fate on the contest depending.

Depending, not long; for the open gateway gave,
    (Though despair fill'd its access, and breasted
The shock of the foeman, that, like a mountain wave,
    Pour'd its force where Hope lingering rested,)

An entrance: since vain against numbers is the pow'r
    Or the effort that fain would oppose them;
For the death-angel gloom'd o'er the struggle of the hour,
    Leaving nought but the slain there to close them.[10]

Literary taste long ago left behind Jones' convoluted poetic fashion. Yet the reading public of the United States and Britain in the 1830s clamored for this kind of labored melancholia. Poems like "A Souvenir" kept alive in the popular conscience the essential story of Fort Mims, in its simplified, mythologized form, as an Indian massacre of whites.

∼

Jones' poem alludes to another increasingly popular element of the evolving myth, the role of drink and other forms of dissipation as contributing factors in the fall of Fort Mims. None of the original battle accounts mention drunkenness among the garrison or the civilian refugees (Figure 20). But American incredulity at the outcome—the destruction of a fully manned fortification at the hands of Indian opponents no better armed than the Americans—led many to consider the possibility of moral failings as the cause of the fort occupants' ill-preparedness. Rather than credit the Redsticks for their prophet-inspired victory, many Americans (battle participants as well as others) looked for immorality in the behavior of their fellow citizens to explain the terrible punishment they had received. Stories soon circulated of Major Beasley's fondness for drink, evident to James Cornells at the very moment before the battle. However, Charles Jones referred in his poem to a broader charge of general licentiousness leveled at the people of the Tensaw.

> All, careless, unarm'd, and, with wassail rout opprest,
> > Its tenants, their revelries keeping,
> Deem'd the red savage foemen, distant far, at rest,
> > In their wilds, round their watch-fires, were sleeping.

Jones attributed the Redsticks' success to nothing more (or less) than the settlers' own "riot madness" and their ensuing "sport-lengthen'd slumbers." Atonement carried a heavy price.

Generations of preachers would recite the parable of Samuel Mims, how he and other former "Indian countrymen" had rejected Protestant teachings and followed a misguided path that led finally to their destruction. According to late-nineteenth-century Methodist historian Anson West, "Samuel Mims . . . associated too intimately with savage life, he had conformed too closely to the manners and customs of barbarous tribes, to have any special appreciation of the Christian religion. Not to speak of worse things, his house was 'a resort of mirth,' a noted place where fiddlers and dancers oft assembled, and spent their time moving in measured step to the sound of musical instruments." Although

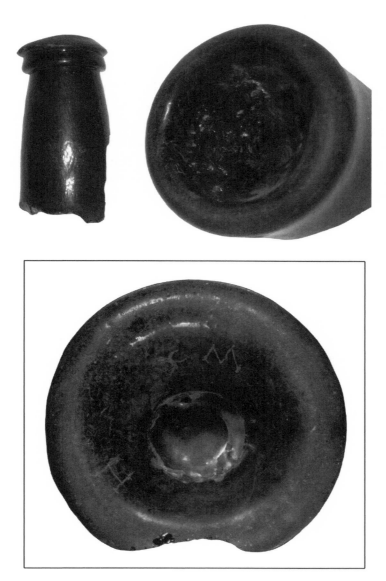

Fig. 20. Wine bottle fragments from archaeological excavations at Fort Mims (3-inch diameter base). Scratched into the bottle base are the initials "HM," possibly those of Captain Hatton Middleton, Mississippi Territorial Volunteers (courtesy of the Alabama Historical Commission, Montgomery).

the itinerant Methodist preacher Matthew Sturdevant did visit "this 'the most spacious house' in the country" during his proselytizing tour of the region in 1807, "he did not succeed in making it a house of prayer. He was unable to exorcise the dancing spirit. The young folks were dancing in that very same house the day that Weatherford and his savage warriors burned it to the ground and massacred its inmates." Since Sturdevant had failed to make a single convert in the Tensaw in 1807, his successors seem to have looked upon the destruction of that hedonistic district with some vindication.[11]

While Protestant evangelists overtly attributed the settlers' bad behavior to time spent among the Indians by some leading figures, such as Samuel Mims, their true grievance lay with the influence of Roman Catholicism in the Tensaw. When Mims and other early American settlers moved to the region in the 1780s, this had been Spanish territory. Spanish officials tolerated Protestant immigrants, but only Catholic priests could minister to the settlers. As a consequence, some *Americanos* converted, among them Samuel Mims. The parish priest in Mobile had solemnized Mims' marriage to Hannah Rains, and five of their children were baptized as Roman Catholics.

This root cause of Protestant hostility toward the residents of Tensaw is best documented in interviews with early residents conducted during the 1840s by historian Albert James Pickett. Hiram Mounger, who came to the region in 1791, told Pickett the Spaniards allowed no religion "but the Catholic," and that consequently "fidling dancing & horse racing was common." Similarly, Pickett heard from old-timer George S. Gaines that "People would collect from all parts of the settlements and dance there [at the Mims house] for several day then go the Duns Thompsons and other Houses. They were fine dancers having been associated much with the Creoles of Mobile." As an afterthought, Gaines recalled, "Taffia & wine were [their] principal drinks." Frontier evangelists read the tale of Fort Mims as divine retribution and a warning for others who might be tempted by frolics and spirits. For the most dedicated, earthly battles between whites and Indians were, in a sense, a distraction that obscured a higher concern for eternal salvation.[12]

The Redstick War Imagined

With the exile of most Indians from the eastern United States largely accomplished by 1840, American literature with an Indian subject took a decided turn toward the romantic. Among the most influential new works was Henry Rowe Schoolcraft's epic poem *Alhalla, or the Lord of Talladega: A Tale of the Creek*

War, published in 1843. In *Alhalla* (from which Henry Wadsworth Longfellow drew inspiration for his famous poem of 1855, *Song of Hiawatha*), Schoolcraft depicted Redstick War events and personages stripped free of all factual detail. William Weatherford, for instance, is transformed into Tuscaloosa, or the Black Warrior, who dies in battle. The character Alhalla, ostensibly a Hillabee Creek, symbolizes Indian rejection of white ways, thereby fulfilling the traditional role of noble savage as vehicle to critique Western civilization. In the opening scene, Oscar, a missionary, chastises the unrepentant Indian Prophet Mongazid for his rejection of the lamented "plan of civilization" (in verse thankfully more lucid than Sewall's or Jones').

> The bliss for which you chase and roam,
> You might more truly find at home,
> If but one tittle of the time
> You give to hunting, war, and crime,
> Were turned, with simple, peaceful hand,
> To stocks or grain upon the land.

After the near-obligatory depiction of Redstick defeats at Tallusahatchee and Talladega and the Tennesseans' treacherous destruction of the Hillabee towns, a demoralized Alhalla vows to abandon his homeland and declaims,

> The poor Muscogee race may say,
> They yet shall see a happier day;
> That happier day I ne'er shall see,
> I deem none happy if not free:
> And with that war—so fates conspire—
> Went out the brave Muscogee fire.
> I, scorning on that soil to be
> No longer honor'd, lov'd, or free!
> Resolved to leave those sunny strands,
> For distant woods and stranger's lands,
> And bending far, still onward hied,
> By vale and torrent, rock and tide,
> With purpose high, and aim severe,
> To close a life of suff'ring here.
> Here in my house, which nature made
> Without the white man's skill or aid,

A few short years shall close my eyes,
And leave my bones in northern skies,
And not a trace be left to show
Alhalla's fate—Alhalla's woe.[13]

With *Alhalla,* Schoolcraft introduced to the genre a sense of regret (and considerable guilt) for America's recent shabby treatment of Indians, while echoing James Fenimore Cooper's earlier theme of the tragic but inevitable extinction of traditional Indian cultures, if not of the people themselves. Interestingly, Fort Mims has no role in this new romantic view of the Redstick War since the Indians have become victims, reversing roles with the white settlers of the earlier myth. Henceforth, the two myths would exist in tandem.[14]

The Redstick War Examined

The next decade witnessed a surge of popular interest in Fort Mims and the Redstick War, beginning in 1851 with the publication of Albert James Pickett's remarkable two-volume *History of Alabama, and Incidentally of Georgia and Mississippi, from the Earliest Period.* Pickett arrived in Alabama (Territory) in 1818, at the age of eight, and grew up among Creek Indians who visited his father's trading house in Autauga County, on the upper Alabama River. In his late thirties, as profits from the labor of his plantation slaves offered him leisure time, and "feeling impressed with the fact that it is the duty of every man to make himself, in some way, useful to his race," Pickett "determined to write a History" of his state. For four years he threw himself into the task, sparing nothing in the pursuit of sources written and oral. Modern historians of the Redstick War should be particularly grateful for Pickett's acquisition of some of Ferdinand Claiborne's personal papers (including the critically important 1813 sketch of Fort Mims) from the general's son, and for his numerous interviews with eyewitnesses to that conflict. Pickett's account of the Redstick War is primarily oral history. His notes from interviews with Dr. Thomas G. Holmes, Jeremiah Austill, Abraham Mordecai and many other careful observers formed the evidentiary basis for his book's hundred pages on the Redstick War, and they remain (in the collections of the Alabama Department of Archives and History) key primary sources to this day.[15]

Like most of the preeminent historians of his era, Pickett was a self-trained gentleman scholar, with a keen ear for engaging anecdote (such as the evocative McGirth tale of captivity and redemption) that complemented his obsession with factual accuracy. The result is a romantic historical narrative, a literary history with "dramatic pacing," as Harper Lee has aptly stated. Because it was both authoritative and readable, Pickett's *History* had enormous influence. Specifically in regard to Fort Mims, his account was cited, quoted, abstracted, or simply lifted in whole or in part by virtually every subsequent historian dealing with the subject for the next century. His reconstruction of that event still seems largely accurate, as does much of the associated information he presented on the Redstick War. Pickett's greatest failing is his treatment of the Redstick Creeks. Perhaps he was too close, emotionally and temporally, to the Redstick War to consider seriously the motivations of a people he considered "savages" and "heathens." Certainly the racism that pervaded his own elitist culture colored his opinions, even of the métis whom he admired (by and large) while routinely referring to them by the derogatory term "half-breed."[16]

There are a few points in his account of the battle at Fort Mims where Pickett failed to live up to his own standards. In some cases, he altered information obtained from his eyewitness interviews, usually (we must assume) to improve the narrative flow. One of his inventions has become a standard element of the tale, as currently told in most modern history books. In his 1851 *History,* Pickett described the opening scene of the battle: "soon the field resounded with the rapid tread of the bloody warriors. The sand had washed against the eastern gate, which now lay open. Major Beasley rushed, sword in hand, and essayed in vain to shut it. The Indians felled him to the earth." Pickett obtained the gist of this scene from a Fort Mims survivor, Doctor Thomas G. Holmes, but altered Holmes' account in the retelling. According to Pickett's own notes of his interview with Holmes, Beasley "rushed sword in hand to the gate and attempted to shut it, but owing to its being made of very heavy materials it had much swagged and the gate was planted on the declivity of the slope & from several heavy rains the earth had washed considerably against said gate and rendered it impossible for Major Beasly with all his phisical powers to shut it." By replacing Holmes' precise but lengthy description with the simpler (and seemingly innocuous) phrase "sand had washed against the eastern gate," Pickett has misled modern historians, including one who imagined the "front gate had been blocked open by sand, perhaps by Red Stick sympathizers inside," and another who suggested (to unintended comic effect) that "the compound's gates were propped open with sandbags." Having excavated at the site of Fort Mims, I can testify the soil there is heavy clay, not sand. But we probably should not be too hard on Pickett for an honest mistake, the only victims of which are a few incautious historians.[17]

More serious, and most controversial, is his implication that the number killed inside the fort approached 500, an overstatement of the actual number by a factor of nearly two. On the basis of his interview with survivor Holmes, Pickett decided that "The whole population of Fort Mims, consisting of whites, Indians, soldiers, officers and negroes," totaled "five hundred and fifty-three souls." Pickett further concluded that "Of the large number in the fort, all were killed or burned up, except a few half-bloods, who were made prisoners, some negroes, reserved for slaves" by the Redsticks, and fifteen named individuals he knew had escaped. His phrase "all were killed" has caused a great deal of confusion because many readers therefore assumed that the death toll at the hands of Redsticks approached 553. As a consequence, estimates of 500 or more killed inside Fort Mims have been widely published with reference to Pickett ever since his book appeared. His initial acceptance of Dr. Holmes' figure of 553 people inside the fort is the root of the problem.[18]

Considerable independent evidence indicates that Dr. Holmes' estimate was too high. We know Major Beasley's tally of soldiers at the post on August 29, 1813 (as recalled later by Ensign Chambliss, a survivor of the battle), totaled 106 Mississippi Territorial Volunteers (including six on leave in Mobile), augmented by 41 or 42 men in Captain Bailey's militia company. The numbers of civilians, free and enslaved, can only be approximated. When General Claiborne first ventured an estimate of losses at Fort Mims, on September 4, he wrote regarding civilians, "how many, I have seen no one that could say." A few days later, after interviewing more survivors, Judge Toulmin came up with probably our best available figures for civilians: "about 24 families of men, women and children in the fort, of whom almost all have perished, amounting to about 160 souls. I reckon, however, among them about six families of half-breeds, and seven Indians. There were also about 100 negroes, of whom a large proportion were killed." Combining these figures gives us around 400 people inside Fort Mims on August 30. (Slightly more than 200 individual participants in the battle have been identified during research for this volume; see Appendix 1, summarized in Tables 1–2).[19]

For numbers of Redsticks involved and their casualties, plausible figures are even more elusive. General Claiborne early on decided there had been about 700 in the Redstick force, revised upward to 725 a few days later based on secondhand reports of statements by Creeks who were attempting to bring the Choctaws into an anti-American coalition. George Stiggins later thought the Redsticks numbered precisely 726, though his statement could be interpreted to include the smaller war party later led by Josiah Francis against the Forks.

Table 1. Summary of documented participants in the battle at Fort Mims, August 30, 1813 (M=men, W=women, C=children, U=unknown)

Outcome	Whites			Africans				Métis Creeks			Redstick Creeks	Totals				Documented Totals	Estimated Totals
	M	W	C	M	W	C	U	M	W	C	M	M	W	C	U		
Killed	61	3	10	15	8	7	0	11	6	9	1	88	17	26	—	131	350
Captured	0	0	1	4	6	11	9	0	3	9	—	4	9	21	9	43	100
Escaped	23	1	0	2	1	2	0	6	2	0	—	31	4	2	—	37	50
Survived	—	—	—	—	—	—	—	—	—	—	13	13	—	—	—	13	600
Documented Totals	84	4	11	21	15	20	9	17	11	18	14	136	30	49	9	224	
Totals by Ethnicity	99			65				46			14						
Estimated Totals	200			100				100			700						1100

Table 2. Numbers and percentages of documented battle participants (excluding Redsticks) killed and captured, calculated by ethnicity and by sex and age.

	# Documented	# Killed	% Killed	# Captured	% Captured	# Escaped	% Escaped
Whites	99	74	74.7	1	1.0	24	24.2
Africans	65	30	46.2	30	46.2	5	7.7
Métis	46	26	56.5	12	26.1	8	17.4
Men	122	87	71.3	4	3.3	31	25.4
Women	30	17	56.7	9	30.0	4	13.3
Children	49	26	53.1	21	42.9	2	4.1
Unknown	9	—	—	9	—	—	—
Totals	210	130	61.9	43	20.5	37	17.6

J. D. Dreisbach, a Weatherford descendant, thought there had been 600 men in the Mims war party. As for casualties, Benjamin Hawkins repeatedly heard low figures for the Redstick dead from his Creek informants, ranging from 30 to 40, but Redstick leaders did not provide such information readily to their enemies. Creek headmen at Coweta, who opposed the Redsticks, interrogated an African who had been taken at Fort Mims and escaped soon afterwards. He said they lost 40 to 50 killed, but these numbers may have only reflected losses suffered by the lower Tallapoosa River towns, where the slave had been held. As we have seen, Captain Kennedy counted, on consecutive visits to the battlefield, 22 and "nearly one hundred." Claiborne's initial speculations on Redstick losses settled on "a hundred & fifty to 2 hundred," a level of casualties corroborated by Sam Jones, a métis survivor of the battle. Stiggins maintained many years later, on the basis of "computations made by the heads of towns," that "such as died of their wounds to and after their return to their homes was two hundred and two, and many that got wounded survived." So we have contemporary estimates ranging from 30 to 202, all apparently guesses at best, with no information from an unbiased source to help us choose among them.[20]

As for counting the dead inside the fort, the burial party's report of 247 bodies deposited in two mass graves sets a minimum number. Pickett had that contemporary report by Captains Kennedy and Blue, which was widely published after the battle, so his preference for Dr. Holmes' figure remains a puzzle.

Some twenty years ago, historian F. Lawrence Owsley, Jr., effectively refuted Pickett, and most recent scholars now follow Owsley's preference for a death toll of 247. But that figure, too, deserves further scrutiny. We might legitimately wonder (as contemporaries did) how the burial party could have accurately counted those consumed by fire in the Mims house or how they discriminated the Redstick battlefield dead from the corpses of Creek residents of the Tensaw. Even a thorough, modern forensic study of human remains in the mass graves and elsewhere on the fort site—something not currently contemplated— would not resolve that last question. So the exact number who died inside Fort Mims will apparently remain uncertain, within a likely range of 250 to 300.[21]

Determining, as best we can, the actual number and identities of those who died at Fort Mims matters principally because later popular writers have claimed that the battle at Fort Mims was one of the greatest massacres of whites perpetrated by Indians in American history. Such claims are inaccurate on at least two scores: they ignore the nature of the hours-long military engagement that preceded the massacre, and most count everyone (or nearly everyone) in the fort as white, which is simply untrue. Those claims arose from, and became part of, the mythologized story of Fort Mims as rallying cry, as a symbol used to justify Indian removal and alienation. Pickett's *History of Alabama* ironically bolstered that myth while simultaneously laying a sound basis for modern historical studies of the Redstick War and the signal event of that conflict, the battle at Fort Mims.[22]

The Redstick War Romanticized

Publication of Pickett's *History* in 1851 spurred another of Alabama's planter-authors to bring to press his own contributions on the history and literature of the Redstick War. Alexander Beaufort Meek's first work, *The Red Eagle: A Poem of the South,* appeared in 1855 to mixed reviews in national literary magazines. The author elevated William Weatherford to epic hero status, a "tragic mulatto" in romantic tension with the fictional Lilla Beazley (destined to be confused by later generations of readers as a presumed daughter of the childless, real-life Major Daniel Beasley), mixed-race daughter of the equally imaginary pioneer hunter, White Wolf, vengeful survivor of Fort Mims. As he explained in the slim volume's introduction, Meek chose his subject because "The love-life of Weatherford,—here truthfully narrated,—his dauntless gallantry, his marvellous personal adventures and hairbreadth escapes, and, chief of all, his wonderful eloquence . . . afford as fine a theme for the poet as any in American history." Despite his preposterously crafted plot and characterizations, Meek did bring Creek métis William Weatherford to the attention of the American public in a positive, though highly distorted and sentimentalized, form.[23]

One stanza from *The Red Eagle* illustrates a fascination with the massacre of civilians common to nearly all works, literary and historical, on Fort Mims.

> Ah! then a deadlier strife began!
> With gun to gun, and man to man,
>   They grapple in terrific close.
> The rifles clubbed are snapped in twain,—
> And skulls are cleft beneath their blows:
> The war-club falls with plunging sound:
>   The tomahawk and scalping-knife
>   Hew down the woodman and his wife;—
> The infant's brains are scattered 'round![24]

American frontier literature (serious works of history, as well as historical fiction like *The Red Eagle*) contains thousands of similarly lurid accounts of atrocities inflicted by Indians on whites and whites on Indians. When evaluating the accuracy of such accounts of Fort Mims, one should recall that essentially all available documentary sources on the Redstick War derive from one side of this conflict. Consequently, most or all of these sources certainly reflect anti-Redstick biases. Apart from a handful of letters written by Redsticks (already cited), the only documents purporting to offer insights into the Redstick perspective were written by George Stiggins, a Tensaw métis who fought against them, and Benjamin Hawkins, whom they considered the agent of the destruction of their culture and nation. We should not accept those accounts, or any others, as factual without evaluating their evidence and arguments very carefully.

Did or did not these atrocities occur at Fort Mims? Some modern historians reject out of hand all descriptions of Indian-on-white atrocities as racist propaganda (while not infrequently accepting accounts of white-on-Indian brutalities without question). Yet recent forensic analyses of whites killed by Indians—remains of British soldiers at Fort William Henry, American Revolutionary War troops at Fort Laurens, and U.S. cavalrymen at the battle of the Little Bighorn—provide definitive evidence that Native American warriors on occasion inflicted evisceration and scalping on their enemies. Some future scientific analysis of the human remains buried in the mass graves at the site of Fort Mims in this case would certainly reveal information, still all too scarce, on the nature of warfare on the southern frontier. In the meantime we must endeavor to interpret the available historical sources as best we can.[25]

Consider, for instance, the numerous claims advanced by Hawkins, Stiggins, and others that women and children were scalped, killed, and mutilated in gruesome ways at Fort Mims. Initial newspaper stories emphasizing the massacre of noncombatants, particularly women and children, incited nationwide outrage at what was generally perceived as an unprovoked attack on American citizens (Figure 21). U.S. military and political leaders responded with public calls for the destruction of the Creek nation. In Tennessee, General Jackson immediately summoned the state militia to "retaliatory vengeance" against the "inhuman blood thirsty barbarians." In a letter to Governor Blount, Jackson expressed a sentiment widely shared in the country, especially in the South, that the United States should "carry a campaign into the heart of the Creek nation and exterminate them." There is no question the deaths of so many civilians at Fort Mims provided a justification (some might say a pretext) for the U.S. military to invade the Creek nation, to carry on a campaign that reached genocidal levels, and finally to confiscate a vast territory.[26]

From an emotional distance of nearly 200 years, however, we can hopefully approach the question more objectively. Did Redstick warriors kill and mutilate women and children at Fort Mims? The killing of many noncombatants certainly occurred. The Redstick William Weatherford is among our most reliable sources on this matter. In conversations with numerous former enemies during the last decade of his life, Weatherford repeatedly expressed regret at the massacre of civilians and explained how he had tried to restrain his warriors at Fort Mims as armed resistance by the white and métis soldiers waned. The great number of eyewitness accounts (by relatives and close acquaintances of the victims) describing murders of women and children is additional compelling evidence that a massacre did occur. Judging the scale of mutilations is more difficult. Most atrocity claims arose from the two visits by Captains Kennedy and Blue and their burial details in the month after the battle, when the bodies had already decomposed and been subject to dismemberment by dogs, pigs, and other animals. Some women apparently were disemboweled, but the historical documentation does not offer definitive proof of other sorts of mutilation. Historian Claudio Saunt considers Redstick mutilations of male and female opponents, in violation of "white codes of warfare," as "the actions of

MASSACRE AT FORT MIMMS.

Fig. 21. "Massacre at Fort Mimms" by Alonzo Chappel, from Dawson, *Battles of the United States by Sea and Land,* vol. 2.

warriors anxious to reestablish their masculinity," which had been challenged by the gender role reversals implicit in the plan of civilization. That métis women seem to have been singled out for disembowelment, however, suggests particular animus directed at the transmitters of Creek identity who had removed their children from participation in their lineage and talwa.[27]

While there is disagreement on the scale of mutilations inflicted by the Redsticks at Fort Mims, there is a great deal of corroboration that scalping occurred on a large scale. Many witnesses saw hundreds of scalps at the Holy Ground, Atasi, Hoithlewaulee and other Redstick towns during the war, all presumably taken at Fort Mims. In fact, since so many scalps were found in Creek towns, contemporary claims must be baseless that Spanish and British provocateurs spurred Redstick atrocities by offering bounties of five dollars per scalp.[28]

The Redstick War Reconsidered

Purveyors of American historical fiction have returned many times to the violent and tragic story of Fort Mims. In 1878, George Cary Eggleston published his take on William Weatherford's life in *Red Eagle and the Wars of the Creek Indians of Alabama* as a volume in the "Famous American Indians" series of the New York publisher Dodd, Mead & Company (Figure 22). Margaret Mitchell's 1936 bestseller, *Gone With the Wind,* features the minor character Grandma Fontaine, who as a child fifty-some years before the Civil War had watched from her hiding place as Redsticks killed her mother, brothers, and sisters, "right after the Fort Mims massacre." A decade later, in 1946, a well-researched historical potboiler set in the War of 1812, *Holdfast Gaines* by Odell and Willard Shepard, introduced another generation of the American public to the Redstick conquest of the Tensaw. By the time a quarter of the U.S. population watched a flaming arrow consume Fort Mims in the opening scene of *Davy Crockett, Indian Fighter,* an episode of the "Disneyland" television program broadcast on December 15, 1954, most Americans were already aware of the Redstick War's historical importance (Plate 8). Mid-twentieth-century history texts aimed at elementary school students all mentioned the Fort Mims massacre, one of the salient events in the bloody century-long struggle by an expanding United States to wrest the bulk of a continent from its native inhabitants. In the midst of a cold war that might erupt at any time into a world-ending catastrophe, the country appreciated a good historical morality tale (set in conflicts like the Redstick War or the War for Texas Independence) in which Americans patriotically rallied, after an initial stunning setback, ultimately to defeat a strong but duplicitous adversary.[29]

But the post–World War II era also was a time when a self-consciously powerful United States began to reevaluate its own history. Along with a slowly growing awareness by America's white majority of current prejudices and unequal treatment of minority segments of the population came an equally gradual reconsideration by academic historians, sociologists, and anthropologists of longstanding historical injustices to minorities, particularly those suffered by African Americans and American Indians. Consequently, Albert James Pickett's original 1851 scholarly interpretation of the Redstick War has intermittently attracted fresh efforts to strip away that pioneering author's antebellum biases and blinders.

A surprisingly successful early reexamination of the Redstick War's course and causes appeared more than a century ago in the form of Halbert and Ball's

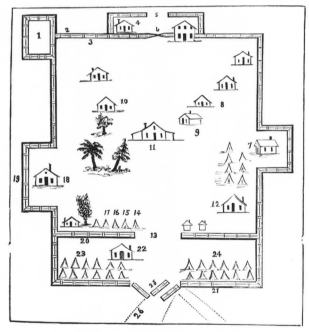

Fig. 22. Fort Mims, from Eggleston, *Red Eagle and the Wars with the Creek Indians of Alabama,* 95.

The Creek War of 1813 and 1814, published in 1895. Henry S. Halbert lived among the Choctaws of Mississippi as a Baptist mission teacher from 1884 through 1899 and became a respected authority on Choctaw (and Creek) culture and history. Baptist minister Timothy H. Ball resided for many years in Clarke County and wrote a detailed history of that region in the Forks of the Tombigbee and Alabama rivers. Their remarkably insightful collaboration uncovered many new firsthand sources on the Redstick War at a time when the last witnesses to that conflict were rapidly disappearing. Halbert's years of conversations with Choctaw elders about their memories of the Prophet's religion and the Redstick movement also recovered unique information from an Indian perspective otherwise almost entirely lacking among the voluminous documentary evidence of the Redstick War. Their book ends with an appeal to "those who dwell along the bright waters which once were held by the free and brave warriors of the great Creek nation, [who] should remember that the children of the forest and the wild had the first and best right to all those beautiful streams, that the white pioneers have nearly always been aggressors upon Indian hunting grounds and burial places, and that the least they can do is, cherishing no animosity for provoked massacres committed in the past, to imitate such virtues as the Creek warriors did possess, and to do their part as American citizens in having henceforth just treatment accorded to all the remaining American Indians."[30] Halbert and Ball made great strides toward understanding the provocations that had preceded the massacre at Fort Mims. It would take the discipline of academic history nearly a century more to adopt their fair-minded, cultural relativist point of view toward the Redsticks, the Tensaw métis, and the Redstick War.

That resurgence of interest finally began in 1981 when cultural anthropologist J. Anthony Paredes produced an ethnohistorical study of the Poarch Band of Creek Indians, descendants of the Tensaw Creeks who remained in south Alabama after the general removal of other Creeks in the 1830s. Paredes' documentation of their consistent self-identification as Indians through one and a half centuries of discrimination and pressure to accept categorization as "colored" (the only option officially open to nonwhites during the era of segregation in much of the South) contributed directly to federal legal recognition of the Poarch Band of Creeks as an Indian tribe and as "a successor of the Creek Nation of Alabama prior to its removal to Indian Territory."[31]

That same year, Frank Lawrence Owsley, Jr., reintroduced the Redstick War into the larger context of the War of 1812 in his book *Struggle for the Gulf Borderlands.* Michael Green soon afterwards traced the consequences of the

Redstick War on the internal politics of the Creek nation in his volume *The Politics of Indian Removal,* which was followed in 1986 by J. Leitch Wright's radical reinterpretation of Muscogee history in *Creek and Seminoles: Destruction and Regeneration of the Muscogulge People.* These three historians reinvigorated Creek studies with rigorous and far-ranging searches for overlooked sources in European and American archives and by applications of ethnohistorical methods of scholarship to their respective domains of military, political, and ethnic history.[32]

In the 1990s two innovative studies of the Redstick War appeared that at last began to reconstruct the multiple perspectives of the Indians involved in that civil conflict. Joel W. Martin's 1991 book, *Sacred Revolt,* upended two centuries of disparagement of the Prophet's movement as misguided pagan delusions or cynical pseudoreligious claptrap by resituating religion—genuine, sincere religion—squarely at the heart of Redstick resistance. By the end of the millennium, Claudio Saunt had taken another tack in *A New Order of Things: Property, Power, and the Transformation of the Creek Indians, 1733–1816* by examining the growing economic disparities that split apart the Creek nation in 1813. His analysis focused particular attention on the Creek métis of the Tensaw, who controlled a huge proportion of their peoples' wealth but largely renounced the reciprocal social obligations that had bound together Creek society for generations.[33] Most recently, Karl Davis has examined the origins and fate of the Tensaw Creeks in his dissertation, *'Much of the Indian Appears': Adaptation and Persistence in a Creek Community, 1783–1854.*[34]

I, too, have devoted a lot of attention to the Tensaw métis in this book. All of this current scholarly interest in the Creeks of the Tensaw, beginning with Paredes in 1981, reflects a fairly recent development in the fields of American Indian ethnohistory and colonial studies. Early anthropological studies of the Creeks, for instance, in the late nineteenth and early twentieth centuries mostly involved searching out men and women with exceptional knowledge of the old ways—traditional songs, dances, ways of healing, religious practices and beliefs, food preparation, craft production—all the myriad elements of earlier Creek culture that seemed on the verge of being lost as Creeks assimilated to mainstream American culture. The search for this kind of information led anthropologists to Oklahoma and Florida, most often to the descendents of Redsticks, to Creeks and Seminoles who respected and sustained their ancient traditions. This sort of anthropology created an invaluable and irreplaceable record of beliefs and customs; interviews documented on paper, sound recordings, and film saved much that would otherwise be gone. But, we now realize, the first anthropologists missed half of the story. So entranced were they by traces of continuity and persistence, by rare remarkable survivals from ancient times, that they overlooked or disregarded innovations and processes of change going on elsewhere, everywhere in Indian cultures. Anthropologists have long since come to appreciate and study the changes that enliven all cultures. Of particular interest to anthropologists are the changes a society undergoes when subjected to colonization, one of the processes responsible for our increasingly less diverse, culturally homogenizing modern world.

A powerful colonizing society severely constrains the adaptive options of the colonized. The Creek nation of the early nineteenth century was colonized by the United States as surely as the British and French colonized areas of Africa later in the nineteenth century. In each case the colonizers left local rulers in positions of apparent authority but manipulated them through subsidies and gifts (as Benjamin Hawkins influenced the Creek national council by presenting or withholding annuity payments to micos). In each case the colonized were permitted to rise only to subordinate or "subaltern" positions of real authority.[35] And in each case the colonizers extracted natural resources and agricultural harvests from the colonized (deerskins, corn, and cotton from the Creeks) in exchange for manufactured goods while severely limiting their means to develop a manufacturing capacity of their own. The colonized might try to make the best of an oppressive situation and assimilate with the colonizers, usually a difficult task, or at least selectively acculturate by adopting some elements of the colonizing culture. Or they could resist passively by refusing to obey the dictates of the colonizers (just as many Creeks in Oklahoma defied official efforts to eliminate the Muscogee language), or they might openly rebel.

The Redstick Creeks chose the last option in 1813 and failed in their bid for independence (though hundreds kept fighting in Florida for decades). Many of their descendents thereafter accepted colonized status but followed a course of passive resistance and thereby managed to maintain elements of traditional culture to the present day. Many others—former Redsticks as well as Creeks who had not followed the prophets' religion—chose the alternative path and opted to acculturate to one degree or another. Each individual in each generation made innumerable decisions to follow custom or innovate in this or that way, often under very difficult economic and political circumstances. In some cases the decisions involved intermarriage with non-Indians, sometimes resulting ultimately in social assimilation with the larger "white" or "black" portions of the population.

It is easy to be judgmental and insist (as early anthropologists evidently thought) that persons should remain true to their ancestral culture. For those of mixed ethnic background, the children of mixed marriages, however, choices must be made, and those choices will inevitably disappoint someone. In the case of the Poarch Band of Creeks, assimilation to American culture is nearly total, yet against great odds they have retained their distinct ethnic identity. Nevertheless, they have suffered more than their share of intolerance. On occasion, others—whites, blacks, Creeks from Oklahoma—still challenge their identity as Indians. Their ancestors, the Creek métis of the Tensaw, faced and endured the same sort of challenges two centuries ago.

10

Reverberations of Fort Mims

An unusual social experiment played out in the Tensaw district of Mississippi
Territory between 1799 and 1813. For more than a decade several hundred white
Americans and Creek Indians lived side by side, engaged in similar economic
activities while linked to a common capitalist trading system, socialized and
in some instances intermarried, and in general got along together quite well.
True, most of the Americans lived on one side of a boundary line and most
Creeks on the other. And each side resorted to its own legal system, by and
large, to resolve internal conflicts, with Benjamin Hawkins serving as a final
court of appeal in situations of overlapping jurisdiction. But the experiment
had worked reasonably well. To proponents of the "plan of civilization," pre-
1813 Tensaw proved that frontier whites and Indians could coexist in peace. But
that dream ended in blood and fire at Fort Mims. One question must have
haunted Benjamin Hawkins in the aftermath, as it has vexed historians ever
since. Could post-1813 America have replicated the Tensaw experiment continent wide?[1]

The Tensaw experience had been unusual, but it was far from unique. The
first whites to reside in many parts of North America had generally done so
peacefully, at the sufferance of Native Americans who tolerated the presence
of foreigners willing to engage with native societies. Many of the whites of the
Tensaw had lived and traded among the Creeks for many years; some married
Creek women and had Creek children. These whites differed from the vast
majority of white Americans with no firsthand knowledge of Indians, and it
would be that second, larger group who would be most embittered by the Fort
Mims massacre. Those white Americans, not the old "Indian countrymen,"

would descend on the Tensaw and other ceded Indian lands after the war's end, and they would overwhelmingly support removal of all Indians from the East.

The Tensaw had been different in other ways, though. The Creeks who moved south to Little River, far from their kin in the traditional talwa towns, did so as much to escape the social limits and obligations expected by their kin as to find new economic and social opportunities in the colonial markets of Mobile and Pensacola. The Creeks who coexisted so well with whites were self-selected; only those strongly motivated to coexist stayed in the Tensaw. The Creeks and whites of the Tensaw further shared a common interest in the institution of chattel slavery. The Africans enslaved on either side of the Creek boundary presumably saw little benefit to them in Benjamin Hawkins' social experiment.

～

Defeat of the Redsticks in the Creek nation resulted (inevitably) in a huge land cession to the United States. By the Treaty of Fort Jackson the Creeks relinquished more than 20 million acres, including all the territory of the Alabama Indians (among the staunchest advocates for war) and, ironically, the Georgia hunting grounds of the Lower Creeks (who had sided overwhelmingly with the Americans). All of the Upper Creeks' great western and southern hunting grounds were also taken to cut off the vestigial stump of the Creek nation from the last Redstick stronghold in Florida. Over the objections of Benjamin Hawkins, General Jackson insisted on treaty terms he knew would be hugely popular in Tennessee and elsewhere in the western United States. For most Americans the perceived benefits were enormous and many. The federal government could sell confiscated Indian lands to pay down the debt incurred by the war. Thousands of American farming families (including former soldiers) could acquire individual land tracts, while politically powerful land speculators could profit from larger developments. Thinly populated Mississippi Territory could be quickly transformed by immigration into one or more (slaveholding) states. The Creeks would be chastised for their treachery, and their harsh treatment at the hands of the United States could serve as a lesson to other native peoples standing in the path of American growth. Finally, for those Americans concerned with the well-being of Indians (and with history's verdict on U.S. treatment of conquered peoples), ceding such a vast tract would promote the plan of civilization. With their land base drastically constricted, the Creeks now must surely give up their hunting economy for plow farming and stockraising.

For want of a viable alternative, the Creek nation did make that economic transformation during the next twenty years, though the transition was most difficult for the Upper Creeks, who had lost nearly all of their wealth and possessions in the war. Even after nearly 600 claims for wartime losses (by "friendly Indians") were processed by the U.S. government, much of the Creek population remained impoverished by the standards of white America, and most families continued to cultivate small fields of corn and beans for their own subsistence. Households steadily dispersed away from the old town squares as families privatized grazing lands—for most of them a novel concept, private land, which undermined the influence of the matrilineages. By the 1830s talwa council houses typically stood alone, out of sight of the communities they had once literally drawn together.[2]

That process of accommodation to the new economic exigencies of the postwar era was equally difficult for the Creek métis of the Tensaw. Their lands had been ceded to the United States by the Treaty of Fort Jackson, and their property losses in the war were immense. However, under a clause in the treaty an influential few, with assistance from Benjamin Hawkins, filed claims for land reservations as "friendly Creeks." Congress granted thirty reservations, twenty-four to Tensaw métis, in 1817. On the list were many familiar names: David Tate, George Stiggins, Josiah Fletcher, the heirs of James Bailey, Lachlan Durant, Samuel Smith, the heirs of William Jones, John Weatherford, Peter Randon, the heirs of John Randon, James Cornells . . . and Zachariah McGirth, who had once again taken to identifying himself as Creek.[3]

Hawkins felt strongly that the Tensaw Creeks should receive compensation under the terms of the peace treaty. As he explained to William Crawford, the new Secretary of War,

> They embraced the plan of civilization first and by their conduct merited the attention of the Agent for Indian affairs. They would not agree in their mode of living or pursuits with their Indian relatives or the Chiefs generally; which produced continual broils between them. This deter-mined the half breeds to apply for, and after several years, to obtain from the Convention of the [Creek] nation leave to settle down on Alabama near the white settlements on the Indian lands. Here they were when the civil war among the Indians commenced.
>
> The Agent for Indian affairs apprehensive for their safety, as well as that of his fellow citizens in this quarter, sent an order to all of them and the whites and the Indians among them to go down, join and make com-

mon cause with their white neighbours. This order they obeyed promptly and willingly. The consequence was a total loss of property in several instances and several of their lives in Fort Mims.

In conclusion, Hawkins confided, "I am of [the] opinion these people will never be suffered by their Chiefs to return again into the nation, unless they will in all things conform to the Indian habits, which from their practical knowledge of the plan of civilization is impossible."[4]

The Creek nation would not risk another social upheaval by again embracing wayward métis who defied the nation's authority. One civil war was one too many. Hawkins hoped the reservation grants would ease métis' assimilation with American society, but the social landscape of Mississippi Territory was about to be transformed. In the next five years, from 1815 to 1820, 100,000 American immigrants with "Alabama fever" would descend on former Creek lands from the Tensaw to Fort Jackson.[5]

When the surviving Tensaw métis returned to their lands in the vicinity of Little River in 1814 and 1815, they found their houses and farm buildings burned, their livestock killed or missing, and their fields overgrown. Those who had found refuge for their slaves at one of the forts south of Mims, at Peirce's Mill or Hinson and Kennedy's Mill in August 1813, had the labor force to rebuild, burn off and plow their fields, and scour the woods for feral animals. David Tate and John Weatherford were still wealthy men at war's end. They quickly brought their reserved lands into production and found the means to set up their brother William with a plantation of his own in newly established Monroe County. By his efforts to reconcile former enemies and by the transparent sincerity of his remorse over the deaths of his own friends and relatives (including sister-in-law Mary Louisa Randon Tate) in the massacre at Fort Mims, William Weatherford forged a fresh life for himself in the rebuilt Tensaw (Figure 23). In 1816 he divorced Supalamy Moniac and married Mary Stiggins, George's sister. They had two children before William's death in 1824. Tate had already assumed the traditional role of eldest male in the matrilineage of Sehoy (who had died shortly before the war) and helped raise his half-sister's son and daughter, the children of Sam Moniac. Of all the Tensaw métis, the Tates and Weatherfords assimilated most easily into the American society around them, which included Dr. Thomas Holmes, Edward and Jesse Steadham, and other white survivors of Fort Mims.[6]

The Moniacs fared worse. At the outbreak of the war, when Sam Moniac fled

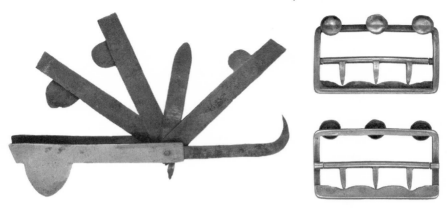

Fig. 23. William Weatherford's fleam, a bloodletting knife (courtesy of the Alabama Department of Archives and History, Montgomery), and his silver shoe buckles, 2.2 inches wide (courtesy of the St. Stephens Historical Commission, St. Stephens, Alabama).

the nation to take refuge with his wife and daughter at the Mount Vernon cantonment, he had been one of the wealthiest of all Creeks. In 1816 he received $12,597.25 (the second highest amount paid to any Creek, after Big Warrior of Tuckaubatchee) for "property destroyed by the hostile Creek Indians." Included in that claim were his dwelling in the Tensaw and his inn on the Federal Road (where he kept 2,000 pounds of coffee, 200 pounds of sugar, and 32 gallons of whiskey), 8 African slaves, 50 horses, 700 cattle, 200 hogs, 48 goats and sheep, a cotton gin house with machinery, looms and spinning wheels, and 500 barrels of corn. His possession of 6 plows, 2 feather beds, and 12 padlocks suggests a man thoroughly acculturated to American frontier life. Moniac claimed land under the Fort Jackson treaty and rebuilt his inn on the Federal Road south of the new American town of Montgomery, a stand that became a popular stop for travelers and post riders from 1816 to 1819 (Figure 24). In 1817 the Creek nation invoked for him the secret clause of Alexander McGillivray's 1790 treaty and obtained a federal subsidy to educate his son David at the U.S. Military Academy. By the 1820s, however, something had gone wrong. David Tate broke the bad news to his cadet nephew in a letter written on April 23, 1822. His father Sam had for some years "kept continually drunk, & made bad trades, & every advantage was taken . . . [until he] has at this time little or no property & has been compeled to move into the nation to save what little he has." Sam Moniac remained in the Creek nation with his relatives of the Taskigi talwa until their removal in 1836. He joined the forced exodus of 17,000 Creek Indians late that winter, traveling by steamboat down the Alabama River and along the coast as far as a deportation camp at Pass Christian, Mississippi. Alexander McGillivray's trusted confidante died there early in 1837, buried with his treasured peace medal given him by President Washington at the New York City conference in 1790.[7]

For other Tensaw métis, disputes with white interlopers began almost immediately. In May 1815, Lachlan Durant (son of Sophia McGillivray and Benjamin Durant) and assorted kin—"not one of us but who lost Relatives both near and dear to us on that memorable day that Fort Mimms was taken by the dreadful massacre that the Hostile Indians made there"—petitioned President Madison for redress of grievances. According to Durant, "Many citizens of the Mississippi Territory have moved over the boundary line betwixt the United States and the Creek Indians on the Alabama River as high up as Fort Claiborne in which distance the greatest number of us who are called Half breeds were born and raised. They have taken forcible possession of our fields and houses and ordered us off at the risk of our lives. They have reproached us with our origins, insulted us with the most abusive language, and not content with that they have even proceeded to blows and committed private injury on our Stocks and property." Although civil authorities refused to intervene on behalf of Creeks outside the nation, Durant's petition resulted in the expulsion of Thomas Boyle and other American squatters by military force. However, the threats and violence continued, and by 1817 several métis, such as Durant and Arthur Sizemore (husband of Mary Bailey), were abandoning their prime river bottomlands for less desirable piney woods to the east, on the Escambia (the ancestral home-to-be of the Poarch Band of Creeks).[8]

For Zach and Vicey McGirth and their girls, their travails did not end with that tearful, joyous reunion on a Mobile dock in 1814. Zachariah filed for and received, as a warrior of the Creek nation, a reservation equivalent to an entire section, one square mile of land in Monroe County. David Mitchell, the federal official overseeing treaty claims, understood McGirth and several others (James Earles, Josiah Fisher, Josiah Fletcher, Michael Ehlert) were white men married to Indian women but accepted their claims as adopted members of the Creek nation, subject to Indian law. McGirth then successfully filed "in the character of a friendly Creek Indian" and received $1,600 for property (valued at $4,000) lost in the war. His luck turned, however, when a congressional claims committee learned he had simultaneously filed for compensation as "a white man, who had resided many years among Indians"; they denied his second claim for $5,300.[9]

Without full compensation for his losses, Zachariah McGirth apparently could not make a success of his newly acquired plantation lands. When General

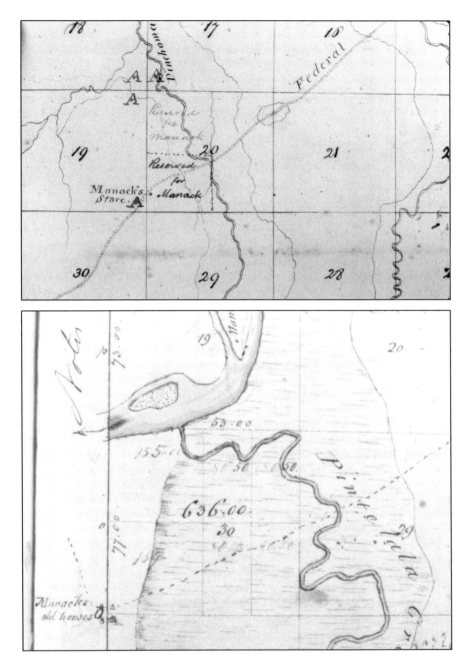

Fig. 24. Locations of Samuel Moniac's inn and store on the Federal Road (*top*), and his plantation near Pintlala Creek and the Alabama River (*bottom*), from U.S. Land Office, Cahaba Land District, Plat Book 2, 1821–1827, p. 85 (T14N, R17E, Section 20), and p. 67 (T16N, R16E, Sections 30 and 31) (courtesy of the Alabama Secretary of State, Montgomery).

Jackson asked him to raise and command a company of rangers in the first Seminole War, McGirth gladly turned warrior once again. As frequently happened during this period, the federal government was exceedingly slow in reimbursing officers for expenses incurred on behalf of their troops. To maintain his ranger company, McGirth assumed a large debt, which he first managed by renting his Monroe County lands. When his "personal responsibilities . . . brought him to the brink of ruin," he moved to the Creek nation "to save his personal property." The McGirths returned to their former talwa, Tuckaubatchee, where they farmed for more than a dozen years, until the Creeks agreed, under duress, to cede their remaining lands in the east to the United States. Zachariah found he could not sell his reservation to settle his debts, since reservations obtained under provisions of the treaty of Fort Jackson reverted to the U.S. government when vacated. He and a willing buyer, Samuel Bradford, petitioned Congress for the right to contract for the sale of his land, but that effort failed. Zachariah and Vicey, now in their mid-sixties, set out with their daughter, Sarah, in 1836 on the long trek west to Indian lands in Arkansas Territory. For the second time in their lives they lost all of their property—the reservation lands, and livestock (2 horses, 20 cows, and 30 hogs) worth $357. Zachariah McGirth's variable ethnic identity puzzled many during his long, eventful life, but he died undeniably a Creek Indian.[10]

∼

Today a state park preserves the site of Fort Mims, a battlefield and gravesite barely contained by a modest five-acre tract. Located in a rural community still known as Tensaw, Fort Mims Park seems far removed from modern life. Yet it lies just 15 miles north of Interstate 65, a modern asphalt offspring of the pathway once grandiosely known as the Federal Road, which Martin Rigdon, Barney O'Riley, and Zach McGirth risked their lives to ride in 1813. The park offers modern-day travelers a contemplative, shaded stroll along the fort's perimeter, where one can scarcely help but marvel at the crowded confines of that horrible event two centuries ago. Brought face to face with a place of great moment, one of those spots where a nation-changing event closed one avenue of history only to lead us all in another collective direction, how can one help but speculate on alternative outcomes? If Major Beasley had only summoned the physical strength and presence of mind to close that gate . . . might the massacre have been avoided, the war been halted before it began, the Creeks' lands saved for the Creeks, even Indian Removal itself averted (Figure 25)?

Such flights of imagination are sources of endless speculation, but they also usefully focus questions of significance and relevance. Did Fort Mims make a

THE FAR SIDE®   BY GARY LARSON

"FLETCHER, YOU FOOL! ... THE GATE! THE GATE!"

Fig. 25. Gary Larson's *The Far Side* (original release date, October 27, 1983).

difference? To the Creek Indians, certainly. Redstick goals had been revolutionary, and consequently their methods had gone beyond the normal bounds of southeastern Indian warfare or political chastisement. By crushing their opponents in the Tensaw with violence that was deliberately excessive, the Redsticks sought not just revenge but the submission of all Creeks who denied the prophets. In turn, the Americans responded with extreme force for equally complex reasons. Andrew Jackson's troops are unlikely to have been so unrestrained in their slaughters at Tallusahatchee and Tohopeka without the visceral motivation of revenge. In the absence of that one great Redstick victory at Fort Mims,

General Jackson probably could not have overridden the desires of his fellow peace commissioners at Fort Jackson who wanted a less punitive land cession. Yet, for the United States, even those 22 million acres, the largest seizure of Indian lands to that point in American history, were not the big payoff. Overwhelming, brutal, justifiable victory over the perpetrators of Fort Mims assured the compliance of other southeastern Indian peoples—peace in the near term and, ultimately, their removal.[11]

Yes, the United States might have found a compromise with the southeastern Indians that could have avoided some of the lasting bitterness caused by the numerous ensuing Trails of Tears. We tend to think of American history as a series of inevitabilities, but many white Americans in the 1820s and 1830s opposed Indian Removal, and Congress only narrowly passed the legislation which enabled that national shame to occur. Indian Removal derived largely from Andrew Jackson's political popularity and his unshakeable will that Removal must occur. And he owed his fame and popularity in no small measure to the military opportunities provided by that opening battle of the Redstick War.

The existence of a Fort Mims massacre, an ever-present reminder in the public mind of mythologized Indian savagery and obstinate rejection of civilized benevolence, posed a high burden of proof to those Americans arguing for peaceful coexistence or assimilation with Indians. In fact, imagery generated by the myth of Fort Mims—of hundreds of helpless white settlers slaughtered by inhuman savages—fueled passions for American conquest of all native peoples for the rest of the century.[12] There had been massacres of whites by Indians before, of course. True, this one had a high death toll, but Fort Mims' impact on white Americans was greater than mere mortality figures would suggest. Many more whites had died in General St. Clair's defeat at the hands of the Shawnees in 1791, just twenty years earlier, yet that event did not have nearly the effect as this battle in the Tensaw. Fort Mims shocked Americans because of the ingratitude it represented. The country's intellectual elite had extended a hand to lift up and ennoble a benighted people. When a large portion of the Creek population rejected that patronizing offer, voiced a strong preference for their own way of life, and fought strenuously to preserve their culture and their country, white Americans took this rejection to heart. That overt rejection of America's best offer, coupled with the murder of women and children, was too much to bear. William Weatherford must have known he had lost the war, and a way of life, when he lost control of his Redstick warriors at the close of the battle at Fort Mims.

Afterword

A Personal Look Back, by Way of Acknowledgment

Convention calls for authors of scholarly volumes to declare up front their intellectual debts and sources of emotional support. There are, I suppose, several good reasons this should be so. Family and friends surely deserve a prominent "thank you" for the encouragement they so selflessly offer a writer, who in turn must invariably in some measure neglect them, no matter how regretfully, if the solitary task of writing is ever to result in a finished book. And authors' biases are often revealed by the professional company they keep, so acknowledgments fairly warn readers from the start. But the nature of this book, and how it came to be written, leads me in a different direction. As I researched and sought to unravel the complex ways the story of Fort Mims has influenced American history, I was surprised to discover at how many points my own life has intersected with this distant historical event.

My earliest contact, albeit indirect, seems to me to have presaged an entire segment of my life. Ethel Morgan, my mother's great-aunt, had grown up in Wayne County, Ohio, and married an Iowan, Roy Dunham, a teacher like herself. Early in the 1930s they began spending summers in Loxley, Alabama, and eventually, in 1952, bought a house in Fairhope, on the eastern shore of Mobile Bay. A group of Iowans had founded Fairhope in 1894 as an experimental "Single Tax Colony" based on the utopian precepts of Henry George, who considered private ownership of land the basis of social inequality. Individuals and families who "settled" the Fairhope colony built homes and made other improvements, which they owned, while the land remained community property. (The system effectively deflated the value of adjacent privately held lands, which remained widely affordable in the Fairhope vicinity for a century, until the real estate boom of the 1990s.) Independent thinkers were attracted to idealistic Fairhope, which became—and remains—a haven for artists and writers. Ethel Morgan Dunham, by all accounts, was one such free spirit. Active at an early age in the suffrage movement, she shocked her staid Methodist family back in Ohio with letters describing nude sunbathing in her hedge-enclosed backyard at Loxley, but she won their approbation by her commitment to temperance, on which she would lecture long and hard at every opportunity. Her modes of self-expression included oil painting and poetry, for which she drew inspiration from the subtropical environs and romantic history of her adopted southern home. In her poem "Sanota," published in 1939, she imagined the emotional impact of the battle at Fort Mims on Zachariah McGirth and his family.

> McGirth was downcast, desperate, and longed
> To die, when with provisions he returned
> To old Fort Mims, and felt that he was wronged
> By massacre through which the fort was burned;
> Felt that he had reared a scalping Indian boy
> (Rejoined into his tribe, an eagle fledged
> For tender prey.) Ingratitude killed joy
> And then cast pain and fury double-edged. . . .
> But six months later there was cause for change
> Of mind, Sanota, fighting hard, was killed
> At Horseshoe Bend. He could not then arrange
> The meeting that his grateful heart had willed;
> Yet, loved ones clasped McGirth, sobbed out the tale
> Of rescue by a brave who did not fail.[1]

I suspect Ethel's limited successes as a published poet are attributable more to persistence than ability, but that is uncharitable of me. Although she died before I could know her, her letters to my mother show that she took a typically exuberant interest in my birth.[2] As I type this now, at my home in Fairhope, a few blocks from the site of her now-vanished cottage on North Section Street, I cannot help but think that my great-great-aunt Ethel's "pioneering discovery" of south Alabama and Fort Mims somehow, subconsciously, had a hand in my eventual retracing of her tracks and interests.

Shortly after I turned two, I, along with much of my generation, was swept away to Frontierland when "Davy Crockett, Indian Fighter" aired December 15, 1954, on the "Disneyland" television program. Forty million Americans saw a

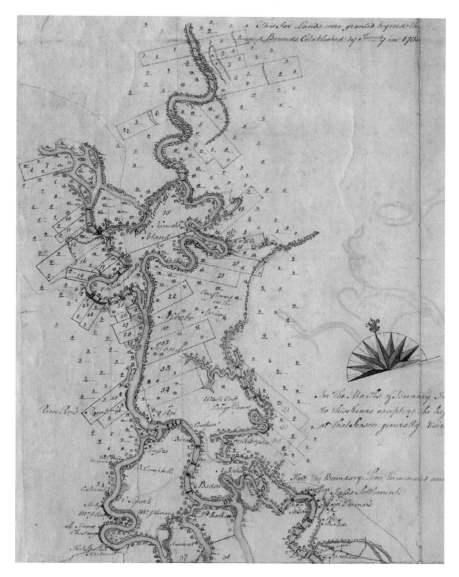

Plate 1. Detail of David Taitt's 1771 map of West Florida, showing the Mobile-Tensaw delta and British land grants in the Tombigbee and Tensaw districts (courtesy of The National Archives, Kew, U.K.).

Plate 2. "A Map of the United States and Part of Louisiana," from *Brookes's General Gazetteer,* 9th edition, by Richard Brookes (Philadelphia, 1808), showing the Louisiana Purchase and Spanish West Florida.

Plate 3. *Benjamin Hawkins and the Creek Indians,* the Plan of Civilization as Allegory (unidentified artist, circa 1805, oil on canvas, 35 ⅞ × 49 ⅞ inches, courtesy of the Greenville County Museum of Art, Greenville, South Carolina. Gift of the Museum Association, Inc., with funds donated by Corporate Partners: Ernst and Young; Fluor Daniel; Director's Circle Members: Mr. and Mrs. Alester G. Furman III; Mr. and Mrs. M. Dexter Hagy; Thomas P. Hartness; Mr. and Mrs. E. Erwin Maddrey II; Mary M. Pearce; Mr. and Mrs. John Pellett, Jr.; Mr. W. Thomas Smith; Mr. and Mrs. Edward H. Stall; Eleanor and Irvine Welling; Museum Antiques Show, 1989, 1990, 1991, Elliott, Davis and Company, CPAs, sponsor; Collector's Group 1990, 1991).

Plate 4. Self-portrait of Hillis Hadjo or Josiah Francis, the Alabama Prophet, in a British military uniform, drawn in England in 1816 (© Copyright The Trustees of the British Museum, London, U.K.).

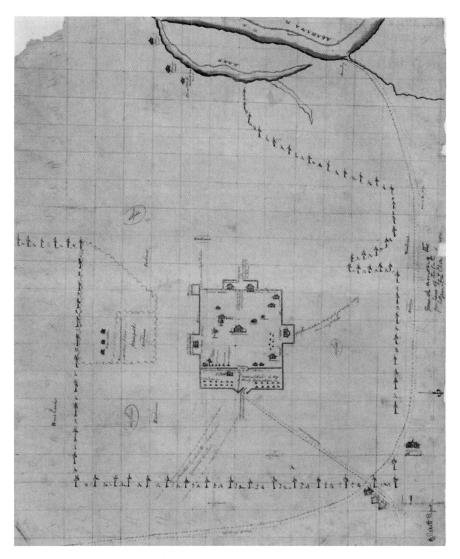

Plate 5. "Claiborne Map" of Fort Mims, 1813, north to the right (courtesy of the Alabama Department of Archives and History, Montgomery).

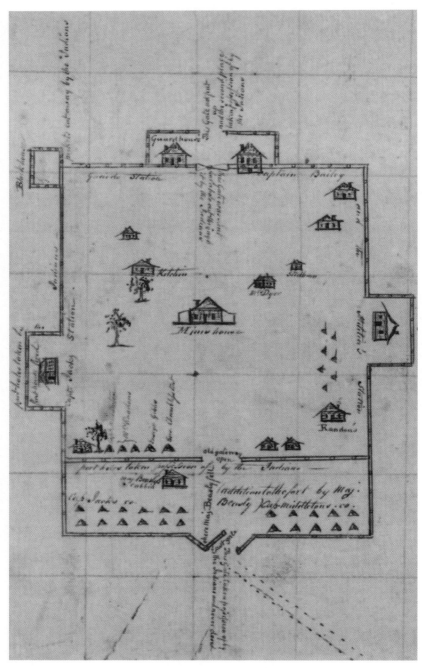

Plate 6. Detail of the "Claiborne Map" of Fort Mims, 1813, north to the right (courtesy of the Alabama Department of Archives and History, Montgomery).

Plate 7. Burned artifacts recovered from archaeological excavations at Fort Mims. *Clockwise from top left:* charred pearlware plate sherds, melted bottle fragments, a melted cast iron Dutch oven (5 inches tall), and an iron writing box (3 inches wide) encrusted with sealing wax (courtesy of the Alabama Historical Commission, Montgomery).

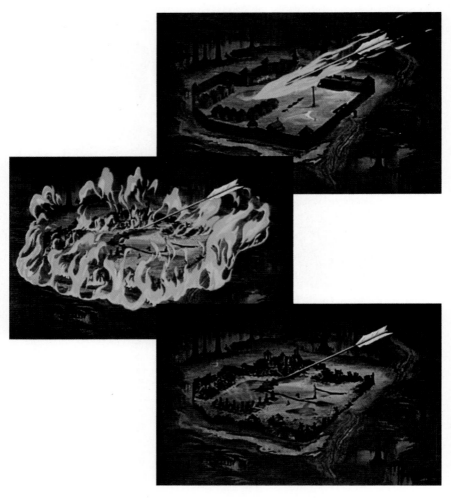

Plate 8. The destruction of Fort Mims, from the opening scene of Walt Disney's *Davy Crockett—Indian Fighter,* 1954 (© Disney Enterprises, Inc.).

flaming arrow consume Fort Mims in the opening scene. While I claim no expertise whatsoever in the academic discipline of American Studies, which reserves popular culture as its principal turf, I suspect this imaginative foray by the Disney Studios into American historical mythology had a deep influence on my age-grade, exceptional numbers of whom later pursued professional careers in history and archaeology. Disney revitalized a two-dimensional, legendary Crockett whose humanity had been sapped by stodgy, didactic textbook treatment. This was no leaden figure in a stale tableau but a believable character with an appealingly iconoclastic view of America's early days. Most significantly, American Indians—particularly the fictional Cherokee family of Charlie Two Shirts, depicted in the second episode, "Davy Crockett Goes to Congress"—were portrayed with more sensitivity than was typical for that era. This series certainly did not transform American attitudes about Indians. (Sadly, an American Indian perspective on early American history would take several more decades to reach the popular media.) And Disney's production team took huge doses of dramatic license with nearly every factual detail. Despite innumerable historical liberties, however, "Davy Crockett" suggested to many children growing up in the 1950s that early America was a place of great interest. We wanted to learn more.

Of course, this may be reading a lot into a television show, especially for viewers in the two-to-three-year-old cohort. Yet family photos support my own vivid recollections from a slightly later age that this was an important source of my future interest in American history. One snapshot taken in 1955 captures me (sporting my prized coonskin cap and fringed jacket) and my brother, Gary, kneeling in a pile of leaves before a split rail fence in our Eastlake, Ohio yard (Figure 26). But the self-absorbed expressions on our faces suggest something else. For us this was no longer suburban Eastlake; we were out there, on some remote frontier of early America. That is not so improbable for a couple of daydreaming youngsters. After all, Davy "kilt him a b'ar when he was only three."[3]

My own "research" on Fort Mims began in 1963 as an assignment for Mr. Green's fifth-grade class at George Washington Elementary School. Tasked with building a diorama of the famous battle site, my project partner, Martin Winters, and I drew on our impressive personal collections of plastic figures—mostly soldiers, of course, struck in frozen poses of martial valor—to populate our miniature, popsicle stick re-creation of the ill-fated stockade. A tiny Major Beasley vainly struggling to close the fort's gate was a particular highlight. Martin, as I recall, expressed some concern that viewers of our masterpiece

Fig. 26. Greg Waselkov (*left*) and Gary Waselkov, Eastlake, Ohio, 1955.

might not grasp the horror of the massacre occurring before them, a defect easily remedied by a liberal dose of red paint. The finished project was a veritable sea of blood and terribly impressed our classmates, though I remember my disappointment with Mr. Green's less enthusiastic reaction. Thinking back after all these years, I realize how naively we had accepted our textbook's interpretation of the battle as simply one of many atrocities perpetrated by Indians in their futile struggle against the inevitable, relentless westward expansion of the United States.

I am not at all certain, however, that we could have found a better, more nuanced treatment of the battle at Fort Mims, or of American Indian history in general, among the library books available to fifth graders in the suburbs of Cleveland in the early 1960s. Most elementary school curricula of that era routinely drew disturbing (albeit, highly questionable) parallels between long-ago native challenges to the young American republic and then current near-hysterical concerns with a looming "red menace." Revisionist historians and ethnohistorians had only begun to reexamine the accumulated pro-expansionist interpretations of American history, a process that had started in earnest not many years before with the first land claims cases brought by American Indian tribes against the federal government. Anthropologists played an important role in this reevaluation by pointing out to scholars and the public alike the ethnocentric, explicitly pro–United States, anti-Indian biases of most earlier written histories and offering in their place a cultural relativist approach to our multicultural past. Cultural relativism is sometimes misconstrued as a value-free approach to human behavioral diversity, with all human actions considered equally valid and acceptable depending upon one's cultural perspective. In fact, cultural relativism simply recommends one try to understand the cultural context of an unfamiliar behavior—its historical origins as well as its social role—and not condemn that behavior out of hand merely because it contradicts one's own ethnocentric cultural norms or values. These anthropological concepts—ethnocentrism and cultural relativism—are now commonly applied by nearly all serious students of America's complex social history. But in 1963 historians had not yet reconsidered Fort Mims from an anthropological perspective. For me, as for most Americans, this battle of 150 years earlier was primarily an historical oddity, a rare victory on a long list of defeats by Indians during four centuries of conquest by whites.

From that time onward, my interests increasingly revolved around history, anthropology, and archaeology, and I became a great reader, devouring books on those broad topics brought home for me by my mother, Elizabeth James Waselkov, a public school librarian. My father, Alexander Waselkov, a public school art teacher, always remained skeptical that this path I stubbornly followed would lead to a career with a living wage. Despite misgivings, they both encouraged my growing mania for the past, especially by humoring my incessant requests to visit historical sites, museums, and parks during our annual summer vacations, which eventually reached all 48 contiguous states, Canada, Mexico, and much of Europe.

My parents gave me something else that has proven helpful in my efforts to understand Fort Mims (and American history, in general), a mixed ethnic heritage. My mother's family origin is English, from Wiltshire. My immigrant ancestors on her side of the family tree came to America between 1640 and 1830, and her immediate forebears settled in rural Ohio before the Civil War. They farmed in southern Wayne County, land on which my grandfather, Carl James, would find many prehistoric stone tools while plowing at a horse's measured pace at the turn of the twentieth century and later while walking other farmers' fields as a soil conservation agent. My father's family, on the other hand, emigrated from the village of Ternovka, near Saratov, in Samara, Russia, on the lower Volga. First to cross the Atlantic was Pyotr (Peter), my grandfather, in 1909, followed a year later by Marja and their young children Tatjana, Ivan, and Pyotr. According to family legend, my grandfather determined to leave the Old World upon surviving the Russo-Japanese War of 1905 as a stoker in the Russian navy. They settled in Colorado, where my father was born in 1913 and where the men folk worked as deep-shaft coal miners for a time. Although he never learned to speak English well himself, my grandfather thought it very important for his family to fit into American society, and he encouraged his boys (though not his girls, following an Old World bias) to attend college.

Of course, my life as the son of an Anglo-American and a second-generation Russian-American must differ immensely from experiences of mixed-race offspring, such as the Creek métis who figure so prominently in the story of Fort Mims. I do, however, draw several insights from my own background that seem relevant to the issues considered in this book. First, America has always been diverse, ethnically and racially, from the earliest days of colonization until the present, and children of mixed ethnic and racial backgrounds have always been an inevitable consequence of that diversity. Americans have long preferred to ignore multiple ethnic and racial identities, and in fact until very recently public policy frequently forced individuals to choose one ethnic or racial identity. The 2000 federal census finally acknowledged mixed descent, and society at large now seems increasingly willing to reexamine this issue historically, as exemplified by the public's interest in the Thomas Jefferson–Sally Hemings paternity debate.

Second, since ethnic and racial diversity is consequently a defining characteristic of American social history, as well as of modern American society, we can all appreciate (in a general way, at least) the difficulties experienced by earlier generations of Americans as they struggled to reconcile the interests of different segments of society, because we struggle to do the same today. Likewise I suspect everyone has suffered some injustice, many of us rarely but some of us routinely, from racial or ethnic prejudice. My experiences have included the occasional insults questioning my patriotism or loyalty to country because of my Russian name, barbs my entire family endured with patience (and pity for the slanderers) throughout the Cold War. Strangely enough, those taunts occurred most often during my childhood, while growing up in the heavily Slavic suburbs of Cleveland. They subsided abruptly when I moved to Alabama, where my name has generated virtually no animosity and little interest beyond some curiosity in its origin. One memorable exclamation came from a puzzled small-town mechanic who asked in a welcoming way, in carefully pronounced English, "So, how do you like it here?"—apparently assuming I had stepped off a steamer from Mother Russia just days before. In the South, families do remain rooted to place, more so than in other parts of our increasing mobile society. Many modern-day residents of the Tensaw trace their ancestors back to survivors of the battle at Fort Mims, and they naturally take a keen, personal interest in their local history. But they also realize that their history resonates throughout the country, and they take considerable pride in sharing it with the rest of us, whether we be recent immigrants from other countries, relocated "Yankees" or Midwesterners, "snowbirds" visiting for the winter, or tourists driving by on the interstate.

My own journey south led first to Columbia, Missouri, where I studied anthropology at that state's university. One of the faculty there, Robert T. Bray, taught historical archaeology, then a new subfield of American archaeology, which had hitherto focused on prehistoric sites occupied before the arrival of Europeans and written histories. Ecstatic to discover a field that combined my three favorite subjects—archaeology, anthropology, and history—I signed up for Bray's field course at the Mormon site of Nauvoo, became his field assistant for a second summer, and stayed on for a year after graduation to direct excavations (under his guidance) at Fort Zumwalt State Park. Like Fort Mims, Jacob Zumwalt's fort had been a settler's residence fortified during the War of 1812 as a precaution against Indian attack. Unlike Fort Mims, no attack transpired and the hewn log fort reverted to farmhouse, falling eventually into picturesque ruin, with the last notched timbers finally succumbing in the 1980s to decay and the campfires of some thoughtless Boy Scouts.

My limited excavations at the site of Zumwalt's fort uncovered little of interest from the War of 1812 era, but the region's history proved fascinating, beginning with French colonization in the 1760s, followed by an influx of ethnic German and English settlers led by Daniel Boone in the 1790s under the Spanish regime, and by American immigration after 1803. That research led me to explore the anthropological literature on frontiers.[4] Historians, beginning with Frederick Jackson Turner in 1891, have conceived of frontiers as the limits of white settlement, where the availability of "free" land was thought to have had profound formative influence on the nature of the American psyche. A few anthropologists in the late twentieth century developed a less Eurocentric conception of frontiers as zones of interaction, where intrusive and indigenous societies meet in active competition, an idea I attempted to apply to the 1812 Missouri frontier, part of the region contested by Tecumseh's northern Indian alliance. Historians more recently have essentially abandoned the Turnerian "frontier" concept in favor of Richard White's "middle ground," the intercultural space created by intersecting societies determined to find means of accommodation, to negotiate and act cooperatively, on the basis of perceived overlaps or congruencies in their worldviews. Initial enthusiasm for "middle ground" has lately been tempered by a renewed appreciation for the essential ethnocentrism of both natives and newcomers, who often actively defended their respective cultural traditions. This is a perspective promoted by anthropological frontier studies, which still have an important role to play in understanding the complex courses of culture change that occurred in early America.[5]

After a few years working on advanced degrees in anthropology at the University of North Carolina in Chapel Hill, and a pleasant eight months spent digging a prehistoric shell midden in Virginia's Northern Neck, my wife, Linda, and I entered the Deep South. At the invitation of John Cottier, I took a research position at Auburn University, where I would piece together my income from contracts and grants for nine hectic years. I had known John since 1971, when he hired this rising sophomore to help excavate the heavy gumbo clays of a Mississippian mound site in Missouri's bootheel. He had grown up in Auburn and spent his youth roaming the lower Tallapoosa Valley, in east-central Alabama, retracing the eighteenth-century journeys of William Bartram and Benjamin Hawkins through Upper Creek country. Inspired by the amazing Creek artifact collections assembled between 1909 and 1945 by members of the Alabama Anthropological Society (now displayed, in part, at the Alabama Department of Archives and History museum in Montgomery), John determined early in life to carry out, someday, a modern scientific study of historic Upper Creek Indian archaeological sites. By the time I arrived, in 1979, he and another native Alabamian, Craig Sheldon, had both obtained faculty positions in the state. The three of us launched the Upper Creek Archaeology Project, a series of excavations at historic Creek town sites—Hoithlewaulee, Fusihatchee, Hickory Ground—all threatened in one way or another by modern development in the Montgomery urban area, by strip mining of valuable gravel deposits (which underlie many sites, to their detriment), and by modern-day looters who systematically despoil Creek graves for the associated artifacts. Excavations at Fusihatchee continued for thirteen years (from 1985 until 1998, ten years after I left central Alabama) as Craig and John, with important assistance from the Poarch Band of Creek Indians, valiantly fought to salvage as much information as they could while gravel quarrying steadily consumed the site. During those years, digging far outpaced analysis, and publications will continue to appear on this work for decades to come.[6]

While at Auburn, I had the additional good fortune to direct (with Craig) two seasons of excavations at an extraordinary National Historic Landmark, Fort Toulouse/Fort Jackson Park, administered by the Alabama Historical Commission in the modern community of Wetumpka. Within the space of a few acres lie the buried remains of two important military outposts: Fort Toulouse (1717–1763, rebuilt several times by the French) and Fort Jackson, established by American forces near the end of the Redstick War in 1814.[7] All of these sites have proved highly instructive, primarily for revealing Creek Indian innovations and adaptations to European and American intrusions into the Southeast.

Despite this intensive effort over the last quarter century, many gaps in our knowledge remain to be filled, of course. Historical archaeologists demonstrate repeatedly how the buried record of humanity, the mundane objects discarded or lost in the course of day-to-day activities, offers an independent perspective on the past, a perspective generally free of the biases embedded in the motivations that led to the creation of written documents. Letters, journal entries, military orders and reports, newspaper articles, reminiscences—all of the sources upon which historians rely—must be meticulously evaluated to discern each author's veracity, accuracy, and motive. While archaeological evidence poses its own considerable interpretive challenges, the presence of a burned wooden stockade or a layer of kitchen debris, as evidence of past behavior, is unlikely to have been manipulated with the intent to persuade or deceive anyone. Archaeology further complements history by providing information on the lives of nonliterate people (who could not create written records) and on highly revealing topics thought at the time to be too commonplace or unimportant (or illegal) to generate much unbiased documentation.

Consider, for instance, how little information we have on the lives of most Creeks during the early nineteenth century in comparison with the very abundant historical record created by and about literate white Americans of that era.[8] Because most documents about the Creeks predating Removal in the mid-1830s were written either by non-Creeks or by literate Creek (usually métis) elites, we stand in great need of more archaeological data on the realities of daily life free from the filters of racial prejudice or political and economic advantage. Consequently, when the Alabama Historical Commission approached me to analyze all previous archaeology accomplished at Fort Mims, I was eager to do so for many reasons. Although I had never perused the collection, I was reasonably sure it contained the possessions of American settlers, enslaved Africans, and Creek métis, and none of those people of the Tensaw had been studied from a modern archaeological perspective. In the course of producing a report on the archaeology of Fort Mims (which I coauthored with Bonnie L. Gums and James W. Parker), I realized that the full history of the battle, its causes and its aftermath, had yet to be written, and I determined to do so.[9]

In bringing this long acknowledgement, and this book, to a close, I am grateful for the help offered by a number of individuals during the last several years of research and writing. At the Alabama Historical Commission, I was fortunate to find encouragement for this volume from Lee Warner and Edwin Bridges (successive executive directors), Thomas O. Maher (state archaeologist), and Mark Driscoll (director of Historic Sites). I hope my research assists their long-term efforts to develop and interpret Fort Mims Park for the public.

As my interest in Fort Mims deepened, I met an extraordinary group of people, most of them descendants of participants in the battle, who live in northern Baldwin County. These kind, determined folks have worked vigorously over the last 50 years to see the site of the battle protected, properly commemorated, and made accessible. They include Robert Leslie Smith (who witnessed the 1953 bulldozer search for the fort ruins) and his cousin H. Davis Smith, currently president of the Fort Mims Restoration Association. Both men are now in their mid-eighties, having waited all their lives (lately with increasing, and understandable, impatience) to see the fort rise again for the education of the American public. I share their frustration with the minimal interpretation so far accomplished at this nationally significant site and hope their dreams will soon be realized.

I am grateful to my academic base, the University of South Alabama, for time to write and for the exceptional support the school, the College of Arts and Sciences, and the Department of Sociology and Anthropology have provided the Center for Archaeological Studies. Most especially, President V. Gordon Moulton, Dean G. David Johnson, and my departmental chair, J. Steven Picou, have been helpful at every turn. In the short span of fourteen years the center's staff members have earned an international reputation for first-rate research, and I very much appreciate their dedication and professionalism. In particular, I thank Bonnie L. Gums for her collaboration on the Fort Mims artifact analysis and Sarah Mattics for her skillful preparation of maps and other illustrations for this volume.

Among my many friends and colleagues who generously shared sources and tried to steer me clear of errors of fact, interpretation, and style, particular thanks goes to Donna and Ed Besch, Kathryn Holland Braund, Charles E. Bryant, Karl Davis, John C. Hall, Jacob Lowrey, Joel Martin, Jacqueline Matte, Jackie McConaha, Stephen R. Potter, Claudio Saunt, Craig T. Sheldon, Jr., and Peter Wood—and most especially to Kathryn and Claudio for their very detailed and constructive comments. Robert Bradley, curator at the Alabama Department of Archives and History, fathomed the vast manuscript and artifact holdings of his institution and surfaced with several items with Fort Mims associations, some authentic and some now disproved. I am pleased he was able to trace a genealogical link to Aaron Bradley, one of the few combatants to survive on the American side. James W. Parker (site director of Fort Toulouse/ Fort Jackson Park) provided invaluable assistance at nearly every stage of this research project. His firsthand experience with field archaeology at Fort Mims and his in-depth knowledge of the 1812-era American military in the South have improved this volume in innumerable ways. I am especially grateful for Jim's generosity in sharing revelatory manuscript references documenting William Weatherford's cooperation with the U.S. military in late spring 1814. Jim also began the painstaking task of compiling and documenting battle participants, a process that Sue Moore and I have continued, with our combined results presented in Appendix 1.

Sue Moore introduced herself to me in November 2002 as "a mother and grandmother" from Longview, Texas, "a retired high school English teacher with a history minor, which should have been major."[10] I've come to know she is every bit a historian. Beginning many years ago with a desire to learn more about her Caller and McGrew ancestors, she has progressed far beyond traditional genealogy and now commands a thorough grasp of the complex and fascinating history of Mississippi Territory. Whenever I had questions about such arcane matters as political alliances among territorial officials or the probable identities of aliases employed in pseudonymous broadsheets and scurrilous satires, Sue either had already puzzled out the answer or quickly did so, always with the unsentimental eye of a top-notch researcher. She is also extraordinarily selfless, freely offering me (and other academics) her archival discoveries and her knowledge simply because history is fun and she enjoys doing it.[11] Over a period of 24 months, Sue emailed to me hundreds of pages of correspondence and transcriptions of historical documents, suggested source leads, and offered her well-reasoned thoughts on the early literature of Alabama, much of which relates directly to Fort Mims and the Redstick War. Among many important contributions, she pieced together the story of the Beasley-Frye duel, which had eluded earlier researchers, and she doggedly pursued genealogical leads with family historians across the country to expand greatly the list of battle participants in Appendix 1. Working with Sue Moore has been a pleasure and an inspiration, and this volume is done sooner and better thanks to her. I hope you like the book, Sue.

To my family I owe my greatest debts: for their unending good humor at an endless succession of hot dusty sites and cold sterile archives and collections repositories, for their forgiveness of my life-long affair with books, for their enthusiasm for learning and their intolerance of sloppy thinking, and for their unsparing capacity for love, I am so grateful. To my wife, Linda, our children, Katherine, Nicholas, and Peter, and my mom, Elizabeth James Waselkov Burge, thank you.

Appendix 1

Participants in the Battle at Fort Mims, August 30, 1813, compiled by Gregory Waselkov, James Parker, and Sue Moore

Our research has identified at least 224 individuals involved in the battle at Fort Mims. A summary of information on individual battle participants, detailed below, highlights some interesting relationships between an individual's race and their likelihood of death (name in **bold**), capture (*italics*), or escape— survival, in the case of Redsticks (plain). Names of those Fort Mims occupants who escaped because they were outside the fort at the time of the attack are underlined. Only 14 Redsticks have been identified by name (Coolajer, Cyrus, Dog Warrior [Efa Tastanagi], **Far-off Warrior [Hopoie Tastanagi]**, Jumper [Otee Emathla], Nahomahteeathle Hopoie, Old Interpreter [James Walsh], Russell, Sanota [Jim Boy], the Shawnee Seekaboo, William Steadham, Paddy Walsh, a chief of Wewocau, and William Weatherford). This is clearly an inadequate sample of the 700 or more Redsticks involved in the fighting, so we draw no inferences from them.

Excluding the 14 known Redsticks, we have evidence for 210 individuals at Fort Mims on August 30, 1813. Our list includes 122 men, 30 women, 49 children, and 9 unknown. Broken down by race, there are 99 whites, 65 Africans, and 46 métis. The Redsticks killed 130 and captured 43; 37 escaped (28 from the fort). Of all these figures, we consider only the count of escapees from the fort (28) close to accurate.[1] All other figures are undercounts. To the overall list of escapees we must add an unknown number of women (and children?) doing laundry on Boatyard Lake who escaped with Peggy Bailey. Approximately twice the number listed here as killed must have died at the hands of the Redsticks. We can assume all or nearly all of the 49 unidentified Volunteers died, since no white or métis men are known to have been captured. Women and children (especially children) of all races are undoubtedly underrepresented in our list, as they are generally in legal documents of the period. If we accept as a minimum the burial party's count of 247 killed on the U.S. side, and estimate about 100 captured and at least 50 escapees, the number of persons inside the fort the morning of the battle minimally totaled around 400.

The Mississippi Territorial Volunteers garrisoning Fort Mims on August 30, 1813, are thought to have totaled 106, minus 6 on leave in Mobile. We have positively identified 34 (Major **Beasley;** Captains **Jack, Middleton;** Lieutenant **Osborne;** Ensigns Chambliss, **Gibbs, McDonald,** [Cornet] **Rankin, Swan;** Sergeants **L. Cathell, Gowan, Kingsbury, Lee, Lowe,** Mountjoy, **E. Steers;** Corporals Daniels, **Holliday;** Musicians **Otis, Shaw;** Privates Bradford, **J. Cathell,** Cook, **Hamilton, Hammond,** Holmes, Inman, **Judkins,** Mathews, Morris, Page, **Tierney, Wade,** Weakley).

The May 4, 1814, issue of the *Washington Republican* carried a public notice of a special Orphans Court scheduled to be held eight days later in Washington, Adams County, Mississippi Territory, to consider administrators for the estates of the following individuals who appear on the rolls of the 1st Regiment of Mississippi Territorial Volunteers: Lewis Brandt (Sergeant Lewis W. Brant), William Bush (Private), Thomas Dozere (Sergeant Thomas Dozier), Matthew Hall (Sergeant), John Judkins (Private),[2] Michael O'Neal (Private Michael Oneal), Edward Steers (Sergeant), and William Steers (Corporal). Such a mass listing for an Orphans Court is highly unusual. Names of two additional privates of the 1st Regiment—Thomas Smith and John Miller—appear in separate court notices published in that issue of the *Washington Republican.* Four others—Robert Green (Corporal), Henry Irby (Private), William McDonald (Corporal), and John Short (Corporal), as well as the previously listed John Miller—appear in other proceedings of the Adams County Orphans Court between January and July 1814.[3] Claiborne County held an Orphans Court on November 8, 1813, that appointed estate administrators for Thomas Evans (Private), Levi Holliday (Corporal), and Simeon Holliday (Private), who had been members of the 1st Regiment, Mississippi Territorial Volunteers, during the summer of 1813.[4] Jefferson County Orphans Court minutes for January and May 1814 list Charles McLaughlin (Private) and William Mays (Musician).[5] We suspect that a great many, perhaps all, of these soldiers died in the battle at Fort Mims. This supposition is strengthened by the appearance of two of these soldiers (Corporal Levi Holliday and Sergeant Edward Steers) on a list of those killed at Fort Mims found among General Claiborne's papers and published by John W. Monette in 1842; that list also includes Sergeants James H. Gowan, Charles Lee, John Lowe; Privates William Hamilton, Peter Tierney,

Henry Wade; and Fifer Zachariah Shaw.[6] In addition, the deaths of Private Jud-kins, Corporal Holliday, and Sergeant Steers at Fort Mims are confirmed by other historical sources. Therefore, from this Orphans Court evidence we pro-pose another 16 likely identifications (Sergeants **Brandt, Dozier, Hall;** Corpo-rals **Green, McDonald, Short, W. Steers;** Musician **Mays;** Privates **Bush, Evans, Holliday, Irby, McLaughlin, Miller, O'Neal, Smith**). This yields a total of 50 white men, 39 killed and 11 escaped (10 from the fort). One eleven-year-old enslaved African known as *Ambrose* (listed below) accompanied the Volunteers as Captain Middleton's personal servant and was taken captive by the Red-sticks.

At least 45 men were enrolled in the Tensaw militia; more or fewer may have been present on August 30. Major Beasley's report to General Claiborne enu-merated 41 fit for duty the morning of August 29.[7] We have identified 15, in-cluding 7 métis (Captain **Dixon Bailey;** Lieutenant P. Randon; lesser Officers and Privates **Daniel Bailey, J. Bailey, Dunn,** Hollinger, Smith) and 8 whites (lesser Officers and Privates **Crawford, Hodge,** J. Hoven, **Plummer, John Rig-don,** Martin Rigdon, Ned Steadham, Jesse Steadham). Another 28 men from the Tensaw are likely to have been members of the militia, including 8 métis (P. Durant, **Dyer, Marlow, James Randon, John Randon,** Socca [Creek, per-haps not métis], **Joel Steadham, Matthew Steadham**) and 20 whites (Beale, Bradley, Cox, Fletcher, **Hatterway,** Jones, **McConnell,** McGirth, **O'Neal,** Perry, **Phillips, J. Rankin, R. Richbourg,** Shaw, **Elijah Steadham, James Steadham, Thomas Steadham,** Stubblefield, **Walker, Whitehead**). Of these 43 men, 26 were killed (16 white, 10 métis) and 17 escaped (12 white [11 from the fort], 5 métis [4 from the fort]).

There are 21 additional whites known, including 6 men (**B. Durant, B. Ho-ven, D. Mims, S. Mims, N. Richbourg, Moses Steadham;** 6 killed), 4 women (**Mrs. Richard Dixon Bailey, Mary Dunn Hoven,** Betsy Hoven, **Mrs. Wiseman Walker;** 3 killed, 1 escaped from the fort), and 11 children (**at least 2 Hoven children, 6 Steadham daughters, at least 2 Walker children,** *white child;* 10 killed, 1 captured), for a total of 19 killed, 1 captured, and 1 escaped from the fort. The mysterious "Spanish deserters" mentioned in two late reminiscences are not counted here.

An additional 31 métis are known from historical records, including 2 men (James Cornells, **Jahomobtee** [Creek, perhaps not métis]; 1 killed, 1 escaped [not from the fort]), 11 women (Margaret "Peggy Bailey, **Nancy Pounds Bailey, Mary Hollinger Dyer, Elizabeth Bailey Fletcher,** *Susannah Stiggins Hatter-way, Mary "Polly" Kean Jones, Levitia "Vicey" Cornells McGillivray McGirth,*

Tura Dyer Randon, <u>Lavinia "Viney" Randon,</u> **Sarah Summerlin, Mary Louisa Randon Tate;** 6 killed, 3 captured, 2 escaped [not from the fort]), and at least 18 children (**Ralph Bailey, 3 James Bailey children, at least 2 Dixon Bailey children,** *Seaborn F. Jones, Samuel Jones, Jeffersonia Hawkins Jones,* **James McGirth,** *4 unnamed McGirth daughters, Sarah McGirth, Elizabeth Randon,* 2 Randon daughters; 9 killed, 9 captured), for a total of 16 killed, 12 captured, and 3 escaped (none from the fort).

No reliable counts or estimates exist for the number of enslaved Africans involved in the battle. We suspect there were around 100, perhaps more. There is historical documentation for apparently 65 individuals; many of these, however, are unnamed, so we cannot be certain that none has been counted twice. We have not listed "some of the McGillivray negroes" that Woodward thought had assisted the Redsticks in setting fire to Fort Mims, because that reference is unspecific in regard to names, number, and owners.[8] Among our total of 65 are 21 men (**Anthony, Bob,** *Caesar, Jack Cato,* **Charles, Cooley, Jack, Jack,** <u>Jo,</u> **Lisbon, Mango, Nead, Negro fellow, Negro fellow, Negro fellow, negro man,** *Negro man,* <u>Negro man,</u> **Negro man, Smith,** *Tom;* 15 killed, 4 captured, and 2 escaped [neither from the fort), 15 women (**Betty,** *Eliza,* Hester, **Jane,** *Lettice,* **Luce, Mary,** *Milley, Milly,* **Nance, Negro Wench,** *Negroe woman,* **Negroe woman,** *Penny,* **Till;** 8 killed, 6 captured, and 1 escaped from the fort), 20 children (*Ambrose,* **Barbara, Beck, Bukton,** *Ginny, India, Jack,* **Jane's child,** *Jim, Jim, Jude, Lizzie,* <u>Negro boy,</u> **Negro boy, Negro boy, Negro girl,** Negro girl, *Peggy, Philis, Wallace;* 7 killed, 11 captured, and 2 escaped [one from the fort]), and 9 captured "Negroes" of unspecified gender and age. Of these 65 Africans, 30 were killed, 30 were captured, and 5 escaped (2 from the fort). This count does not include the African Cyrus, who fought with the Redsticks and is included in their number (above).

Several individuals have been identified by descendants as survivors or victims of the battle at Fort Mims, based entirely on family tradition and oral history. While we have been unable to substantiate these claims with independent information, we recognize that the families' records and traditions eventually may be proven correct with more research. We provide this list of names in the hope that others will be able to determine any relationship they may have to this pivotal event and that the identities of many more participants—white, black, Redstick, *métis*—will someday be discovered. Our "unproven" list includes: Thomas and Elizabeth Adcock,[9] Harriet Allen,[10] John and Margaret Carter Allen,[11] James Boon, Thomas J. Downing,[12] Cornelius Dunn,[13] Capt. Robert Dunn,[14] Penelope Farr,[15] Samuel Fillingim and Esther Boggs,[16] Walter

Griffin, Mrs. Bernard Riley, Mr. Sinquefield,[17] Aletha and Aletha Ann Smith,[18] George Weekley and unnamed wife,[19] and William Whitmire. Other family traditions of ancestral involvement in the battle at Fort Mims seem demonstrably erroneous, based on conflicting historical evidence: Mrs. Daniel Beasley and Lilla Beazley,[20] Lazarus John Bryars,[21] Robert Fillingim,[22] Audley L. Osborne and Ephraim Brevard Osborne,[23] and William and Mary Miller Tarvin.[24]

Table 3. Participants in the Battle at Fort Mims, August 30, 1813

Name	Sex	Age	Slave	Slave Owner	Fate	Notes
———, Ambrose[25]	M	11	X	Clark Middleton	Captured	(African descent) "Negro," private servant of Captain Hatton C. Middleton, surrendered by Redsticks at Fort Jackson on July 15, 1814
———, Anthony[26]	M	22	X	Samuel Mims	Killed	(African descent) "Negro man," Tensaw resident
Bailey, Daniel[27]	M	~15			Killed	Creek métis (Creek-English, Wind clan), member of Tensaw militia, brother of Dixon and James
Bailey, James[28]	M	~27			Killed	Creek métis (Creek-English, Wind clan), member of Tensaw militia; brother of Dixon and Daniel Bailey
Bailey, Margaret "Peggy"[29]	F				Escaped	Creek métis (Creek-English, Wind clan), Tensaw resident, sister of Dixon, Daniel, and James Bailey;

Continued on the next page

Name	Sex	Age	Slave	Slave Owner	Fate	Notes
						"working on the lake then swam the Alabama"
Bailey, Nancy [Durant?] Pounds[30]	F	23			Killed	Creek métis (Creek-English-French), Tensaw resident, wife of James Bailey, perhaps granddaughter of Sophia McGillivray Durant and Benjamin Durant
Bailey, Ralph[31]	M	14			Killed	Creek métis (Creek-English), Tensaw resident, son of Dixon Bailey
Bailey, Richard Dixon[32]	M	~35			Killed	Creek métis (Creek-English, Wind clan), from Atasi, son of Richard Bailey (from England) and Mary (member of Wind clan), elected Captain of Tensaw militia in early August 1813, wounded while fleeing fort at the end of the battle, died in the woods of his wounds
Bailey, ——— [Mrs. Richard Dixon (Sarah?)][33]	F				Killed	(English descent? from South Carolina?), Tensaw resident, wife of Dixon Bailey
Bailey children[34]					Killed	Creek métis (Creek-English), children of James Bailey, including two by

Name	Sex	Age	Slave	Slave Owner	Fate	Notes
Bailey children[35]					Killed	Nancy [Durant?] Pounds and one by Nancy Summerlin Creek métis (Creek-English), children of Dixon Bailey
——, Barbara[36]	F	13	X	John Randon	Killed	(African descent) "Negro girl," Tensaw resident
Beale, James[37]	M				Escaped	(English descent) Resident of Washington County, MT
Beasley, Daniel[38]	M	47			Killed	(English descent) Major, Mississippi Territorial Volunteers, post commander; from Chesterfield County, Virginia; resided in Greenville, Jefferson County, MT; "shot in the bowels" or dispatched with a war club while rushing toward the fort's open gate
——, Beck[39]	F	12	X	Josiah Fletcher	Killed?	(African descent) "Negro girl," Tensaw resident
——, Betty[40]	F	17	X	Moses Steadham, Sr.	Killed	(African descent) "Negroe woman," Tensaw resident
——, Bob[41]	M	25	X	Josiah Fletcher	Killed	(African descent) "Negro man," Tensaw resident
Bradford, Elemuel[42]	M				Escaped	(English descent) Private, Mississippi Territorial Volunteers

Continued on the next page

Name	Sex	Age	Slave	Slave Owner	Fate	Notes
Bradley, Aaron[43]	M				Escaped	(English descent) Tensaw resident
——, Bukton[44]	M	12	X	Josiah Fletcher	Killed	(African descent) "Negro boy," Tensaw resident
——, Caesar[45]	M		X	Mrs. B. Riley (O'Riley?)	Captured	(African descent) Tensaw resident, captured on the Tallapoosa
Cathell, Joshua[46]	M				Killed	(English descent) Private, Mississippi Territorial Volunteers, from Baldwin County, Georgia
Cathell, Levin[47]	M				Killed	(English descent) Sergeant, Mississippi Territorial Volunteers, from Baldwin County, Georgia
Cato, Jack[48]	M	~18	X	Wyche Cato	Survived	(African descent) "colored resident of Clarke County . . . a drummer in the War of 1812 . . . claims to have been at Fort Mims"
Chambliss, William R.[49]	M				Escaped	(English descent) Ensign in Captain Jack's rifle company, Mississippi Territorial Volunteers, shot with two arrows and a musket ball, found a boat and floated to Mt. Vernon, "died ten years afterwards;" resided in Port Gibson, Claiborne County, MT

Name	Sex	Age	Slave	Slave Owner	Fate	Notes
——, Charles[50]	M	25	X	David Mims, Sr.	Killed	(African descent) "Negro man," Tensaw resident
Cook, Joseph[51]	M				Escaped	(English descent) Private, Mississippi Territorial Volunteers
Coolajer (Light Maker)[52]	M				Survived	Redstick war leader, from an Alabama town, also called Dog Warrior; said to have led attack on Fort Sinquefield in early September
——, Cooley[53]	M	45	X	Samuel Mims	Killed	(African descent) "Negro man," Tensaw resident
Cornells, James[54]	M	~41			Survived	Creek métis (Creek-English), Tensaw resident, son of Joseph Cornells and brother of Vicey McGirth; tried to warn those inside Fort Mims of the imminent Redstick attack
Cox, Fletcher[55]	M				Escaped	(English descent) Tensaw resident?
Crawford, ——[56]	M				Killed	(English descent) Tensaw resident, member of Tensaw militia, elected Ensign in early August 1813, dismissed as Ensign after discovery that he once deserted from the U.S. Army

Continued on the next page

Name	Sex	Age	Slave	Slave Owner	Fate	Notes
———, Cyrus ("Siras")[57]	M	50	X	Samuel Moniac	Survived	Redstick, (African descent) "Negro man," Tensaw resident; either captured by or joined the Redsticks at Samuel Moniac's plantations and joined them in the attack on Fort Mims where he "cut down the pickets"
Daniels, Abner[58]	M				Escaped	(English descent) Corporal, Mississippi Territorial Volunteers, from Jefferson Co., MT
Dog Warrior, Efa Tastanagi (*Efv Tustunuke*)[59]	M				Survived	Redstick Creek, from Atasi, saved Susannah Stiggins Hatterway, Elizabeth Randon, and Lizzie, a little black girl; killed at the battle of Atasi in November 29, 1813
Dunn, Thomas[60]	M	24			Killed	Creek métis (Creek-English), Tensaw resident, member of Tensaw militia, stepped down as Ensign in early August 1813
Durant, Benjamin (also known as Peter Durant)[61]	M	~59			Killed	(French Huguenot descent) born in South Carolina; Tensaw resident, husband of Sophia McGillivray, father of Nancy and Lachlan Durant

Name	Sex	Age	Slave	Slave Owner	Fate	Notes
Durant, Peter[62]	M				Escaped	Creek métis (Creek-French), Tensaw resident, relative of Benjamin, left fort before battle to pick grapes across river
Dyer, Mary Hollinger[63]	F				Killed	Choctaw métis (French-Choctaw-English), Tensaw resident, wife of Rueben Dyer, half-sister of William Hollinger
Dyer, Rueben[64]	M	63			Killed	Creek métis (Creek-English), Tensaw resident, husband of Mary Hollinger Dyer
——, Eliza[65] (Lizzie?)	F		X	David Tate	Captured	(African descent) Tensaw resident; Susannah Stiggins Hatterway requested of Andrew Jackson that Eliza be turned over to David Tate, which was done on October 28, 1818.
Far-off Warrior, Hopoie Tastanagi (*Hopvyē Tustunuke*)[66]	M				Killed	Redstick Creek (Bear clan) war leader from Taskigi, son of Efa Haujo (Mad Dog) and Big Woman
Fletcher, Elizabeth Bailey[67]	F	37			Killed	Creek métis (Creek-English, Wind clan), Tensaw resident; sister of Dixon, James, and Daniel Bailey, wife of Josiah Fletcher

Continued on the next page

Name	Sex	Age	Slave	Slave Owner	Fate	Notes
Fletcher, Josiah[68]	M	47			Escaped	(English descent) Tensaw resident, lay among hogs after escape, then met with Lt. Davis' command; husband of Elizabeth Bailey Fletcher in 1796
Gibbs, George H.[69]	M				Killed	(English descent) Ensign, Mississippi Territorial Volunteers
———, Ginny[70]	F	4	X	James Earle	Captured	(African descent) "Negro," Tensaw resident, surrendered at Fort Jackson on July 15, 1814
Gowan, James H.[71]	M				Killed	(English descent) Sergeant, Mississippi Territorial Volunteers, Captain Jack's company
Hamilton, William[72]	M				Killed	(English descent) Private, Mississippi Territorial Volunteers, Captain Middleton's company
Hammond, Thomas[73]	M				Killed	(English descent) Private, Mississippi Territorial Volunteers
Hatterway, Henry[74]	M				Killed	(English descent) Tensaw resident, husband of Susannah Stiggins Hatterway
Hatterway, Susannah Stiggins[75]	F	18			Captured	Natchez métis (Natchez-English), Tensaw resident, wife of Henry

Name	Sex	Age	Slave	Slave Owner	Fate	Notes
——, Hester[76]	F		X	Benjamin Steadham	Escaped	Hatterway, George Stiggins' sister, daughter of Joseph Stiggins and Haw, rescued by Efa Tastanagi, Dog Warrior of Atasi (African descent) "Negroe woman," Tensaw resident, wounded in arm during escape through the pickets
Hodge, Alexander ("Alex") Elliott[77]	M				Killed	(English descent) Tensaw resident, from Georgia, member of Tensaw militia
Holliday, Levi[78]	M				Killed	(English descent) Corporal, Mississippi Territorial Volunteers, Captain Middleton's company
Hollinger, William Randon[79]	M	30			Escaped	Creek métis (Creek-English), Tensaw resident, private in the Tensaw militia, half-brother of Mary Hollinger Dyer; wounded at the battle of Burnt Corn Creek
Holmes, Thomas Golphin[80]	M	33			Escaped	African métis (African-Irish), Assistant Surgeon and Private, Mississippi Territorial Volunteers, Tensaw resident; from

Continued on the next page

Name	Sex	Age	Slave	Slave Owner	Fate	Notes
Hoven, Benjamin[81]	M	54			Killed	Silver Bluff, South Carolina; escaped fort at end of battle (Dutch descent) Tensaw resident, from South Carolina, husband of Mary Dunn
Hoven, Mary Dunn[82]	F				Killed	(English descent) Tensaw resident, from Georgia, wife of Benjamin Hoven, probably a sister of Cornelius Dunn
Hoven, John[83]	M	19			Escaped	(Dutch-English descent) Tensaw resident, private in the Tensaw militia, son of Benjamin and Mary Hoven; escaped by swimming
Hoven, —— [Betsy][84]	F				Escaped	(Dutch-English descent) Tensaw resident, sister of John Hoven, escaped through an opening in the wall, caught an officer's horse and rode to St. Stephens
Hoven children[85]					Killed	(Dutch-English descent) Several children
——, India[86]	F	6	X	Josiah Fletcher	Captured	(African descent) "Negro," Tensaw resident, surrendered at Fort Jackson on July 15, 1814

Name	Sex	Age	Slave	Slave Owner	Fate	Notes
——, Jack[87]	M	10–13	X	Wiseman Walker	Captured	(African descent) Tensaw resident
——, Jack[88]	M	17	X	Josiah Fletcher	Killed	"Negro boy," Tensaw resident
——, Jack[89]	M		X	Cornelius Dunn	Killed	(African descent) "Negroe man," Tensaw resident, "supposed to have been killed"
Inman, Richard[90]	M	30			Escaped	(English descent) Private, Mississippi Territorial Volunteers
Jack, William[91]	M	27			Killed	(English descent) Captain, Mississippi Territorial Volunteers; from Adams County, MT, resided in Jefferson County, MT
Jahomobtee[92]	M				Killed?	Creek, pro-American faction, "shot three Indians in the act of tomahawking white women"
——, Jane[93]	F	19	X	Josiah Fletcher	Killed	(African descent) "Negro woman," Tensaw resident
——, Jane's child[94]			X	Josiah Fletcher	Killed	(African descent) Tensaw resident, child of Jane ("Negro woman")
——, Jim[95]	M	3	X	James Earle	Captured	(African descent) "Negro," Tensaw resident, surrendered at Fort Jackson on July 15, 1814
——, Jim[96]	M	8–10	X	Wiseman Walker	Captured	(African descent) Tensaw resident

Continued on the next page

Name	Sex	Age	Slave	Slave Owner	Fate	Notes
——, Jo[97]	M		X	Zachariah McGirth	Captured, Escaped, Captured?	(African descent) Sent to McGirth's plantation to gather corn before battle, captured by Redsticks, escaped and returned to fort; recaptured or joined Redsticks
Jones, Mary "Polly" Kean[98]	F	25			Captured	Creek métis (Creek-English), Tensaw resident, daughter of John Kean and Lucy Cornells, half-sister of Samuel Smith, niece of James Cornells, wife of William Samuel Jones, taken to Wewocau, "delivered up" at Fort Jackson
Jones, Seaborn F.[99]	M	9			Captured	Creek métis (Creek-English), Tensaw resident, son of Polly and William Samuel Jones, taken to Wewocau, "delivered up" at Fort Jackson
Jones, Samuel[100]	M	7			Captured	Creek métis (Creek-English), Tensaw resident, son of Polly and William Samuel Jones, taken to Wewocau, "delivered up" at Fort Jackson
Jones, Jeffersonia Hawkins[101]	F	4			Captured	Creek métis (Creek-English), Tensaw resident, daugh-

Name	Sex	Age	Slave	Slave Owner	Fate	Notes
						ter of Polly and William Samuel Jones, taken to Wewocau, "delivered up" at Fort Jackson
Jones, William Samuel[102]	M	~39			Escaped	(English descent), Tensaw resident, husband of Mary "Polly" Kean Jones wounded in thigh during escape
———, Jude[103]	F	8	X	Josiah Fletcher	Captured	(African descent) "Negro girl," Tensaw resident, returned by General Jackson
Judkins, John[104]	M	31			Killed	(English descent) Private, Mississippi Territorial Volunteers, resided in Adams County, MT
Jumper, Otee Emathla (*Ohta Emahlv*)[105]	M				Survived	Redstick Creek warrior, "rushed through the gate at Fort Mims," later fought with Micanopy in the Seminole Wars
Kingsbury ("Rishbury"), Daniel[106]	M				Killed	(English descent) Sergeant, Mississippi Territorial Volunteers, "a soldier died from pure fear"
Lee, Charles[107]	M				Killed	(English descent) Sergeant, Mississippi Territorial Volunteers, Captain Painboeuf's company

Continued on the next page

Name	Sex	Age	Slave	Slave Owner	Fate	Notes
——, Lettice[108]	F	18	X	James Earle	Captured	(African descent) "Negro," Tensaw resident, surrendered at Fort Jackson on July 15, 1814.
——, Lisbon (Lesbon)[109]	F	27	X	Robert McConnell	Killed	(African descent) Tensaw resident
——, Lizzie[110]	F	X			Captured	(African descent) "a little colored girl"
Lowe, John[111]					Killed	(English descent) Sergeant, Mississippi Territorial Volunteers, Captain Painboeuf's company
——, Luce (Lucy)[112]	F	17	X	Moses Steadham, Jr.	Killed	(African descent) "Negroe woman," Tensaw resident
——, Mango (Marengo)[113]	M	35	X	Josiah Fletcher	Killed	(African descent) "Negro man," Tensaw resident
Marlow, James[114]	M				Killed	Creek métis (Creek-English), Tensaw resident
——, Mary[115]	F	40	X	Josiah Fletcher	Killed	(African descent) "Negro woman," Tensaw resident
Mathews, Samuel[116]	M				Escaped	(English descent) Private, Mississippi Territorial Volunteers, called "Sergeant" by survivors, accused of cowardice
McConnell, Robert[117]	M				Killed	(English descent) Tensaw resident
McDonald, Young R.[118]	M				Killed	(English descent) Ensign, Mississippi Territorial Volunteers, Captain

Name	Sex	Age	Slave	Slave Owner	Fate	Notes
"McGillivray Negroes"[119]	M				Unknown	Painboeuf's company, resident of Amite County, from South Carolina (African descent) helped the Redsticks set fire to Fort Mims
McGirth, James[120]	M	child			Killed	Creek métis (Creek-English), Tensaw resident, son of Vicey and Zachariah McGirth
McGirth daughters[121]	F				Captured	Creek métis (Creek-English), Tensaw resident, four unnamed daughters of Vicey and Zachariah McGirth
McGirth, Sarah[122]	F	child			Captured	Creek métis (Creek-English), Tensaw resident, daughter of Vicey and Zachariah McGirth
McGirth, Levitia "Vicey" Cornells McGillivray[123]	F	~43			Captured	Creek métis (Creek-English), Tensaw resident, daughter of Joseph Cornells and sister of James Cornells, previously married to Alexander McGillivray, wife of Zachariah McGirth; captured by Sanota or Jim Boy
McGirth, Zachariah[124]	M	43			Escaped	(English descent) Tensaw resident,

Continued on the next page

Name	Sex	Age	Slave	Slave Owner	Fate	Notes
						husband of Vicey McGirth, left the fort moments before the Redstick attack
Middleton, Hatton C.[125]	M	29			Killed	(English descent) Captain, Mississippi Territorial Volunteers, resident of Adams County, MT
——, Milley[126]	F	40	X	Rueben Dyer	Captured	(African descent) "Negro," mother of Peggy, Tensaw resident, surrendered at Fort Jackson on July 15, 1814
——, Milly[127]	F	40	X	Alex Hodge	Captured	(African descent) "Negro," mother of Philis, Tensaw resident, surrendered at Fort Jackson on July 15, 1814
Mims, David[128]	M	76			Killed	(English descent) Tensaw resident, from Albemarle County, Virginia, shot while entering the bastion from the Mims house; brother of Samuel Mims
Mims, Samuel[129]	M	66			Killed	(English descent) Tensaw resident, from Albemarle County, Virginia, brother of David Mims, husband of Hannah Rains Mims

Name	Sex	Age	Slave	Slave Owner	Fate	Notes
Morris ("Maurice"), A. J.[130]	M	22			Escaped	(English descent) Private, Mississippi Territorial Volunteers, escaped through the pickets.
Mountjoy, John[131]	M				Escaped	(English descent) Sergeant, Mississippi Territorial Volunteers
Nahomahteeathle Hopoie (*Enhomahtvhorre Hopvyē,* "foremost man in danger in time of battle")[132]	M				Survived	Redstick Creek prophet, from Jim Boy's town
———, Nance (Nancy)[133]	F	27	X	Moses Steadham, Sr.	Killed	(African descent) "Negroe woman," Tensaw resident
———, Nead (Ned)[134]	M	19	X	Josiah Fletcher	Killed	(African descent) "Negro boy," Tensaw resident
"Negroe"[135]			X	Dixon Bailey	Killed?	(African descent) Tensaw resident
"Negroe"[136]			X	Dixon Bailey	Killed?	(African descent) Tensaw resident
"Negroe"[137]			X	Dixon Bailey	Killed?	(African descent) Tensaw resident
"Negro"[138]			X	George Cornells	Captured	(African descent) Tensaw resident, recaptured on the Chattahoochee
"Negro"[139]			X	George Cornells	Captured	(African descent) Tensaw resident, recaptured on the Chattahoochee
"Negro"[140]			X	George Cornells	Captured	(African descent) Tensaw resident, recaptured on the Chattahoochee

Continued on the next page

Name	Sex	Age	Slave	Slave Owner	Fate	Notes
"Negro"[141]			X	George Cornells	Captured	(African descent) Tensaw resident, recaptured on the Chattahoochee
"Negro"[142]			X	George Cornells	Captured	(African descent) Tensaw resident, recaptured on the Chattahoochee
"Negro"[143]			X	Ann Turvin (Tarvin)	Killed or Captured	(African descent) Tensaw resident
"Negro boy"[144]	M		X	John Randon	Escaped	(African descent) Tensaw resident, went to the fort at Peirce's Mill immediately before the attack
"Negro boy"[145]	M		X	John Randon	Killed?	(African descent) Tensaw resident
"Negro boy"[146]	M	15	X	Nathaniel Richbourg	Killed	(African descent) Tensaw resident
"Negro boy"[147]	M	15	X	Nathaniel Richbourg	Killed?	(African descent) Tensaw resident
"Negro fellow"[148]	M		X	James Earle	Killed	(African descent) Tensaw resident
"Negro fellow"[149]	M		X	Mary Dyer	Killed	(African descent) Tensaw resident
"Negro fellow"[150]	M		X	Mary Dyer	Killed	(African descent) Tensaw resident
"[Negro] girl"[151]	F	10	X	Mary Dyer	Killed	(African descent) Tensaw resident
"Negro girl"[152]	F		X	John Randon	Escaped	(African descent) Tensaw resident
"negro man"[153]	M		X	Eli Shaw	Killed	(African descent) Tensaw resident
"Negro man"[154]	M		X		Captured	(African descent) taken to Wewocau, escaped and re-ported to Benjamin Hawkins
"Negro man"[155]	M		X	Zachariah McGirth	Escaped	(African descent) Tensaw resident, left fort with

Name	Sex	Age	Slave	Slave Owner	Fate	Notes
"Negro man"[156]	M	19	X	Samuel Edmunds	Killed	McGirth immediately before Redstick attack (African descent) Tensaw resident
"Negro Wench"[157]	F		X	Elizabeth Bailey & Mrs. David Allen	Killed	(African descent) Tensaw resident
"Negroe woman"[158]	M		X	Richard Turvin (Tarvin)	Killed or Captured	(African descent) Tensaw resident
"negro woman"[159]	F	30	X	Samuel Edmunds	Killed	(African descent) Tensaw resident
Old Interpreter (James Walsh?)[160]	M				Survived	Redstick warrior (Irish descent-métis?), probably stepfather of Paddy Walsh, helped "cut the fort down"
O'Neal, Benjamin[161]	M				Killed	(English descent) Tensaw resident, neighbor of Samuel Mims, whose house on the road to Mims' Ferry was burned by the Redsticks
Osborne, Spruce McKay[162]	M	28			Killed	(English-Scots descent) Second Lieutenant and surgeon, Mississippi Territorial Volunteers; from Iredell County, North Carolina attended West Point Military Academy; resided in Wilkinson County, MT; died in Patrick Mahoney's loom house

Continued on the next page

Name	Sex	Age	Slave	Slave Owner	Fate	Notes
Otis, James[163]	M				Killed	(English descent) Musician (drummer), Mississippi Territorial Volunteers, resided in Amite County, MT
Page, Nehemiah Scott[164]	M	26			Escaped	(English descent) Private and hostler, Mississippi Territorial Volunteers, from North Carolina, resident of Washington County, MT; asleep in stable outside fort when attack began
———, Peggy[165]	F	12	X	Rueben Dyer	Captured	(African descent) "Negro," Tensaw resident, daughter of Milly, surrendered at Fort Jackson on July 15, 1814
———, Penny[166]	F	40	X	James Earle	Captured	(African descent) "Negro," Tensaw resident, surrendered at Fort Jackson on July 15, 1814
Perry, Joseph[167]	M				Escaped	(English descent) Escaped through the pickets
———, Philis[168]	F	1	X	Alex Hodge	Captured	(African descent) "Negro," Tensaw resident, daughter of Milly, surrendered at Fort Jackson on July 15, 1814
Phillips, Jeremiah[169]	M	37+			Killed	(English descent) Tensaw resident, occupied plantation on Nannahubba Island,

Name	Sex	Age	Slave	Slave Owner	Fate	Notes
Plummer, _____[170]	M				Killed	mentioned along with Wiseman Walker as deceased on documents claiming reparations for property lost at Fort Mims (English descent) Tensaw resident, member of Tensaw militia, "acted cowardly" at Burnt Corn Creek battle, stepped down as Ensign in early August 1813
Randon, Elizabeth[171]	F	4			Captured	Creek métis (Creek-French-English), Tensaw resident, daughter of John Randon and Tura Dyer Randon, rescued by Susannah Hatterway and Efa Tastanagi, the Dog Warrior of Atasi
Randon, James[172]	M	43			Killed?	Creek métis (Creek-French, Panther clan), Tensaw resident, brother of John Randon
Randon, John[173]	M	47			Killed	Creek métis (Creek-French, Panther clan), Tensaw resident, from Burke County, GA; brother of James Randon, husband of Tura Dyer Randon

Continued on the next page

Name	Sex	Age	Slave	Slave Owner	Fate	Notes
Randon, Peter[174]	M	23			Escaped	Creek métis (Creek-French-English), elected Ensign, then Lieutenant of Tensaw militia in mid-August 1813, son of John Randon and Roseanna Holmes
Randon, Tura Dyer[175]	F				Killed	Creek métis (Creek-English), Tensaw resident, wife of John Randon, daughter of Rueben Dyer and Mary Hollinger
Randon, Lavinia ("Viney")[176]	F	~15			Escaped	Creek métis (Creek-French-African) Tensaw resident, possibly a niece of John Randon, left fort before battle to pick grapes across river
Randon daughters[177]	F				Killed	Creek métis (Creek-French-English) Tensaw resident, two daughters of John Randon and Roseanna Holmes
Rankin, Joseph[178]	M	24			Killed	(English descent) Tombigbee resident, born in Kentucky, brother of Thomas Berry Rankin, possibly a member of the Tensaw militia
Rankin, Thomas Berry[179]	M	30			Killed	(English descent) Cornet, Mississippi Territorial Volunteers, com-

Name	Sex	Age	Slave	Slave Owner	Fate	Notes
						manded dragoons, Tombigbee resident, born in Virginia, brother of Joseph Rankin
Richbourg, Nathaniel[180]	M	67			Killed	(French descent, probably Huguenot) Tensaw resident, from Craven County, South Carolina, father of Renna Richbourg
Richbourg, René ("Renna")[181]	M				Killed	(French descent) Tensaw resident, adult son of Nathaniel Richbourg
Rigdon, John[182]	M	19			Killed	(English descent) Tensaw resident, Private and drummer in Tensaw militia; born in Lincoln County, North Carolina, musician in U. S. 2nd Regiment until May 8, 1813
Rigdon, Martin[183]	M	17			Escaped	(English descent) Tensaw resident, Private and drummer in Tensaw militia; from Georgia, musician in U. S. 2nd Regiment until May 8, 1813, escaped through the pickets at Fort Mims, reenlisted at Mobile

Continued on the next page

Name	Sex	Age	Slave	Slave Owner	Fate	Notes
Rigdon family[184]					Killed	Point November 1, 1813, died in New Orleans in 1816 (English descent) Tensaw residents, possibly recently arrived from Georgia
Russell, ———[185]	M				Survived	Redstick Creek métis (Creek-English), "son of Hoithlewaule," captured the "negro man" who escaped and reported to Benjamin Hawkins
Sanota (Jim Boy?)[186]	M	20			Survived	Redstick Creek warrior who captured the McGirth females; killed at Horseshoe Bend, March 1814
Seekaboo[187]	M	42			Survived	Métis (Shawnee-Creek-English?), relative of Tecumseh; prophet fighting with the Redsticks
Shaw, Eli[188]	M				Killed	(English descent) Tensaw resident
Shaw, Zachariah[189]	M				Killed	(English descent) Fifer (musician), Mississippi Territorial Volunteers, Captain Middleton's company
———, Smith[190]	M	30	X	George Weekley	Killed	(African descent) "Negroe man," Tensaw resident
Smith, Samuel[191]	M				Escaped	Creek métis (Creek-English) in Tensaw militia, son of

Name	Sex	Age	Slave	Slave Owner	Fate	Notes
Socca[192]					Escaped	Lucy Cornells and Samuel Smith, escaped through the pickets Creek, "a friendly Indian"
"Spanish deserters"[193]	M				Killed	(Spanish) from four to eight sailors or soldiers from Pensacola, "killed around the well"
Steadham daughters[194]	F				Killed	(Swedish-English descent), six daughters of Moses Steadham and Elizabeth ———
Steadham, Edward (Ned)[195]	M	27			Escaped	(Swedish-German descent), Tensaw resident, son of Moses Steadham and Winifred Eppinger, twin (?) brother of Thomas, private in Tensaw militia, finger of the left hand shot off while escaping.
Steadham, Elijah[196]	M	35			Killed	(Swedish-German descent) Tensaw resident, son of Moses Steadham and Winifred Eppinger
Steadham, James Moses[197]	M	29			Killed	(Swedish-German descent) Tensaw resident, son of Moses Steadham and Winifred Eppinger

Continued on the next page

Name	Sex	Age	Slave	Slave Owner	Fate	Notes
Steadham, Joel[198]	M	43			Killed	Creek métis (Creek-Swedish), Tensaw resident, son of John Steadham, brother of Matthew and half-brother or brother of William Steadham
Steadham, John Jesse[199]	M	26			Escaped	(Swedish-German descent) Tensaw resident, son of Moses Steadham and Winifred Eppinger, member of Tensaw militia, escaped through the pickets, shot through the thigh
Steadham, Matthew[200]	M	23			Killed	Creek métis (Creek-Swedish), Tensaw resident, son of John Steadham, brother of Joel and half-brother or brother of William Steadham
Steadham, Moses[201]	M	65			Killed	(Swedish descent) Tensaw resident, from Beaufort, South Carolina, son of Benjamin Steadham, half-brother of John Steadham
Steadham, Thomas[202]	M	27			Killed	(Swedish-German descent), Tensaw resident, son of Moses Steadham and Winifred Eppinger, twin (?) brother of Edward

Name	Sex	Age	Slave	Slave Owner	Fate	Notes
Steadham, William[203]	M				Survived	Redstick Creek métis warrior (Creek-Swedish), Tensaw resident, son of John Steadham, brother or half-brother of Joel and Matthew Steadham
Steers, Edward[204]	M				Killed	(English descent) Sergeant, Mississippi Territorial Volunteer, Captain Middleton's company
Stubblefield, William Henry[205]	M	20			Escaped	(English descent) wounded by arrow, saved by Samuel Smith
Summerlin, Sarah[206]	F				Killed	Creek métis (Creek-English?) Tensaw resident, wife of John Summerlin
Swan, Robert[207]	M	28			Killed	(English descent) Ensign, Mississippi Territorial Volunteers, Captain Middleton's company, resident of Natchez, arrived at Fort Mims on August 12 with supplies
Tate, Mary Louisa Randon[208]	F	27			Killed	Creek métis (Creek-French-English) Tensaw resident, daughter of John Randon, sister of Peter Randon, wife of David Tate

Continued on the next page

Name	Sex	Age	Slave	Slave Owner	Fate	Notes
Tierney, Peter[209]	M				Killed	(English descent) Private, Mississippi Territorial Volunteers, Captain Middleton's company
———, Till[210]	F	40	X	Josiah Fletcher	Killed	(African descent) "Negro woman," Tensaw resident
———, Tom[211]	M		X	Dixon Bailey	Survived	(African descent) Tensaw resident, escaped carrying Ralph Bailey but returned to fort.
———, Tony[212]	M	34	X	Judge Harry Toulmin	Captured	(African descent) "Negro," Tombigbee resident, taken to Holy Ground
Wade, Henry[213]	M				Killed	(English descent) Private, Mississippi Territorial Volunteers, Captain Middleton's company
Walker, Wiseman[214]	M				Killed	(English descent) Tensaw resident
Walker, ———[215]	F				Killed	(English descent) Tensaw resident, wife of Wiseman Walker
Walker children[216]					Killed	(English descent) Tensaw residents, children of Wiseman Walker
———, Wallace[217]	M	4	X	Benjamin Steadham	Captured	(African descent) "Negro," Tensaw resident, surrendered at Fort Jackson on July 15, 1814

Name	Sex	Age	Slave	Slave Owner	Fate	Notes
Walsh, Paddy[218]	M				Survived	Redstick Creek métis prophet (Alabama-?), from Tawasa town, wounded during the battle
Weatherford, William, Hopnicafutsahia (war name)[219]	M	33			Survived	Redstick Creek métis leader (Creek-English, Wind clan), Tensaw resident
Weakley, Buford[220]	M	43			Survived	(English descent) Private, Mississippi Territorial Volunteers, Tensaw resident, from Barnwell, South Carolina
Wewocau, a chief of[221]	M				Survived	Redstick Creek, led first warriors into Fort Mims
"White child"[222]	F				Captured	
Whitehead, Benjamin[223]	M				Killed	(English descent) Tensaw resident

Appendix 2

Places to Visit: Mississippi Territory and the Creek Nation, ca. 1813

The rural nature of much of southern Alabama and Mississippi belies two centuries of change that have radically altered both cultural and natural elements of the environment. William Weatherford, Dixon Bailey, and Daniel Beasley would probably see little familiar in our mechanized farmscapes dominated by monoculture fields of hybridized corn, cotton and soybeans, eroded hillsides (largely stripped of topsoil after 1814) now covered by invasive plants like kudzu and cogon grass, and clear-cut-harvested forests nearly devoid of the fire-climax canebrakes and longleaf pines that once dominated the landscape. Look closely, though, and one can still find traces of that not too distant past—most often just artifacts buried in the ground but occasionally standing structures that have miraculously survived the last two centuries of use and progress. Even when nothing visible remains above ground, the places remain—those spots where historic events occurred, from the spectacularly violent, like the epic battle at Fort Mims, to the humdrum activities of daily frontier life. Echoes of 1813 still reverberate for the historically curious explorer.

Note: Before setting out, wise travelers will search the Internet for websites on the attractions mentioned below, to obtain current information on opening and closing times, admission fees, camping facilities, and handicap accessibility. Detailed road maps are also valuable when navigating rural areas, where highway signs can be scarce.[1]

Southwest Alabama

No structures survive in Mobile from the Redstick War era, but an accurate, partial reconstruction of **Fort Condé,** downtown on Royal Street, serves as this

300-year-old city's welcome center. The original, crumbling, century-old masonry citadel had been seized from Spain by American troops commanded by Major General James Wilkinson in April 1813 and renamed Fort Charlotte. The fort was razed in 1820 to make way for urban construction as the city's population swelled with thousands of immigrants. Between 1967 and 1972, archaeologists from the University of Alabama excavated the site of the fort to clear a path for the Wallace Tunnel, which carries Interstate 10 beneath the Mobile River. Diagonally across the street from Fort Condé is the **Museum of Mobile,** occupying the old city hall and market, which contains modern exhibits on the region's social and military history.

On the campus of the University of South Alabama, in west Mobile, is **the Toulmin house,** now known as Alumni Hall. Harry Toulmin was appointed federal judge of Washington County, Mississippi Territory, by President Jefferson in 1804. He played an important role in the events leading to the outbreak of the Redstick War. On the evening after the battle at Fort Mims, Judge Toulmin penned an impassioned letter as he watched smoke rise over the Tensaw from his vantage point across the delta at Fort Stoddert. This Creole Cottage-style home, built by his son Theophilus in 1828, was moved in 1977 from its original location in the Toulminville area of north Mobile and now houses the Office of Alumni Affairs for the university.

From Mobile, drive across Mobile Bay on the elevated Bayway of Interstate 10 or, better yet, on the water-level Causeway constructed in the 1920s for U.S. Highways 90 and 31, and ascend the bluff at Spanish Fort, highest point on the Gulf coast. Take a glance back at the extensive bay, marsh, and delta that occupy the Mobile graben, a massive "downthrown" fault block. Southwestern Alabama is a region of considerable geological faulting, which probably accounts for the confluence of two major river systems, the Tombigbee and the Alabama, not far to the north. The bluffs lining the east side of Mobile Bay are escarpments, "upthrown" fault blocks on the edge of the graben. Few natives know they live in a geologically active fault zone.[2]

Drive north 5 miles on State Highway 225 to **Historic Blakeley State Park** (Figure 27). In 1812, Josiah Blakeley, a speculator from Connecticut, purchased from Spanish authorities a large land tract on the east side of the Mobile-Tensaw delta. His initial newspaper advertisements of lots for sale in the proposed town of Blakeley, which appeared in the *Washington Republican* early in October 1813, attracted little interest because roaming Redstick war parties had emptied the entire region of American settlers.[3] Despite his bad timing, Blakeley did soon attract buyers and the town for a time rivaled Mobile in population, until decimated by a yellow fever outbreak in 1822. For centuries this site had been the head of a trading path leading deep into the interior Southeast. During the early colonial period, Apalachee Indians here operated a flatboat ferry across the delta to Mobile. Excavations by University of South Alabama archaeologists have uncovered remnants of the Apalachee village, the Joseph Badon plantation (occupied during the British colonial period, in the 1770s), and the townsite of Blakeley, all encompassed by an 1865 Civil War battlefield. Visitors today can watch birds, hike, bicycle, and ride horseback on 15 miles of park trails; some camping facilities are available.

Park staff operates tours of the **Mobile-Tensaw delta** on certain Saturdays throughout the year via the *Delta Explorer,* a 50-passenger pontoon boat. Unlike other large swamps in the Southeast, such as the Atchafalaya in Louisiana and the Okefenokee in Georgia, the Mobile-Tensaw delta remains largely uncommercialized and little visited by the public. Numerous private landings offer launch access for canoes, kayaks, and motorboats, but fishing is currently the delta's main attraction, leaving its historic, scenic, and recreational potential essentially untapped. In the heart of the delta, and accessible only by boat, is the **Bottle Creek archaeological site** on Mound Island, late prehistoric capital of the Pensacola culture, a chiefdom that ruled the north-central Gulf coast from A.D. 1250 to 1400. This impressive site has over a dozen earthen mounds; each served as a platform for a house or a temple in a village of several thousand occupants. Today Mound Island is covered in mature cypresses, tupelo gums, and tulip poplars reminiscent of the giant trees timbered out of this bottomland forest in the late nineteenth and early twentieth centuries. The Alabama Historical Commission maintains Bottle Creek as an undeveloped preserve. As at Historic Blakeley State Park and other state-owned sites mentioned here, digging or metal detecting for artifacts is strictly forbidden. Violators are subject to prosecution and confiscation of property used in the commission of looting. These parks safeguard important portions of our archaeological heritage, as well as critical plant and animal habitats. Visitors are encouraged to enjoy these wonderful preserves and to assist park staff in their protection from vandalism and theft.

Continuing due north from Historic Blakeley State Park for 32.8 miles on State Highways 225 and 59 takes you to the modern crossroads community of Tensaw. In 1813, this was the northernmost extent of American settlement on the southern boundary of the Creek nation. Turn west onto County Road 80 and follow the signs 3.4 miles to **Fort Mims Park,** a 5-acre tract owned by the Alabama Historical Commission and maintained by the Baldwin County

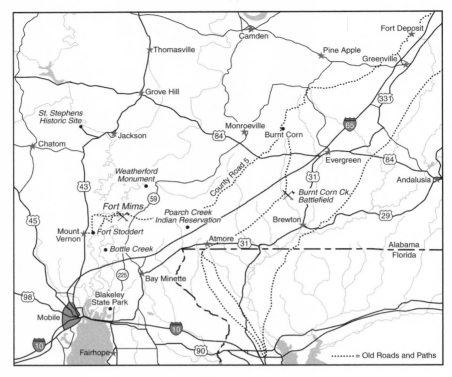

Fig. 27. Historic sites in southwest Alabama.

Commission. The park has a picnic pavilion and interpretive markers that explain the locations of fort features revealed by archaeological investigation. A portion of the western fort wall has been reconstructed recently. The attacking Redstick force charged the fort from their hiding place in a ravine east of the park. The few defenders who escaped the fort during the battle fled to a swamp in the woods to the northwest. A two-day commemoration of the battle takes place every August. Hosted by the Fort Mims Restoration Association, this popular annual event features a living history encampment and reenactments of the battles at Burnt Corn Creek and Fort Mims.

A short (¼-mile) drive west on County Road 80 brings you to Boatyard Lake, where women from the fort were washing clothes when the Redstick attack occurred. A two-mile jaunt down Holley Creek Landing Road leads to the site of Samuel Mims' Ferry (now Holley Creek Landing) on the Alabama River. Here the Federal Road crossed the Mobile-Tensaw delta on the route west to Fort Stoddert. Retracing your path to State Highway 59 and continuing across, ¼-mile east on County Road 80, leads to Montgomery Hill Baptist Church (built in 1854), located near where the Redsticks camped the night after the battle.[4] Numerous descendants of William Weatherford, Jesse Steadham, Dr. Thomas G. Holmes, and other participants in the battle at Fort Mims still live in the vicinity of Tensaw, from Little River to Stockton.

Twelve miles to the north, State Highway 59 crosses Little River, around which Alexander McGillivray and his métis kin established their plantations and cattle pens beginning in the 1780s.[5] In the vicinity, the **William Weatherford Monument** marks the graves of "Red Eagle" and his mother, Sehoy III, two miles west on County Road 84, near the Alabama River at a spot called Tate's Brickyard. Descendants of some of the Little River Creek métis live today around the town of Poarch, 15 miles to the southeast, near Atmore. The annual Thanksgiving Day Powwow at the **Poarch Creek Indian Reservation** features competitive Indian dance groups from across the country, as well as an opportunity to try traditional Creek foods such as fry bread and sofki (*osafke*), fermented corn soup.

Continuing north and east on State Highway 59 for 13 miles, through Chrysler and Uriah, and traveling south 3.3 miles on State Highway 21 brings you to Little River State Forest and Claude D. Kelley State Park. Both offer fishing, hiking, and camping. Three miles farther south on State Highway 21, turn left (east) on County Road 30, just north of the rural community of Huxford; after 2.4 miles, turn left (north) onto County Road 45. Proceed 3.7 miles, then veer right (northeast) onto Old Stage Road, the path of the 1811 **Federal Road** that ran from Milledgeville, Georgia, entered the Creek nation at Benjamin Hawkins' Creek Agency on the Flint River, and emerged near Samuel Mims' ferry where it continued on to Fort Stoddert. Created to expedite delivery of the U.S. mail between New Orleans and Washington, D.C., the Federal Road greatly accelerated the westward movement of American settlers into the Natchez and Mobile districts. In bisecting the Creek nation it also created much discontent among the Creeks, which contributed to the Redstick War of 1813–1814.

One can drive along more than 50 miles of the old Federal Road by following the boundary between Monroe and Conecuh counties (where you may occasionally see "Blue Star" signs placed years ago to commemorate the historic route). Old Stage Road ends at U.S. Highway 84, but the Federal Road continues 2.6 miles to the northeast on an unpaved, narrow lane that is impassable at its northern end without a good four-wheel-drive truck and some luck. (Be warned!) However, that section can be bypassed by taking U.S. Highway 84 east 2 miles to Repton. Turn left (north) onto Burnt Corn Road at the old schoolhouse and drive north toward Bermuda on Conecuh County Road 5, rejoining—in about 2½ miles—the Monroe-Conecuh county line and the Federal Road. Less than 2 miles north of Bermuda, you will cross the headwaters of Burnt Corn Creek; a mile farther north, and 300 yards off the road to the left, is **Burnt Corn Springs,** site of James Cornells' plantation, where Peter McQueen's Redsticks kidnapped Cornells' wife in July 1813 prior to the Battle of Burnt Corn Creek. At the terminus of County Road 5, past Skinnerton, continue north on State Highway 83 to Midway.

From that point, several interesting options lay open to the adventurous traveler. The truly daring may wend their way farther on the Federal Road, following county roads diagonally across Butler county to **Fort Deposit,** location of a supply depot that General Ferdinand Claiborne's Mississippi Territorial Volunteer army created on their approach to the Holy Ground. Others might choose to head west on State Route 47 to Beatrice and back to Monroeville, to continue a circuit of the Mobile-Tensaw delta. Or you may drive south through Evergreen to the Conecuh National Forest.[6] The southern 15-mile stretch of the Federal Road, south of U.S. Highway 84, is a mixture of paved and graveled sections; the rest of the way to Skinnerton is paved. Even so, this drive through sparsely populated farmland and woods takes the modern traveler out of fast-paced modern America to a place where one's historical imagination has a fighting chance. Most evocative of all is the lane immediately north of U.S. Highway 84, where the deeply entrenched narrow road most closely resembles its former self (Figure 28). If you are so fortunate as to travel any portion of the old Federal Road, notice how few streams are bridged on this route. This is a sure sign that the parties of axmen who cut the original mail route in 1806 and 1807 were following, and to a large extent simply widening, well-established Indian trails that stayed whenever possible on the ridges that divide stream drainages. Such efficient paths evolved over millennia, incorporating innumerable corrections gained from an increasingly detailed collective knowledge of the terrain. Fords—crossing places with hard sand bottoms across major streams—were rare and carefully selected to avoid natural obstacles, such as the extensive swamps and impenetrable canebrakes that lined most creek banks.

Modern thoroughfares have diverged from the Federal Road route because they connect towns that grew up later along the major rivers (which the Federal Road avoided) and along the railroads. Some authors of Alabama history texts maintain that Interstate 65 follows the old Federal Road, but fortunately that is not so. Interstate 65 today crosses paths with the old Federal Road at only

Fig. 28. Conecuh County Road 5, on the path of the Federal Road, 2004.

one point, north of Exit 142 at the State Highway 185 overpass. The old road still exists, here and elsewhere in the state, in bits and pieces of the county road systems, rarely recognized and seldom appreciated for its antiquity and its connection to earlier peoples and places.

Longleaf pine savanna, the natural habitat through which much of the Federal Road passed, can no longer be found anywhere along that route, even though this type of open forest once covered vast portions of the southern coastal plain, an estimated 93 million acres from Virginia to Texas. Fire suppression and modern logging practices—especially the selective replanting of fast-growing loblolly and slash pines in place of the longleaf—has almost eliminated an entire open-savanna ecosystem with bluestem and wiregrass growing under widely spaced 100-foot-tall pines. Fortunately, the U.S. Forest Service has encouraged restoration of longleaf pines (*Pinus palustris*) in the Southeast since the 1940s.[7] In **Conecuh National Forest,** 60 miles east of Atmore, on either side of State Route 137, the 20-mile-long Conecuh Hiking Trail winds through parklike longleaf pine savannas in the uplands. Here one sees patches of rivercane (*Arundinaria gigantea*), miniature exemplars of the expansive

canebrakes that originally covered thousands of acres of river bottoms throughout the South before fire prevention, cattle grazing, and clearing for agriculture
destroyed that habitat.[8]

Returning to our circumnavigation of the Mobile-Tensaw delta: head west
from Monroeville on U.S. Highway 84 to visit the region of the Tombigbee
settlements. (Monroeville boasts the Old Courthouse Museum, where a nationally celebrated amateur production of a play based on Harper Lee's *To Kill
a Mockingbird* is performed throughout May every year.) Where the highway crosses the Alabama River, General Claiborne's Mississippi Territorial Volunteers established Fort Claiborne in mid-November 1813. At Grove Hill the
route intersects with U.S. Highway 43. East of that modern-day town, Josiah
Francis and one to two hundred Redstick warriors unsuccessfully attacked Fort
Sinquefield, a settler stockade on Bassett's Creek, three days after the fight at
Fort Mims. South of Grove Hill is **"the Forks,"** formed by the confluence of
the Alabama and Tombigbee rivers, where about 15 small forts were built by
settlers prior to the Fort Mims battle.

Take U.S. Highway 43 to Jackson and across the Tombigbee River. At Leroy,
County Road 34 leads northwest to **Historic Old St. Stephens,** which in 1813
marked the northernmost limits of American settlement in the region. Old
Washington County Courthouse, a building dating to 1853, houses a small museum. The townsite of Old St. Stephens, 3 miles away, is a remarkable ghost
town. Dozens of house foundations made from locally quarried limestone are
plainly evident, aligned along still visible streets. Originally the site of a Spanish fort ceded to the Americans in 1799, a small American community soon
grew around the Choctaw Indian factory into a city of several thousand residents. After the Redstick War, St. Stephens became the capital of Alabama Territory, from 1817 until statehood was declared in 1819 and the seat of government moved to Cahawba. Most businesses and residents left soon afterward,
but the town lingered on for another three decades. A few years ago generous
landowners donated the townsite, where historians and archaeologists have
been piecing together the story of this lost town. However, recent cuts in state
funding now threaten the continued existence of this exceptional state park.

Thirty-two miles south on U.S. Highway 43 brings you to Mount Vernon.
East on County Road 96 leads to the site of **Fort Stoddert,** now a public landing
on the Tombigbee River. Construction of the landing parking lot largely destroyed the fort's archaeological remains. Taking that same road a mile west of
U.S. Highway 43 brings you to Searcy Hospital, a mental health facility on the
grounds of **Mount Vernon Cantonment,** established by the U.S. Army just

prior to the Redstick War. Farther west, County Road 96 intersects Red Fox Road, where the **MOWA Choctaw Tribal Center** is located (at 1080 West Red Fox Road, Calvert, AL). About 6 miles south of Mount Vernon, on U.S. Highway 43, two historical markers note the approximate locations of the **Ellicott Stone** and **Old Mobile** (original site of the French colonial settlement, dating 1702 to 1711). The former can be visited by hiking a short trail into the woods, where one will find, beneath a metal shelter, a boundary stone with an eroded inscription left by the joint American-Spanish team that in 1799 surveyed the 31st parallel, establishing the international boundary between American and Spanish lands. Five miles farther south, U.S. Highway 43 intersects with Interstate 65, which leads to Mobile.

Central Alabama

The U.S. government's Indian Removal policy of the 1830s forcibly exiled central Alabama's Creek Indian population, leaving only Muskogee place-names and archaeological sites where the Creek nation once existed. Today the original Creek Indian nation may in some sense be "nothing more than a pink hue on a map or an answer on a test," but we can grasp something of that lost human landscape by visiting places still important to the modern Creeks.[9] Immediately north of modern-day Montgomery were the towns of the Alabama division of the Upper Creeks (Figure 29). **Coosada,** home of the Sehoy women, lay east of the modern town of that name, on the upper Alabama River. Twenty miles west of Montgomery, on County Road 40, is **Holy Ground Battlefield.** In December 1813, General Claiborne's American army destroyed a Redstick refuge in a small fight with warriors led by William Weatherford. The site is maintained by the U.S. Army Corps of Engineers as a public landing at the junction of Cypress Creek and the Alabama River, adjacent to the Lowndes Wildlife Management Area.

The **Alabama Department of Archives and History** (624 Washington Avenue, across the street from the state capitol in Montgomery) houses a spectacular collection of artifacts excavated from Upper Creek archaeological sites in the area. The Indian exhibits display a remarkable variety of native-made items and imported trade goods, which the Creeks creatively combined to form a distinctive and highly original culture.

Driving north from Montgomery on U.S. Highway 231, you will cross the **lower Tallapoosa River.** For the best view of the valley of that river, which was lined with a dozen Creek towns in 1813, take County Roads 8 and 4 east to Tal-

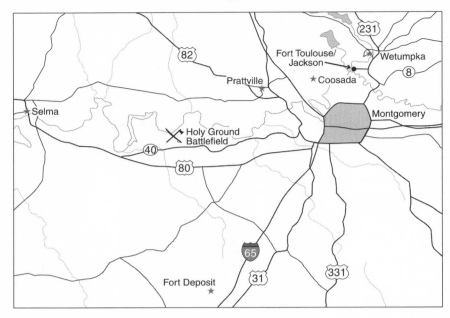

Fig. 29. Historic sites in central Alabama.

lassee. This road approximately follows the route of General Andrew Jackson's army during the final phase of the Redstick War, in mid-April 1814. The large Creek town of Tuckaubatchee, where Tecumseh addressed the Creek national council in 1811, was located south of Tallassee, partially on land now farmed by Auburn University Agricultural Extension. State Highway 229, south from Tallassee, will take you across the Tallapoosa River again, to Interstate 85. In this vicinity, Governor Floyd's Georgia State Militia troops burned the Creek town of Atasi in November 1813 and, upon their return two months later, were surprised by a Redstick attack while encamped along Calebee Creek.

If one continues north from Montgomery, on U.S. Highway 231 toward Wetumpka, Fort Toulouse–Fort Jackson Road to the west leads to the historical park of that name. Operated by the Alabama Historical Commission, the park contains the densest concentration of important archaeological sites in Alabama. At this strategic confluence of the Coosa and Tallapoosa rivers, prehistoric Indians lived in large villages for centuries. In 1717, the French established **Fort Toulouse** among the Alabama towns to serve as a center for trade with the Upper Creeks. This is where Captain Marchand met Sehoy I and quelled a mutiny of his troops in the early 1720s. In May 1814 American forces constructed

Fort Jackson astride the ruins of Fort Toulouse. Here William Weatherford surrendered to General Jackson in the tent camp just outside the fort, and in August assembled leaders of the Creek nation signed the Treaty of Fort Jackson, ceding some 22 million acres of land to the United States as reparation for the war. The park has a small visitors' center, boat launch facilities, a campground, and an arboretum trail dedicated to the Quaker naturalist William Bartram, who visited this spot in 1775.

Continuing another 2 miles north on U.S. Highway 231, into Wetumpka, notice the Riverside Entertainment Center, a bingo and electronic gaming establishment owned by the Poarch Band of Creek Indians. The center stands on the site of **Hickory Ground,** where the Creek national council met frequently from the 1780s until 1813. Alexander McGillivray's principal home, Little Tallassee, was located about 6 miles farther north, on the east bank of the Coosa River. From U.S. Highway 231, just north of Julia Tutwiler Prison for Women, take Elmore County Road 211. At Thelma Church, on the left, notice the historical marker erected by the Alabama Anthropological Society in 1930 near McGillivray's "apple grove."

Ninety-five miles northeast of Montgomery, near the town of Dadeville, is **Horseshoe Bend National Military Park.** On March 27, 1814, General Jackson's army destroyed a force of 1,000 Redsticks led by Menawa, effectively ending organized Redstick military resistance in the Creek nation. This unit of the National Park Service preserves the sites of the Redstick barricade, their village of Tohopeka, and the earlier Creek town of Nuyaka in a 2,040-acre park that contains an excellent nature trail and an interpretive center.

Southwest Mississippi

Most of the men serving in the Mississippi Territorial Volunteers stationed at Fort Mims enlisted from the four counties of Adams, Jefferson, Wilkinson, and Amite, in the southwest corner of the territory adjacent to Louisiana (Figure 30). Although Natchez was the largest and oldest settlement in the area, the small town of **Washington,** 6 miles east of Natchez, served as territorial capital from 1802 until 1817. In Washington one can visit Jefferson College, the first school chartered in the territory, which opened in 1811. While sheriff of adjacent Jefferson County in 1806, Daniel Beasley helped create competing Franklin Academy, which "sunk into oblivion" a short while later. Visitors are able to tour the restored West Wing, kitchens, Prospere Hall (which houses interpretive exhibitions, a gift shop, and restrooms), and the T. J. Foster Nature

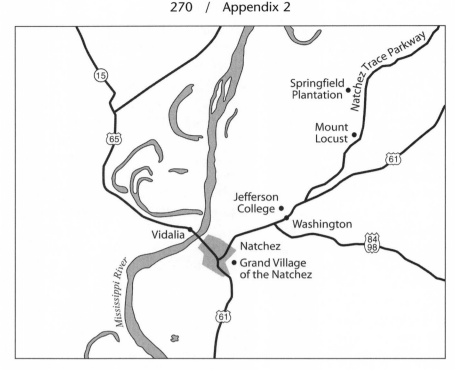

Fig. 30. Historic sites in southwest Mississippi.

Trail on the Jefferson College campus, where the itinerant Methodist preacher Lorenzo Dow held revivals as early as 1804. Elsewhere in town, behind the Washington United Methodist Church, one can see the dilapidated Federal/ Greek Revival–style house of Cowles Mead, a governor of the territory.[10]

Natchez contains a remarkable number of historic structures, including several constructed during the 1790s under Spanish colonial dominion, such as the home of Territorial Governor David Holmes (207 S. Wall Street) and Airlie (9 Elm Street), and territorial-era Texada (222 S. Wall at Washington Street). These are now private residences but can occasionally be visited during the annual Natchez Spring and Fall Pilgrimages. The town was the southern terminus of the **Natchez Trace,** an early road that connected the salt licks of central Tennessee with the lower Mississippi Valley. The National Park Service has resurrected the 444-mile Trace, and after 67 years of intermittent reconstruction the scenic parkway was at last declared officially completed, in May 2005 (even though a segment through Jackson, Mississippi, and the last 8 miles into Natchez remain unfinished). Driving any portion of the Natchez Trace Parkway is worthwhile (and relaxing for those resolved to the enforced speed limits of 45 and 50 mph), but the last 20-mile approach to Natchez is perhaps the most intriguing. There the old road cut deeply into the unstable Pleistocene loess soils of the Natchez Hills, creating a picturesque sunken lane through the forest (best seen at mile post 8.7). Sitting atop a late prehistoric Indian mound is **Mount Locust** (at mile post 15.5), one of the few surviving "stands" that once served as inns for travelers on the Trace. At the end of the Trace sits **Connelly's Tavern,** on the hill overlooking Natchez where Major Andrew Ellicott challenged Spanish control of the region by raising the American flag in 1797. The tavern, built a year later, is a museum operated by the Natchez Garden Club. One mile off the Trace (near mile post 20, at Fayette) is **Springfield Plantation,** begun in 1789, where Andrew Jackson married Rachel Robards in 1791, which suggests the deep social ties that bound Jackson to his compatriots in arms from Mississippi Territory during the multipronged American campaign against the Redstick Creeks.[11]

This selection of historic and natural places highlights some of the fascinating sites and sights awaiting discovery in the lands of the old Creek nation and Mississippi Territory. I hope you are inspired to visit these survivors of the past, explore further, and help preserve our cultural and natural treasures.

Notes

Abbreviations

ADAH	Alabama Department of Archives and History
AGI	Archivo General de Indias
ASP	*American State Papers*
Draper, WHS	Lyman Draper Manuscript Collection, Wisconsin Historical Society
MDAH	Mississippi Department of Archives and History
NARA	National Archives and Records Administration
NCDCR	North Carolina Department of Cultural Resources
PKY	P. K. Yonge Library, University of Florida
RG	Record Group
WHS	Wisconsin Historical Society
WPA	Works Progress Administration

Introduction

1. See Peggy Samuels and Harold Samuels, *Remembering the Maine.*

2. See Robert D. Ballard and Spencer Dunmore, *Exploring the Lusitania: Probing the Mysteries of the Sinking That Changed History.*

3. See Stephen L. Hardin and Gary S. Zaboly, *Texian Iliad: A Military History of the Texas Revolution, 1835–1836;* Richard D. Flores, *Remembering the Alamo: Memory, Modernity, and the Master Symbol;* William C. Davis, *Lone Star Rising: The Revolutionary Birth of the Texas Republic;* James E. Crisp, *Sleuthing the Alamo: Davy Crockett's Last Stand and Other Mysteries of the Texas Revolution.*

4. Hawkins to John B. Floyd, September 30, 1813, in C. L. Grant, ed., *Letters, Journals and Writings of Benjamin Hawkins,* 669.

5. Jackson to Willie Blount, December 29, 1813, in John Spencer Bassett, ed., *Correspondence of Andrew Jackson,* 1:417.

6. Marvin T. Smith, *Archaeology of Aboriginal Culture Change in the Interior Southeast: Depopulation during the Early Historic Period*; Kristen J. Gremillion, "Comparative Paleoethnobotany of Three Native Southeastern Communities of the Historic Period."

7. Gregory A. Waselkov, "Seventeenth-Century Trade in the Colonial Southeast"; Gregory A. Waselkov and Marvin T. Smith, "Upper Creek Archaeology"; John E. Worth, "The Lower Creeks: Origins and Early History"; Gregory A. Waselkov, "Exchange and Interaction since 1500." I am indebted to John C. Hall for the apt description of bezoars as "gastric pearls."

8. Smith, *Archaeology of Aboriginal Culture Change;* Peter H. Wood, "The Changing Population of the Colonial South: An Overview by Race and Region, 1685–1790."

9. In this book, I preferentially employ John R. Swanton's spellings of Creek—or Muskogee—words, as he used them in "Social Organization and Social Usages of the Indians of the Creek Confederacy." His spellings may already be familiar to some readers, and they generally permit English speakers to approximate Muskogee pronunciation without employing special phonetic characters. However, Muskogee writers now use their own orthography, so I have included the modern spelling in italics as each word is introduced. In some instances, I have also provided an English translation or, in the case of plant names, the genus and species represented by the Muskogee word. For an authoritative reference to modern Muskogee, see Jack B. Martin and Margaret McKane Mauldin, *A Dictionary of Creek/Muskogee, with Notes on the Florida and Oklahoma Seminole Dialects of Creek.* Readers should note that four letters found in English represent very different sounds in written Muskogee. English approximations of these four sounds are:

v as in English *a*go
i as in English h*ey*
c as in English in*ch*
r as in English fif*thl*y

10. Gregory A. Waselkov and John W. Cottier, "European Perceptions of Eastern Muskogean Ethnicity"; Joshua Piker, *Okfuskee: A Creek Indian Town in Colonial America,* 7–10.

11. Swanton, "Social Organization," 113–70, 195–304.

12. Two other linguistic groups, the Alabamas and the Koasatis, play an important role in Upper Creek and Tensaw history. Their terms for town are *oola* and *ó:la,* respectively. See Cora Sylestine, Heather K. Hardy, and Timothy Montler, *Dictionary of the Alabama Language,* and Geoffrey D. Kimball, *Koasati Dictionary.*

13. Swanton, "Social Organization," 171–90. For a review of recent ethnohistorical considerations of historic Creek talwas, see Piker, *Okfuskee,* 1–12.

14. Gregory A. Waselkov, "Changing Strategies of Indian Field Location in the Early Historic Southeast"; William E. Doolittle, *Cultivated Landscapes of Native North America,* 136, 192–93.

15. John R. Swanton, "Religious Beliefs and Medical Practices of the Creek Indians," 481–84, 538, 625–70; Major Caleb Swan, "Position and State of Manners and Arts in the Creek, or Muscogee Nation in 1791"; David Lewis, Jr., and Ann T. Jordan, *Creek Indian Medi-*

cine Ways: The Enduring Power of Muskoke Religion, 78–105, 151–62; Jean Chaudhuri and Joyotpaul Chaudhuri, A Sacred Path: The Way of the Muscogee Creeks, 46–55. On plant physics, also see Notes furnished A. J. Pickett by the Rev Lee Compere, Pickett Papers, ADAH.

16. Swanton, "Religious Beliefs," 546–614.

17. For the creation of the Creek nation and formation of a national council, see Steven C. Hahn, The Invention of the Creek Nation, 1670–1763, 229–77.

18. See Michael Yellow Bird, "What We Want to Be Called: Indigenous Peoples' Perspectives on Racial and Ethnic Identity Labels."

19. Willard B. Walker, "Creek Confederacy Before Removal," 390–91.

20. The development of Creek racial attitudes is thoughtfully discussed by Claudio Saunt in the following: A New Order of Things: Property, Power, and the Transformation of the Creek Indians, 1733–1816, 117–20; "The Graysons' Dilemma: A Creek Family Confronts the Science of Race"; and Black, White, and Indian: Race and the Unmaking of An American Family." See also Tiya Miles, Ties That Bind: The Story of an Afro-Cherokee Family in Slavery and Freedom, and Nancy Shoemaker, A Strange Likeness: Becoming Red and White in Eighteenth-Century North America. In contrast, Theda Perdue argues that the Creeks rejected American racialist concepts during the early nineteenth century until forced to do so under economic duress imposed by the U.S. government; see Perdue, "Mixed Blood" Indians: Racial Construction in the Early South, ix, and Andrew K. Frank, Creeks and Southerners: Biculturalism on the Early American Frontier, 1–10.

A Muskogee-English dictionary published in 1890 revealingly offers a Creek translation for "half-breed," Estē hvtkē hayv, literally "white person maker," suggesting that racial intermarriage was by then considered a way children of Indians could become white—not a goal of Creeks earlier in the century. R. M. Loughridge and D. M. Hodge, English and Muskokee Dictionary, Collected from Various Sources, 36.

21. An important early work on the Red River Métis of the northern Plains is Marcel Giraud, Le Métis canadien: son rôle dans l'histoire des provinces de l'Ouest. For recent considerations of expanded concepts of métis and métissage, see Jacqueline Peterson and Jennifer S. H. Brown, eds., The New Peoples: Being and Becoming Métis in North America; Serge Gruzinski, La pensée métisse; Gilles Havard, Empire et métissages: Indiens et Français dans le Pays d'en Haut, 1660–1715. These terms are not without their own complex connotations, and scholars disagree over the advisability of their use beyond areas of French settlement.

The Spanish terms mestizo and mestizaje have undergone a similar rehabilitation at the hands of postcolonial scholars and are equally appropriate for discussion of the racial terrain of the historical Southeast. See Barbara Krauthamer, Tiya Miles, Celia E. Naylor, Claudio Saunt, and Circe Sturm, "Rethinking Race and Culture in the Early South," and Néstor García Canclini, Hybrid Cultures: Strategies for Entering and Leaving Modernity.

Chapter 1

1. Gregory A. Waselkov and Bonnie L. Gums, Plantation Archaeology at Rivière aux Chiens, ca. 1725–1848, 32–34.

2. Ibid., 37–38; K. G. Davies, ed., Documents of the American Revolution, 1770–1783, vol.

3, *Transcripts 1771*, 132, 218–19, 222, vol. 5, *Transcripts 1772*, 33–34, 74, 165, 224; Kathryn E. Holland Braund, "'Like a Stone Wall Never to be Broke': The British-Indian Boundary Line with the Creek Indians, 1763–1773."

Delta land between the Alabama Cut-off, also known as Bayou Conunga or Coonungo, and the confluence of the Alabama and Tombigbee rivers comprises Naniaba Island, where the fields of the Naniaba Indians had been located early in the eighteenth century. David Taitt, "A Plan of part of the Rivers Tombecbe, Alabama, Tensa, Perdido, & Scambia In the Province of West Florida, ca. 1771," Geography and Map Collection, Library of Congress; Anonymous, "Land Granted and Surveyed on the River and Bay of Mobile, ca. 1775" (photograph ibid.).

3. Robert R. Rea, *Major Robert Farmar of Mobile*, 114, 124, 131–35.

4. Taitt, "A Plan of part of the Rivers . . . In the Province of West Florida, ca. 1771." George Stiggins recorded a garbled version of this story of the Tensaw. In the 1840s he wrote, "The first settlement we find in tracing the Alabama (a branch of the Creek or Ispocoga tribe) is at the confluence of the Alabama river and Tensaw lake near the Town of Stockton in Baldwin County. Their settlements extended up the lake & river as far as Fort Mimbs their town sites and other settlements they called Towassee, and at this time they Call that extent of Country Towassee Talahassee which is Towassee old Town. The white settler of the place call it the Tensaw Settlement." Stiggins, "A Historical narration of the Genealogy traditions and downfall of the Ispocaga or Creek tribe of Indians, written by one of the tribe," Draper, WHS, 1. An accurate version of Stiggins' manuscript was published by Theron A. Nuñez, Jr., ed., "Creek Nativism and the Creek War of 1813–1814." However, the editorial conventions for historical transcription have changed somewhat since Nuñez's day. For this volume, I have relied upon a modern transcript prepared by Kathryn E. Holland Braund, which she graciously made available.

5. Governor Peter Chester to Earl of Hillsborough, Pensacola, August 13, 1772, in Davies, *Documents of the American Revolution*, 5:165.

6. The Creeks objected to English plantations near an old Spanish cowpen on the Escambia and intended themselves to settle in an old field across the Conecuh River from an abandoned Spanish fort. Davies, *Documents of the American Revolution*, 3:218–19, 5:74 (quote); Braund, "'Like a Stone Wall,'" 53–80. On November 22, 1772, David Taitt wrote to John Stuart that "The Fighter and Emistisiguo," from Little Tallassee, "are gone towards Pensacola to hunt and afterwards to war against the Choctaws, there are some Cowetas and most of the Tallipouses and Savannahs [Shawnees] are gone down towards Pensacola and Tensa to hunt," in Davies, *Documents of the American Revolution*, 5:224–25.

7. Yet 159 British inhabitants of the Mobile district did sign an oath of fidelity to Spain in 1780; F. de Borja Medina Rojas, *Jose de Ezpeleta: Gobernador de la Mobila, 1780–1781*, 173–75.

8. Wood, "Changing Population of the Colonial South," 38, 58; J. Anthony Paredes and Kenneth J. Plante, "A Reëxamination of Creek Indian Population Trends: 1738–1832."

9. William S. Coker and Thomas D. Watson, *Indian Traders of the Southeastern Spanish Borderlands: Panton, Leslie & Company and John Forbes & Company, 1783–1847*, 55–176.

10. After McGillivray's initial dismay at the prospect of a loyalist exodus to West Florida—"we have disorderly people enough already among us"—he quickly saw the advantage, to Creeks as well as Spaniards, of welcoming "respectable" men and their families to the Ten-

saw. McGillivray to Governor Arturo O'Neill, in John Walton Caughey, *McGillivray of the Creeks*, 63 ("disorderly," December 5, 1783), 69 ("respectable," February 5, 1784).

11. Albert James Pickett, *History of Alabama, and Incidentally of Georgia and Mississippi, from the Earliest Period*, 2:123–24; Jack D. Holmes, "Alabama's Forgotten Settlers: Notes on the Spanish Mobile District, 1780–1813," 88, 90; Karl Davis, "'Remember Fort Mims': Reinterpreting the Origins of the Creek War," 614–18.

12. Thomas S. Woodward, *Woodward's Reminiscences of the Creek, or Muscogee Indians, Contained in Letters to Friends in Georgia and Alabama*, 77. An early settler told Jeremiah Austill that the Mims brothers had been Tories; Notes taken from the lips of Hiram Mounger . . . by Col J Austill, Pickett Papers, ADAH. Historians have generally assumed Mims was a loyalist, most recently Frank, *Creeks and Southerners*, 40.

13. Pedro de Favrot, Noticia y Nombres de los Habitantes en General, de la Plaza y Jurisdiccion de la Mobila; en 1.° de Enero de 1786 [Census of the Mobile District, Mobile, Jan. 1, 1786], legajo 2360, fol. 50, Papeles procedentes de la Isla de Cuba, AGI, Seville, Spain.

14. Pedro de Favrot, Total General de la Jurisdicción de la Mobila del Primero de Enero del Año de 1787 [Census of the Mobile District, Mobile, Jan. 1, 1787], legajo 206, Cuba, AGI.

15. WPA, Historical Record Survey, *Transcriptions of Manuscript Collections of Louisiana: No. 1, The Favrot Papers*, vol. 3, *1781–1792*, 83–84, Spanish Oath of Allegiance taken by residents of Tensas, January 4, 1797; also see 86–88.

16. Samuel Mims and Hannah Rains, both residents of the Tensa River, were married by the pastor of Mobile on January 23, 1788. Cathedral of the Immaculate Conception, Marriage Book 1 (1724–1832), fol. 186, act 186; Baptismal Records Book 2 (1781–1850), fol. 3, act 4; Book of the Baptisms of the Americans of Tombicbee . . . 1801, 2, Diocese of Mobile Sacramental Records. Also see Sam Mims, *Leaves from the Mims Family Tree: A Genealogic History*, 31.

Samuel Mims and Hannah Rains were both white, of English descent. I have been unable to find evidence for any intermarriage with Indians among their ancestors. Nevertheless, many historians have assumed one or both were Indians or métis. See Michael Paul Rogin, *Fathers and Children: Andrew Jackson and the Subjugation of the American Indian*, 148; Robert V. Remini, *Andrew Jackson and the Course of American Empire, 1767–1821*, 189; Frank L. Owsley, Jr., "Prophet of War: Josiah Francis and the Creek War," 280; J. Leitch Wright, Jr., *Creeks and Seminoles: Destruction and Regeneration of the Muscogulge People*, 173; Lynn Hastie Thompson, *William Weatherford: His Country and His People*, 329; Thomas D. Clark and John D. W. Guice, *The Old Southwest, 1795–1830: Frontiers in Conflict*, 133; Karl Davis, *'Much of the Indian Appears': Adaptation and Persistence in a Creek Community, 1783–1854*, 116, 147; Frank, *Creeks and Southerners*, 32 (an "Indian countryman" married to "a Creek woman"), 125 ("Samuel Mims, the Creek leader"). Starting from a mistaken notion of Samuel Mims' Creek ethnicity, Frank compounds his error by marveling that a politically and economically successful Mims descendant, Robert Jemison, Jr., did not find his "Creek lineage or 'Indian blood'" socially inhibiting.

17. For the Tombigbee, see Walter Lowrie, ed., *American State Papers, Public Lands*, vol. 1, *March 4th, 1789, to February 27th, 1809*, 574, 586, 635, 697, 712; WPA, *Interesting Transcripts of the British, French, & Spanish Records of the City & District of Mobile, State of Alabama, found in Probate Court in two volumes in the City of Mobile, 1715–1812*, 1:39–40, 214; Marilyn Davis

Hahn, *Old St. Stephens' Land Office Records and American State Papers, Public Lands*, vol. 1, *1768–1888*, 7.

For Mobile, see Asbury Dickins and John W. Forney, eds., *ASP, Public Lands*, vol. 5, *1827–1829*, 496; WPA, *Interesting Transcripts*, 1:145–46; Hahn, *Old St. Stephens' Land Office Records*, 2.

18. Lowrie, *ASP, Public Lands*, 1:554, 555, 575, 578 (quote), 589, 591, 592, 745–47, 763, 766, and 2:87; Walter Lowrie and Walter S. Franklin, eds., *ASP, Miscellaneous, Commencing May 22, 1809 and ending March 3, 1823*, 154. In a request for a town lot, dated July 22, 1796, he is described as "Samuel Mims an inhabitant of Tensaw River"; WPA, *Interesting Transcripts*, 1:145–46. The land Mims eventually occupied was first patented by Henry Fairchild in 1766 (described as "200 acres on mainland and 300 on opposite Island"), relinquished by him in 1768 to Alexander Frazier, and apparently obtained by William Clark in 1778; none of these English colonists is known to have actually occupied the property. See Clinton N. Howard, *The British Development of West Florida, 1763–1769*, 77, 97, 106. Mims' Spanish grants to Tensaw lands were confirmed by Congress in 1810–11. See Lowrie, ed., *ASP, Public Lands*, 2:87; Lowrie and Franklin, *ASP, Miscellaneous*, 154; Richard Peters, ed., *The Public Statutes at Large of the United States of America*, vol. 6, *The Private Statutes at Large of the United States of America*, 99–100.

Samuel Mims and Hannah Rains had six children. According to Baptismal Records, Diocese of Mobile Catholic Sacramental Records, they were Henrica, born November 17, 1788 (f. 30, no. 133); twins Sara and Joseph, baptized on June 30 and July 1, 1794 (f. 46, nos. 200, 210); Alexander born in October 1796 (f. 56, no. 256); Prudence born May 11, 1799 (f. 3, no. 4); and David born July 20, 1800 (f. 3, no. 4).

19. Waselkov and Gums, *Plantation Archaeology*, 70–71. By 1800 the Tombigbee district's population was one-third black; James F. Doster, "Early Settlement on the Tombigbee and Tensaw Rivers," 93.

20. Favrot, Noticia y Nombres . . . 1786; Total General . . . 1787. By 1803 Samuel Mims was the second-largest slaveholder in the Tensaw when he paid taxes on 31 slaves; five years later he owned 46 slaves. Ben Strickland and Jean Strickland, comps., *Washington County, Mississippi Territory, 1803–1816 Tax Rolls*, 1, 37.

21. Ira Berlin, *Many Thousands Gone: The First Two Centuries of Slavery in North America*, 325–57.

22. Waselkov, "Changing Strategies of Indian Field Location."

23. Favrot, Noticia y Nombres . . . 1786; Total General . . . 1787.

24. Waselkov and Gums, *Plantation Archaeology*, 63–90.

25. Peter H. Wood, *Black Majority: Negroes in Colonial South Carolina from 1670 through the Stono Rebellion*, 30–31.

26. White developed the concept of "Middle Ground" to understand the new métis society that arose in the Great Lakes region prior to American settlement; Richard White, *The Middle Ground: Indians, Empires, and Republics in the Great Lakes Region, 1650–1815*.

27. Caughey, *McGillivray*, 62 (O'Neill to Captain General Jose de Ezpeleta, October 19, 1783), 163 (McGillivray to O'Neill, November 20, 1787), 213 (McGillivray to John Linder, December 28, 1788); Dr. Marion Elisha Tarvin, "The Muscogees or Creek Indians, 1519 to 1893," 133.

28. Many factors contributed to the decline in prices for deerskins. For instance, the French Revolution and subsequent wars in Europe effectively blockaded the French industrial market, which had been the principal European consumer of North American deerskins. Paul Chrisler Phillips, *The Fur Trade*, 2:100–101, 209.

29. For a thorough examination of evolving concepts of masculinity on all sides of the Upper Tennessee frontier, see Nathaniel J. Sheidley, *Unruly Men: Indians, Settlers, and the Ethos of Frontier Patriarchy in the Upper Tennessee Watershed, 1763–1815*. For documentation of the effects of the Georgia border conflict, see Joel W. Martin, "Cultural Contact and Crises in the Early Republic: Native American Religious Renewal, Resistance, and Accommodation," 241–42.

30. Waselkov, "Changing Strategies of Indian Field Location," 185–93.

31. Saunt, *A New Order of Things*, 49.

32. Caughey, *McGillivray*, 157 (Governor O'Neill to Sonora, July 11, 1787, English translation).

33. The foremost work on early federal Indian policy is Reginald Horsman, *Expansion and American Indian Policy, 1783–1812*, viii–ix, 57–58. Also see Francis Paul Prucha, *American Indian Policy in the Formative Years: The Indian Trade and Intercourse Acts, 1790–1834*; Bernard W. Sheehan, *Seeds of Extinction: Jeffersonian Philanthropy and the American Indian*; Anthony F. C. Wallace, *Jefferson and the Indians: The Tragic Fate of the First Americans*. For the Black Legend of the Spanish conquests, see David J. Weber, *The Spanish in North America*, 336–41. Because of their prominent role in the "plan of civilization" and their disruptive effects on traditional Creek agriculture, cattle would become a principal target of Redstick aggression during the 1813–1814 war. See Virginia DeJohn Anderson, *Creatures of Empire*, 245.

34. Treaty with the Creeks, 1790, in Charles J. Kappler, comp. and ed., *Indian Affairs: Laws and Treaties*, 28.

35. For instance, see Reginald Horsman, "The Indian Policy of an 'Empire for Liberty.'"

36. Swan, "Position and State of Manners and Arts," 252.

37. Kathryn H. Braund, "Guardians of Tradition and Handmaidens to Change: Women's Roles in Creek Economic and Social Life in the Eighteenth Century"; Davis, "'Remember Fort Mims,'" 619.

38. Fort Stoddert (commonly misspelled Stoddart or Stoddard or Stodderd, then and later), established in July 1799, was named for Benjamin Stoddert, President John Adams' secretary of the Navy from 1798 to 1801. See Peter J. Hamilton, *Colonial Mobile: An Historical Study*, 377, 415n.1; Jack D. L. Holmes, "Fort Stoddard in 1799: Seven Letters of Captain Bartholomew Shaumburgh," 231.

39. Lowrie and Franklin, *ASP, Miscellaneous*, 154; Clarence Edward Carter, ed., *The Territorial Papers of the United States*, vols. 5–6, *The Territory of Mississippi, 1798–1817*, 5:292–95, 671–73, 6:183–85.

40. Rev. Anson West, *A History of Methodism in Alabama*, 25; Lowrie, *ASP, Public Lands*, 1:744–45; Bureau of Land Management, General Land Office Records, Private Land Claim, Patent Number 246341; Jeremiah Austill, Notes taken from the lips of Hiram Mounger . . . by Col J Austill, Pickett Papers, ADAH.

41. Florette Henri, *The Southern Indians and Benjamin Hawkins, 1796–1816*, 62. On Feb-

ruary 1, 1802, Hawkins wrote to Henry Dearborn, "Mr. Hill one of my assistants is of opinion that nearly 500 persons have passed through this agency during the winter from Georgia to Tombigbee and Natchez"; Grant, *Letters, Journals and Writings,* 433. Benjamin Hawkins' role as symbol of the plan of civilization is explored in Martha R. Severens and Kathleen Staples, "Benjamin Hawkins and the Creek Indians: A Study in Jefferson's Assimilation Policy."

42. Henry deLeon Southerland, Jr., and Jerry Elijah Brown, *The Federal Road through Georgia, the Creek Nation, and Alabama, 1806–1836,* 14–32; Carter, *Territorial Papers,* 6:405n.43.

43. Carter, *Territorial Papers,* 5:322–26 ("imperfectly known," and long quote).

Chapter 2

1. H. Thomas Foster II, ed., *The Collected Works of Benjamin Hawkins, 1796–1810,* 30s, 39–40, 99–100.

2. Ibid., 35s; Swanton, "Social Organization," 204.

3. Mark F. Boyd, "The Expedition of Marcos Delgado from Apalache to the Upper Creek Country in 1686," 26.

4. The name Sehoya or Sehoy is thought to be of Muskogee origin, although commonly used by the Koasatis. Geoffrey D. Kimball, *Koasati Grammar,* 16n.5, 390.

5. American Indian genealogical research can be challenging. Researchers often must rely heavily on family oral traditions because written documents are scarce, particularly for the early historic period. Individuals can be difficult to track through time because, prior to the modern era, many Indians took several names in the course of their lives, and names were often transcribed phonetically in imaginative but inconsistent ways by bureaucrats not fluent in Indian languages. Of course, historically prominent people, like William Weatherford, often have better documented genealogies than others.

6. Albert James Pickett elicited the family legend from Lachlan Durant; see Pickett, *History of Alabama,* 1:264–67. Pickett's surmise that warriors from Hickory Ground assisted in apprehending the mutineers cannot be correct, since Hickory Ground was not established until the 1760s. The earliest account of the Marchand-Sehoy relationship appears in Louis LeClerc Milfort, *Memoirs or a Quick Glance at My Various Travels and My Sojourn in the Creek Nation* [1802], 135; Sehoy was "a Creek woman of the Wind family (clan), an illegitimate daughter of a French officer who formerly commanded Fort Toulouse near the Alibamons Nation." In the original French, the initial phrases read "une sauvage creek de la famille du Vent, et fille naturelle d'un officier français"; [Jean-Antoine Leclerc-Milfort], *Chef de Guerre, Chez les Creeks,* 212.

Pickett thought the mutineers killed Marchand (a mistake repeated by innumerable historians), but he lived on and served in the colonial Troupes de la Marine until 1734. See Daniel H. Thomas, *Fort Toulouse: The French Outpost at the Alabamas on the Coosa,* 19–20); Waselkov, "Introduction," ibid., xxxii; Carl E. Brasseaux, *France's Forgotten Legion: Service Records of French Military and Administrative Personnel Stationed in the Mississippi Valley and Gulf Coast Region, 1699–1769,* pt. 2, 10–11; Craig T. Sheldon, Jr., John W. Cottier, and Gregory A. Waselkov, "A Preliminary Report on the Subsurface Testing of a Portion of the Creek Indian Property at Hickory Ground," 5. Earlier in the eighteenth century, Coosada was located "in the forks of the Coosa and Tallapoosa Rivers about a quarter mile below the old French fort"; David Tait, "Journal to and through the Upper Creek Nation," in Davies, *Documents of the American Revolution*, 5:267.

The town affiliation of Sehoy I and Sehoy II is uncertain. Of the two leading candidates, Taskigi or Coosada, Coosada seems most likely. The Taskigis were situated on the Chattahoochee River, among the Lower Creeks, in 1716 and 1718; they relocated to the middle Coosa Valley perhaps as early as 1718 and settled near the forks of the Coosa and Tallapoosa sometime between 1725 and 1733, too late to have assisted Marchand in quelling his troops' mutiny. If the Sehoys were affiliated with Coosada, then Alexander McGillivray was an Alabama-Koasati, not an Abeka or a Tallapoosa, as is commonly thought. See Mark F. Boyd, "Diego Peña's Expedition to Apalachee and Apalachicolo in 1716," 26, and "Documents Describing the Second and Third Expeditions of Lieutenant Diego Peña to Apalachee and Apalachicolo in 1717 and 1718," 134; Marvin T. Smith, *Coosa: The Rise and Fall of a Southeastern Mississippian Chiefdom*, 79–80. Some modern anthropologists suspect the people of Taskigi originally spoke the Koasati language. Karen M. Booker, Charles M. Hudson, and Robert L. Rankin, "Place Name Identification and Multilingualism in the Sixteenth-Century Southeast," 430, 439.

7. Sehoy II had a half-brother and a step-brother (following European reckoning) both named Red Shoes, headmen of Coosada. "Red Shoes" seems to have been a title or hereditary name of Koasati headmen. For references to McGillivray's maternal uncle, Red Shoes II (Sehoy II's half-brother), who died in 1784, see Caughey, *McGillivray*, 62–63, 66, 72, 158. "Red Shoes brother [of] one of my uncles" is mentioned in 1788; ibid., 185. This second individual was "the Coosada Chief Red Shoes [III]," from 1789 until at least 1793, but McGillivray never called him uncle, implying their affiliation with separate matrilineages; ibid., 230, 240, 246, 343, 351; Walter Lowrie and Matthew St. Clair Clarke, eds., *ASP, Indian Affairs*, 1:385. Another or the same Koasati Red Shoes was interviewed by Woodward in Texas; Woodward, *Reminiscences*, 14. For a recent study of the Yamasee War, its origins, and significance, see Steven J. Oatis, *A Colonial Complex: South Carolina's Frontiers in the Era of the Yamasee War, 1680–1730*.

8. Two nineteenth-century writers thought Sehoy II was not a métis but rather a "full blood" woman of Taskigi, an Alabama-affiliated town adjacent to Fort Toulouse. See Woodward, *Reminiscences*, 53, and J. D. Dreisbach to Lyman C. Draper, July 1874, Draper, WHS. These, however, are secondhand accounts dated a century after Sehoy II's death. More reliable is a letter of August 16, 1784, from Vincente Zéspedes, Governor of East Florida, to Bernardo de Gálvez, describing Sehoy II's son, Alexander McGillivray, as "a quarter Indian Englishman," which of course implies that Sehoy II was half Indian; Lawrence Kinnaird, ed., "Spain in the Mississippi Valley, 1765–1794, Part II: Post War Decade, 1782–1791," 108. As Amos Wright astutely comments on the Zéspedes letter, "the Spanish were very class conscious and kept up with these matters"; Wright, *The McGillivray and McIntosh Traders on the Old Southwest Frontier, 1716–1815*, 185.

9. The principal secondary source on Lachlan McGillivray is Edward J. Cashin, *Lachlan McGillivray, Indian Trader: The Shaping of the Southern Colonial Frontier*, 71–80. On Lachlan McGillivray's plantation, see John Pope, *A Tour through the Southern and Western Territories of the United States of North-America*, 46–48.

10. The later marriages of Sehoy II have created much confusion among historians, mainly because Thomas Woodward's discussion of Sehoy's life, written in 1858, has gener-

ally been interpreted to mean that McPherson married Sehoy II in the 1730s, before her marriage to McGillivray; Woodward, *Reminiscences,* 52, 77; see Wright, *McGillivray and McIntosh Traders,* 188–94. As Lynn Hastie Thompson has pointed out, this is not possible, since their granddaughter, Roseannah Weatherford, was born in 1804, so Roseannah's mother, Sehoy III, could have been born no earlier than the late 1750s. If Sehoy III's father, McPherson, had married Sehoy II prior to Lachlan McGillivray's arrival in the Southeast, Sehoy III's birth year could have been no later than 1744, making her sixty years old in 1804. Thompson estimates that her birth occurred in 1759 or later in *William Weatherford,* 14, 836. Wright located a number of references that establish Malcolm McPherson II's role as headman of Little Tallassee and Hickory Ground; Wright, *McGillivray and McIntosh Traders,* 191–92; Foster, *Collected Works,* 45. His son fought with William Weatherford as a Redstick at the Holy Ground in December 1813; Stiggins, "Historical narration," 70–71. See also Saunt, *New Order of Things,* 170.

11. For references to this family legend, see Henry S. Halbert and Timothy Ball, *The Creek War of 1813 and 1814,* 28; L. J. Newcomb Comings and Martha M. Albers, *A Brief History of Baldwin County,* 28.

12. Edward J. Cashin, *The King's Ranger: Thomas Brown and the American Revolution on the Southern Frontier,* 166 ("King and Head Warrior"). "Alexander McGillivray, half-breed, has been elected king of Creeks"; Lieut. Colonel Brown to Lord North, St. Augustine, October 24, 1783, in Davies, *Documents of the American Revolution,* 441.

13. Jacob (also known as William Dixon) Moniac was the father of Sam Moniac; Jacob raised Sehoy III when she was orphaned, then either married her or cohabited briefly. See Woodward, *Reminiscences,* 78, 95; Caughey, *McGillivray,* 137; Wright, *McGillivray and McIntosh Traders,* 260–64. He was trading among the Tallapoosa Creeks as early as 1764; John T. Juricek, ed., *Early American Indian Documents: Treaties and Laws, 1607–1789,* vol. 12, *Georgia and Florida Treaties, 1763–1776,* 12. For Jacob's activities as an interpreter from 1772 until his death in 1787, see David Taitt, "Journal of David Taitt's Travels from Pensacola, West Florida, to and through the Country of the Upper and the Lower Creeks, 1772," 536, 542, 544; Caughey, *McGillivray,* 82, 84, 134, 148; Cashin, *Lachlan McGillivray,* 292; Juricek, *Early American Indian Documents,* 12:137, 163, 175, 179, 181.

14. Their children were Peggy, who married Charles Cornells, a métis; Alexander, who died in England in 1802 at around the age of twenty-two; and Lizzy, who married Captain Sam Isaacs, a métis. Woodward, *Reminiscences,* 57; William Panton to Lachlan McGillivray, April 10, 1794, in Caughey, *McGillivray,* 363; Wright, *McGillivray and McIntosh Traders,* 269, 275–76.

15. Vicey moved back to Tuckaubatchee a year after Alexander died, when she married Zachariah McGirth. Her sister Lucy had lived in the Tensaw with her husband John Keane, whose daughter Polly was born there. Brother James eventually established a plantation and cowpens at Burnt Corn Springs, where the Wolf Trail intersected the trail to Tuckaubatchee, northeast of the Tensaw. See Caleb Swan, "Position and State of Manners and Arts in the Creek, or Muscogee Nation in 1791," 5:252; Wright, *McGillivray and McIntosh Traders,* 267; Foster, *Collected Works,* 36–37; Woodward, *Reminiscences,* 84–85, 96–97.

16. Milfort and Jennet McGillivray's son, Will Milfort, was a Redstick warrior killed by Sam Dale in a skirmish preceding the Canoe Fight in November 1813. Milfort, *Memoirs,* 136–

38; Pickett, *History of Alabama*, 1:264; J.F.H. Claiborne, *Life and Times of Gen. Sam. Dale, the Mississippi Partisan*, 120–21; Cashin, *Lachlan McGillivray*, 76; Foster, *Collected Works*, 43; Wright, *McGillivray and McIntosh Traders*, 206–7, 211–16; O'Neill to Ezpeleta, October 19, 1783, in Caughey, *McGillivray*, 62 (quote).

17. Pickett, *History of Alabama*, 2:268; Woodward, *Reminiscences*, 78; Wright, *McGillivray and McIntosh Traders*, 260; Thompson, *William Weatherford*, 21.

18. The anthropological literature on structures of non-Western marriage systems is vast. For an interesting discussion of female agency in patrilineal marriage alliances, see Marshall Sahlins, *Apologies to Thucydides: Understanding History as Culture and Vice Versa*, 221–36.

19. Historians have been generally reluctant to accept David Taitt's paternity of David Tate. Pickett assumed this relationship, based on the testimony of an old trader; see Notes taken from the lips of Abram Mordecai, Pickett Papers, ADAH. But Woodward sowed confusion by identifying the father, whom he characterized as "the last agent the English Government ever had among the Creeks" (a fair description of David Taitt), as John Tate. Pickett, *History of Alabama*, 2:268; Woodward, *Reminiscences*, 52 (quote), 78; J. D. Dreisbach Letter to Lyman Draper, July 1874, Draper, WHS; Tarvin, "Muscogees or Creek Indians," 129; Thompson, *William Weatherford*, 19–22; Charles E. Bryant, *The Tensaw Country North of the Ellicott Line, 1800–1860*, 367; Wright, *McGillivray and McIntosh Traders*, 189, 194–202, 269. Cf. Cashin, *Lachlan McGillivray*, 77, 335n.40; Benjamin W. Griffith, Jr., *McIntosh and Weatherford, Creek Indian Leaders*, 36–37. I am indebted to Kathryn Holland Braund for pointing out the coincidence of Taitt's years of residence at Little Tallassee and the dates of conception of Sehoy's children Eloise and David. See David H. Corkran, *The Creek Frontier, 1540–1783*, 289–320; Davies, *Documents of the American Revolution*, 14:95, 147, and 15:33, 188 (quote); Cashin, *King's Ranger*, 81–82, 93, 98; Medina Rojas, *Jose de Ezpeleta*, 149–54; Juricek, *Early American Indian Documents*, 12:84 and 431 (for documentation of a 1772 visit), 441 (1774), 369; Kenneth Donovan, *Slaves in Cape Breton, 1713–1815*.

20. Woodward, *Reminiscences*, 77. Charles Weatherford sold nine enslaved Africans to William Clark, in the Tensaw, on June 26, 1779, perhaps placing a date on his arrival in the region; Robin F. A. Fabel, *The Economy of British West Florida, 1763–1783*, 236.

21. Thompson, *William Weatherford*, 23–24, 872; Cashin, *King's Ranger*, 43; Griffith, *McIntosh and Weatherford*, 5. American agent James Seagrove thought Weatherford was white; see Lowrie and Clarke, *ASP, Indian Affairs*, 1:305, 469. Also see Alan Ray's Weatherford family webpage at http://freepages.genealogy.rootsweb.com/~walanray/pafg52.htm. For various guesses about Charles Weatherford's ethnic background, see Halbert and Ball, *Creek War*, 27–28; Griffith, *McIntosh and Weatherford*, 40; Saunt, *New Order of Things*, 74, 99, cf. 167; Wright, *McGillivray and McIntosh Traders*, 204–5. Only two historians have understood his mixed descent, based on research in Spanish colonial documents. See Helen Hornbeck Tanner, *Zéspedes in East Florida, 1784–1790*, 90; J. Leitch Wright, Jr., *William Augustus Bowles, Director General of the Creek Nation*, 166.

22. George Cary Eggleston, *Red Eagle and the Wars with the Creek Indians of Alabama*, 41; Pickett, *History of Alabama*, 2:92, 130, 190; Swan, "Position and State of Manners and Arts," 255; Grant, *Letters, Journals and Writings*, 23; Wright, *McGillivray and McIntosh Traders*, 204; Foster, *Collected Works*, 170. A 1793 report to Governor William Blount of Tennessee

Territory mentions the theft by Creek Warriors of four horses from the Cumberland, including "Drumgold's roan race horse"; Lowrie and Clarke, *ASP, Indian Affairs*, 1:446.

23. In 1799, Jesse Rountree of Edgefield County, South Carolina, filed a complaint against Charles Weatherford over a "negro man slave named Aster," who had run away from Rountree to the Creek nation ten years before. Rountree had given Weatherford a bill of sale from his original purchase of Aster from Stephen Tillman, thinking it would persuade Weatherford to return his slave, but Weatherford apparently argued that possession of Rountree's bill of sale was authorization to sell Aster himself. Deposition of June 14, 1799, Jesse Rountree Papers, Duke University Rare Book, Manuscript, and Special Collections Library.

24. Griffith, *McIntosh and Weatherford*, 40–44. McGillivray to O'Neill, December 3, 1786 in Caughey, *McGillivray*, 141; McGillivray to Miró, January 10, 1788, ibid., 167 (first quote); O'Neill to Miró, October 28, 1788, ibid., 205. Lowrie and Clarke, *ASP, Indian Affairs*, 1:387 (second quote).

25. Grant, *Letters, Journals and Writings*, 187–88 (quote), 195.

26. Ibid., 256–57 ("malady"), 24–25 ("expensively"); Tanner, *Zéspedes in East Florida*, 194. Griffith, *McIntosh and Weatherford*, 18, identifies the horse malady as infectious equine anemia. On October 20, 1796, "Seehoye Weatherford & Robert Walton" posted $1,000 bond with the U.S. government agent to trade in the towns of the "Towassees & Powaghtee in the Alabama upper Creeks," immediately downriver from Coosada; Records of the Office of Indian Trade, Records of the Creek Agency East, Correspondence and Other Records, 1794–1818, RG 75, NARA.

Sisters Sehoy III Weatherford, Sophia Durant, and Jennet Milfort Crook claimed the properties of Alexander McGillivray and Malcolm McPherson II, upon the deaths of their brothers, for themselves and their own children, as was customary under Creek law. See Kathryn E. Holland Braund, "The Creek Indians, Blacks, and Slavery," 631; Saunt, *New Order of Things*, 89, 169–71; Perdue, *"Mixed Blood" Indians*, 59.

27. Wright, *William Augustus Bowles*, 2–3, 128–41, 166–67; Griffith, *McIntosh and Weatherford*, 50–53; Woodward, *Reminiscences*, 78; J. D. Dreisbach Letter to Lyman Draper, 1874, Draper, WHS. Abram Mordecai recollected Bowles' capture by Moniac and other young warriors, who threw him down and bound his arms with wahoo ropes; Notes taken from the lips of Abram Mordecai, Pickett Papers, ADAH. Bowles died in 1805, still in Spanish custody at Morro Castle in Havana, Cuba.

28. Sandra Riley, *Homeward Bound: A History of the Bahama Islands to 1850, with a Definitive Study of Abaco in the American Loyalist Period*, 195, 208. On cropping, see William Bartram, *Travels through North & South Carolina, Georgia, East & West Florida, the Cherokee Country, the Extensive Territories of the Muscogulgees, or Creek Confederacy, and the Country of the Choctaws*, 213, 448–49, 515. Dr. Thomas G. Holmes told historian Albert James Pickett a very different story about the end of Charles Weatherford's life. Holmes maintained that Weatherford died in the Tensaw "at David Tates House about 1811." Notes taken from the lips of Dr Thos G. Holmes, Pickett Papers, ADAH.

29. Halbert and Ball, *Creek War*, 175; John Spencer Bassett, ed., "Major Howell Tatum's Journal," 14; Davis, "'Much of the Indian Appears,'" 90. "Point Thlolly" is an attempt to transcribe the name of the stream near Weatherford's home, Pintlala Creek.

30. Daniel McGillivray to John Panton, September 28, 1799, July 27, 1800, Panton Leslie

Papers, cited in Wright, *McGillivray and McIntosh Traders,* 259; Baptismal Records, Diocese of Mobile Sacramental Records, folio 3, number 4—"On the Eleventh day of November 1801, at Tensaw, in Mr. Randon's house, I, John Francis Vaugeois Rector of Mobile, Christened with the Ceremonies of the holy Catholic Church Prudence born on the 11th of May 1799, and David born on the 20th of July last, both of them Lawful son and daughter of Samuel Mims from Maryland, and Ana Rain of St. Augustine in florida. the godfather and godmother of the girl were David Tate and Mary Ana Randon."

31. Albert James Pickett, "McGillivray and the Creeks," 136; James Lamar Appleton and Robert David Ward, "Albert James Pickett and the Case of the Secret Articles: Historians and the Treaty of New York of 1790," 33–34 (quote); Gregory A. Waselkov and Kathryn E. Holland Braund, *William Bartram on the Southeastern Indians,* 190–91; Indian Committee Records, Philadelphia Society of Friends Yearly Meeting, Quaker Collection, Haverford College Library.

32. *Pennsylvania Packet and Daily Advertiser* (July 15, 29, 1790). The issue of July 29 identifies the two boys as "David Frances, a young half breed, Kinsman to Col. M'Gillivray" and "David Tate, Nephew to Col. M'Gillivray." I am grateful to Kathryn Holland Braund for generously providing these sources on Tate and Frances, as well as the Indian Committee Records reference cited above. David Frances, or Francis, was a distant matrilineal relation of McGillivray, perhaps a brother of Josiah Francis of Autauga town. See Pickett, *History of Alabama,* 2:245; Stiggins, "Historical narration," 70–72; Owsley, "Prophet of War," 273. "David Francis," presumably a trader, "lived sometimes at Aconchautee [Red Ground] and sometimes among the Autaugas"; Notes taken from the lips of Abram Mordecai, Pickett Papers, ADAH.

33. Carlos Howard to Governor Juan Quesada, September 24, 1790, Caughey, *McGillivray,* 283, 323n.317; Tarvin, "Muscogees or Creek Indians," 134–35; Grant, *Letters, Journals and Writings,* 299, 556; Marie Taylor Greenslade, "William Panton," 116–18. According to Tate's son-in-law, J. D. Dreisbach, Tate stayed in Scotland, returning only after Alexander McGillivray, Jr., had died. J. D. Driesbach to Lyman Draper, July 1874, Draper, WHS.

34. Only Sam Moniac joined him in American court proceedings, in the September Term 1807, "John Brown vs. Saml. Monyack, alias Fi-Fa, no debt." Also see May Term 1807: "Admrs. F. Killingsworth vs. David Tate, Fi-Fa, debt $113.50, Levied on one negro boy name unknown & [?] by David Tate and a parcel of Indians; September Term 1807: T. B. Singleton vs. David Tate, alias Fi-Fa, no debt; John Mills vs. David Tate, alias Fi-Fa, debt $735.00, no property found; Admrs. of Francis Killingsworth vs. David Tate, alias Fi-Fa, debt $113.50, no property found"; Collections of the St. Stephens Historical Society, St. Stephens, Alabama, Lower Court Docket Book, 1807–1812, Washington County, Mississippi Territory. "Fi-Fa" stands for *fieri facias,* "a writ of execution commanding the sheriff to levy and make the amount of a judgment from the goods and chattels of the judgment debtor;" Henry Campbell Black, *Black's Law Dictionary: Definitions of the Terms and Phrases of American and English Jurisprudence, Ancient and Modern,* 565. Also see Grant, *Letters, Journals and Writings,* 565–66; March Court 1812, Superior Court, Book C, Washington County, Mississippi Territory (LDS Film 1752975); Frank, *Creeks and Southerners,* 65–66.

35. Some English-language correspondence from Spanish Governor González Manrique was taken from Weatherford's house after the battle at the Holy Ground, suggesting that

he could read. See González Manrique to Josiah Francis, Old King, Old Interpreter and Mougaioulchie, September 29, 1813, and Manrique to my Friend and Brother, November 15, 1813, in Letterbook F, Letters and Papers Relating to the Indian Wars, 1812–1816, J.F.H. Claiborne Collection, MDAH. In a letter to David Moniac, Tate conveyed regards from Moniac's uncles, John and William Weatherford. There are no extant letters written by Weatherford. David Tate, "David Tate to Cadet David Moniac, Letter of 1822."

36. A. B. Meek, *Romantic Passages in Southwestern History,* 267–70. J. D. Dreisbach to Lyman Draper, July 1874, Draper, WHS. Dreisbach described Weatherford as "6 feet and 2 inches in hight, and weighed about 175 lbs, with a form of perfect mould." See also Eggleston, *Red Eagle,* 44–45. For descriptions of the Creek ball game, see Swanton, "Social Organization," 456–68; Charles M. Hudson, *The Southeastern Indians,* 235–36 ("the little brother to war").

37. Meek recounts "the words of an old Indian woman who knew him at this period, 'The squaws would quit hoeing corn, and smile and gaze upon him as he rode by the cornpatch'"; *Romantic Passages,* 267. A highly biased account, written shortly after the Redstick War by General Ferdinand Claiborne's nephew, described Weatherford as exhibiting "genius, eloquence and courage," despite his "avarice, treachery, and a thirst for blood. . . . Fortune, in her freaks," according to this author, "sometimes gives to the most profligate an elevation of mind, which she denies to men whose propensites are the most virtuous"; Nathaniel Herbert Claiborne, *Notes on the War in the South,* 18. For a tale of Weatherford's rowdy prewar behavior, see Mrs. Dunbar [Eron] Rowland, *Mississippi Territory in the War of 1812,* 86–87.

38. A. B. Meek, *The Red Eagle: A Poem of the South,* and *Romantic Passages,* 263. Dreisback, "Weatherford—'The Red Eagle,'" ("poet"). Woodward, *Reminiscences,* 76 (alternate names). The Muskogee word *lane* means yellow or brown in English; Martin and Mauldin, *Dictionary of Creek/Muskogee,* 70. See John H. Moore, "Mvskoke Personal Names."

39. Claudio Saunt, "Taking Account of Property: Stratification among the Creek Indians in the Early Nineteenth Century," 735, 751.

40. Taitt, "Journal to and through the Upper Creek Nation," 258–59 (first quotes); Dorothy Williams Potter, *Passports of Southeastern Pioneers, 1770–1823,* 48; Juricek, *Early American Indian Documents,* 12:398 (final quote).

41. Grant, *Letters, Journals and Writings,* 22; *Georgia Gazette* [Savannah], August 21, 1783. In 1788, Alexander McGillivray wrote to Governor O'Neill that Bailey "had fallen under my displeasure for his former roguery & bad behaviour," and had moved to the Spanish settlement on the Tensaw, where he was enumerated in a census the year before; Caughey, *McGillivray,* 169 (quote); Gwendolyn Midlo Hall, ed., *Databases for the Study of Afro-Louisiana History and Genealogy, 1699–1860: Computerized Information from Original Manuscript Sources.*

42. Grant, *Letters, Journals and Writings,* 21–22 (quotes), 26. Hawkins noted also the presence of "20 bee hives" at the plantation. "Mr. Bailey keeps some good rum in his house, and it is remarkable in him that he neither drinks or smokes tobacco. By the former I mean, to excess; he every day takes a glass of grog or two and that's all." Hawkins added, regarding Mrs. Bailey, "She presides at her table which is always neat and well supplied with coffee or tea, butter of her own make, meat and well made bread." Regarding the treatment of slaves

by the Creeks, "The black people here are an expense to their owners except in the house where I am. They do nothing the whole winter but get a little wood, and in the summer they cultivate a scanty crop of corn barely sufficient for bread"; ibid., 22, 28–29. By 1799, Hawkins regretfully concluded that Mary Bailey's example had no beneficent effect "on the Indians, even her own family, with the exception of her own children"; ibid., 293. For a location map of Bailey's plantation, see Robbie Ethridge, *Creek Country,* 69. For an illustration of the kind of spinning wheel made for the Creeks by Moravian missionary Karsten Petersen from 1807 to 1813, see Severens and Staples, "Benjamin Hawkins," 23.

43. Severens and Staples, ibid., 27–28 (quotes), 322–23; Perdue, "Mixed Blood" Indians, 20.

44. Grant, *Letters, Journals and Writings,* 28.

45. Ibid., 186–87 (quotes), 195; Foster, *Collected Works,* 168.

46. Grant, *Letters, Journals and Writings,* 67–68, 94 (quotes), 104–105, 168, 180.

47. Ibid., 293 (quotes). Frank misinterpreted Hawkins' correspondence to mean Dixon and Richard, Jr., were two sons of Richard, Sr., and that one embraced and one rejected Indian life; Frank, *Creeks and Southerners,* 75. A careful reading of Hawkins makes clear the single identity of Richard Dixon Bailey, which is confirmed by testimonies of William Hollinger and Gilbert C. Russell, who alternatively referred to the captain of militia at Fort Mims as Richard Bailey or Dixon Bailey; Testimony of William Hollinger, April 21, 1854, and Testimony of Gilbert C. Russell, February 15, 1855, File 222, Probate Court Records, Monroeville, Monroe County, Alabama.

48. Hawkins to Henry Dearborn, Creek Agency, June 1, 1801, in Grant, *Letters, Journals and Writings,* 359–360 ("the new order of things"); Dixon Bailey still resided on the plantation west of Atasi in January 1802; Foster, *Collected Works,* 82j.

49. Grant, *Letters, Journals and Writings,* 643.

50. Of course, the original rationale behind Creek settlement at Tensaw was for Alexander McGillivray and like-minded, wealthy métis to raise cattle near the market provided by Spanish Pensacola. See Tarvin, "Muscogees or Creek Indians," 133; Davis, "'Remember Fort Mims,'" 613–16.

51. Grant, *Letters, Journals and Writings,* 518–19 (quote), 588; Davis, *'Much of the Indian Appears,'* 102–106. Construction of the Federal Road through the Creek nation in 1811 devastated Alabama hunting grounds, as well; Michael D. Green, *The Politics of Indian Removal: Creek Government and Society in Crisis,* 40. According to Pickett, Isaacs' actual name was "Tourculla" or "Towerculla." On Isaacs' ties to Coosada, see Pickett, *History of Alabama,* 2:134, 191; Notes taken from the lips of Abram Mordecai, Pickett Papers, ADAH; Woodward, *Reminiscences,* 33.

52. Notes taken from the lips of Dr Thos G. Holmes, Pickett Papers, ADAH (quotes); cited in Davis, *'Much of the Indian Appears,'* 140–42.

Bailey's ferry was a major crossing point for traffic to Natchez and New Orleans. In 1809 the Choctaw Boundary survey team crossed "the great path from Baileys Ferry on the Alabama, to Callers Ferry on Tombigbee"; Silas Dinsmoor and Levin Wailes, "Journal and Field Notes on the Boundary lines Between The United States and The Chaktaw nation of Indians Surveyed Pursuant to a Treaty concluded at Mount Dexter on the 16th day of November 1805," 185, Old Case F File, Item 1, RG 49, NARA.

53. Saunt, *New Order of Things,* and "Taking Account of Property"; Sheehan, *Seeds of Extinction*; Sheidley, *Unruly Men,* 235, 244; Davis, "'Remember Fort Mims,'" 625–26; Joel W. Martin, *Sacred Revolt: The Muskogees' Struggle for a New World,* 104.

54. See Grant, *Letters, Journals and Writings,* 668–69. Specifically, in 1813, the murders of many wealthy micos immediately preceded a unified attack on the Tensaw by warriors from thirteen Alabama, Abeka, and Tallapoosa towns.

Chapter 3

1. Pickett, *History of Alabama,* 2:35; T. S. Arthur and W. H. Carpenter, *The History of Georgia, from Its Earliest Settlement to the Present Time,* 126–27; Lorenzo Sabine, *Biographical Sketches of Loyalists of the American Revolution, with an Historical Essay,* 64–65; Thomas J. Kirkland and Robert M. Kennedy, *Historic Camden,* 297–305; Wilbur Henry Siebert, *Loyalists in East Florida, 1774–1785,* 1:44, 46, 58–59, 72, 164–67, 174, 179, 2:44, 48, 237, 328–30; Cashin, *King's Ranger,* 98, 105, 168; *Tanner, Zéspedes in East Florida,* 39–46 ("banditti"), 189, 225; Joseph B. Lockey, trans., "The St. Augustine Census of 1786," 23 (quotes). Jerry G. Braddock, Sr., kindly provided me with information and references on McGirth family history.

2. By 1796 the McGirths already had one child, a daughter. For the location of the Cornells plantation, see Ethridge, *Creek Country,* 69. Foster, *Collected Works,* 36–37, 219–20, 259–60, 495 (first quote); Grant, *Letters, Journals and Writings,* 291–92 (second quote).

3. Siebert, *Loyalists in East Florida,* 2:178–79; Wright, *William Augustus Bowles,* 146, 148.

4. Creek métis Linn McGee, later Dixon Bailey's ferry boatman, signed on as an early mail rider; Lieutenant H. R. Graham to Gideon Granger, March 20, 1807, no. 9, Joseph Wheaton Papers, University of Georgia Libraries, Athens. Henry Richard Graham was a first lieutenant in the Second U.S. Infantry at Fort Stoddert; Francis B. Heitman, *Historical Register and Dictionary of the United States Army,* 467–68; I am grateful to James W. Parker for this reference. Henry deLeon Southerland, Jr., and Jerry Elijah Brown, *The Federal Road through Georgia, the Creek Nation, and Alabama, 1806–1836,* 22–32; Joseph Wheaton to Gideon Granger, November 28, 1806, no. 2 (quotes), and Gideon Granger to Caleb Swan and John VanNess, March 21, 1808, no. 1, Wheaton Papers, University of Georgia Libraries. It seems unfair to attribute McGirth's change of heart to "his shortcomings as a postman," as does Davis, "'Much of the Indian Appears,'" 128n2.

5. On June 13, 1807, "Zachie McGirth" still resided at Tuckaubatchee, where he witnessed a document conveying to Big Warrior power of attorney in the Creek nation to recover debts owed to Daniel McGillivray; Very curious old M.S. furnished me [Pickett] by Mr Edward Hamrick, Section 8, no. 12, Pickett Papers, ADAH.

6. Mississippi Territory, *U.S. Census of Population*; population estimate for 1813 from John W. Monette, *History of the Discovery and Settlement of the Valley of the Mississippi,* 2:392.

7. David Hackett Fischer and James C. Kelly argue, in *Bound Away: Virginia and the Westward Movement,* xvi, that a frontier "was not, in the fashionable sense, a 'zone of interaction' between cultures but a place where one culture rapidly established a hegemony which persists to this day." Their usage dismisses hundreds of years of colonial interaction as irrelevant in contrast to the later massive waves of American migration, thereby ignoring the lasting impact of colonial-era interactions on modern regional populations. It also con-

verts "frontier" from a process to a transitory event, the implications of which, neverthe-less, took decades to play out. I find it more useful to consider the westward migrations of nineteenth-century America as a particular kind of frontier phenomenon, one that acceler-ated the frontier process (of interaction) and often rapidly devastated native populations in its wake. Quick imposition of American hegemony in no way lessened interaction with na-tive peoples, which is the essence of an anthropological approach to frontiers. For more on migrations of Virginians into the Old Southwest, see ibid., 129, 137–40. On Africans in the Natchez District, see Berlin, *Many Thousands Gone*, 338–57, and Ira Berlin, *Generations of Captivity: A History of African-American Slaves*, 146–57.

8. For more on the early history of Mississippi Territory, see Monette, *History of the Discovery and Settlement of the Valley of the Mississippi*, 2:339–90; Isaac Joslin Cox, *The West Florida Controversy, 1798–1813*, 482–85; Hamilton, *Colonial Mobile*, 379–415; Claiborne, *Missis-sippi*, 244–314; Clark and Guice, *The Old Southwest*, 19–116; Frank L. Owsley, Jr., and Gene A. Smith, *Filibusters and Expansionists: Jeffersonian Manifest Destiny, 1800–1821*, 61–81; Garry Wills, *"Negro President": Jefferson and the Slave Power*, 185–87. Kemper's main force crossed the Mobile-Tensaw delta at Nannahubba Island and camped near Mims' ferry, where they learned of the defeat of their compatriots. See Notes furnished by Doct Thos G. Holmes, Pickett Papers, ADAH.

Among old Mobilians, the name Caller is pronounced "kaller," not "collar," and the name Toulmin is pronounced "tollman" (as in the eponymous Mobile neighborhood, Toulmin-ville), not "toolman."

9. I am indebted to Martha W. McCartney for researching primary documentation on Daniel Beasley's life in Virginia. Her sources and interpretations form the basis for my brief summary. Martha W. McCartney, "Daniel Beasley," manuscript on file at the Center for Ar-chaeological Studies, University of South Alabama, Mobile.

10. Alberta Marjorie Dennstedt, "The Cheatham Family of Colonial Virginia," 102–4; Virginia Land Office Patent Books, 1623–1762 (microfilm on file at the Rockefeller Library, Colonial Williamsburg Foundation, Williamsburg, Va.), 12:254, 15:223, 16:130, 22:572, 30:136; Amelia County, Virginia, Deed Books (microfilm on file, Library of Virginia, Richmond), 4:388, 12:174; Chesterfield County, Virginia, Deed Books 1–9, 1749–1783 (microfilm on file, Library of Virginia, Richmond), 1:362, 3:174–75, 4:621, 5:505, 6:1, 8:113, 9:72.

11. Elizabeth A. Fenn, *Pox Americana: The Great Smallpox Epidemic of 1775–82*, 46, 115–34; Chesterfield County Will Book 5:4 (quote).

12. Will of Benjamin Beasley, December 12, 1781, Chesterfield County Will Book 3:301. The Beasleys' ten slaves were named Nell, Moses, Jack, Bowser, Lyddy, Hoe, Judy, John, Edy, and Sam. A few modern historians have mistakenly assumed, because Beasley fought at Fort Mims in the Tensaw, that he was a métis. See Clark and Guice, *Old Southwest*, 133; Thomp-son, *William Weatherford*, 306. This is clearly a baseless assumption. Accounts of estate executors Stephen Beasley (in Amelia County) and Mathew Cheatham (in Chesterfield County) are summarized in McCartney, "Daniel Beasley."

13. Beasley vs. Beasley Legatees, March 1794, 1794-17, Box 6, Chesterfield County Chan-cery Court Records; Nottoway County Land Tax Lists, 1789–1799, Nottoway County Personal Property Tax Lists, 1790–1797, and Chesterfield County Personal Property Tax Lists, 1796–1803, Virginia Historical Society, Richmond. For comparative data on economic class struc-

ture in Chesterfield and York counties, see Martha W. McCartney, "The Hatcher-Cheatham Site (44CF259): A Middling Farmstead in Rural Chesterfield" (manuscript on file, Department of Anthropology, James Madison University, Harrisonburg, VA), and "Middling Farm Households in York County, Virginia" (manuscript on file, Yorktown Victory Center, Yorktown, Va.).

A like-named cousin of Daniel's (son of Benjamin's brother John) posted a bond with John Page to operate an ordinary in Nottoway County, southwest of Amelia County, in 1805, postdating our Daniel Beasley's move to the Natchez District by two years. Bond Concerning an Ordinary, October 3, 1805, MSS4 N8493b6, Nottoway County Court Papers, 1790–1817, Virginia Historical Society, Richmond.

14. Will of Daniel Beasley, March 7, 1813, Will Book A (1800–1833), p. 17, Chancery Clerk's Office, Jefferson County Courthouse, Fayette, Mississippi. Daniel willed his possessions to his nearest relations, nieces Polly and Obedience Beasley, daughters of his deceased brother Thomas, whose family remained in Chesterfield County, Virginia. Ann Brown, of Lorman, Mississippi, kindly provided me with a copy of Daniel Beasley's last will and testament.

15. Dunbar Rowland, ed., *Letter Books of W.C.C. Claiborne*, 1:167–68 (quote); Jefferson County Deed Book B1 (1804–1813), pp. 57, 191, 217–18, 221, 232 (microfilm #12008), MDAH; Court Records, Jefferson County, Mississippi Territory, pp. 106, 176–77 (Church of Latter Day Saints, Family History Library, Salt Lake City); Notices, *Weekly Chronicle* [Natchez, Mississippi Territory] (August 24, September 7, 1808), (October 7, 1809, March 26, 1810); Tax receipt of Isaac Guion, September 7, 1808, in Book F, J.F.H. Claiborne Collection, MDAH; John Shaw vs. George B. Watson, February 5, 1805, to January 9, 1813, John Shaw Papers, Center for American History, University of Texas at Austin. Beasley resigned as Sheriff on February 26, 1813; Papers of the Mississippi Territory, RG 2, Territorial Governors Papers, Letters, certificates, and commissions, 8:136, MDAH. I am indebted to Sue Moore for these and most of the following references to Daniel Bailey's career in the Natchez District.

16. Franklin Academy, *Mississippi Messenger* [Natchez, Mississippi Territory] (February 11, 1806); Monette, *History of the Discovery and Settlement of the Valley of the Mississippi*, 2:351; Dunbar Rowland, ed., *Encyclopedia of Mississippi History*, 1:742–43; Sue Burns Moore, "Time Line for Dr. John Shaw."

The four competing newspapers that began publishing in Natchez at the beginning of the century were a powerful force for partisanship, particularly after the rapid decline of the Federalist party in the South and nationally. See Jeffrey L. Pasley, "'*The Tyranny of Printers:'*" *Newspaper Politics in the Early American Republic*, 21, 218, 229, 235, 351.

17. Dunbar Rowland, ed., *Third Annual Report of the Director of the Department of Archives and History of the State of Mississippi from October 1, 1903 to October 1, 1904, with Accompanying Historical Documents Concerning the Aaron Burr Conspiracy*, 55–56, 97, 104.

18. John Doherty to Messrs. John W. Winn & Co. [Publisher], *Weekly Chronicle* (June 18, 1810):3.

19. On Trigg, King, & Co., see Notice, *Weekly Chronicle* (August 24, 1808, February 5, June 25, 1810). Quotes from Elliott to Beasley, Greenville, May 28, 1810, and Beasley to Elliott, Greenville, May 29, 1810, *Weekly Chronicle* (June 25, 1810):3.

20. Wood to Beasley, Greenville, May 31, 1810, *Weekly Chronicle* (June 25, 1810):3.

21. Beasley [to Publisher], *Weekly Chronicle—Extra* (July 2, 1810):1. A gallery is a raised,

covered porch running an entire length of an exterior wall. In the lower Mississippi valley, many French-style creole cottages have galleries wrapping around two, three, or four sides. The phrase "he lost his priming" means the gunpowder in the priming pan of Elliott's pistol had fallen out and the gun would not fire.

22. Beasley to Wood, Greenville, June 16, 1810, *Weekly Chronicle—Extra* (July 2, 1810):1; Wood to the Publick, Port Gibson, June 20, 1810, and Daniel Beasley, Greenville, June 21, 1810, *Weekly Chronicle* (June 25, 1810):2.

23. Governor Holmes appointed Samuel Frye Attorney at Law on April 20, 1808; see Papers of the Mississippi Territory, RG 2, Territorial Governors Papers, Register of Appointments (1805–1817), MDAH. As a practicing attorney he put his name to two petitions in 1809 requesting a judge be appointed for Madison County, on the Tennessee River; Carter, *Territorial Papers*, 5:722–23, 742–43. See two fragmentary undated letters of Nathaniel Frye, Jr. [1811], in Samuel Frye Papers, AR 85–311, Center for American History, University of Texas, Austin; Samuel Frye, Genealogical Records of the Frye Family [n.d.], Fryeburg Historical Society, Fryeburg, Maine; J.F.H. Claiborne, *Mississippi, as a Province, Territory and State,* 389n; Anne Mims Wright, *A Record of the Descendants of Isaac Ross and Jean Brown,* 69–71.; Mary T. Logan, *Mississippi-Louisiana Border Country: A History of Rodney, Miss., St. Joseph, La., and Environs,* 23. Sources disagree as to which daughter of Isaac Ross was to wed Samuel Frye. Most sources say Margaret A. Ross, who later married Senator Thomas B. Reed. But a family history compiled by relatives of the women indicates the betrothed was Isaac's youngest daughter, Martha B. Ross, who was seventeen at the time of the duel and died in 1818; Wright, *Descendants of Isaac Ross,* 71n.

The duel took place west of Petit Gulf (Rodney), across from the mouth of Coles Creek, perhaps on the Vidalia sandbar known as the "Duelling Ground" where Jim Bowie had a famous fight in 1827; see James L. Batson, *James Bowie and the Sandbar Fight: Birth of the James Bowie Legend & Bowie Knife,* 5.

24. According to Claiborne, in his 1860 book, *Life and Times of Gen. Sam Dale,* 115, Beasley "had an affair of honor with Mr. Fry, a rising member of the bar, of the same county. They fought opposite Rodney, and the latter fell. It was peculiarly distressing, for he was on the eve of marriage with a most beautiful woman. This rendered Beasley very unhappy. He wrote to General Claiborne to obtain a commission in the army. The general appointed him his aid." Also see Claiborne, *Mississippi,* 389n; Logan, *Mississippi-Louisiana Border Country,* 24; Charles E. Bryant, *Oh God, What Have I Done,* 7–21.

25. Robert Lowery and William H. McCardle, *A History of Mississippi,* 218 (Beasley description). Also see J. R. Hutchinson, *Reminiscences, Sketches and Addresses Selected from My Papers During a Ministry of Forty-five Years in Mississippi, Louisiana, and Texas,* 51–60; Dickson D. Bruce, Jr., *Violence and Culture in the Antebellum South,* 21–43; Jack K. Williams, *Dueling in the Old South: Vignettes of Social History;* Bertram Wyatt-Brown, *Honor and Violence in the Old South,* 142–53; Thomas Fleming, *Duel: Alexander Hamilton, Aaron Burr, and the Future of America,* 7–8; Joanne B. Freeman, *Affairs of Honor: National Politics in the New Republic.* According to Freeman, in "Dueling as Politics: Reinterpreting the Burr-Hamilton Duel," 301–2, a small percentage of duels resulted in fatalities or even injuries.

26. Harry Toulmin, *A Digest of the Laws of the State of Alabama,* 261–66, quoted in Peter A. Brannon, "Dueling in Alabama," 97. Also see Harry Toulmin, *Statutes of the Mississippi Ter-*

ritory. Although Beasley and Frye fought their duel in Concordia Parish, Louisiana, sections 2 and 3 of the 1803 Mississippi Territorial statute expressly forbade such a subterfuge.

> SEC. 2. *And be it further enacted,* That if any person or persons residing or being in this territory, shall promote, concert, plan, or in any manner encourage the fighting of a duel between persons residing or being in this territory, whether the same duel be fought or not within this territory or elsewhere, such person or persons shall be subject to the pains and penalties prescribed in the preceding section of this act.
>
> SEC. 3. *And be it further enacted,* That if any person resident or being in this territory, do hereafter actually fight a duel, and either of the combatants be killed; the survivor, with such other person or persons who may have aided or assisted in the said duel, shall be deemed guilty of wilful murder, and on conviction thereof, shall suffer death. (Toulmin, *Digest,* 261)

By his persistence in this matter, Beasley probably gained the approbation of politically influential Ferdinand Claiborne, who had met fellow militia officer Benjamin Farrar on the field of honor on November 30, 1806; see Robert Dabney Calhoun, "A History of Concordia Parish," 631.

27. Election, *Weekly Chronicle* (May 27, 1809); Dunbar Rowland, ed., *Mississippi: Comprising Sketches of Counties, Towns, Events, Institutions, and Persons, Arranged in Cyclopedic Form,* 1:76–82; D. Clayton James, *Antebellum Natchez,* 105.

28. Papers of the Mississippi Territory, RG 2, Territorial Governors Papers, Letters, certificates, and commissions, and Tavern Licenses, Jefferson County, Mississippi Territory, MDAH; Mississippi Territory, 1810 U.S. Census Returns, *U.S. Decennial Census Publications, 1790–1970.*

Beasley's financial interest in this tavern and the several mentions of stands and taverns in the Beasley-Frye duel accounts suggest how important such establishments were to the many single white men in the Natchez District. Frontier Americans at the turn of the nineteenth century obtained stalls and fodder for their horses, lodging, meals, and drinks at an ordinary, a combination roadside inn and public house. Depending on the establishment, one might also find illegal gambling and prostitution, although these were by no means ubiquitous. Drinking seems to have been the principal form of amusement at such places. For an excellent recent study of the social role of taverns in early English-speaking America, see Sharon V. Salinger, *Taverns and Drinking in Early America.*

On the Beasley Petition, so-called because Daniel Beasley was the first signatory, see Carter, *Territorial Papers,* 6:339–41, 358; Norman E. Gillis, comp., *Early Inhabitants of the Natchez District;* Clark and Guice, *Old Southwest,* 214–15, 299n17.

Chapter 4

1. Grant, *Letters, Journals and Writings,* 292–93; Gregory Evans Dowd, "The American Revolution to the Mid-Nineteenth Century," 143.

Few "progressive" Creek males openly defied traditional gender norms. The wealthiest men opted instead to compel slaves to tend cattle and cultivate the soil, thereby skirting sticky questions about Creek male conceptualization of division of labor. But the adoption of race slavery must have left Creek women conflicted, when (by that innovation) they no longer engaged directly in agricultural labor. The growing reliance of the Tensaw métis on human chattel, and the acceptance of an American definition of race-based slavery, was a profound break from traditional Creek beliefs. For two views of this issue, see Theda Perdue, "Race and Culture: Writing the Ethnohistory of the Early South," 707; Krauthamer et al., "Rethinking Race and Culture."

2. Wallace, *Jefferson and the Indians*, 220–21 (quote), citing Thomas Jefferson to General Andrew Jackson, February 16, 1803, in Albert Ellery Bergh, ed., *The Writings of Thomas Jefferson*, 10:357–59. Federal insistence on Indian land cessions stiffened Indian resistance to the civilization policy, which in turn led President Jefferson to increase pressure for assimilation during his second term. See Horsman, "Indian Policy," 49–55; Joyotpaul Chaudhuri, "American Indian Policy: An Overview."

3. Eric Wolf, *Europe and the People without History*, 96.

4. Saunt, "Taking Account of Property."

5. James Mooney, *The Ghost Dance Religion and the Siouan Outbreak of 1890*, 672–75, and "Tenskwatawa"; Ralph Linton, "Nativistic Movements," 230; Anthony F. C. Wallace, "Revitalization Movements," and *Revitalization and Mazeways: Essays on Culture Change*, 3–56; Nuñez, "Creek Nativism," 3–17.

6. The following discussion of Creek revitalization builds on Gregory A. Waselkov and Brian M. Wood, "The Creek War of 1813–1814: Effects on Creek Society and Settlement Pattern."

7. Some of the finest American ethnohistorical research of the last several decades has been devoted to the Delaware, Shawnee, and Creek revitalization movements. See R. David Edmunds, *The Shawnee Prophet*, and *Tecumseh and the Quest for Indian Leadership*; Martin, *Sacred Revolt*, and "Cultural Contact and Crises"; Gregory Evans Dowd, *A Spirited Resistance: The North American Indian Struggle for Unity, 1745–1815*, and *War Under Heaven: Pontiac, the Indian Nations, and the British Empire*; John Sugden, *Tecumseh: A Life*. For excellent studies of the Chickamaugas, see James Paul Pate, "The Chickamaugas: A Forgotten Segment of Indian Resistance on the Southern Frontier," and Peter H. Wood, "George Washington, Dragging Canoe, and Southeastern Indian Resistance." Gordon M. Sayre characterizes Tenskwatawa's prophetic visions as "spiritual responses to colonization, syncretic spiritual road maps for political rebellion," in *The Indian Chief as Tragic Hero*, 38.

8. Paradise quote from Edmunds, *Shawnee Prophet*, 33. A notable exception to general white dismissal of Indian religions is the account of Shaker Brother Richard McNemar, who interviewed Tenskwatawa in March 1807. See J. P. MacLean, "Shaker Mission to the Shawnee Indians" (final quote).

9. James H. Howard, *Shawnee! The Ceremonialism of a Native American Tribe and its Cultural Background*, 201 (text quote), from a letter by Thomas Forsyth to William Clark, December 23, 1812, quoted in Emma H. Blair, ed., *The Indian Tribes of the Upper Mississippi Valley and Region of the Great Lakes*, 2:274–78; MacLean, "Shaker Mission," 224–25 ("weep and tremble" and "cry and tremble"); Edmunds, *Tecumseh*, 76–83. According to an American who claimed intimate knowledge of the Shawnee Prophet's teachings, Tenskwatawa instructed his followers that "Spirituous liquor was not to be tasted by any Indians on any

account whatever"; Daniel K. Richter, *Facing East from Indian Country: A Native History of Early America*, 228–29.

10. Edmunds, *Shawnee Prophet*, 36–41; Joel W. Martin, *The Land Looks After Us: A History of Native American Religion*, 48–57. Howard equated the "Dance of the Lake" with the Little River Men's Dance of the Absentee Shawnee of Kansas, which he witnessed in the 1970s. He thought that the Shawnee, Alligator, Fish, and Bear dances of the modern-day central Algonquian peoples (all involving two concentric circles of dancers, a line of women paired with a line of men who switch places on musical cue) are versions of a dance introduced by the Shawnee Prophet "simply for amusement." See Howard, *Shawnee!*, 202–3, 274–85, 319–21 (quote). For the positive nature of the Prophet's message, see Martin, *Sacred Revolt*, 171–86; Tom Mould, *Choctaw Prophecy: A Legacy of the Future*, 5–6.

11. Edmunds, *Shawnee Prophet*, 42–93, and *Tecumseh*, 83–134; Sugden, *Tecumseh*, 143–214.

12. Halbert and Ball, *Creek War*, 40–57; John Sugden, "Early Pan-Indianism: Tecumseh's Tour of the Indian Country, 1811–1812," 278–83; Gideon Lincecum, *Pushmataha: A Choctaw Leader and His People*, 90. On an effort by the Shawnees among the Upper Creeks to "form a Confederacy of all the Western and Southern Nations" in 1769, see Juricek, *Early American Indian Documents*, 330.

13. Edmunds, *Shawnee Prophet*, 29, *Tecumseh*, 19–20; Sugden, *Tecumseh*, 13–23.

14. Hawkins to William Eustis, September 21, 1811, in Grant, *Letters, Journals and Writings*, 591 (quote), 601; Sugden, "Early Pan-Indianism," 283–85. On the presumed Shawnee origin of the Tuckaubatchee people, see John Swanton, *Early History of the Creeks and Their Neighbors*, 277–82; Sugden, *Tecumseh*, 14.

15. Grant, *Letters, Journals and Writings*, 687.

16. For thorough reviews of contemporary and later accounts, see Sugden, "Early Pan-Indianism," 286–89, 302n.43, and *Tecumseh*, 244–49. For additional interpretations, see Grant, *Letters, Journals and Writings*, 601; Halbert and Ball, *Creek War*, 66–69.

17. Stiggins, "Historical narration," 43–44 (quote). Strong tremors were felt at the Creek Agency in central Georgia in January and February; Carl Mauelshagen and Gerald H. Davis, eds., "Partners in the Lord's Work: The Diary of Two Moravian Missionaries in the Creek Indian Country, 1807–1813," 67–68. For other accounts, see Thomas L. McKenny and James Hall, *History of the Indian Tribes of North America*, 1:64–65; William G. McLoughlin, *Cherokees and Missionaries, 1789–1839*, 83; Sugden, *Tecumseh*, 4 ("Shooting Star"), 249–52; James Lal Penick, Jr., *The New Madrid Earthquakes*, 101–27; Jake Page and Charles Officer, *The Big One: The Earthquake that Rocked Early America and Helped Create a Science*, 34–36; Jay Feldman, *When the Mississippi Ran Backwards: Empire, Intrigue, Murder, and the New Madrid Earthquake*, 160–61.

18. Stiggins, "Historical narration," 42; Sheidley, *Unruly Men*, 287. Sugden discovered an account linking Tecumseh to the comet and the earthquake dating as early as June 1812, published in *The Halcyon Luminary*, a New York newspaper. An even earlier article, in the *New York Herald* of December 21, 1811, quoted an Indian who thought "the Shawanoe Prophet has caused the Earthquake to destroy the whites." Sugden, "Early Pan-Indianism," 288–91, 303n.69 (note quote), and *Tecumseh*, 246–47, 249–51, 440n.11.

For discussion of a similar messianic movement among the Cherokees, see William G. McLoughlin, ed., *The Cherokee Ghost Dance*, 125–30.

19. Some historians of religion have recently criticized the terms "Great Awakening" and "Second Great Awakening" for implying a unity and a discreteness that these long-term, popular, evangelical movements conspicuously lacked. The Second Great Awakening certainly had no single origin but rather evolved spontaneously along a broad front as American population shifted abruptly westward after the American Revolution. Richard McNemar, *The Kentucky Revival*; Robert F. Berkhofer, Jr., *Salvation and the Savage: An Analysis of Protestant Missions and American Indian Response, 1787–1862,* 1; Dickson D. Bruce, Jr., *And They All Sang Hallelujah: Plain-Folk Camp-Meeting Religion, 1800–1845;* Frank Lambert, *Inventing the 'Great Awakening,'* 5, 16, 90–102; Philip N. Mulder, *A Controversial Spirit: Evangelical Awakenings in the South,* 4, 126–29, 136; Russell Bourne, *Gods of War, Gods of Peace: How the Meeting of Native and Colonial Religions Shaped Early America,* 332. On Lorenzo and Peggy Dow, including their impressions of the New Madrid quakes, see Lorenzo Dow, *The Dealings of God, Man, and the Devil: As Experienced in the Life, Experience, and Travels of Lorenzo Dow,* 155–57, and Peggy Dow, *Vicissitudes in the Wilderness,* 223; Notes taken from the lips of Hiram Mounger . . . by Col J Austill, Pickett Papers, ADAH.

20. The South Carolina Conference assigned Matthew P. Sturdevant to the Tombigbee district in December 1807. Sturdevant attributed his failure to make a single convert in the following year to the "lawless and licentious" nature of the population; Walter B. Posey, "The Advance of Methodism into the Lower Southwest," 445–46. The dramatic upswing in Christian religious conversions in the aftermath of the New Madrid earthquakes may have forestalled interest by Africans in the Creek prophets' movement. During 1812, Methodist membership in the Tensaw-Tombigbee settlements increased by 71 whites and 40 blacks; West, *History of Methodism in Alabama,* 58.

21. For example, see recent interpretations of Mississippian iconography in Richard F. Townsend, ed., *Hero, Hawk, and Open Hand: American Indian Art of the Ancient Midwest and South.*

22. "*Hisákidamissi,* freely rendered, 'Master of Breath' (*hisákida* 'act of breathing,' *imíssi,* 'its controller'). In how far this concept has been influenced by Christian ideas in former times it is now impossible to say. As no other culture-hero, in the broadest sense of the term, is remembered at the present day by the Taskigi, all creations, when thought about at all, and nearly all reasons for the existence of things, are simply attributed to Master of Breath." Quoted from Frank G. Speck, "The Creek Indians of Taskigi Town," 134.

For a description of the Master of Breath based on mid-1770s observations, see Bartram, *Travels,* 498; Waselkov and Braund, *William Bartram on the Southeastern Indians,* 145, 148–49. Adair's comments are based on earlier experience with the Creeks; James Adair, *The History of the American Indians,* 149. Joel Martin does not speculate on the antiquity of the Master of Breath but writes of the creator as "mythic"; Martin, *Sacred Revolt,* 24. Some modern-day Muskogees think Christians reinterpreted the Master of Breath as the Christian God; see Chaudhuri and Chaudhuri, *Sacred Path,* 15. A recent book by Buffalo Tiger places "Breathmaker" at the heart of traditional as well as modern Miccosukee religion; Buffalo Tiger and Harry A. Kersey, Jr., *Buffalo Tiger: A Life in the Everglades,* 4 and passim. The great network of spirits in the Choctaw cosmos did not include a supreme being; see Mould, *Choctaw Prophecy,* 123.

23. MacLean, "Shaker Mission," 217 (first quote), 224–25, 226 (second quote); Sugden,

Tecumseh, 138–42. Apart from a few brief comments on apparent cross influences of native Indian and American Christian religions, this topic has not yet attracted sustained academic interest. For some considerations of selective Christian syncretism in Indian religions, see Edmunds, *Shawnee Prophet,* 40; Dowd, *Spirited Resistance,* 29–33, 126–27; Martin, "Cultural Contact and Crises"; Jane T. Merritt, "Dreaming of the Savior's Blood: Moravians and the Indian Great Awakening in Pennsylvania," 725, 735; Alfred A. Cave, "The Delaware Prophet Neolin: A Reappraisal." Only Russell Bourne has developed a book-length treatment of the issue, and it focuses primarily on missionary influences. He maintains that certain elements of Mormonism, a religion that appeared in the 1820s, suggest that the influences have gone both ways. See Bourne, *Gods of War, Gods of Peace,* 242–43, 323, 328, 376–86. More numerous are studies documenting the lack of success by Christian missionaries among the Indians during the early Federal period. Some examples include Rayner W. Kelsey, *Friends and the Indians, 1655–1917,* 89–106; Edmund Schwarze, *History of the Moravian Missions among Southern Indian Tribes of the United States,* 88–99; Earl P. Olmstead, *Blackcoats among the Delaware: David Zeisberger on the Ohio Frontier;* Mauelshagen and Davis, "Partners in the Lord's Work"; McLoughlin, *Cherokees and Missionaries.*

24. Seekaboo may have been Creek as well as Shawnee, associated in some way with the people of Tuckaubatchee. See Woodward, *Reminiscences,* 33; Sugden, "Early Pan-Indianism," 279; Dowd, *Spirited Resistance,* 146; cf. Halbert and Ball, *Creek War,* 40. Sugden thinks he was "Tusseki Abbee," who helped organize armed resistance to the Americans among the Seminoles in the fall of 1812, although that name probably refers to Tussekiably, a Seminole leader; Sugden, *Tecumseh,* 320–21, 448n.21. Hawkins identified him as "Tusseki Abbee of Nauchee," the Natchez town among the Upper Creeks; Grant, *Letters, Journals and Writings,* 442, 624 (quote), obviously distinct from the Shawnee Seekaboo.

25. Stiggins, "Historical narration," 41 (quote).

26. Lewis and Jordan, *Creek Indian Medicine Ways,* 49–43, 138–39; Theodore Stern, "The Creeks," 442; Swanton, "Religious Beliefs," 614–17.

27. Seymour Feiler, trans. and ed., *Jean-Bernard Bossu's Travels in the Interior of North America, 1751–1762,* 149.

28. Stiggins, "Historical narration," 46 (quote); also Martin, *Sacred Revolt,* 221n.20 on Captain Isaacs; Mereness, ed., *Travels in the American Colonies,"* 536–37, 546. Josiah Francis and Paddy Walsh later exposed Captain Isaacs as an evil witch and drove him from the prophets' movement; Stiggins, "Historical narration," 49. For the necessity to proscribe witchcraft in a revitalization movement, see Howard, *Shawnee!,* 202; Dowd, *Spirited Resistance,* 170. Joel Martin convincingly argues that Isaacs conversed with "the powerful Tie-Snake," a mystical underworld spirit familiar to the Creeks, "who recklessly shook the earth and unleashed a new force for recreating the world"; Martin, *Sacred Revolt,* 25–26, 124.

29. Grant, *Letters, Journals and Writings,* 687. For shaking earth, see ibid., 647–48; Lowrie and Clarke, *ASP, Indian Affairs,* 1:846; Stiggins, "Historical narration," 44, 47; Edmunds, *Shawnee Prophet,* 38; Martin, "Cultural Contact and Crises," 249–50.

30. John Innerarity, "A Prelude to the Creek War of 1813–1814, in a Letter of John Innerarity to James Innerarity," 251; quote from "Deposition of Samuel Manac, of lawful age, a Warrior of the Creek Nation . . . 2d day of August, 1813," in Halbert and Ball, *Creek War,*

91–93. According to Stiggins, High-head Jim was called "cussetaw Tus to nug gie" (war name) and "Cussetaw Haujo" (prophet name); "Historical narration," 52, 77.

Samuel Moniac's name inspired much creative spelling by his contemporaries, with McNac, Manac, and Macnac all popular variations, perhaps based on the mistaken notion the name was Scots instead of Dutch. Puzzlement over his name continued well after his death and to the present day. In one notable editorial blunder, Walter Lowrie and Matthew St. Clair Clarke, compilers of the first *Indian Affairs* volume of the *American State Papers* series, transcribed his name as "some maniac"; Lowrie and Clarke, *ASP, Indian Affairs*, 1:847 (Talosee Fixico to Hawkins, July 5, 1813).

31. Stiggins, "Historical narration," 52 (quote). Ojibwa prophets inspired by Tenskwatawa carried four strings of beans, "made of the flesh itself of the prophet," which believers would draw through their hands, perhaps influenced by Catholic rosaries. "This was called shaking hands with the prophet, and was considered as solemnly engaging to obey his injunctions"; quoted in Howard, *Shawnee!*, 208.

32. Grant, *Letters, Journals and Writings*, 324; Swanton, "Religious Beliefs," 573, 587, 601; Waselkov and Wood, "Creek War," 5; Saunt, *New Order of Things*, 258.

33. Grant, *Letters, Journals and Writings*, 322, 648 (quote), 683; Swanton, "Religious Beliefs," 605; Waselkov and Wood, "Creek War," 5; Martin, *Sacred Revolt*, 131.

34. Grant, *Letters, Journals and Writings*, 655; Lowrie and Clark, *ASP, Indian Affairs*, 1:847, 858.

35. Stiggins, "Historical narration," 41 (quote); Mooney, "Ghost Dance Religion," 676.

36. Lowrie and Clarke, *ASP, Indian Affairs*, 1:846–47.

37. Richard S. Lackey, comp., *Frontier Claims in the Lower South: Records of Claims Filed by Citizens of the Alabama and Tombigbee River Settlements in the Mississippi Territory for Depredations by the Creek Indians During the War of 1812*, xiv, 22–23; Lowrie and Clarke, *ASP, Indian Affairs*, 1:849, 854; Sheidley, *Unruly Men*, 287. Resistance to the Americans involved selective, culturally informed, pragmatic reevaluations. Marshall Sahlins describes the general practice in this way: "It seems that encounters with foreigners were not necessarily marked by a politics of blanket opposition so much as by culturally informed processes of interpretation and adaptation." Marshall Sahlins, "Preface to Outside Gods: History Making in the Pacific."

38. Stephanie A. May, "Alabama and Koasati," 412. This style of notched war club remained in use among the Ponca Indians of the western prairies in the early nineteenth century; see David C. Hunt and Marsha V. Gallagher, eds., *Karl Bodmer's America*, 331, 336.

Halbert and Ball repeated a story (probably apocryphal, and retold by them with little conviction), first published by Thomas McKenney in 1833. McKenney believed the name referred to bundles of red sticks Tecumseh supposedly presented to his followers to count the days until they should rise against the Americans. John Sugden located an article published in *The National Intelligencer*, September 5, 1818, attributing the name to "a red wand which Tecumseh had carried on his tour and which he was alleged to have used for magical purposes." Thomas L. McKenney and James Hall, *The Indian Tribes of North America*, 1:103; Sugden, "Early Pan-Indianism," 288–89, but see Sugden, *Tecumseh*, 440n.10; David S. Heidler and Jeanne T. Heidler, eds., *Encyclopedia of the War of 1812*, 444; Sayre, *Indian Chief as Tragic Hero*, 259.

39. Stiggins, "Historical narration," 35 ("shaped like a small gun"); Sewall, *The Miscellaneous Poems of Lewis Sewall,* 27 ("a kind of war club"). Henry Halbert elicited a detailed description from an unnamed informant, a member of the burial detail at Fort Mims:

> The winter hackleberry and the white oak runner were the forest growth exclusively used in making the red stick, as the wood of both is exceedingly hard and tough. The warrior would select a bush having a single, large, bending root. He cut his stick about three feet long, leaving about seven inches to the root, or club end. After stripping off the bark, he began about two inches from the end of the root, and beveled down two sides of the bend to a sharp edge, about five inches long, so that this beveled part bore some resemblance to the curving blade of a hatchet. After this, the stick was thoroughly seasoned over a fire, the warrior giving an additional hardness to the sharp edge of the bend by rubbing over it as much tallow as the heated wood would absorb. The stick was then painted red, with the exception of the club end, which part the warrior expected to dye red in the blood of an enemy. The paint generally used was made of a soft, red stone, found in different portions of Alabama, but sometimes use was made of the red juice of the pokeberry, and the puccoon root. The stick received several coats of paint. After the last coat had become dry, a hole was then bored through the handle, about five inches from the end, and a strong loop of buckskin or deer's sinew was fastened therein. The red stick was now complete and ready for service. In using the weapon, which was always weilded in one hand, the wrist of the warrior was inserted in the loop, so that, if in any manner the stick should be knocked out of the owner's grip, he could easily regain his hold, as he would find it hanging by the loop from his wrist. In action, the warrior always smote his victim on the head with the sharp edge of the bend, a single stroke not unfrequently causing death. (Henry S. Halbert, "The Creek Red Stick.")

"Hackleberry" is an ambiguous folk term, used alternatively for hackberry and huckleberry, very different plants. I assume Halbert meant the tree, hackberry (*Celtis occidentalis*). Red paint was made by grinding hematite (an iron oxide), and extracted from poke (*Phytolacca americana*) and puccoon (*Sanguineria canadensis* or *Lithospermum canescens*). Also see John Reid and John Henry Eaton, *The Life of Andrew Jackson: The Original 1817 Edition,* 29.

40. Grant, *Letters, Journals and Writings,* 675, 685, 709, 722, passim; Halbert and Ball, *Creek War,* 65, 134 ("honorable appellation"). Chiefs of the Red Stick Nation to Commanding Officer of His Britannic Majesty's Forces, Pensacola, January 9, 1814, Papers of Admiral Alexander Forrester Inglis Cochrane, PKY, microfilm roll 65M, 1:28–28v. Opothleyoholo, postwar speaker of the Creek nation, likewise suggested how the term had been used by the anti-American faction when, in 1825, he insisted "with great emphasis—indeed, indignation" that "I NEVER WAS A RED STICK." *U.S. Serials Set 161, House Report 98, 19th Con., 2nd sess.,* 449. Modern-day Muskogee speakers refer to the historical Redsticks as *ēcatēcvlke,* literally Red (*catē*) People (*cvlke*). In the Muskogee language, the war symbolism was reinforced by the double meaning of *cate* as "red" and "blood." See Martin and Mauldin, *Dictionary of Creek/Muskogee,* 20.

Some modern scholars have opted for the contraction "Redstick" in favor of the traditional "Red Stick." While I prefer the former on stylistic grounds (since it seems analogous to other compound words that came to symbolize groups of people: Redcoats, rednecks, Blackshirts, etc.), I realize this break with historical precedence has not found universal acceptance. Martin, in *Sacred Revolt*, seems to have been the first to adopt "Redstick." I appreciate Kathryn E. Holland Braund's willingness to argue the point in a series of lively emails (or e-mails, as she prefers!).

The term "White Sticks" has recently come into use as a label for those Creeks opposed to the Redstick movement. I have not been able to determine the source of the phrase, but can find no evidence that it dates to the era of the Creek War. Not only does the phrase "White Sticks" lack historical legitimacy, it violates the logic of traditional Creek color symbolism. The Creeks of the eighteenth and early nineteenth centuries did frequently oppose red and white to symbolize, roughly speaking, war and peace. But the idea of "White Stick," referring either to a war club—an atássa, the emblematic symbol of war—painted white for peace or to a peaceful warrior, makes no sense in Creek cultural context. For recent uses of the unfortunate phrase "White Sticks," see Chaudhuri and Chaudhuri, *Sacred Path*, 22 and passim; Jacqueline Jones, Peter H. Wood, Thomas Borstelmann, Elaine Tyler May, and Vicki L. Ruiz, *Created Equal: A Social and Political History of the United States*, 249–50.

41. Grant, *Letters, Journals and Writings*, 605, 609, 615–17, 631–34, 757; *Message from the President of the United States, Transmitting a Report of the Secretary of War Relative to Murders Committed by the Indians, in the State of Tennessee*, 4–12 ("decoyed"); Lowrie and Clarke, *ASP, Indian Affairs*, 1:841, 843; Stiggins, "Historical narration," 49; Waselkov and Wood, "Creek War," 1; Martin, *Sacred Revolt*, 125–28; George E. Lankford, "Red and White: Some Reflections on Southeastern Symbolism," 66. According to Thomas Woodward, "if [William] Lott had not been killed at the time he was," Sam Moniac thought "the war could have been prevented"; *Reminiscences*, 32–34 (quote), 83.

42. The murders of many micos and other headmen at the outset of the civil war (at Coosa, Oakfuskee, Wewocau, and elsewhere) indicate that they were principal targets of the prophets. See Edmunds, *Shawnee Prophet*, 152; Grant, *Letters, Journals and Writings*, 641, 644–48, 651–52, 660, 687 (quote); Lowrie and Clarke, *ASP, Indian Affairs*, 1:843, 846. Although his wife was killed by the Redsticks, Captain Isaacs escaped the attempt on his life, contrary to statements by several modern authors based on an error of Hawkins. Martin, *Sacred Revolt*, 132; Extract of a Letter from Mr. Limbaugh, *The War* [New York] (July 20, 1813):1; Pickett, *History of Alabama*, 2:250–51; Woodward, *Reminiscences*, 33. Hawkins to Halsted, Creek Agency, April 26, 1813, in Letters Received by the Office of the Secretary of War Relating to Indian Affairs, Creek Indian Factory Records, RG 75, NARA.

43. Andrew Jackson, *Andrew Jackson Papers*, vol. 4, *Military Papers* (microfilm), 874, Library of Congress; Stiggins, "Historical narration," 68; Dow, *Dealings of God, Man, and the Devil*, 144; Lowrie and Clark, *ASP, Indian Affairs*, 1:857 (quote). Gregory Dowd notes that Pontiac's War broke out in 1763 in regions far removed from white settlement; *War under Heaven*, 175.

44. Factions based on relationships with French and British officials and traders were highly influential in Creek society from 1715 to 1763. Creek willingness to tolerate competing

factions was key to their diplomatic success in negotiations with European colonial leaders. Factional divisions became less clear-cut after the abandonment of Louisiana by the French in 1763, and especially after the American Revolution. British traders and military officers continued to vie for influence with American officials and traders from bases in Pensacola and elsewhere. So we should not entirely discount the importance of pro-British and pro-American factions among the Creeks between the 1780s and 1814, although the bases of those factional affiliations themselves remain unclear.

45. Ross Hassig, "Internal Conflict in the Creek War of 1813–1814," 261.

46. Saunt, *New Order of Things,* 255, and (especially) "Taking Account of Property," 733–60; Douglas Barber, "Council Government and the Genesis of the Creek War," 172–73; Waselkov and Wood, "Creek War," 7–8.

47. See Stiggins, "Historical narration," 58.

48. Karl Davis discovered apparent evidence of Francis' Tensaw connection in the Spanish archives; Manuel de Lanzos to Arturo O'Neill, Mobile, March 21, 1793, in Archivo General de Indias, Papeles procedentes de la Isla de Cuba, legajo 64 (PKY, microfilm roll 440, doc. 50, p. 31), cited in Davis, "'Much of the Indian Appears,'" 152. This letter from the Spanish commandant at Mobile to the governor reads as follows, in translation (graciously provided by my University of South Alabama colleague Richmond Brown):

Yesterday an English resident of Tensaw named Juan Francis brought here a black female of Don Tomas Comin who remains imprisoned in one of the prison cells of this Fort. The Englishman related to me that the black male [slave] of the same owner, and in this estate on Little River killed a male Tallapoosa [Creek] Indian, and injured another gravely. The Indian wife of the dead man retaliated and with a machete cut the head of the black male, and would have done the same with the black female had not she been stopped by a son of the aforementioned Francis named Josias, the bearer of this letter to be presented to your honor. I ordered Comin to pay the 100 pesos negotiated with the Indians for the ransom of the black female. Your honor, after having heard this, may decide on the appropriate amount, as well as if Don Tomas Comin should pay for the costs of her maintenance.

May God give your honor many years, Manuel de Lanzos

If this cryptic correspondence refers to the same Josiah Francis who became the Alabama Prophet, the young man serving as cultural intermediary for the Little River métis community in its formative years became a radical Creek nativist sometime in the subsequent two decades.

See Owsley, "Prophet of War," passim; Stiggins, "Historical narration," 47–48, 72. Francis put his mark, a shaky X, to a letter penned for him in Pensacola on June 9, 1814, found in the Papers of Admiral Cochrane, PKY microfilm, roll 65M, no. 1, p. 28. In a deposition to Judge Toulmin at Fort Stoddert on August 2, 1813, Sam Moniac stated how "my sister [his half-sister, Hannah Moniac, Francis' wife] and brother [John], who have joined the war party, came and got off a number of my horses and other stock, and thirty-six of my negroes" from his plantation in July; Halbert and Ball, *Creek War,* 91–92. Hawkins wrote to John Armstrong on July 28, 1813:

The prophets party have destroyed in several places at the upper towns all the cattle, hogs and fowls. They have moved out of the towns into the woods where they are dancing 'The dance of the Indians of the Lakes.' . . . Two chiefs with a party went out foraging from Tookaubatche in the cattle range of that town, saw hogs and cattle killed and was in the stench of them for fifteen miles. Josiah Francis a prophet, half brother [actually, half brother-in-law] of Sam Macnac, John Macnac, his brother and Sam's son destroyed all his property and burnt his houses. The declaration of the prophets is to destroy every thing received from the Americans, all the Chiefs and their adherents who are friendly to the customs and ways of the white people, to put to death every man who will not join them and by those means to unite the nation in aid of the British and Indians of the Lakes, against their white neighbours as soon as their friends the British will be ready for them. (Quoted from Grant, *Letters, Journals and Writings,* 651–52)

Francis and other Redstick leaders had confronted Moniac earlier that year and demanded he join their movement or die. According to Thomas Woodward, "Moniac snatched a war-club from his [Francis'] hand, gave him a severe blow and put out [on his horse], with a shower of rifle bullets following him"; *Reminiscences,* 83–84.

49. Woodward, *Reminiscences,* 34 ("countrymen"), 84 ("fate"). Weatherford's argument anticipates the logic of Robert E. Lee's famous decision nearly half a century later to side with the Confederacy and reluctantly break his oath to defend the United States because he could not bear to turn against the state of Virginia and his people.

A descendant, J. D. Dreisbach, gave this account of Weatherford's 1811 response to Tecumseh in the square ground at Tuckaubatchee, which agrees in substance with Woodward's assessment of Weatherford's reluctance to join the Redsticks:

He was always to be found on the side of the weak and defenseless, and from the first days of his manhood believed that his peoples' rights had been trampled upon by the whites, but nevertheless he was opposed to his people joining the British in a war against the US. He used all the powers of his eloquence to induce them to remain neutral; told them that when the Americans were weak, and unprepared for war, they made the 'British Lion howl, and drove him back to his den,' that now the Americans were strong, and would be more certain to conquer again, That it would be ruin to his people to join either side, That both the Americans and English were their enemies, that England talked to them with a forked tongue, as did the Americans, That the Palefaces were the enemies of the Red Man, and cared not for his welfare, or distruction, That he was willing to lay down his life for his people if it would benefit them, and drive the white man from their country, but that he was satisfied this would not be accomplished by their joining either side, These were some of the arguments he used to induce them to remain neutral. (J. D. Dreisbach to Lyman Draper, July 1874, 7–8, Draper, WHS)

50. Davis, " 'Much of the Indian Appears,' " 77–79, ("struggled"). Driesbach, "Weatherford— 'The Red Eagle' " (long quote); a similar passage appears in J. D. Dreisbach, "A Short Addenda

to the paper furnished by the writer on June the 28th, 1877, Baldwin County, Ala.," July 28, 1883, ADAH.

51. According to Dreisbach's romanticized family legend, she was "said to be the most beautiful forest maiden of the tribe, noted for her musical voice, and powers of song; could charm the stern red warrior, and make him forget for the moment the war-path and the chase, by the cadence of her voice; whilst the wild bird stopped in its flight to drink in the sweet refrain." Driesbach, "Weatherford—'The Red Eagle.'" A similar passage appears in Dreisbach, "A Short Addenda."

52. Stiggins, "Historical narration," 57 (final quote). Susan Sizemore (formerly, Susan Stiggins Hatterway) maintained that Supalamy remained married to William Weatherford until he "quit her" in March 1816 and married Mary Stiggins three months later. Supalamy gave birth to William Weatherford, Jr., in July of that year. While a prisoner of the Redsticks, Sizemore saw Supalamy and William Weatherford together in the Creek nation during the war. Weatherford vs. Weatherford, Case No. 1299 (1846), Document 10: Testimony of Susan Sizemore, February 26, 1847, Mobile County Chancery Court Records, University of South Alabama Archives, Mobile.

Sam Dale thought Weatherford joined the Redsticks "Through the influence of Tecumseh"; Claiborne, *Life and Times of Gen. Sam. Dale,* 128–29. Robert James' tale of Weatherford's sick wife being removed from the camp at Holy Ground, across the river to a tent in Dutch Bend, where she died two days after the battle there, seems baseless; Notes taken from the lips of Col Robert James, Pickett Papers, ADAH.

53. Stiggins, "Historical narration," 56–59; Griffith, *McIntosh and Weatherford,* 89. According to Dreisbach, "The Indians had Weatherfords wife & children and threatened to put them to death if he did not join them." J. D. Driesbach to Lyman Draper, July 1874, 9, Draper, WHS. Lynn Hastie Thompson points out that Sam Moniac, in his deposition of August 2, 1813, did not mention his own family so treated, although that had been rumored as well; *William Weatherford,* 274. Moniac did testify "that many, particularly the women among them [the Redsticks], (two daughters of the late Gen. McGillivray, who had been induced to join them to save their property,) were very desirous to leave them, but could not"; quoted in Halbert and Ball, *Creek War,* 93. For the Chickasahay meeting, see Dreisbach, in Draper, WHS; Claiborne, *Mississippi,* 487 ("secret interview"); Henry S. Halbert, "Some Inaccuracies in Claiborne's History in Regard to Tecumseh," 102–3; Woodward, *Reminiscences,* 83; Halbert and Ball, *Creek War,* 95–96.

Chapter 5

1. McLoughlin, *Cherokee Ghost Dance,* 125–27, 134.
2. "The following sketch . . . [from] the Nashville (Ten.) *Clarion,*" in *Weekly Register* (September 26, 1812):52–53.
3. Samuel Moniac claimed "my houses on my river plantation, as well as those of James Cornells and Leonard McGee," were burned and cattle stolen; Halbert and Ball, *Creek War,* 93. After the war, Moniac's plantation was valued at $12,595.25, including livestock valued at $5,300 (700 cattle, 48 goats and sheep, and 200 hogs), a fully equipped cotton gin, his home, and scores of other items; Clark and Guice, *Old Southwest,* 126.

4. Deposition of Samuel Manac, in Halbert and Ball, *Creek War,* 92–93. Joel Martin interprets the Redsticks' probably groundless claim to have letters of introduction from a British general as an example of the Creek prophets' intention to co-opt the power of literacy. See Martin, "Cultural Contact and Crises," 236n.24, and *Sacred Revolt,* 160, 221; also Mereness, *Travels in the American Colonies,* 536–37, 546. "Josiah Francis a half blooded Frenchmen, who was of the prophets, received an order from the master of breath, to meet him every day at a certain place, as he intended to teach him the different languages that he would want to use, and writing so as he would be enabled to transact his own and the national affairs"; Stiggins, "Historical narration," 47–48.

5. Grant, *Letters, Journals and Writings,* 650; Claiborne, *Life and Times of Gen. Sam. Dale,* 68–69. Immediately after his seizure of Mobile, General Wilkinson received a letter from four prominent Tombigbee residents about a "Serious apprehension" by the inhabitants of their district "of a hostile disposition in the Creek Indians toward the Americans." John Hanes, William McGrew, James Wood, and George S. Gaines to Wilkinson, St. Stephens, April 17, 1813, *Papers of Panton Leslie, and Co.,* ed. William S. Coker, microfilm, roll 19, University of South Alabama Library. On June 29, the general wrote Judge Toulmin of rumors that a Redstick force had assembled near the Alabama towns: "One Josiah Francis, who lived on the road, pretends he has had a visit from the Lord, who has revealed many things to him, which are shaped and detailed in the manner most impressive on his barbarian auditors. . . . Francis and his followers, to the number of more than three hundred, are assembled at a camp on the Alabama, eight miles below the mouth of Pithlula Creek, and about sixteen above the big swamp [the Holy Ground location]. . . . the party thus encamped, were about to move down the river to break up the half-breed settlements and those of the citizens in the forks of the river"; quoted in Claiborne, *Mississippi,* 322. Moniac's message reinforced a deposition given the previous day by James Cornells, who claimed the Redsticks had "uniformly declared their determination to cut of [off] all Americans & their friends & to burn & destroy as they go. That they will proceed Westward burning all before them with their prophet at their head, to the Mississippi & establish themselves on red River where they would have a home & more game, & fish." Deposition of James Curnels to A. L. Osborne, Cantonment Mount Vernon, August 1, 1813, in Letterbook F, J.F.H. Claiborne Collection, MDAH.

Karl Davis cites two early accounts by Tombigbee settlers of warnings from Tensaw métis that the Redsticks planned to attack the whites. Tandy Walker to William McGrew, April 17, 1813, and the letter of Hanes, McGrew, Wood, and Gaines to Gen. Wilkinson, April 17, 1813, cited above, from the *Papers of Panton Leslie, and Co.* Davis, *'Much of the Indian Appears,'* 146n.25.

6. For instance, Caleb Swan reported similar methods used to chastise Alexander McGillivray during his rise to power in the 1780s. The old Tallassee King, "Opilth Mico, who, with his clan, pronounced M'Gillivray a boy and an usurper, taking steps that must be derogatory to his family and consequence. And under these circumstances he undertook to treat separately with the Georgians. The consequences were, his houses were burnt in his absence, and his corn and cattle destroyed"; Swan, "Position and State of Manners," 281.

7. Hawkins to Thomas Pinckney, Milledgeville, July 9, 1813, in Grant, *Letters, Journals and Writings,* 645 ("badly armed"); Saunt, *New Order of Things,* 262, citing González Man-

rique to Ruiz Apodaca, 23 July 1813, AGI, Papeles procedentes de la Isla de Cuba, legajo 1794, 1417 (PKY, roll 112).

8. Betsy Coulter "was sold to Madame Baronne, a French lady, for a blanket"; Halbert and Ball, *Creek War,* 126–29. Also see Woodward, *Reminiscences,* 84–85, 96–97. William Hollinger accompanied Peirce and Tate to Pensacola; Deposition of David Tate, August 2, 1813, in Letterbook F, J.F.H. Claiborne Collection, MDAH. The Creek who rescued McGirth was Jim Boy, possibly the same man known as High-head Jim, though probably not.

9. Elizabeth H. West, ed., "A Prelude to the Creek War of 1813–1814 in a Letter of John Innerarity to James Innerarity," 254 (quote). According to Benjamin Hawkins, "When the war party went to Pensacola, . . . They received 25 small guns"; Hawkins to Floyd, September 30, 1813, in Grant, *Letters, Journals and Writings,* 668–69; Lowrie and Clarke, *ASP, Indian Affairs,* 1:854. Whether the Redsticks also obtained ammunition from González Manrique later in the war is similarly uncertain. Spanish documents indicate Peter McQueen was refused arms and ammunition during a visit to Pensacola in January 1814, and received only food. See Sugden, *Tecumseh,* 452n.28. However, Stiggins thought Weatherford and High-head Jim, with an escort of 390 mounted men, had gone to Pensacola in December 1813, after the battle at Autossee: "On their arrival in that metropolis in pursuance of the mission of the hostile authorities they demanded to have an audience and a Tete a tete with his Excellency   in their Tete a tete they pleased his Excellency so well that he made them a present of three horse loads of powder and lead with which they returned to Cluwallee camps"; "Historical narration," 55, 78 (quote).

10. West, "Prelude to the Creek War," 256–57 (quote); Owsley, "Prophet of War," 278.

11. Stiggins, "Historical narration," 56; Notes furnished by Col G. W. Creagh, Notes furnished by Gen Patrick May, and Notes of Doctor Thomas G. Holmes, all in Pickett Papers, ADAH. These last three, all battle participants, disagreed as to when the battle commenced: 10 A.M. (Creagh), 11 A.M. (May), or noon (Holmes). Halbert and Ball, *Creek War,* 130–33, identified the battlefield location very precisely. The Redstick camp, they maintain, was situated about sixty yards northwest of Cooper's Spring, "about half a mile nearly east of the [trail] crossing, and about one hundred and fifty yards south of the road. . . . the battle ground of Burnt Corn is in Escambia County, one-half a mile from the line of Conecuh County, on the north."

Halbert and Ball were confused about the names of trails in this area. The path crossing Burnt Corn Creek near the battlefield was called the Wolf Trail in 1813, and later came to be known as the Pensacola Road. I suspect the Wolf Trail was named for the Wolf King (Tastanagi Emathla or Yaha Mico) of Mucklassa, an influential Upper Creek leader who in 1764 advocated abandonment of the old trading path from Okfuskee to Augusta in favor of a route south from the Tallapoosa towns to Pensacola. See Juricek, *Early American Indian Documents,* 12:2, 11–12, 130, 181–82, 298, 506.

12. Claiborne to Bailey, Tait & Moniac, July 31, 1813, in Letterbook F, J.F.H. Claiborne Collection, MDAH; Pickett, *History of Alabama,* 2:256–62; Halbert and Ball, *Creek War,* 125–42. Creagh thought American losses were two killed and 18 to 20 wounded, while the Redsticks lost "some 20 killed and a good many wounded;" Notes furnished by Col G. W. Creagh, Pickett Papers, ADAH.

13. Benjamin Hawkins informed David B. Mitchell on August 17, 1813, that McQueen's

Redsticks "were attacked at 'Burnt Corn' by a party from Tensaw but met with no loss which puts them in high spirits. The destruction of every American is the song of the day"; Grant, *Letters, Journals and Writings,* 656. Larry Owsley, following Stiggins, thought the Redsticks altered their plans to attack the Lower Creeks at Coweta because the families of those killed and wounded at Burnt Corn Creek demanded vengeance against Dixon Bailey and the other métis who had fought against them alongside the whites; Owsley, "Prophet of War," 280.

14. G. W. Creagh, a militia lieutenant wounded in the battle, always maintained that the militia successfully carried off the Redsticks' packhorses: "As soon as the first order to fall back had been given Major Phillips left with a portion of his own and of the other Battalions left the Battle Ground and looked out for their safety in flight taking with them the greater part of the pack Horses & their loads"; Notes furnished by Col G. W. Creagh, Pickett Papers, ADAH. One militia officer captured a horse loaded with "Liverpool Salt," which is interesting in light of the Creek prophets' injunction against the use of salt; Notes furnished by Gen Patrick May, Pickett Papers, ADAH. Some Redsticks, like Peter McQueen, may have decided to violate that prophets' proscription and salt the meat of slaughtered domesticates for the coming winter. A "good deal of salt" was found in the houses at Chattucchufaulee, Peter McQueen's home, during a raid by Lower Creeks after the Burnt Corn Creek battle; Grant, *Letters, Journals and Writings,* 657. Also see Hawkins to Secretary of War, August 23, 1813, in Lowrie and Clarke, *ASP, Indian Affairs,* 1:852. Hawkins' statements specify this was one of several late July raids against McQueen and other Redsticks emanating from Coweta, on the Chattahoochee, not led by Dixon Bailey from the Tensaw, as Karl Davis asserts (without documentation) in *"Much of the Indian Appears,"* 148–49, and "'Remember Fort Mims,'" 629–30. An anonymous correspondent (Judge Toulmin?) at Fort Stoddert in mid-August thought William McIntosh had led the Coweta raid against McQueen's town. That same source maintained that "The Indians lost about 200 lbs. of powder and some other articles" of the "1000 lbs. of powder" they had received from the Spanish governor; "Indian Expedition," *The War* (September 21, 1813):1.

Territorial Governor Holmes reported to the secretary of war on August 30, 1813, that "Some time in July last the citizens on Tombigbee recieved information that a party of unfriendly Creeks, consisting of about three hundred, had gone to Pensacola for the purpose of procuring arms and ammunition to be used against the frontier inhabitants. About one hundred and eighty citizens placed themselves under the command of Colo Caller of the militia, with the intention to intercept them upon their return. They came upon forty Indians at a place called the Wolf path and immediately commenced an attack. The Indians returned the fire and in a short time all Colo Caller's party except twenty or thirty sought safety by flight. The few that remained maintained the contest with bravery. By the address of a half breed Indian [Dixon Bailey], who acted with the whites, the ammunition, and some clothing which the party had procured at Pensacola was taken and secured. The expedition was irregular and unauthorized by me, but I am confident there existed good grounds to believe that the Indians meditated an attack upon the settlements"; Carter, *Territorial Papers,* 6:396–97.

15. Notes furnished by Gen Patrick May, Pickett Papers, ADAH; Arthur H. Hall, "The Red Stick War: Creek Indian Affairs During the War of 1812," 279–80; Hawkins to Floyd, September 30, 1813, in Lowrie and Clarke, *ASP, Indian Affairs,* 1:854.

16. Pickett, *History of Alabama*, 2:264; Notes taken from the lips of Dr Thos G. Holmes, Pickett Papers, ADAH. Benjamin Hawkins wrote in 1816 that he had been "apprehensive for their safety [referring to the Tensaw métis, the "half breeds," as he called them], as well as that of his fellow citizens in this quarter, [and] sent an order to all of them and the whites and the Indians among them to go down, join and make common cause with their white neighbours. This order they obeyed promptly and willingly"; Grant, *Letters, Journals & Writings*, 768.

"Peirce" is the proper spelling of the surname of the mill-owning brothers, although their contemporaries frequently ignored their preference. See Robert Leslie Smith, *Gone to the Swamp*, 28. On September 25, 1809, a survey party lodged that night "at Messrs. Peirce on the Alabama [River]"; Silas Dinsmoor and Levin Wailes, "Journal and Field Notes on the Boundary lines Between The United States and The Chaktaw nation of Indians," p. 164, RG 49, NARA. Also see David A. Bagwell, "The Treaty of Mount Dexter of 1805 and The Old Indian Treaty Boundary Line of 1809" (manuscript). Mr. Bagwell kindly furnished me with a photocopy of the 1809 journal and his manuscript.

17. Governor David Holmes to Secretary of War, July 27, 1813, in Carter, *Territorial Papers*, 6:388–89.

18. Margaret Eades' remarkable reminiscence of her Tombigbee childhood, "Early Life of Margaret Ervin Austill," is preserved (as a typed copy of the privately owned manuscript) in the Jeremiah Austill Papers, Library of the University of North Carolina, Chapel Hill. This copy is marred by many apparent errors in transcription; I have drawn quotes from a published version, "Life of Margaret Ervin Austill." The original, said in the 1940s to be held by the Jere Austill family of Mobile, has not been located.

19. William and J. Peirce to Judge Harry Toulmin, Tensaw, July 18, 1813, in Lackey, *Frontier Claims*, 10.

20. Quote from Joseph Carson, Col. Volunteers, to Gen. Claiborne, July 29, 1813, in Claiborne, *Life and Times of Gen. Sam. Dale*, 79–80; Frank H. Akers, Jr., "The Unexpected Challenge: The Creek War of 1813–1814," 147; "A Roll of officers educated at West Point who have been Killed in the Service of the United States," J. G. Swift to Secretary of War, New York, February 4, 1817, R1815, Letters Received by the Secretary of War, Unregistered Series (microform 222, roll 7), RG 107, NARA.

21. Claiborne to Governor of Georgia, Fort Stoddert, August 14, 1813, in Letterbook F, J.F.H. Claiborne Collection, MDAH; West, ed., "Prelude to the Creek War of 1813–1814," 263. "On the 28th of June I received an order to march from Baton Rouge with the volunteers, for the eastern frontier of our territory. At the time of the receipt of this order, the quarter master general advanced me two hundred dollars for the transportation of about five hundred and fifty men three hundred miles, with their baggage, camp equipage, ammunition, &c. . . . With this pitiful sum it was impossible for the troops to proceed. . . . I borrowed on my own responsibility the necessary funds for the transportation of the troops." See Claiborne to Editor of Mississippi Republican, *Supplement to the Mississippi Republican* [Washington, Mississippi Territory] (March 25, 1814):1.

22. Holmes to Toulmin, July 29, 1813, Papers of the Mississippi Territory, RG 2, Territorial Governors Papers, vol. 32:1647, MDAH, quoted in Jack D. Elliott, Jr., "The Plymouth Fort and the Creek War: A Mystery Solved," 343.

23. Claiborne to Editor of Mississippi Republican, *Supplement to the Mississippi Republican* (March 25, 1814):1. "Captain Dent was despatched to Oaktupa, where he assumed the command of a fort with two block-houses within a mile of the Choctaw line"; John Simpson Graham, *History of Clarke County,* 34.

24. Brigadier General Thomas Flournoy to Governor Holmes, Aug. 6, 1813, in Carter, *Territorial Papers,* 6:397–98 (from "a quantity" to "lives"); Claiborne to Editor of Mississippi Republican, *Supplement to the Mississippi Republican* (March 25, 1814):1 ("in the land" and "skulking").

25. "Carsons Ferry, Bill, August 3, 1813, "for ferry of troops from Mt. Vernon Cantonement for Mims Blockhouse   102 men 2 horses   also Cornet Rankin & 9 Dragoons" and ten horses [signed by Major Beasley], RG 94, Box 220 (Z), NARA. Mims Ferry, Bill, August 2, 1813, "for ferraige of Major Beasley   112 men & 12 horses to Mim's Blockhouse, paid September 20, 1813 in Mobile," RG 94, Box 219, NARA. James Parker kindly provided these references. Four years before, the Choctaw Boundary survey team traversed the same road, and had camped in "Mr. Mim's field on Nannahubba Island"; Silas Dinsmoor and Levin Wailes, "Journal and Field Notes on the Boundary lines," p. 165, RG 49, NARA.

On July 28, Lt. Spruce Osborne offered his opinion that "this Stockade is in Good Condition, and I am sure will be well defended"; S. M. Osborne to Col. Jos. Carson, Mims Stockade, July 28, 1813, in Letterbook F, J.F.H. Claiborne Collection, MDAH, and quoted in Claiborne, *Life and Times of Gen. Sam. Dale,* 79–80. See Akers, *Unexpected Challenge,* 147.

26. Major Daniel Beasley to General Claiborne, Mims' Block House, August 6, 1813, in Letterbook F, J.F.H. Claiborne Collection, MDAH, quoted in James F. Doster, ed., "Letters Relating to the Tragedy of Fort Mims: August–September, 1813," 270–71. Karl Davis claims that "Bailey held the position of *tustunuggee thlucco,* or big warrior, in Tensaw"; "'Much of the Indian Appears,'" 121–22. Such a title seems unlikely for a member of the Wind clan, but Davis offer no documentation in any case.

27. Beasley to Claiborne, Mims' Block House, August 7, 1813, in Letterbook F, J.F.H. Claiborne Collection, MDAH.

28. J.F.H. Claiborne's historical notes, ibid.

29. Beasley to Claiborne, Mims' Block House, August 7, 1813 ("one of the militia"), ibid.; William and J. Peirce to Judge Harry Toulmin, July 18, 1813, in Lackey, *Frontier Claims,* 10 ("Rigdon"), 12. Also see Pickett, *History of Alabama,* 2:251 (who misidentified Rigdon as "Greggs"); Claiborne, *Life and Times of Gen. Sam. Dale,* 79; Mrs. Dunbar (Eron) Rowland, *Andrew Jackson's Campaign against the British or the Mississippi Territory in the War of 1812,* 68–69; Toulmin to Claiborne, Fort Stoddert, July 23, 1813, ADAH; Toulmin to Claiborne, Fort Stoddert, July 31, 1813, in Letterbook F, J.F.H. Claiborne Collection, MDAH. On the briefly occupied Perdido fort, see Notes obtained from a conversation with Major Reuben Chamberlain, Pickett Papers, ADAH. The apparently landless Rigdons moved every few years as the father and sons, all professional soldiers, were reassigned to different military posts across the South. Other members of the Rigdon family present at Fort Mims are not known for certain; they might have included father Enoch Rigdon (age forty-four), mother Sophia Shittle Rigdon, and unnamed sisters (one may have been named Nancy, married to Reuben Hart). Records of Men Enlisted in the U.S. Army Prior to the Peace Establishment, May 17, 1815, Registers of Enlistments in the U.S. Army, 1798–1914, M-233, Reel 10 (P–R), p. 244, RG

94, NARA; Monte George, pers. comm., March 9, 2003. I am very grateful to Mr. George for sharing his remarkably well documented family history with me.

30. Lieutenant George F. Wilkinson, Charges, Cantonment Washington, February 8, 1814, Document 15, Papers of the Mississippi Territory, Series 487: Military Papers, 1807–1815, MDAH.

31. Copy of Instructions, Claiborne to Beasley, Mimms' Station, August 7, 1813, in Letter-book F, J.F.H. Claiborne Collection, MDAH; Claiborne, *Life and Times of Gen. Sam. Dale,* 101.

32. Copy of Instructions, Claiborne to Beasley, ibid. Regarding the Tensaw militia, Claiborne added, "On thirty persons enrolling allow them the privalige of appointing their own Captain & an Ensign & should forty five enroll give them the privalige of electing a Lieutenant & for a complete Company of seventy six add a 2d Lieutenant to their number of officers, to serve for three months unless sooner discharged by the Commanding General Officer of the 7th Military District."

After the war, Claiborne recalled his impressions of Fort Mims during his visit of August 7: "I found the fort in such a situation as would not enable it to resist should an attack ensue. Impressed with this fact, I instantly issued orders to major Beasley to strengthen the piquets, to build two additional block-houses, and to put the garrison in every respect in a perfect and secure state of defence"; Claiborne to Editor of Mississippi Republican, *Supplement to the Mississippi Republican* (March 25, 1814):2. Claiborne's political enemies scoffed at his claims, maintaining he had never publicly read those orders on parade and had, in fact, not ordered any improvements to the fortification at all: "How does this agree with your remark on the same day after viewing its situation, that 'there was no cause of alarm unless a more formidable enemy than the Indians were to arrive and begin to batter the pickets over their heads with six-pounders, it would then be time enough to be alarmed'—that this remark was made by you in the presence of the officers and some of the citizens, will not be denied." One of the Volunteers, Mobile, May 2, 1814, *Washington Republican* (May 25, 1814):2–3.

Claiborne also endured criticism for dividing his forces to garrison mills owned by wealthy, influential citizens. According to his biographer and son, "Pierces & Henson & Kennedys mills were deemed important. the latter were actually in the employ of Government to prepare timbers for the completion of the works at Mobile Point (now Fort Bowyer) and for the repair of the Fort at Mobile which from the length of time it has existed was fast molding away & falling into total decay. No private motive induced the General to guard those places"; [J.F.H. Claiborne], Fort Mimms, in Letterbook F, J.F.H. Claiborne Collection, MDAH.

33. Beasley to Claiborne, Mims' Block House, August 12, 1813, ibid.

34. On August 14, Major Beasley wrote General Claiborne, "At the time of receiving your dispatch, Mr. Pierce & Mr. Tate was with me on the Subject of furnishing a guard, at the Mill, I will send one there to night. Capt. Bailey has as many men as to entitle his Company to a Lieutenant" Beasley to Claiborne, Mims' Block House, August 14, 1813, ibid.

35. Quote from Hawkins to Floyd, September 30, 1813, in Grant, *Letters, Journals and Writings,* 668, and Lowrie and Clarke, *ASP, Indian Affairs,* 1:854. Stiggins, "Historical narration," 59 (quote). Redstick attacks against Coweta did commence on the first of August but were limited to skirmishes.

36. Quotes from Judge Harry Toulmin, "Indian Warfare, Mobile, September 7," 105–6.

37. "War parties leaving the town were always headed by a man of proved physical prowess and cunning, and his title as leader was *pakádja łákko*. Another individual, called *hobáya*, 'prophet,' accompanied such forays. He was versed in songs and rituals with which he could weaken the enemy and blind the eyes of their warriors. He could also foretell events and determine whether raids or hunting excursions would be successful or not"; Speck, "Creek Indians of Taskigi Town," 114; Stiggins, "Historical narration," 60 (quotes). The quotes on "war physic" and "war food" from Hawkins to Floyd, October 4, 1813, in Lowrie and Clarke, *ASP, Indian Affairs,* 1:855, refers to preparations for a later battle with Georgia troops, although the same sort of preliminaries must have preceded the march on the Tensaw. On the war physic, an emetic concoction made from *mēkko-hoyvnēcv* or red root (*Salix humilis*) and *passv* or button snake root (*Eryngium yuccifolium*), see Grant, *Letters, Journals and Writings,* 324–25; Martin, *Sacred Revolt,* 34, 143–44; Lewis and Jordan, *Creek Indian Medicine Ways,* 78–79, 151–54. I am grateful to Jacob Lowrey (pers. comm. November 12, 2004) for confirming the identity of Big Flat Creek, in Monroe County, Alabama, as the Flat Creek mentioned in George Stiggins' account. Lowrey points out that modern-day Big Flat Creek is labeled Flat Creek on the 1825 Tanner map of Alabama.

38. Beasley to Claiborne, Mims' Block House, August 14, 1813, in Letterbook F, J.F.H. Claiborne Collection, MDAH.

39. "On the 21st Inst. a Chaktaw Indian Known by the Name of Baker's hunter came in to Easlys fort and Told that in Six days at farthest from that time the Creeks would be down and would Attack their fort that a part of the Creeks were then embodied at a little Chaktaw Town about twelve or fifteen Miles above the line, the Chaktaw said from the best information he could get about four hundred Creek Indians would come down against the whites, the Indian appeared Much Alarmed Said the White people were at liberty to take him into the settlement Tye him & Keep him, and if at the expira[tion] of his Six days the fort was not attacked he would agree to have his throat Cut": statement made by Hugh Cassitty to Colonel Joseph Carson, Fort Madison, August 23, 1813, ibid.; Toulmin, "Indian Warfare," 106 (text quote).

40. "At this time there is verry little necessity for my Medical services at this post. The men with one exception are able to do duty or convalescent. Their temperance & the lightness of their duties will I expect keep them so. I entered the service with the prospect and wish to continue in it as soldier during the war; my present employment will render me less fit for promotion. I cannot help often thinking what a small share of glory would fall to my lott in the event of actual hostility. . . . I would be asked at the end of this campaign, where were you on such a day when the enemy were routed?" Osborne to Claiborne, "Mims B^k House," August 24, 1813, in Interesting Papers . . . by Col John F. H. Claiborne, Pickett Papers, ADAH; Stiggins, "Historical narration," 60 (quote). For accounts of the several war parties converging on the Tensaw and Tombigbee settlements, see Foster, *Collected Works,* 83s–84s; Toulmin to Holmes, August 27, 1813, and Toulmin to Flournoy, August 30, 1813, in Doster, ed., "Letters," 278–84.

41. According to the U.S. Naval Observatory website, www.aa.usno.navy.mil, the new moon rose on August 26, 1813. On August 29, the night before the attack on Fort Mims, the moon was a waxing crescent with 17 percent of the visible disk illuminated. Moonset oc-

curred at 8:47 P.M. Woodward, *Reminiscences,* 86 ("convenient"); Toulmin, "Indian Warfare," 106 ("credit"); Stiggins, "Historical narration," 60.

42. Toulmin, "Indian Warfare," 106 (first quote); Stiggins, "Historical narration," 61 (second quote). Also see Claiborne to Editor of Mississippi Republican, *Supplement to the Mississippi Republican* (March 25, 1814).

"The mail rider also from the Chickasaw agency was informed by the Choctaw chief Pooshamattahaw that the Creeks had been or were assembled on the Black Warrior, dancing the war dance, and would certainly break in upon us in about eight days. It must have been 3 days ago that he saw the Chief"; Toulmin to Holmes, August 27, 1813, in Doster, ed., "Letters," 278–81.

43. Claiborne to Editor of Mississippi Republican, *Supplement to the Mississippi Republican* (March 25, 1814); Toulmin, "Indian Warfare," 106 ("greater exertions"); Halbert and Ball, *Creek War,* 166–67 ("drunken frolic").

44. Stiggins, "Historical narration," 61–62 (quotes). J. D. Dreisbach to Lyman Draper, July 1874, Draper, WHS.

45. First quotes from J. D. Dreisbach to Lyman Draper, ibid., 5–6; Dreisbach added, "there was several attempts made during the night to assassinate him." Stiggins, "Historical narration," 61–62 (later quotes, from "a few Indians" onward).

46. Stiggins, ibid., 62–63, 66 (quotes).

47. On Shawnee and Shawnee-inspired battle tactics, see John Sugden, *Blue Jacket: Warrior of the Shawnees,* 117–27; Edmunds, *Shawnee Prophet,* 110–13; Sugden, *Tecumseh,* 28–29, 232–36; Frank L. Owsley, Jr., *Struggle for the Gulf Borderlands: The Creek War and the Battle of New Orleans, 1812–1815,* 56–58.

Chapter 6

1. In a campaign later in the Redstick War, the Carolina brigade organized the day by "the beat of the drum," a practice typical of U.S. military units of this era; April 26, 1814, Orderly Books, Joseph Graham Papers, NCDCR.

2. Woodward, *Reminiscences,* 80 ("inmates"); J. D. Dreisbach Letter to Lyman Draper, July 1874, Draper, WHS; Claiborne Map, Pickett Papers, ADAH.

3. The map may have been sketched by Lieutenant Benjamin F. Salvage, regimental quartermaster, or perhaps by Captain Joseph P. Kennedy, commanding the burial party. An early derivative of this map appeared in the *Mississippi Republican* on December 1, 1813, accompanying an article highly critical of General Claiborne. For an even simpler version, see Halbert and Ball, *Creek War,* 149. The original map ended up among the general's personal papers, which were inherited by his son J.F.H. Claiborne; he gave the sketch to historian Albert James Pickett in the late 1840s. Pickett reproduced a simplified engraved version in his 1851 *History of Alabama,* 2: facing 265. The original resides among Pickett's papers at the ADAH in Montgomery, where it is cataloged as "Ferdinand Leigh Claiborne's Map of Fort Mims and Environs" [1813], CB-23.

4. Sworn statements with accompanying exhibits of sundry inhabitants of the Mississippi Territory, September–November, 1815, praying for relief from Indian depredations, 14th Cong., 1st sess., House of Representatives, Other Select Committees, January 2, 1816, RG 233,

NARA, quoted in Lackey, *Frontier Claims*, 31. Other property itemized in the Mims claim petition includes:

1 Feather Bed	25—
100 Head of Sheep killed @ $4	400—
16 ditto of Horses, averaged @$70	1120—
5 ditto @$40	200—
200 ditto Hogs @$2	400—
415 ditto stock cattle killed @$6	2490—
1 work ox	20—
1 negro man named Anthony 22 years old	450—
1 negro man named Cooley 45 years old	300—
1 Pair handmill stones burnt	25—
2 Riding Saddles, one @ $35 and one @ $25	60—
1 Riding Saddle	30—

5. Just two are mentioned in the Creek War claims petition—the Mims home and the dwelling place of William and John Peirce, who operated a sawmill about two miles south of the Mims plantation; Lackey, *Frontier Claims*, 31. Hiram Mounger, an early American settler, told Jere Austill in 1848, "People at my Coming [in 1791] & for some years after lived in log cabbins except the French who lived in Dirt houses, plastered within & without generally—during the Spanish times." Notes taken from the lips of Hiram Mounger . . . by Col. J. Austill, Pickett Papers, ADAH.

6. "[S]et fire to an old framed house in the center of the pickets . . . the old men, women and children who were in a upper room were burnt to death . . . " Lewis Sewall & Others, Fort St. Stephens, Oct. 4, 1813, Secretary of War, Letters Received, Main Series (1801–1870), RG 107, NARA. The Mims house could not have been erected more than 15 years earlier, but perhaps its style of construction during the previous Spanish administration qualified it as "old."

7. Pickett, *History of Alabama*, 2:273.

8. Woodward, *Reminiscences*, 86.

9. Pickett, *History of Alabama*, 2:272–73 ("loom-house" and "bastion"); Halbert and Ball, *Creek War*, 148. According to Doctor Holmes, the place referred to by Pickett as "Patrick's loom-house" was the home of Patrick Mahoney, a weaver; Notes taken from the lips of Dr Thos G. Holmes, Pickett Papers, ADAH. Mahoney may have survived the Redstick War. A seventy-nine- to eighty-year-old Patrick Mahoney, maybe the Mims' plantation weaver, purchased land in Baldwin County in 1831; Hahn, *Old St. Stephens Land Office Records*, 37.

10. Halbert and Ball, *Creek War*, 166–67; Henry S. Halbert, "An Incident of Fort Mimms." Halbert's source was James Welsh, of Neshoba, Mississippi, who knew Page. He gathered further details on the stable from Dick Embry, an "old negro" who was "often at Mims' house." Embry said the stables, which had been built especially for the Volunteers' horses, "stood about 80 yards southeast of the east gate of the fort, and on the edge of the potato patch." Henry S. Halbert, "Fort Mims Incident—1813, November 10, 1882," in Series YY: Tecumseh Papers, Draper, WHS.

11. Pickett, *History of Alabama*, 2:264–65 ("board shelters"), 272; Stiggins, "Historical narration," 64. Dick Embry described to Halbert "the potato patch adjoining the fort on the south . . . [as] comprising about six acres, the fence joining the picketing on the southeast and southwest corners." Halbert, "Fort Mims Incident—1813, November 10, 1882." The Claiborne Map shows the fenced "Potatoe patch" detached from the fort, a considerable distance south. For information on excavated features of Fort Mims, see Gregory A. Waselkov, Bonnie L. Gums, and James W. Parker, "Archaeology at Fort Mims: Excavation Contexts and Artifact Catalog."

12. Pickett, *History of Alabama*, 2:264–65 (quote).

13. James W. Parker suggests the fort's gunpowder may have been stored in the block-house; pers. comm., 2003. Toulmin, "Indian Warfare, 106; Grant, *Letters, Journals and Writings,* 667, 768–69; Letter report from Kennedy to Claiborne, Mt. Vernon, Sept. 9, 1813, in Interesting Papers . . . by Col John F. H. Claiborne, Pickett Papers, ADAH; "Massacre at Fort Mimms" by Alonzo Chappel, from *Battles of the United States by Sea and Land,* by Henry B. Dawson, vol. 2, n.p.

14. For a discussion of the architectural range of pioneer forts from mid- to late-eighteenth-century Kentucky and Virginia, see Nancy O'Malley, 'Stockading Up;' A Study of Pioneer Stations in the Inner Bluegrass Region of Kentucky, 23–29; W. Stephen McBride, Kim Arbogast McBride, and Greg Adamson, *Frontier Forts in West Virginia: Historical and Archaeological Explorations.* Heirs of Joshua Kennedy, Feb. 3, 1848, *U.S. Congressional Serial Set, House Report 155, 30th Cong., 1st sess.,* cited in McDonald Brooms, *Archaeological Investigations at the Kennedy Mill Site: 1Ba301 in Baldwin County, Alabama,* 24.

Among contemporary accounts, only Captain Kennedy's report of the initial reconnaissance party's visit after the battle mentions a stockade. See Kennedy to Claiborne, Sept. 9, 1813, in Interesting Papers . . . by Col John F. H. Claiborne, Pickett Papers, ADAH. Contrasted with the word "stockade," which conveys a sense of stoutness, a certain flimsiness seems implied by contemporary commentators' preference for "pickets" and "picketing" in their descriptions of the Fort Mims walls. One of the Fort Mims survivors, Dr. Thomas G. Holmes, chopped through two of the fort's pickets to escape; Pickett, *History of Alabama*, 2:273.

The uprights certainly would not have been driven into the ground, since use of pile drivers was limited exclusively at that era to building foundations in waterlogged soils, such as along the banks of river or in marshes. Unfortunately, Pickett's surviving notes do not reveal the source or inspiration for his description of the fort's outer wall. I directed an excavation by a group of volunteers on November 29, 2004 and on several other Saturdays that fall and the following spring, that uncovered a small portion of the west palisade trench of Fort Mims. Permission from the Alabama Historical Commission to conduct this limited excavation and assistance from the Fort Mims Restoration Association (particularly first cousins H. Davis Smith and R. Leslie Smith, descendants of Jesse Steadham) are gratefully acknowledged.

15. According to George Stiggins' account of William Weatherford's nighttime reconnoiter, "the port holes . . . were four foot high and about four foot apart all around"; "Historical narration," 62.

16. Pickett, *History of Alabama*, 2:266 (quote); Toulmin, "Indian Warfare."

17. On the establishment of the Mount Vernon cantonment on Mound Bend, west of Fort Stoddert, see Notes taken from the lips of Mr. George S. Gaines, Notes obtained from a conversation with Major Reuben Chamberlain, and Notes taken from the lips of Hiram Mounger . . . by Col. J. Austill, all in Pickett Papers, ADAH. "Being in the month of August & the Fort situated near the alabama swamp; the garrison & inmates had experienced great deal sickness"; Notes of Doctor Thomas G. Holmes, ibid.

18. On the Baileys' cleanly ways, see Foster, *Collected Works,* 30s, 39–40, 47–48. "One of our Soldiers died the night before last and from the report enclosed you will see that we have a good many on the Sick report; but none of them dangerous"; Beasley to Claiborne, Mims' Block House, Aug. 12, 1813, in Letterbook F, J.F.H. Claiborne Collection, MDAH. Also see Beasley to Claiborne, Mims Block House, August 7, 1813, and Beasley to Claiborne, Mims' Block House, August 30, 1813, ibid. General Claiborne's son thought the "ill-constructed stockades" built prior to the battle at Fort Mims were "scourged within with typhus, scarlatina [scarlet fever], and dysentery"; Claiborne, *Life and Times of Gen. Sam. Dale,* 84. Pickett, *History of Alabama,* 2:265 ("out-houses"); Remarks, *Washington Republican* (December 1, 1813):2 ("filthy pens").

19. Samuel Mims had been in St. Stephens paying taxes and filing for land as late as August 17, 1813; Hahn, *Old St. Stephens Land Office Records,* 11. Halbert and Ball, *Creek War,* 166–67; Remarks, *Washington Republican,* ibid.; Grant, *Letters, Journals and Writings,* 665–67.

20. "The years from 1805 to 1820 were the coldest era in Europe, eastern North America, and Japan" during the Little Ice Age. "1812 was probably the coldest year in the last four centuries." From Helmut E. Landsberg, "Past Climates from Unexploited Written Sources," in *Climate and History: Studies in Interdisciplinary History,* ed. Robert I. Rotberg and Theodore K. Rabb, 61. In 1816, the famous "year without a summer," summer monthly temperatures in northern latitudes were 2.3° to 4.6°C colder than the two-century mean; Brian Fagan, *The Little Ice Age: How Climate Made History, 1300–1850,* 170.

21. Using grape harvest dates as temperature proxies has a venerable history in France, beginning in 1883. See Emmanuel Le Roy Ladurie, *Times of Feast, Times of Famine: A History of Climate Since the Year 1000,* 7–79; Emmanuel Le Roy Ladurie and Micheline Baulant, "Grape Harvests from the Fifteenth through the Nineteenth Centuries." Quotes from Edmund P. Gaines to Gideon Granger, February 1, 1807, no. 6, Joseph Wheaton Papers, University of Georgia Libraries. In August 2004, wild muscadines growing in Fairhope, Alabama, on the eastern shore of Mobile Bay, ripened by mid-August and were gone by month's end. On August 28, I scoured the woods around Fort Mims Park for muscadines and could find none of the fallen fruit, although vines are abundant in the area.

22. The normal high temperature for August 30, measured at Bay Minette, Alabama, between 1971 and 2000, was 88° F; daily station normals from the National Climatic Data Center, National Oceanic and Atmospheric Administration, http://www5.ncdc.noaa.gov/climatenormals/. A partial 1807–8 temperature record, along with the promotional comment, is found in John Melish, *Travels through the United States of America in the Years 1806 & 1807, and 1809, 1810, & 1811,* 391 ("seldom oppressive"). Edmund P. Gaines presumably provided this information to Melish, who acknowledged his source only as "a register kept near Fort Stoddart." In 1807 the mean high in July was 86°F, with daytime highs of 88° on August 2

and 95° on September 5. In the Natchez district, August 30, 1813, was the hottest day of the month, with a high of 94°, a low of 80°, and cloudy with thunderstorms late in the day; Meteorological Register, *Washington Republican* (September 1, 1813):3.

23. J.F.H. Claiborne's historical notes, Chambliss' Certificate, and Beasley to Claiborne, Mims' Block House, August 30, 1813, in Letterbook F, J.F.H. Claiborne Collection, MDAH; Extract of a letter from Lieut. Montgomery of the Mississippi Volunteer Regiment to his father, Samuel Montgomery, Esq. of this county, dated Mobile, Sept. 4, 1813, *Washington Republican* (September 29, 1813):3; For the Washington Republican, Gen. F. L. Claiborne, *Washington Republican* (April 30, 1814); Stiggins, "Historical narration," 64. Montgomery's detachment at Fort Peirce totaled 20 Volunteers, with another 18 under Ensign Isaac Davis at Hinson and Kennedy's Mill, according to Notes of Doctor Thomas G. Holmes, Pickett Papers, ADAH. References counting 26 men at Hinson and Kennedy's Mill and 40 at Peirces' Mill probably add militia to the Volunteer counts.

24. Beasley to Claiborne, Mims' Block House, August 30, 1813, in Letterbook F, J.F.H. Claiborne Collection, MDAH.

25. Stiggins, "Historical narration," 63.

26. Remarks, *Washington Republican* (December 1, 1813):2; David Crockett, *A Narrative of the Life of David Crockett of the State of Tennessee*, 104–5; Grant, *Letters, Journals and Writings*, 666, and *ASP, Indian Affairs*, 1:853; Toulmin, "Indian Warfare," 106. One of McGirth's slaves captured on Saturday, "a very intelligent negroe named Joe," suggested to the Redsticks their attack should coincide with the noon drum beat, when the garrison and civilians would be preoccupied with meal preparations, according to Notes of Doctor Thomas G. Holmes, Pickett Papers, ADAH. Joe later fought with the Redsticks; he was badly wounded in a battle and taken prisoner by Major Russell's regular troops in Pensacola in December 1814; Notes taken from the lips of Dr Thos G. Holmes, Pickett Papers, ADAH.

27. Remarks, *Washington Republican* (December 1, 1813):2; Toulmin, "Indian Warfare," 106; Woodward, *Reminiscences*, 86 ("red cattle"); Grant, *Letters, Journals and Writings*, 665 ("in two circles"), 666–67, and *ASP, Indian Affairs*, 1:853; Benjamin Hawkins to John Floyd, "Extract of a Letter to John Floyd, Sept. 26, 1813"; Notes taken from the lips of Col Robert James, Pickett Papers, ADAH; Crockett, *A Narrative*, 104; Notes of Doctor Thomas G. Holmes, and Notes taken from the lips of Dr Thos G. Holmes, Pickett Papers, ADAH.

28. Woodward, *Reminiscences*, 86; Stiggins, "Historical narration," 63. While most first-hand accounts agree that the attack took place around noon, Lieutenant Montgomery, at Peirces' Mill two miles away, thought the battle began at 11 A.M., as did an informant of Judge Toulmin; Montgomery, Extract, *Washington Republican* (September 29, 1813):3; Toulmin, "Indian Warfare," 106.

29. Woodward, *Reminiscences*, 84; Stiggins, "Historical narration," 62–63 ("playing cards" and "the Indians, the indians"); Crockett, *Narrative*, 104–105; Halbert and Ball, *Creek War*, 166–67 ("rushing"); Lackey, *Frontier Claims*, 31; Toulmin, "Indian Warfare," 106 ("Indians"). "Judge Toulmin, in a letter to General Claiborne, . . . 'Mr. Fletcher Cox (one who escaped) tells me that the Indians were within thirty steps of the gate before they were seen'"; Claiborne, *Life and Times of Gen. Sam. Dale*, 109. None of these writers acknowledged the considerable irony of white troops crying "Indians" at the sight of Redsticks when a formidable contingent of their own force consisted of Creek Indians of the Tensaw.

"Every Indian was provided with a gun, war club a bow and arrows pointed with iron spikes. With few exceptions they were naked—around the waist was drawn a girdle from which was tied a cows tail runing down the back and almost draging the ground. It is impossible to imagine people so horibly painted. Some were painted half red & half black Some were adorned with feathers—their faces were painted so as to show their horrible contortions"; Notes of Doctor Thomas G. Holmes, Pickett Papers, ADAH. J.F.H. Claiborne offered a correction regarding the cow tails, suggesting these were actually buffalo tails and only Shawnee warriors fighting with the Redsticks wore them; comments of J.F.H. Claiborne in Notes taken from the lips of Abram Mordecai, Pickett Papers, ADAH.

30. Toulmin, "Indian Warfare," 106 ("war-whoop"); Grant, *Letters, Journals and Writings,* 667, and Hawkins, Extract, *New-York Spectator* (October 16, 1813):4. Beasley "had been dispatched with a war club," according to Notes of Doctor Thomas G. Holmes, Pickett Papers, ADAH.

31. Stiggins, "Historical narration," 62–64 ("foremost man"); Woodward, *Reminiscences,* 86; Monette, *History,* 2:406; Claiborne to ———, Cantonment Mount Vernon, September 6, 1813, in Letterbook F, J.F.H. Claiborne Collection, MDAH; Grant, *Letters, Journals and Writings,* 672 ("cuting"), and *ASP, Indian Affairs,* 1:852; Notes of Doctor Thomas G. Holmes (rifles and shotguns), Pickett Papers, ADAH; Toulmin, "Indian Warfare," 106.

32. Stiggins, "Historical narration," 66 ("enter the fort").

33. Answers, *Washington Republican* (December 1, 1813):2 ("Carpenters tools"); Toulmin, "Indian Warfare," 106; Grant, *Letters, Journals and Writings,* 665; Monette, *History,* 405; Crockett, *Narrative,* 104–5; Pickett, *History of Alabama,* 2:272–73; Claiborne to ———, September 6, 1813, in Letterbook F, J.F.H. Claiborne Collection, MDAH. Doctor Holmes attested to the "many acts of bravery on the part of the females" among the fort's defenders, singling out Daniel Bailey's wife who "loaded guns during the whole engagement for the defenders of the Bastion." One of the burial details, Holmes further noted, found inside the blockhouse the body of a soldier in Captain Jack's company still clutching his jaeger rifle in one hand and his ramrod in the other. See Notes of Doctor Thomas G. Holmes, Pickett Papers, ADAH.

34. Notes of Doctor Thomas G. Holmes, ibid.; Stiggins, "Historical narration," 64–65 ("sufficiently humbled"); Woodward, *Reminiscences,* 80–81 ("advised"); J. D. Dreisback Letter to Lyman Draper, July 1874, 6–7, Draper, WHS. There seems no basis for Karl Davis' speculation that the Redsticks withdrew temporarily "to remove safely those inhabitants sympathetic to their cause"; "'Remember Fort Mims,'" 631.

35. According to Woodward, *Reminiscences,* 86, the Shawnee, "Seekaboo, and some of the McGillivray negroes got behind some logs that were near the Fort, kindled a fire, and, by putting rags on their arrows and setting them on fire, would shoot them into the roof of Mims' smokehouse." Also see Claiborne Map, and Kennedy to Claiborne, Mt. Vernon, Sept. 9, 1813, in Interesting Papers . . . by Col John F. H. Claiborne, Pickett Papers, ADAH; Woodward, *Reminiscences,* 80–81; Stiggins, "Historical narration," 64; Grant, *Letters, Journals and Writings,* 665 ("matches"), and *ASP, Indian Affairs,* 1:853; Toulmin, "Indian Warfare," 106; Notes taken from the lips of Dr Thos G. Holmes, Pickett Papers, ADAH; Pickett, *History of Alabama,* 2:273.

The Creeks in earlier days had tortured and killed war captives (non-Creeks) by burning.

In the nineteenth century, death by fire was deemed an appropriate punishment for Creeks who had betrayed their own people. In 1825, as William McIntosh (Tastanagi Hutki) fought off a force sent by the Creek national council to assassinate him, his wives begged the executioners to let him emerge from his burning house and "not to burn him up for he was an indian like themselves." Since McIntosh had negotiated the sale of Creek lands, the council had decided he was no longer truly Creek. Conversation with James Moore, in Notes taken from the lips of Abram Mordecai, Pickett Papers, ADAH.

36. "There was much silver money in the house melted, and run about and some dollars blacked only." Grant, *Letters, Journals and Writings*, 665, and *ASP, Indian Affairs*, 1:853.

37. Grant, *Letters, Journals and Writings*, 665–67 (quotes), and *ASP, Indian Affairs*, 1:853; Hawkins, Extract, *New-York Spectator* (October 16, 1813):4.

38. Stiggins, "Historical narration," 64 ("surrounded"); Toulmin, "Indian Warfare," 106 ("despond"); Notes of Doctor Thomas G. Holmes and Notes Taken from the lips of Dr Thos G. Holmes, Pickett Papers, ADAH; Pickett, *History of Alabama*, 2:272 ("the women"); Claiborne to ———, September 6, 1813, in Letterbook F, J.F.H. Claiborne Collection, MDAH. See Appendix 1 of this volume.

39. Notes of Doctor Thomas G. Holmes (quotes), Pickett Papers, ADAH; Pickett, *History of Alabama*, 2:274.

40. Crockett, *Narrative*, 105; Dr. A. B. Clanton, "Massacre of Fort Mims," *Meridian Daily News* [Meridian, Mississippi], clippings in Clanton Papers, ADAH; Halbert and Ball, *Creek War*, 157 (citing Clanton, they say 14 escaped at once), 160; Pickett, *History of Alabama*, 2:277–78; Claiborne, *Life and Times of Gen. Sam. Dale*, 102; Notes taken from the lips of Dr Thos G. Holmes, Pickett Papers, ADAH.

41. Graham, *History*, 52–53; Halbert and Ball, *Creek War*, 157, 161, 174 (quote), 175. After some months of captivity in the Creek nation, Susannah Hatterway and the two little girls were taken eventually to Pensacola by Efa Tastanagi and released to some friends. Fletcher made his way to Hinson and Kennedy's Mill and joined Ensign Davis' command; Notes taken from the lips of Dr Thos G. Holmes, Pickett Papers, ADAH. On August 30, 1813, the sun set in Mobile at 6:18 P.M., according to the U.S. Naval Observatory's website <http://mach.usno.navy.mil/cgi-bin/aa_rstablew.pl>; therefore, the battle ended around 5 P.M.

42. Notes taken from the lips of Col Robert James, Pickett Papers, ADAH (McGirth quotes); Grant, *Letters, Journals and Writings*, 667, and Extract, *New-York Spectator* (October 16, 1813):4; Montgomery, Extract, *Washington Republican* (September 29, 1813):3.

43. Toulmin to Flournoy, Mount Vernon, August 30, 1813, in Doster, ed., "Letters," 283.

44. Ibid., 283–84.

45. Toulmin, Indian Warfare, *Weekly Register* (October 16, 1813):106 (quote); Grant, *Letters, Journals and Writings*, 666, and *ASP, Indian Affairs*, 1:853; Halbert and Ball, *Creek War*, 166–67; Toulmin to Flournoy, Mount Vernon August 30, 1813, in Doster, ed., "Letters," 283–84. "A negro woman named Hester belonged to Benjamin Stedham . . . swam the Alabama River and kept the road [across Nannahubba Island] to the Tombigbee River and swam that and on the next morning by 8 oclock she was the first to tell the news at Mt Vernon to Genl Claiborne"; Notes of Doctor Thomas G. Holmes, Pickett Papers, ADAH.

46. Pickett, *History of Alabama*, 2:279–80; Notes taken from the lips of Col. Robert James,

Pickett Papers, ADAH (quotes). McGirth, himself, cast some doubt on the chronology of his battlefield visit, by telling Benjamin Hawkins (on September 26, 1813) that he "went to the fort the fourth day after the battle to hunt for his family." Grant, *Letters, Journals and Writings,* 667. "Hundreds of abandoned red sticks lay everywhere"; Henry S. Halbert, "The burial of the dead at Fort Mims," March 3, 1887, Series YY: Tecumseh Papers, Draper, WHS.

47. Claiborne, *Life and Times of Gen. Sam. Dale,* 102 ("fire"); Pickett, *History of Alabama,* 2:275–78; Claiborne Map, Pickett Papers, ADAH; Grant, *Letters, Journals and Writings,* 664–65, 667 ("boy"), and Hawkins, "Extract," *New-York Spectator* (October 16, 1813):4; Notes taken from the lips of Dr Thos G. Holmes, Pickett Papers, ADAH.

48. Notes taken from the lips of Dr Thos G. Holmes, Pickett Papers, ADAH; Pickett, *History of Alabama,* 2:276–77.

49. Stiggins, "Historical narration," 66 (quotes); Grant, *Letters, Journals and Writings,* 664–65.

Chapter 7

1. Stiggins, "Historical narration," 67.

2. Claiborne, *Life and Times of Gen. Sam. Dale,* 114; Grant, *Letters, Journals and Writings,* 665–66 (quotes), and *ASP, Indian Affairs,* 1:853. According to Robert James, Mrs. McGirth and her daughters were held at Hickory Ground; Notes taken from the lips of Col Robert James, Pickett Papers, ADAH.

3. Montgomery, Extract, *Washington Republican* (September 29, 1813):3 (quotes); An Old Soldier, *Washington Republican* (October 27, 1813):2; Notes taken from . . . Col Robert James, Pickett Papers, ADAH.

4. Peggy Bailey's grandson, Dixon Bailey Reed, proudly recalled her heroism when interviewed in 1908; The Eastern Cherokee vs. No. 23,214 The United States "Creek File Testimony" Taken before Guion Miller, Special Commissioner, February 1908, Creek Testimony, U.S. Court of Claims, RG 123, NARA. Henry S. Halbert, "Ensign Isaac W. Davis and Hanson's Mill" (quotes), and Anonymous, "Notes and Queries: Ensign Isaac W. Davis."

5. These Redstick towns were located in the Black Warrior River Valley, west of the traditional limits of Creek settlement in the Coosa Valley. Families discontented with the rising influence of the Creek national council had formed those communities a few years earlier; they quickly joined the Redstick movement when civil war broke out in 1813.

6. Extract of a letter from Gen. Ferdinand L. Claiborne to Gen. Flournoy, commanding the 7th Military District, Cantonment, Mount Vernon, 3rd September, 1813, *Richmond Enquirer, Extra* (October 9, 1813), in Letterbook F, J.F.H. Claiborne Collection, MDAH; Grant, *Letters, Journals and Writings,* 663–65, and *ASP, Indian Affairs,* 1:853; F. L. Claiborne, "From the Mississippi Republican Extra, Mount Vernon, Sept. 21st. 1813," and "Extract of a letter from Capt. Alexander Calvit, aid-de-camp to Gen. Claiborne, Cantonment, Mount Vernon, Sept. 23, 1813," *Supplement to the Washington Republican—Sept. 29, 1813* (September 30, 1813):1; Notes Furnished by Col Jeremiah Austill and Notes furnished by Col G. W. Creagh (quote), Pickett Papers, ADAH; Pickett, *History of Alabama,* 2:285–87; Halbert and Ball, *Creek War,* 177–99. Saunt has confused Lieutenant James Bailey with the Baileys of the Tensaw in *New Order of Things,* 263n.79.

7. Stiggins, "Historical narration," 67–68 (quotes). Karl Davis seems to question the ethnicity of the Sinquefield attackers, calling them "a small group of unidentified 'Indians'"; "'Remember Fort Mims,'" 633. George Stiggins testified in 1822 that John Crook, a Redstick métis with one of Josiah Francis' war parties, participated in the burning of Hinson and Kennedy's mills, lumber, cotton house, cotton gin, and cotton and killed some sheep, all shortly after the departure of Ensign Davis' garrison. "Heirs of Joshua Kennedy," Feb. 3, 1848, *U.S. Congressional Serial Set, 30th Cong., 1st sess.*, 10, 18–19.

8. Guice, Introduction to Lackey, *Frontier Claims*, xiv ("depredations"); Saunt, *New Order of Things*, 264. "They [Redsticks] have nothing to live on in the nation & mean to live on our crops as is said by those that have deserted them"; Claiborne to ———, Cantonment Mount Vernon, September 6, 1813, in Letterbook F, J.F.H. Claiborne Collection, MDAH.

9. Toulmin, "Indian Warfare," 107.

10. Joseph Caldwell to David Holmes, Pearl River, September 1813, Papers of the Mississippi Territory, Territorial Governors Papers 33:1783, MDAH, quoted in Elliott, "Plymouth Fort," 344.

11. Claiborne to B. Dent, Fort St. Stephens, September 4, 1813, and Claiborne to Carson, Mount Vernon, September 4, 1813, in Letterbook F, J.F.H. Claiborne Collection, MDAH.

12. Claiborne to Carson, ibid. ("enterprize"), and Claiborne to ———, Cantonment Mount Vernon, September 6, 1813 (subsequent quotes), ibid. For a brief note on Ensign Ferdinand Claiborne's service with General Anthony Wayne against the Shawnees in 1794, see Alan D. Gaff, *Bayonets in the Wilderness: Anthony Wayne's Legion in the Old Northwest*, 183.

13. Jesse Griffin to parents, St. Stephens, September 5, 1813, Jesse Griffin Manuscript Letter, W. S. Hoole Special Collections Library, University of Alabama, Tuscaloosa.

14. Austill, "Life of Margaret Ervin Austill," 97.

15. Captain Blue's troops were transferred from Mobile Point; Claiborne to ———, September 6, 1813, in Letterbook F, J.F.H. Claiborne Collection, MDAH. Of the 20 militia forts occupied a few days earlier, only McGrew's station and Carney's stockade remained; Claiborne, *Supplement to the Washington Republican—Sept. 29, 1813* (September 30, 1813):1.

16. Holmes to Capt. Thos. Hinds, Washington, M.T., September 10, 1813, and Holmes to Doctor Lewis, Washington, M.T., September 14, 1813, ("melancholy intelligence"), in Papers of the Mississippi Territory, Executive Journal of David Holmes (February 1, 1813–1814), 334, 344, MDAH; "Postscript, Mr. William R. Cox, (surgeon's Mate in Gen. Claiborne's brigade,) arrived in town last evening from the vicinity of Fort St. Stevens, by whom we have received the following: Extract of a letter from Judge Tolmin, to General Flournoy, dated Sept 1," *Washington Republican* (September 8, 1813):2. Cox imagined Peirces' Mill had been "carried by storm." Col. John A. Watkins, "The Mississippi Panic of 1813," 487 ("I was then . . ."); Halbert and Ball, *Creek War*, 296–300.

17. Claiborne, "Extract," *Richmond Enquirer, Extra* (October 9, 1813), in Letterbook F, J.F.H. Claiborne Collection, MDAH; Toulmin, "Indian Warfare"; Grant, *Letters, Journals and Writings*, 664–66, and *ASP, Indian Affairs*, 1:853. According to Stiggins, Ikanachaki alternatively meant "sacred or beloved ground"; "Historical narration," 67.

The Choctaw town of Nanifalia was located in the vicinity of modern-day Nanafalia, Alabama, a community in Marengo County, on the east side of the lower Tombigbee River.

The name means "long hill" and was applied to a region, "the hills of *Nanna Falaya*," visited by Bernard Romans in 1772; see Romans, *A Concise Natural History of East and West Florida*, 281; Halbert, "Choctaw Indian Names in Alabama and Mississippi," 69; William A. Read, *Indian Place Names in Alabama*, 44.

18. Stiggins, "Historical narration," 67–70 (quotes). On population and casualties, see a discussion in Saunt, *New Order of Things*, 270, esp. n.125; Paredes and Plante, "Reëxamination of Creek Indian Population Trends," 15–18.

19. Grant, *Letters, Journals and Writings*, 652, 663, 674.

20. On James Walsh, see Stiggins, "Historical narration," 82. Josiah Francis, the Old King, Old Interpreter, and Mougceweihche to Governor González Manrique [August 1813], Papeles procedentes de la Isla de Cuba, PKY.

21. 1810 U.S. Census of Population, January 28, 1811, Mississippi Territory, Aggregates, *U.S. Decennial Census Publications*.

22. Claiborne, Extract, *Richmond Enquirer, Extra* (October 9, 1813), in Letterbook F, J.F.H. Claiborne Collection, MDAH; Flournoy to Claiborne, St. Stephens, October 12, 1813, in Interesting Papers . . . by Col John F. H. Claiborne, Pickett Papers, ADAH ("All negroes"); Governor Claiborne, Circular to Colonels of Militia, New Orleans, Sept. 8, 1813, in Rowland, *Official Letter Books of W.C.C. Claiborne*, vol. 6, *1801–1816*, 265 ("discipline"); Neal Smith, "Letter of Dr. N. Smith to the Rev. James Smylie"; Frank L. Owsley, Jr., "The Fort Mims Massacre," 202.

23. Grant, *Letters, Journals and Writings*, 664–66 (first quote), 670; "Report of Col Pearsons Expedition Against the Hostile Creeks on the Alabama . . . June 1st 1814, Enclosure in Pinckney to Secretary of War, June 28, 1814, Letters Received by the Secretary of War, (M221, roll 65, P27), RG 107, NARA. In 1815, Euphrasie Lacoste of Bon Secour filed a compensation claim with the federal government for $280 "Cash paid to the Indians to redeem 13 slaves" during the Redstick War; Lackey, *Frontier Claims*, 66; Lowrie and Clarke, *ASP, Indian Affairs*, 1:853–55; Wright, *Creeks and Seminoles*, 173; Karl Davis, "'Remember Fort Mims,'" 633.

24. Tacitus, "For the Washington Republican" (quotes).

25. This previously unpublished report is reproduced here in its entirety. Major Joseph Kennedy and Captain Uriah Blue to General Claiborne, Mt. Vernon, September 9, 1813, in Interesting Papers . . . by Col John F. H. Claiborne, Pickett Papers, ADAH.

26. In the eighteenth century, Creek men cut the cartilage of their outer ear, stretched it into a large hoop, and wrapped it with copper or silver wire. By the early nineteenth century, they merely perforated the ear lobe and outer ear for suspension of earbobs and other small ornaments. See Adair, *History of the American Indians*, 202–3.

On the ball game, see Albert James Pickett, "Conversations with George S. Gaines," in James P. Pate, ed., *The Reminiscences of George Strother Gaines, Pioneer and Statesman of Early Alabama and Mississippi, 1805–1843*, 136. Gaines quoted Pushmataha, the Choctaw leader: "You know the Tensaw people—they were our friends. We have played ball with them & whenever we journeyed to Pensacola we stoped at their houses and they fed us. What has become of these good people. Most all of them killed in one day in that [large] slaughter pen. Their Bones ly there now."

Major Beasley and other senior officers at Fort Mims may have purchased some elements of uniforms on their own, in Natchez or Mobile.

27. Ferdinand Claiborne to Brig. Gen. Flournoy, Mount Vernon, 21st Sept. 1813, Ferdinand Leigh Claiborne Papers, ADAH. Also see Holmes to Claiborne, Washington, MT, September 13, 1813; Holmes to Lt. Col. Stocket, Washington, MT, September 13, 1813; Holmes to Capt. I. G. Richardson, 4th Wilkinson Troop of Cavalry, Washington, MT, September 14, 1813; Holmes to Sec. of War John Armstrong, Washington, MT, September 14, 1813; Holmes to Doct. Lewis, Washington, MT, September 14, 1813; Holmes to Maj. Thomas Hinds, Washington, MT, September 28, 1813; Holmes to Gen. Jackson, Washington, MT, September 29, 1813; Holmes to Jackson, Washington, MT, October 5 1813, all in Papers of the Mississippi Territory, RG 2, Executive Journal of Governor David Holmes (1813–14), MDAH.

28. Claiborne to Capt. J. P. Kennedy, Brigade Major, Mount Vernon, September 22, 1813 (quotes), in Letterbook F, J.F.H. Claiborne Collection , MDAH; Notes of Doctor Thomas G. Holmes, Pickett Papers, ADAH.

29. Kennedy to Claiborne, Mount Vernon, September 26, 1813, in Letterbook F, J.F.H. Claiborne Collection, MDAH.

30. Zachariah McGirth told Robert James he accompanied Kennedy's burial party and helped collect "the bodies of a woman & eight children comprising his family [so he thought] and buried them in the general vault—a hole." Notes taken from the lips of Col Robert James, Pickett Papers, ADAH.

31. Notes of Doctor Thomas G. Holmes (quote), ibid. Halbert related an impression of the battlefield from "an aged survivor" of the burial party: "Everywhere could be seen the evidence of terrific strife; Ten feet from where stood the eastern gate, and on the northern side of the road leading thereto, stood a persimmon tree about a foot in diameter, the trunk of which all around was absolutely riddled with bullets, showing how terrible and desperate had been the fire of both besieged and besiegers." Halbert's informant described how "the soldiers dug two large pits in the potato patch, one about forty yards southwest of the fort, the other about thirty yards south of this. The soldiers then dragged the bodies to these pits and threw them in. About midday the burial task was finished." Henry S. Halbert, The burial of the dead at Fort Mims, March 3, 1887, in Series YY: Tecumseh Papers, Draper, WHS.

32. Tacitus, "For the Washington Republican," and T. [Tacitus], "Questions, Answers, Remarks"; Claiborne, "To the Editor of Mississippi Republican."

33. Peter A. Brannon, ed., "Journal of James A. Tait for the Year 1813," 232; Grant, Letters, Journals and Writings, 664–65; Jackson to the Tennessee Volunteers, Sept. 24, 1813, in Harold D. Moser and Sharon McPherson, eds., The Papers of Andrew Jackson, 2:428; Events of the War, Weekly Register (October 16, 1813):117.

34. Governor Claiborne to Flournoy, St. Tammany Parish, September 17, 1813, in Rowland, Official Letter Books of W.C.C. Claiborne, 6:268–69.

35. Claiborne, "Extract," Richmond Enquirer, Extra ("Col. Hawkins' . . . "), in Letterbook F, J.F.H. Claiborne Collection, MDAH; Events of the War, Weekly Register (September 4, 1813):7, (October 16, 1813):117; Toulmin, "Indian Warfare"; Holmes to Armstrong, Washington, MT, September 14, 1813, in Papers of the Mississippi Territory, RG 2, Executive Journal of Governor David Holmes, MDAH; Claiborne to Toulmin, Mount Vernon, September 12, 1813 ("Civil War story"), and Judge W. C. Mead to Claiborne, Baton Rouge, September 26, 1813 (final quotes), in Letterbook F, J.F.H. Claiborne Collection, MDAH.

36. [Dr. John Shaw], "Extract from the New Military Dictionary."

37. Tacitus, "For the Washington Republican."

38. T. ["Tacitus"], "Questions, Answers, Remarks."

39. Claiborne, [An Address] To the Public, n.d. ("vindicate" to "errors"), and Certification by W. R. Chambliss, Lieut. Miss. Volunteers, July 16, 1814, in Letterbook F, J.F.H. Claiborne Collection, MDAH. One of the Volunteers, "To Gen. F. L. Claiborne, Mobile, May 2, 1814"; Claiborne, "To Editor of Mississippi Republican," 2 (final quote). General Claiborne died on March 22, 1815, at his home, Soldier's Retreat; Died, *Richmond Enquirer* (April 26, 1815):3. His son-in-law, John H. B. Latrobe, painted a watercolor of Soldier's Retreat during a visit in 1834; Samuel Wilson, Jr., ed., *Southern Travels: Journal of John H. B. Latrobe, 1834,* facing p. 43, 63–64. The house no longer stands.

The general left his family burdened by debts he incurred during the campaign against the Holy Ground. Governor Claiborne comforted his widowed sister-in-law as they together endeavored to save Soldier's Retreat from creditors: "Your esteemed Husband although not favored by Fortune bequested to his children an incalculable heritage. He left them the example of a Life well passed, and exclusively devoted to honorable perseverity. Be it your care to rear them up in knowledge and let it be theirs to emulate their Father's virtues." W.C.C. Claiborne to Magdalene Claiborne, August 20, 1815, Claiborne Letters, Magdalene H. Claiborne Collection, University of North Carolina, Chapel Hill.

Chapter 8

1. Grant, *Letters, Journals and Writings,* 201, 665, 667, 675; *ASP, Indian Affairs,* 1:853–84. Barney O'Riley was the son of trader John O'Riley and a Taskigi woman; Frank, *Creeks and Southerners,* 30.

2. Extract of a Letter, Mount Vernon, Feb. 10, 1814, *Washington Republican* (February 23, 1814):2; Notes taken from the lips of Col Robert James, Pickett Papers, ADAH (quotes); Grant, *Letters, Journals and Writings,* 673, 681; *ASP, Indian Affairs,* 1:855, 857; Pickett, *History of Alabama,* 2:338. On his last two rides, McGirth carried correspondence between Colonel Russell and General Floyd. James Cornells, while riding "an express from Fort Madison to Floyd's Army" in November, narrowly evaded a Redstick party, who fired upon and chased him to the Alabama River; Henry S. Halbert, "Creek War Incidents," 101.

3. Halbert and Ball, *Creek War,* 219–22; Claiborne to Flournoy, St. Stephens, October 22, 1813 (text quotes), in Letterbook F, J.F.H. Claiborne Collection, MDAH. Several other Redstick probes into the Forks in October are described in Halbert, "Creek War Incidents," 104–7. According to Claiborne, the skirmish took place near Tallahatta Creek on October 12, and he found "one Indian who was killed in that action"; Claiborne to Peter Isler, Camp Pine Level, October 29, 1813, in Letterbook F, ibid.

According to Jeremiah Austill, Claiborne's men derisively dubbed his ineffective march around the Forks the Potato Expedition for the sweet potatoes that constituted the bulk of their provisions during that week. Isaac Heaton (or Hayden), of Fort Sinquefield fame, "was shot through the mouth cutting his tong nearly in two and loosing several of his teeth on each side. This hapened in camp going for watter—not an Indian was seen upon the expedition that I am apprised of." Notes furnished by Col Jeremiah Austill, Pickett Papers, ADAH.

4. The precise date of this episode remains in doubt. It occurred between October 22 and November 1, when Claiborne moved his command to Pine Level. Holmes to Hinds, Washington, MT, November 9, 1813, in Papers of the Mississippi Territory, RG 2, Executive Journal of Governor David Holmes, 394, MDAH. Service records for Hinds' battalion compiled late in 1814 list 22 African-American waiters and private servants accompanying the officers, an extraordinary number reflecting the wealth and high social status of battalion officers. See Compiled Service Records of Volunteer Soldiers Who Served during the War of 1812 in Organizations from the Territory of Mississippi (M678, rolls 13–15), RG 94, NARA. For accounts of this little-known massacre, see Claiborne to Holmes, East Bank of the Alabama, November 21, 1813, in Letterbook F, J.F.H. Claiborne Collection, MDAH; John Griffing Jones, *A Complete History of Methodism as Connected with the Mississippi Conference of the Methodist Episcopal Church, South*, 319–20 ("Indian hunt"); final quotes from *Washington Republican* (November 24, 1813):3; Pickett, *History of Alabama*, 2:319; Rowland, ed., *History of Mississippi*, 460–61; Owsley, *Struggle for the Gulf Borderlands*, 46. I am indebted to Sue Moore for noting the significance of this event.

5. Quotes from Notes furnished by Col Jeremiah Austill, Pickett Papers, ADAH. Austill described Caesar as "a Black or Dark Middle Sized Free Negro who lived with the freindly Indians." Also see Claiborne to Isler, November 25, 1813, in Letterbook F, J.F.H. Claiborne Collection, MDAH; Pickett, *History of Alabama*, 2:306–13; Woodward, *Reminiscences*, 75; Halbert and Ball, *Creek War*, 231–34; Jeremiah Austill, [Autobiography].

According to J.F.H. Claiborne, Sam Dale said he killed Will Milfort, the métis son of Louis le Clerc Milfort and Jennet McGillivray, in a skirmish among the canebrakes just prior to the Canoe Fight. He also identified the "chief" of Austill's account as "Tar-cha-chee, a noted wrestler, and the most famous ball-player of his clan." See Claiborne, *Life and Times of Gen. Sam. Dale*, 119–27.

Caesar furnished the Volunteers and militia with canoes. According to Austill, he lived near the scene of the fight with the family of Creek métis Josiah Fisher, "who had taken protection in our Fort [Madison]" and with whom he remained "until his death about Ten years after the Canoe fight." Austill to Lyman C. Draper, Clarke County, Alabama, July 11, 1854, Draper, WHS; Pickett, *History of Alabama*, 2:307–12; Halbert and Ball, *Creek War*, 206–7. Halbert gave a very different account of Caesar's later years, stating he was purchased some years after the war by Sam Dale, then sold to a family in Lauderdale County, Mississippi, in 1843, and died in Kemper County in 1866. See Halbert, "Creek War Incidents," 98.

6. Halbert and Ball, *Creek War*, 241–42. The Monroe County community of Claiborne occupies the site of Fort Claiborne.

7. Jackson to the Tennessee Volunteers, September 24, 1813, in Moser and McPherson, *Papers of Andrew Jackson*, 2:428.

8. From a 1797 statement by Richard Thomas, General Clerk of Georgia, in Foster, *Collected Works*, 250.

9. These battles occurred on November 3 (Tallusahatchee), 9 (Talladega), and 18 (Hillabee towns). Jackson, "To Gov. Blount, With the Creek Indians, November 4, 1813 ("retaliated"); Daniel C. Sanders, *A History of the Indian Wars*, 189; Halbert and Ball, *Creek War*, 269–73; Owsley, *Struggle for the Gulf Borderlands*, 61–71. Also see Vernon James Knight, Jr., "Fort Leslie and Upper Creek Ceramics of the Early Nineteenth Century."

David Crockett wrote a famous account of the battle at Tallusahatchee, where he saw 46 Redsticks burned inside a single structure. The Tennesseans found a cellar beneath that building, full of sweet potatoes cooked from "the oil of the Indians we had burned up on the day before"; *Narrative*, 88–89.

10. Grant, *Letters, Journals and Writings*, 700. By the end of 1814, Hawkins had 100 Creek warriors at his agency, more than 600 at Coweta, and 200 more at Fort Decatur. A month later, 1,405 had enrolled as warriors "in the service of the U. States under the command of Col. Hawkins"; ibid., 711, 716–17.

11. Edmund Shackelford to Ann and Frances Shackelford, Camp Armstrong, Chata-hoocha, December 11, 1813 ("The Indians loss . . . "), National Anthropological Archives, Smithsonian Institution, Suitland, Md.; Stiggins, "Historical narration," 74–77; Halbert and Ball, *Creek War*, 273; John Floyd to Miss Mary H. Floyd, December 5, 1813, in Floyd, "Letters of John Floyd, 1813–1838," 236 ("scalps"); Owsley, *Struggle for the Gulf Borderlands*, 51–60. I thank Glen C. Beckwith for providing Sue Moore and me with a trove of information on his ancestor, Edmund Shackelford, who wrote this letter to his sisters, then living in Hanover County, Virginia.

12. Memorial quoted in Halbert and Ball, *Creek War*, 244–45; Notes taken from the lips of Dr Thos G. Holmes, Pickett Papers, ADAH; Claiborne, *Mississippi*, 328–29.

13. Lieutenant Joseph M. Wilcox to General Joseph Wilcox, Fort Claiborne, January 1, 1814, in Anonymous, *A Narrative of the Life and Death of Lieut. Joseph Morgan Wilcox, Who was Massacred by the Creek Indians, on the Alabama River, (Miss. Ter.) on the 15th of January, 1814*, 5–6.

14. Neal Smith to James Smiley, St. Stephens, January 8, 1813 [1814] ("scalps"), ADAH; Governor González Manrique to Messrs Josiah Francis, Old King, Old Interpreter and Mou-gaioulche (copy), Pensacola, September 29, 1813 ("great satisfaction"), in Letterbook F, J.F.H. Claiborne Collection, MDAH. For the letter that prompted the Spanish governor's reply, see Josiah Francis, the Old King, Old Interpreter, and Mougceweihche to González Manrique, August [1813], Papeles de Cuba (PKY microfilm roll 311). Also see Claiborne to Blount, Fort Claiborne, January 1, 1814, in Letterbook F; Stiggins, "Historical narration," 70–71; Pickett, *History of Alabama*, 2:319–25 ("parching corn"); Lewis Sewall to Claiborne, Land Office, St. Stephens, MT, January 14, 1814, in Letterbook F; Woodward, *Reminiscences*, 87–88; Clai-borne, *Life and Times of Gen. Sam. Dale*, 140–41 ("prophets" and "shivering"); Neal Smith, Letter, 2–3, ADAH; Halbert and Ball, *Creek War*, 241–65; Austill, [Autobiography], 86 (fire-hunting); Owsley, *Struggle for the Gulf Borderlands*, 46–48. On the splitting of scalps for multiple trophies, see Notes of Doctor Thomas G. Holmes, Pickett Papers, ADAH.

There seems to have been a second town, Pintlala or "Prophet's Town," at or near Moniac's plantation, where the Americans burned 50 to 60 houses. Wilcox to Wilcox, January 1, 1814, in *Narrative of the Life and Death of Lieut. Joseph Morgan Wilcox*, 6.

According to Weatherford's relative Robert James, "Weatherford's wife became sick while he was encamped at the Holy Ground & hearing of the approach of Claiborne, he removed her to the Autauga side, 2 miles, now in the Dutch Bend & placed her in a tent. two days after the battle she died. Taking his only child, about 12 months old his rifle & a little negro girl named Abigail he departed on his Grey steed for the Hickory Ground settlements"; Notes taken from the lips of Col Robert James, Pickett Papers, ADAH. Later, convincing testimony refutes the apparently romanticized notion that Supalamy, Weatherford's second wife, died after the battle at Holy Ground; instead, Weatherford divorced her in 1816. Just as Weatherford's marriage to Supalamy signified his commitment to the Redstick cause, his abandonment of her symbolized his abandonment of the Redstick movement. See Weatherford vs. Weatherford, especially Testimony of Susan Sizemore, February 26, 1847, Mobile County Chancery Court, University of South Alabama Archives, Mobile.

15. Rowland, *Mississippi Territory in the War of 1812,* 77 (quote); Dunbar Rowland, "Military History of Mississippi, 1803–1898," 392. Early in 1813, Governor Holmes asserted that "From the time the detachment were bound to serve I have always believed that they were entitled in justice to a blanket each if not six months clothing; . . . some have received blankets from the public while others have furnished themselves." Holmes to Claiborne, Washington, M.T., February 20, 1813, p. 262, in Papers of the Mississippi Territory, Executive Journal of Governor David Holmes, MDAH.

16. I speculate that the undated letter was found among Weatherford's possessions at the Holy Ground. A penciled note on this letter states only that it was "Obtained during the Creek War by Gen. Claiborne." Reference to "two powerful armes in our country" probably refers to the Tennessee and Georgia armies that retreated in November before Claiborne's campaign began. John Durant to Alickander [Sandy] Durant "at the Apperlachcola," n.d., Ferdinand Leigh Claiborne Papers, ADAH. Judging from the Durant and Griffin letters, punctuation was considered superfluous by correspondents on the Creek frontier.

17. The following letter to General Claiborne expresses a sentiment widely held by his American contemporaries, who generally regarded the prophets' movement with contempt:

> The more I reflect on the consequences likely to result from your late expedition to the "Holy ground" on the Alabama, the more I am impress'd with its importance. . . . The Imposters (Colo. Hawkin's "prophets") who had gain'd . . . an extraordinary ascendancy over the minds of the Indians unfriendly to civilization, will exert this influence no more! The *Unhallowed* footsteps of your troops have profaned the *Sanctuary,* and the *sacrifice* of the *"Prophets,"* is necessary for an *atonement!* Religious superstitions form a powerful *bond of union* among the Ignorant and unenlighten'd, and approaches their minds with more facility than reason. . . . The *fallacy* of the Prophesies being clearly established by the defeat of the Indians, and destruction of their "Holy Towns" by your troops, will produce such a despondency, as must terminate in their Submission, or total *abandonment* of the country.

From Lewis Sewall to Claiborne, St. Stephens, January 13, 1814, in Letterbook F, J.F.H. Claiborne Collection, MDAH.

After the Redstick defeat at Horseshoe Bend, John, Sandy, and Betsy Durant followed McQueen to east-central Florida. Sandy died at Tampa Bay soon afterwards; John went to Nassau, in the Bahamas. See Woodward, *Reminiscences,* 38, 40.

18. Stiggins, "Historical narration," 78 (quotes); Owsley, *Struggle for the Gulf Borderlands,* 56, 73. Just two weeks after his defeat at the Holy Ground, Josiah Francis was in Pensacola, where he sent a message to the commander of a British fleet anchored off St. George's Island, at the mouth of the Apalachicola River:

We the Chiefs of the red Stick Nation beg Leave to adress You these few Lines . . . Our Case is really miserable and lamentable, driven from House and Home without Food and Clothes to cover our Bodies by disasters and an Enemy who has sworn our Ruin, . . . Our Spirits begone allready to sink, . . . We have already send a Letter to His Grace the Duke of Manchester, Governor of Jamaica, by the same Hand who writtes this Letter, but before the begining of our Misfortune stating Our Want of Arms and Powder and other Articles to cary on a vigorous War, but We till now recived no Answer. . . . We have hopes to gett Relive in our present miserable Condition, as We have determined to make no Peace with the United States of America without the britisch Government Consent.

The letter bears the marks of "Yahollasaptko," "Hopoyhisck Yaholla," and "Joshea francis." Chiefs of the Red Stick Nation to the Commanding Officer of His Britannick Magesty Forces, Panzacola, January 9, 1814, Papers of Admiral Cochrane, PKY microfilm reel 65M, 1:28–28v.

19. Pickett, *History of Alabama*, 2:329–35 (quote); Halbert and Ball, *Creek War*, 273–74; Owsley, *Struggle for the Gulf Borderlands*, 73–76. Many town, stream, and battle locations are placed erroneously on the maps in Owsley's book. He and many other modern authors apparently have not realized that the Redstick strongholds at Emuckfau and Horseshoe Bend were one and the same.

20. Stiggins, "Historical narration," 78–81; Pickett, *History of Alabama*, 2:336–39; Owsley, *Struggle for the Gulf Borderlands*, 57–59. Woodward, a member of the Georgia Militia at Calebee Creek, recalled overhearing Redstick warriors "asking each other to 'give me some bullets—give me powder.'" He added, "Jim Boy and Billy McDonald, or Billy McGillivray, as he was best known, said that they had between 1800 and 2000 men; but many of them were without guns, and only had war-clubs and bows and arrows"; Woodward, *Reminiscences*, 88–89.

21. Brannon, ed., "Journal of James A. Tait," 236–37.

22. Extract of a Letter to the Editors, Mount Vernon, Feb. 10, 1814, *Washington Republican* (February 23, 1814):2; Stiggins, "Historical narration," 81; Owsley, *Struggle for the Gulf Borderlands*, 49–50.

23. Stiggins, "Historical narration," 81–82; Pickett, *History of Alabama*, 2:339–46; Halbert and Ball, *Creek War*, 275–77 (quote); Owsley, *Struggle for the Gulf Borderlands*, 78–83; Joel W. Martin, "'My Grandmother Was a Cherokee Princess': Representations of Indians in Southern History," 143. For archaeological studies of Tohopeka and the Redstick barricade, see Charles H. Fairbanks, *Excavations at Horseshoe Bend, Alabama*; Roy S. Dickens, Jr., *Archaeological Investigations at Horseshoe Bend, National Military Park, Alabama*; Gregory A. Waselkov, "A Reinterpretation of the Creek Indian Barricade at Horseshoe Bend."

24. Redstick bands continued to raid the Tensaw, harassing American settlers who reoccupied their farms for spring planting. Three whites—Gerald Byrne and two neighbors named Taylor and Hatcher—and an unnamed African were killed in late April 1814 four miles north of Blakeley. See "Mr Byrne's account of the Death of his father," Pickett Papers, ADAH.

In the winter of 1814–15, Dr. Thomas G. Holmes accompanied 170 troops of the 39th U.S.

Infantry and 300 Chickasaw warriors commanded by Major Uriah Blue on a march to intercept a band of Alabama Redsticks encamped on the east bank of the Yellow River. Blue's force surrounded the Redsticks who were "engaged in the war dance." When one of his force shouted to the Redsticks in Muskogee to surrender, their leader "the old Alabama King" replied, "die first!" The Americans and Chickasaws fired, killing 30 and taking another 70 prisoner, including the Alabama King, who was tomahawked to death and scalped later in the day by Captain Brown commanding a company of Chickasaws. Quotes from Notes taken from the lips of Dr. Thos. G. Holmes, Pickett Papers, ADAH. This incident exemplifies the ferocity of the continuing war between the Americans and surviving Redsticks in West Florida and southeastern Mississippi Territory after the latter's presumably definitive defeat at Horseshoe Bend. Another notable battle involved nearly 600 Redsticks and escaped slaves who participated in an unsuccessful British naval and land assault on Fort Bowyer, at Mobile Point, in mid-September 1814. The full story of this late phase of the Redstick War remains to be chronicled by historians.

25. For a list of Creek towns destroyed in the war, see Waselkov and Wood, "Creek War," 12–14. For counts of refugees, see Grant, *Letters, Journals and Writings,* 680–81; Bassett, *Correspondence of Andrew Jackson,* 2:24–25; Letter of May 15, 1814, Graham Papers, NCDCR; Andrew Jackson Papers, Military Papers, 4:874, 893, Library of Congress.

A version of Weatherford's speech that circulated in newspapers within months brought him immediate fame throughout the United States. On June 8, 1814, the *Washington Republican* repeated the following story (apparently based on John Reid's account of the speech) from a Nashville paper, under the headline "Indian Eloquence."

The following is a specimen of that bold eloquence which nature seldom bestows, and which still less seldom bursts forth from the uncultivated mind. Wetherford, the speaker, has been thro' this war one of the most active and enterprising chiefs. As a partizan leader he has frequently opposed his enemy where he was little expected. Seeing that it was in vain any longer to resist, he voluntarily came in and delivered himself up: in a private interview with general Jackson, he made the following short, though forcible and bold address, which was forwarded by a person who was present:

"I fought at fort Mims; I fought the Georgia army; I did you all the injury I could; had I been supported as I was promised, I would have done you more. But my warriors are all killed, I can fight you no longer. I look back with sorrow, that I have brought destruction on my nation. I am now in your power, do with me as you please, I am a soldier."

For some accounts of Weatherford's surrender, see Reid and Eaton, *The Life of Andrew Jackson,* 165; Pickett, *History of Alabama,* 2:347–51; Woodward, *Reminiscences,* 79–81, 89; Eggleston, *Red Eagle,* 333–42; Driesbach, "Weatherford—'The Red Eagle'"; Halbert and Ball, *Creek War,* 284–85; William Gates Orr, "Surrender of Weatherford"; Owsley, *Struggle for the Gulf Borderlands,* 83–85. Woodward thought Benjamin Hawkins had sent word to Weatherford through his cousin Sam Moniac that he could come in safely to treat with Jackson.

26. Pickett, *History of Alabama,* 2:350–51 ("surrender"); Woodward, *Reminiscences,* 81;

Meek, *Romantic Passages,* 287–89; Eggleston, *Red Eagle,* 342 ("year"); Griffith, *McIntosh and Weatherford,* 155.

27. General Joseph Graham to Jackson, near Fort Jackson, June 7, 1814, Correspondence, Graham Papers, NCDCR; quotes from "Report of Col Pearsons Expedition Against the Hostile Creeks on the Alabama," enclosure in Pinckney to Secretary of War, June 28, 1814, Letters Received by the Secretary of War (M221, roll 65, P27), RG 107, NARA. I am most grateful to James Parker for sharing this important documentation of Weatherford's whereabouts after his surrender in April.

28. Weatherford seems to have been haunted by the final stages of the battle at Fort Mims. According to his relative Robert James, "He did not like to allude much to the fall of Fort Mims, but wuld sometimes talk to his intimate friends about it & regret the destruction of the women & children & observe that he endeavoured to restrain his warriors & save their lives but could not"; Notes taken from the lips of Col Robert James, Pickett Papers, ADAH. Also see Woodward, *Reminiscences,* 81; Claiborne, *Life and Times of Gen. Sam. Dale,* 128–29. According to Dale (via Claiborne), "[William Weatherford] often deplored to me his inability to arrest the carnage on that occasion; 'but my warriors,' said he, 'were like famished wolves, and the first taste of blood made their appetites insatiable.'"

29. "A party of American horsemen about 40 (no Choctaws) headed by Colonel Carson, and joined by Wm Weatherford an Indian Chief, are pursuing the Creek Indians and are Killing them wherever they meet them, they were yesterday at Mr. Marshalls about 16 miles off, the other side of this [Escambia] Bay, and Killed 7 or 8 Indians there, they then went to Mr. Millers Plantation but did no damage there. they have also attackd a new Indian settlement called Coneta, and Killed all the Indians they could lay hands on, have taken what Women & Children could be found." In [?] to Lieutenant Jackson of the Cockchafer, Pensacola, June 9, 1814, Papers of Admiral Cochrane (PKY microfilm roll 65M), 1:31v–32) (endnote and text quotes); cited in Reid and Eaton, *Life of Jackson,* xxxi–xxxii, and Saunt, *New Order of Things,* 277n.16. Thomas Holmes described the same events to Pickett but did not mention the presence of William Weatherford; Notes taken from the lips of Dr Thos G. Holmes, Pickett Papers, ADAH.

30. Notes taken from the lips of Col Robert James, Pickett Papers, ADAH (endnote quote); Pickett, *History of Alabama,* 2:281–82.

Many years before the fall of Fort Mims an indian lad nearly starved to death, homeless & friendless caled at McGirths house. Mrs McGirth took care of him & raised him as an adopted son. He grew to be a stout athletic man & for some unaccounted cause left McGirths family & joined Weatherfords party. While the bloody malee was going in the Fort, this man was bold & active in killing the unfortunate inmates. With uplifted tomahaw[k] he was slaying the women & children when he came across his foster Mother Mrs McGirth surrounded by her children. He suddenly stoped. Pity & gratitude took possession of his savage soul. He determined to save them by claiming them as his slaves. Thrusting them in a corner, he nobly made his heart a rampart for their protection. The next morning this noble savage placed his assumed Mother & her children upon horses & carried them up among the upper Creeks at Hickory Ground. Here he maintained them for some time & guarded their persons from the assaults of the hostiles. When the indians were preparing to fight Jackson at the Horse Shoe this man told Mrs McGirth that she must take care of herself in future. He might get killed in battle & [s]he must in future provide for herself. Soon afterwards he lay among the slain at Tehopeca. Mrs McGirth now deprived of her only friend & in a hostile land took her children & fled on foot for the old Tensaw settlements.

On April 18, 1814, General Jackson wrote Governor Blount, "Many of the negroes who were taken at Ft. Mimms have been delivered up [at Fort Jackson]; and one white woman (Polly Jones) with her three children." Bassett, *Correspondence of Andrew Jackson,* 1:503.

31. Notes taken from the lips of Col Robert James, Pickett Papers, ADAH.

32. Austill, "Life of Margaret Ervin Austill," 97–98.

Chapter 9

1. Communiqué, *Courrier de la Louisiane* [Nouvelle-Orleans] (September 8, 1813):2; Events of the War, *Weekly Register* (October 16, 1813):105–7, 117; Massacre at Fort Mims and Indian Warfare, *New-York Spectator* (October 16, 1813):2, 4; Southern Border-War, Massacre at Tensaw, *The War* 2 (October 19, November 16, 1813).

2. Toulmin, "Indian Warfare," 106–7.

3. "Patriotism of Tennessee," *Weekly Register* (October 16, 1813):105 (quotes).

4. Claiborne, *Notes on the War in the South,* 23 ("fall of Fort Mims"), 43 ("reclaim," "chymerical," and "countenance"), 44 ("reason"), 46 (long quote). Three of the earliest histories of the Redstick War consist essentially of letters and reports of American participants quoted at length. See T. H. Palmer, *The Historical Register of the United States,* 1:118–32, 328–47; J. Russell, *The History of the War between the United States and Great Britain,* 233–35; Sanders, *History of the Indian Wars,* 187–96.

5. This enormous topic is discussed in many excellent references. Among the more important are William Penn [pseudonym for Jeremiah Evarts], *Essays on the Present Crisis in the Condition of the American Indians;* Francis Paul Prucha, "Andrew Jackson's Indian Policy: A Reassessment"; Rogin, *Fathers and Children;* Green, *The Politics of Indian Removal.*

6. "Excluded" and "invisible from Steven Conn, *History's Shadow: Native Americans and Historical Consciousness in the Nineteenth Century,* 1–2, based on David Levering Lewis, *W. E. B. DuBois: Biography of a Race,* 72.

7. [Lewis Sewall], *The Last Campaign of Sir John Falstaff the II; or, The Hero of the Burnt-Corn Battle, A Heroi-Comic Poem,* 14–15 (first verse), 19–20 (final verses). For a modern literary criticism, see Philip D. Beidler, "Literature and the Art of Political Payback in an Early Alabama Classic," and *First Books: The Printed Word and Cultural Formation in Early Alabama,* 14–22, 154n.18 (final quote).

8. Beidler, *First Books,* 32–46 ("romantic stature"); "Don Pedro Casender" [M. Smith?], *The Lost Virgin of the South: An Historical Novel, Founded on Facts, Connected with the Indian War in the South, in 1812 to '15.*

9. Sewall, *Miscellaneous Poems,* 29–33.

10. Once again I am indebted to Sue Moore, in this instance for tracking down this long overlooked early work of Alabama literature. Charles L. S. Jones, *American Lyrics; Compris-*

ing the Discovery, A Poem; Sapphic, Pindaric and Common Odes; Songs and Tales on American and Patriotic Subjects, and also Imitations from the Greek, Latin, French, and Spanish, 152–53 (quote). Also see Jacqueline Anderson Matte, *The History of Washington County: First County in Alabama*, 50.

11. For Cornells' accusation of Beasley's drunkenness, see Woodward, *Reminiscences*, 86; poetic quote from Jones, *American Lyrics*, 152; final quotes from West, *History of Methodism in Alabama*, 84.

12. Mims family sacraments documented in Marriage Book 1:186 (Act. 186); Baptisms Book 2:3 (Act. 4), 57 (Act. 146), 85 (Act. 213), 89 (Act. 224), 108 (Act. 269), Cathedral of the Immaculate Conception, Mobile. Notes taken from the lips of Hiram Mounger . . . by Col J Austill (quotes) and Notes taken from the lips of Mr George S. Gaines, Pickett Papers, ADAH (final quotes).

13. Poetic quotes from [Henry Rowe Schoolcraft], *Alhalla, or the Lord of Talladega. A Tale of the Creek War*.

14. The expulsion of Acadians eerily anticipated in many details the tragedy of Indian Removal nearly a century later. Poet Henry Wadsworth Longfellow's immensely popular idyll, *Evangeline, A Tale of Acadie* (1847), spellbound a portion of the American public already outraged by the Cherokees' Trail of Tears and eager to identify with similarly mistreated white settlers oppressed by British imperialism. See John Mack Faragher, *A Great and Noble Scheme: The Tragic Story of the Expulsion of the French Acadians from Their American Homeland*.

15. Pickett, *History of Alabama*, 1:viii–x ("a History"); Michael O'Brien, *Conjectures of Order: Intellectual Life and the American South, 1810–1860*, 2:631–36.

16. Pickett, *History of Alabama*, passim ("savages," "heathens," "half-breed"). See Harper Lee, "Romance and High Adventure," 13–20 ("dramatic pacing"); Beidler, *First Books*, 63–75. For one influential popular author who relied on Pickett's account of the battle at Fort Mims, see Benson J. Lossing, "Scenes in the War of 1812, War with the Creek Indians," and *The Pictorial Field-Book of the War of 1812*, 738–82.

17. Pickett, *History of Alabama*, 2:270 ("soon the field . . . sand . . . "). See fort map in *Washington Republican* (Wednesday, December 1, 1813); Notes of Doctor Thomas G. Holmes ("rushed"), Pickett Papers, ADAH. For other contemporary mentions of the eastern gate, see Grant, *Letters, Journals and Writings*, 667, and Hawkins, "Extract of a Letter to John Floyd," in which "[William Samuel] Jones . . . says that they had not time to shut the fort gate." Also see Woodward, *Reminiscences*, 86 ("The Fort gate was open and could not be shut."). For modern misinterpretations of Pickett's account, see Davis, "'Remember Fort Mims,'" 631 ("Red Stick sympathizers"); Richter, *Facing East from Indian Country*, 232 ("sandbags").

18. Pickett, *History of Alabama*, 2:266 ("five hundred and fifty-three souls"), 276 ("all were killed"). Also see Notes of Doctor Thomas G. Holmes, and Notes taken from the lips of Dr Thos G. Holmes, Pickett Papers, ADAH. Even Henry Halbert, who was highly critical of Pickett in other matters, accepted Pickett's figure of 500 dead inside the fort; Halbert and Ball, *Creek War*, 157, 162–63; Frank L. Owsley, Jr., "Editor's Notes," ibid., 339. For a recent use of an inflated casualty figure, see Susan K. Barnard and Grace M. Schwartzman, "Tecumseh and the Creek Indian War of 1813–1814 in North Georgia," 499–500.

19. Chambliss' Certificate, and Claiborne to Col. Carson, Mount Vernon, September 4,

1813 ("how many"), in Letterbook F, J.F.H. Claiborne Collection, MDAH; Toulmin, "Indian Warfare," 106 (final quote).

Samuel D. Carrick interviewed eyewitnesses at St. Stephens and concluded there had been between 350 and 400 people inside Fort Mims, counting those who escaped or were taken captive; Owsley, "Editor's Notes," 339–40. George Stiggins thought the occupants numbered 340; "Historical narration," 64. See also Claiborne to ——, September 6, 1813, in Letterbook F, J.F.H. Claiborne Collection, MDAH; Flournoy to Willie Blount, Bay St. Louis, Sept. 15, 1813, Letters Received by the Secretary of War (M221, roll 50, B333), RG 107, NARA; Grant, *Letters, Journals and Writings,* 667, and Hawkins, "Extract of a Letter"; Governor Claiborne, Circular to Colonels of Militia, New Orleans, Sept. 8, 1813, in Rowland, *Official Letter Books of W.C.C. Claiborne,* 6:265. The only early high estimate, "nearly six hundred souls," emanated from an anti-Claiborne writer calling himself "Tacitus," whose letters appeared in the *Washington Republican* throughout late 1813; T. [Tacitus], "Questions, Answers, Remarks."

20. Claiborne to Carson, Mount Vernon, September 4, 1813, and Claiborne to ——, September 6, 1813, in Letterbook F, J.F.H. Claiborne Collection, MDAH; Stiggins, "Historical narration," 60, 64–65 (quotes); J. D. Dreisbach to Lyman Draper, July 1874, Draper, WHS; Grant, *Letters, Journals and Writings,* 663–65, 667, and Hawkins, "Extract of a Letter."

21. Owsley, "Editor's Notes." Overall losses in the fort were at first estimated at "upwards of two hundred persons killed"; Claiborne to ——, September 6, 1813, in Letterbook F, J.F.H. Claiborne Collection, MDAH. Zach McGirth thought he saw 250 bodies during his twilight tour of the battlefield; Notes taken from the lips of Col Robert James, Pickett Papers, ADAH. Holmes recalled "over four hundred persons" interred in the mass graves; Notes of Doctor Thomas G. Holmes, Pickett Papers, ADAH. Judge Toulmin's calculations placed the number of dead at around 300, a figure generally used in official correspondence throughout the rest of the Redstick War; "Indian Warfare," 106. See Appendix 1 of this book for information on individuals known to have died at Fort Mims.

22. Statements exaggerating the scale and nature of the massacre at Fort Mims have appeared most commonly in popular literature, not scholarly historical works. For instance, see Bryant, *Oh God, What Have I Done,* i ("the worst massacre that ever occurred on American soil"); Sean Michael O'Brien, *In Bitterness and in Tears: Andrew Jackson's Destruction of the Creeks and Seminoles,* xv ("the worst frontier massacre in U.S. history").

23. Meek, *The Red Eagle: A Poem of the South,* 14–15 (quote). His later works of prose and poetry, *Romantic Passages* and *Songs and Poems of the South,* contain little original information useful to the historian. Anonymous, "Editorial Notes—Literature." See Philip D. Beidler, "A. B. Meek's Great American Epic Poem of 1855; or, the Curious Career of the Red Eagle," and *First Books,* 76–86; O'Brien, *Conjectures of Order,* 2:722–24; Gordon M. Sayre, *The Indian Chief as Tragic Hero: Native Resistance and the Literatures of America, from Moctezuma to Tecumseh.*

In *Redstick: Or, Scenes in the South,* B. R. Montesano poked bawdy fun at Meek's epic pretensions by setting the opening of his picaresque novella in "The Spread Eagle" tavern.

24. Meek, *Red Eagle* (1914 ed.), 46–47.

25. For instance, Karl Davis, in "'Much of the Indian Appears,'" 157, suspects newspaper accounts "amplified the severity of atrocities and . . . exaggerated the deaths of Red Sticks"

at Fort Mims. For modern studies based on forensic evidence from other American contexts, see Paul W. Sciulli and Richard M. Gramly, "Analysis of the Ft. Laurens, Ohio, Skeletal Sample"; Douglas D. Scott, Richard A. Fox, Jr., Melissa A. Connor, and Dick Harmon, *Archaeological Perspectives on the Battle of the Little Big Horn*, 85–86; Maria A. Liston and Brenda J. Baker, "Reconstructing the Massacre at Fort William Henry, New York"; P. Willey and Douglas D. Scott, "'The Bullets Buzzed Like Bees': Gunshot Wounds in Skeletons from the Battle of the Little Bighorn"; Douglas D. Scott, P. Willey, and Melissa A. Connor, *They Died with Custer: Soldiers' Bones from the Battle of the Little Big Horn*, 302–17; David R. Starbuck, *The Great Warpath: British Military Sites from Albany to Crown Point*, 83–98. A remarkable study of battle-related trauma based on analysis of human remains from the War of the Roses is found in Veronica Fiorato, Anthea Boylston, and Christopher Knüsel, eds., *Blood Red Roses: The Archaeology of a Mass Grave from the Battle of Towton, AD 1461*, 90–102.

The archaeology of battlefields is a new specialized field of study with great popularity. Recent books of interest include Douglas D. Scott and Richard A. Fox, Jr., *Archaeological Insights into the Custer Battle: An Assessment of the 1984 Field Season*; Richard Allan Fox, Jr., *Archaeology, History, and Custer's Last Battle: The Little Big Horn Reexamined*; Tony Pollard and Neil Oliver, *Two Men in a Trench: Battlefield Archaeology—The Key to Unlocking the Past*, and *Two Men in a Trench II: Uncovering the Secrets of British Battlefields*; Jerome A. Greene and Douglas D. Scott, *Finding Sand Creek: History, Archeology, and the 1864 Massacre Site*.

26. Prucha, "Andrew Jackson's Indian Policy," 529, citing General Orders, September 19, 1813; see Basset, *Correspondence of Andrew Jackson*, 1:319–20 ("retaliatory vengeance"); Jackson to Willie Blount, Ft. Strother, December 29, 1813, ibid., 1:417 ("exterminate"). As Daniel Richter expresses it, "This 'Fort Mims Massacre' freed Whites to declare open season on the Red Sticks"; *Facing East from Indian Country*, 232.

27. Only two women, both Creek métis and relatives of Dixon Bailey, are known to have been eviscerated: Nancy Pounds (Mrs. James) Bailey and Sarah Summerlin.

28. On Weatherford's remorse over the slaughter of civilians, see "Report of Col Pearsons Expedition Against the Hostile Creeks on the Alabama . . . June 1st 1814," Letters Received by the Secretary of War, Registered Series, (M221, roll 65, P27), RG 107, NARA; Claiborne, *Life and Times of Gen. Sam. Dale*, 128–29. Grant, *Letters, Journals and Writings*, 667, and Hawkins, "Extract of a Letter to John Floyd"; Tacitus, "For the Washington Republican"; Floyd, "Letters of John Floyd," 236; Neal Smith to James Smiley [Amite Co.], St. Stephens, January 8, 1813 [1814], Neal Smith Collection, ADAH; Bassett, "Correspondence of Andrew Jackson," 1:504–5; Crockett, *Narrative*, 105. Saunt, *New Order of Things*, 267 (quotes). Rev. John Brown, the son of a member of the burial detail, told Halbert that "white persons, Indians, negroes, men, women and children, [were] all mutilated in every conceivable manner. The bodies of many of the women, stripped naked, were impaled on stakes driven in the ground. . . . the heads and faces of many of the slain had been bruised and crushed by the blows of the Creek war club." Henry S. Halbert, The burial of the dead at Fort Mims, March 3, 1887, in Tecumseh Papers, Draper, WHS. For references to a bounty, see Pickett, *History of Alabama*, 2:275; Benson J. Lossing, *Our Country: A Household History for All Readers*, 5:1258. Cf. David Pierce Mason, *Five Dollars a Scalp: The Last Mighty War Whoop of the Creek Indians*.

29. Eggleston, *Red Eagle*; Margaret Mitchell, *Gone With the Wind*; Odell Shepard and

Willard Shepard, *Holdfast Gaines*, 377–90; *Davy Crockett, Indian Fighter* (Burbank, Calif.: Walt Disney Studios, 1954); Max Byrd, *Jackson: A Novel.*

30. Halbert and Ball, *Creek War*, 293–94. Unfortunately this fine piece of scholarship was hardly noticed outside of Alabama and had little effect on synthetic histories until very recently. Typical of writings on the Redstick War from the mid-twentieth century is an error-ridden synopsis of the Redstick War in John Tebbel and Keith Jennison, *The American Indian Wars*, 163–79.

31. J. Anthony Paredes, "Anthropological Report on the Poarch Band of Creeks"; Anonymous, Federal Acknowledgment of the Poarch Band of Creeks; Proposed Finding, *Federal Register* 49 (January 9, 1984):1141 (quote). Also see J. Anthony Paredes, "Back from Disappearance: The Alabama Creek Indian Community," and "Kinship and Descent in the Ethnic Reservation of the Eastern Creek Indians."

32. Owsley, *Struggle for the Gulf Borderlands;* Green, *Politics of Indian Removal,* and "The Expansion of European Colonization to the Mississippi Valley, 1780–1880"; Wright, *Creeks and Seminoles.* More recently, Robert V. Remini has repackaged his 1977 analysis of the Redstick War as *Andrew Jackson and His Indian Wars;* see also his *Andrew Jackson and the Course of American Empire.*

I added an archaeological dimension to the discussion with Gregory A. Waselkov, Brian M. Wood, and Joseph M. Herbert, *Colonization and Conquest: The 1980 Archaeological Excavations at Fort Toulouse and Fort Jackson, Alabama;* Waselkov and Brian M. Wood, "The Creek War"; and Waselkov, "A Reinterpretation of the Creek Indian Barricade at Horseshoe Bend." Earlier archaeological research was accomplished by Fairbanks, "Excavations at Horseshoe Bend, Alabama," and Dickens, *Archaeological Investigations at Horseshoe Bend.*

33. Martin's book was preceded by publication of Natchez métis George Stiggins' very important manuscript on the Redstick War, with an excellent anthropological introduction, by Theron A. Nuñez, Jr., "Creek Nativism." Nuñez first identified the rise of the Redsticks as a revitalization movement with a nativistic religious basis. Also see Martin, *Sacred Revolt,* and "Cultural Contact and Crises"; Saunt, *New Order of Things* and "Taking Account of Property."

The impact of this scholarship is mixed. Some recent books on the War of 1812 nearly ignore the Redstick War altogether; see Donald R. Hickey, *The War of 1812,* 146–51; Carl Benn, *The War of 1812,* 62–63; Andrew Burstein, *The Passions of Andrew Jackson,* 97–106. On the other hand, several others include lengthy, sophisticated discussions of the Redstick War; see John Buchanan, *Jackson's Way: Andrew Jackson and the People of the Western Waters;* O'Brien, *In Bitterness and in Tears;* Walter R. Borneman, *1812: The War that Forged a Nation.*

34. Davis, "'Much of the Indian Appears.'" Davis' interpretation differs from Saunt's and mine in his insistence that many Tensaw métis sided with the Redsticks. While many prominent Redsticks had close ties of kinship to the Tensaw métis, they were not part of the Tensaw Creek community, which was uniformly pro-American during the Redstick War.

35. See Peter S. Wells, *The Barbarians Speak: How the Conquered Peoples Shaped Roman Europe,* 132, 222, 264–66. Wells describes how the ancient Romans granted citizenship in conquered territories to encourage certain behaviors of indigenous elites, while indigenous people often manipulated the Roman colonial system for their own social and political benefit. Many parallels can be drawn between his case study and American-Indian relations in

the early nineteenth century. For an explicitly comparative approach to colonial tactics and responses, see Chris Gosden, *Archaeology and Colonialism: Cultural Contact from 5000 BC to the Present.*

Chapter 10

1. "Had it not been for this unfortunate massacre, something entirely new in American Indian relations seemed close at hand"; Owsley, "Fort Mims Massacre," 204.

2. Saunt, "Taking Account of Property," 748; Waselkov, "Changing Strategies of Indian Field Location." After David Tate's death in 1829, his estate was valued at $47,982.75, an extraordinary accumulation of wealth for that era. Estate Case Files of David Tate, et al., Baldwin County Probate Case 381, ADAH.

3. Application of Sundry Half-breeds of the Creek Nation to Sell Their Reservations of Land in Alabama, and List of Claims for Such Reservations [doc. no. 539], in Asbury Dickins and James C. Allen, eds., *ASP, Public Lands*, vol. 4, *Commencing December 1, 1823, and Ending March 3, 1827*, 858–60.

4. Hawkins to Willam H. Crawford, January 19, 1816, in Grant, *Letters, Journals and Writings*, 768–69.

5. Thomas P. Abernethy, *The Formative Period in Alabama*, 50–56.

6. David Tate, "David Tate to Cadet David Moniac"; Bryant, *Tensaw Country*; Tarvin, "Muscogees or Creek Indians"; Thompson, *William Weatherford*.

7. An Act for the Relief of Samuel Manac, *U.S. Serials Set 173, House Document 200, 20th Congress, 1st Session*, 3–17 ("property destroyed"); Carter, *Territorial Papers*, vol. 18, *The Territory of Alabama, 1817–1819*, 354, 508; Tate, "David Tate to Cadet David Moniac," 407 ("what little he has"); Davis, " 'Much of the Indian Appears,' " 167–69, 174–75, 200; Woodward, *Reminiscences*, 82.

8. Records of the Bureau of Indian Affairs, Letters Received by the Office of the Secretary of War Relating to Indian Affairs, 1800–1823, Petition of Laughlin Durant & other half-breeds, Relatives of Alexr. McGilvray, a Creek Chief, May 29, 1815 (quotes), and Petition of Sundry Half breeds, enclosed in Hawkins to Secretary of War, January 19, 1816, RG 75 (M271), NARA. For the outcome of the dispute with Thomas Boyle, see Bureau of Land Management, Laughlin Durant Certificate No. 12, RG 49, NARA. Davis, " 'Much of the Indian Appears,' " 173–74, 185–86, documents a similar land grab by future Alabama governor John Gayle.

For an unusually detailed biography of a nineteenth-century métis, in this case a Cheyenne-American, see David Fridtjof Halaas and Andrew E. Masich, *Halfbreed: The Remarkable True Story of George Bent*.

9. Report of David Mitchell, Agent for Indian Affairs, December 10, 1818, Special Acts, Treaty of Fort Jackson 1814, RG 49, NARA; "Act for the Relief of Certain Creek Indians," *U.S. Serials Set 173, House Document 200, 20th Cong., 1st sess.*, 29; Walter Lowrie and Walter S. Franklin, eds., "Losses Sustained by the War with the Creek Indians, February 9, 1818 [doc. no. 386]," *ASP, Claims*, 550 (quotes).

10. Quote from "Zachariah McGirth and Samuel Bradford," June 24, 1834, and *House Bill 547, House Reports*, vol. 4, *U.S. Serials Set 263, House Document 540, 23rd Cong., 1st sess.*; Bu-

reau of Indian Affairs, Property Left in 1836 in Tallassee and Chehaw Towns, May 6, 1838, RG 75, NARA; Pickett, *History of Alabama*, 2:282; Woodward, *Reminiscences*, 97; Clanton, "Reminiscences of Ft. Mims," Clanton Papers, ADAH.

Also see "Memorial on Behalf of Sundry Individuals Belonging to the Creek Indians," February 15, 1832, *U.S. Serials Set 213, Senate Document 65*, vol. 2, *22nd Cong., 1st sess.*; Davis, "'Much of the Indian Appears," 195–202.

11. In my interpretations of the Redstick War, I have benefited from Marshall Sahlins' theoretical writings, particularly his *Apologies to Thucydides*, 7, 96, 106.

12. As historian Richard White has eloquently argued, "Americans had to transform conquerors into victims. The great military icons of American westward expansion are not victories, they are defeats: the Alamo and the Battle of the Little Bighorn [and, I would add, Fort Mims]. We, these stories say, do not plan our conquests . . . We just retaliate against barbaric massacres." White, "Frederick Jackson Turner and Buffalo Bill," in *The Frontier in American Culture*, ed. James R. Grossman, 27, quoted in Crisp, *Sleuthing the Alamo*, 164.

Afterword

1. Ethel Morgan Dunham, *Echoes of Alabama*, 5.

2. She died on my eighth birthday, in 1960.

3. "The Ballad of Davy Crockett," lyrics by Tom Blackburn (Burbank, Calif.: The Walt Disney Company, 1954). Catherine L. Albanese reviewed the earlier mythology of Crockett in "Savage, Sinner, and Saved: Davy Crockett, Camp Meetings, and the Wild Frontier."

4. Professor Lewis B. Atherton's course on frontier history at the University of Missouri greatly influenced my thinking about history, historical anthropology, and historical archaeology.

5. On anthropologically influenced reformulations of the frontier concept, see Walker D. Wyman and Clifton B. Kroeber, eds., *The Frontier in Perspective*; Joseph B. Casagrande, Stephen I. Thompson, and Philip D. Young, "Colonization as a Research Frontier: The Ecuadorian Case"; Miller and Steffen, eds., *The Frontier: Comparative Studies*. For my own application to archaeological research, see Gregory A. Waselkov, "Zumwalt's Fort: An Archaeological Study of Frontier Process"; Gregory A. Waselkov and Robert Eli Paul, "Frontiers and Archaeology."

White, *Middle Ground*, 52–53, 93. For evidence of a resurgence in interest in the frontier concept among historians, see Oatis, *Colonial Complex*, 4–9.

6. Some results of the Upper Creek Archaeology Project have appeared in Waselkov and Cottier, "European Perceptions of Eastern Muskogean Ethnicity," 23–45; Gregory A. Waselkov, ed., "Culture Change on the Creek Indian Frontier"; Waselkov and Wood, "Creek War"; Waselkov, "Reinterpretation of the Creek Indian Barricade at Horseshoe Bend"; Gregory A. Waselkov and Craig T. Sheldon, Jr., "Cataloguing and Documenting the Historic Creek Archaeological Collections of the Alabama Department of Archives and History"; Gregory A. Waselkov, John W. Cottier, and Craig T. Sheldon, Jr., "Archaeological Excavations at the Early Historic Creek Indian Town of Fusihatchee (Phase 1, 1988–1989)"; Gregory A. Waselkov, "French Colonial Trade in the Upper Creek Country"; Gregory A. Waselkov, "Historic Creek Indian Responses to European Trade and the Rise of Political Factions"; Gremil-

lion, "Comparative Paleoethnobotany of Three Native Southeastern Communities of the Historic Period"; Cameron B. Wesson, "Households and Hegemony: An Analysis of Historic Creek Culture Change"; Gregory A. Waselkov, "The Eighteenth-Century Anglo-Indian Trade in Southeastern North America"; Waselkov and Smith, "Upper Creek Archaeology"; Barnet Pavao-Zuckerman, "Vertebrate Subsistence in the Mississippian-Historic Transition," and "Culture contact and subsistence change at Fusihatchee (1EE191)."

7. Waselkov, Wood, and Herbert, *Colonization and Conquest*; Gregory A. Waselkov, *Fort Toulouse Studies*; Gregory A. Waselkov, "Introduction: Recent Archaeological and Historical Research."

8. One exception (apart from several excavated Redstick War sites, mentioned elsewhere in this volume) is an investigation of an isolated Creek homestead near Tuckaubatchee; Gregory A. Waselkov, "Intensive Subsurface Archaeological Investigations at the I-85 Shorter-Milstead Interchange, Alabama."

9. Waselkov, Gums and Parker, *Archaeology at Fort Mims*.

10. Sue Moore to Greg Waselkov, email correspondence, November 27, 2002.

11. She has also corresponded with Philip Beidler regarding his article, "Literature and the Art of Political Payback."

Appendix 1

1. Judge Toulmin estimated "not more than 25 or 30 escaped and of these many were wounded." Toulmin, "Indian Warfare," 106.

2. Rowland, *Mississippi Territory in the War of 1812*, 176–86.

3. Notices, *Washington Republican* (May 4, 1814):3–4. Smith was a resident of Jefferson County, and Miller had lived in Adams County. Neither estate was sufficient to pay the debts of the deceased; Court Minutes, 1803–1835, Orphans Court, Washington, Adams County, Mississippi, Latter Day Saints, Family History Center.

4. Court Records, 1805–1826, Port Gibson, Claiborne County, Mississippi, Latter Day Saints, ibid.; Rowland, *Mississippi Territory in the War of 1812*, 178, 180.

5. Orphans Court Minutes, Greenville, Jefferson County, 1804–14 (microfilm), Latter Day Saints, ibid.; Rowland, *Mississippi Territory in the War of 1812*, 176, 182.

6. Monette, *History*, 2:407n.

7. J. Claiborne's historical notes, in Letterbook F, J.F.H. Claiborne Collection, MDAH.

8. Woodward, *Reminiscences*, 85–86.

9. According to Adcock family genealogical records provided by Mark Migura, pers. comm., Tensaw residents Thomas and Elizabeth Adcock, husband and wife, died during the battle at Fort Mims; Thomas was about fifty-eight years of age, from Franklin County, Georgia.

10. A mid-nineteenth-century daguerreotype of a woman and her infant, in the collections of the Museum of Mobile, is associated with a label that reads, "Harriet Allen, a survivor of the Fort Mims massacre." Nothing more is known about the photograph's origin or donor. However, the young woman in the photo, who was perhaps in her twenties, does not seem old enough to have been at Fort Mims, even as an infant herself.

11. Allen family genealogical information from Jayne Allen Lipe of Bellevue, Washing-

ton, indicates that John and Margaret Carter Allen, husband and wife, were killed at Fort Mims. A cenotaph of recent age in the Jesse Carter Allen private cemetery in Allentown, Florida, marking the graves of Wade Leslie Allen, Jr., and his wife Ruth Kizer, lists the genealogy of the Allen family line, from John and Margaret Allen, "killed—Aug. 30, 1813 by Creek Indians at Ft. Mims, AL."

12. An obituary in *Raymond Gazette* [Hinds Co., Miss.] (August 15, 1845) for Thomas J. Downing, Sr., of Raymond, Mississippi, states, "He was one of the few who escaped the massacre at Fort Mims." Born in County Tyrone, Ireland, October 18, 1770, he resided in Adams County, Mississippi Territory, married, and had one child before the war and one afterwards. Family genealogical records provided by Walter D. Downing, Jr., of San Antonio, Texas.

13. Lackey, *Frontier Claims*, 25, 27, 34.

14. Bryant, *Tensaw Country*, 260.

15. Penelope Farr, age thirty-eight, wife of James DePriest, is said to have died at Fort Mims.

16. Samuel Fillingim and Esther Boggs, Tensaw residents, moved from Craven County, North Carolina. According to a family oral history written in 1922, "During the War of 1812, Robert & Samuel Fillingim moved to South Alabama. . . . They lost their families in the Fort Mims Massacre, Aug. 30, 1813. Robert Fillingim married again to Miss Esther Boggs in 1820, one of the few survivors of the Fort Mims Tragedy"; Lil King, pers. comm., August 30, 2003.

17. Elizabeth d'Autrey Riley, *The Evergreen Old Historical Cemetery in Evergreen, Alabama, Conecuh County*, 27–28. According to that reference, Mr. Sinquefield was "one of the THREE who escaped Fort Mimms, going through the country giving the alarm, telling the horrors of the massacre and warning the people the Indians were on the rampage." In the absence of any corroboration, we suspect the author has confused the battle at Fort Mims with an attack a few days later on Fort Sinquefield, another settlers' fort in the forks of the Alabama and Tombigbee; cf. Halbert and Ball, *Creek War*, 184–99.

18. Dess L. Sangster and Tom Sangster, *Fort Mims and the Tensaw Settlement*, 57.

19. Weekley family genealogy by Mrs. Donald Jones; Lackey, *Frontier Claims*, 25, 27, 34.

20. There is no record of Major Daniel Beasley ever having been married. Lilla Beazley is a fictional character in Meek's poem, *Red Eagle*. She was accepted as historical by David Pierce Mason, *Massacre at Fort Mims*, 165.

21. Lazarus filed a compensation claim for losses during the Redstick War and died in 1827; Lackey, *Frontier Claims*, 27, 57. Genealogical information on the Bryars family was provided by Cody Phillips and Gary Aiken, pers. comm.

22. Robert Fillingim died in 1799; Questel family genealogical records provided by Nick Questel, pers. comm.

23. "Family History," in the Edwin Augustus Osborne Papers, Southern Historical Collection, University of North Carolina, Chapel Hill. From his station at St. Stephens on September 9, 1813, 1st Lieutenant Audley L. Osborne, adjutant in the Mississippi Territorial Volunteers and Lieutenant Spruce Osborne's brother, asked General Claiborne to inform his father of Spruce's death; Interesting Papers . . . by Col John F. H. Claiborne, Pickett Papers, ADAH.

24. In a lengthy family reminiscence, including much about Fort Mims, a descendant

placed their deaths "about 1812"; see Tarvin, "Muscogees or Creek Indians," 136; Lackey, *Frontier Claims*, 63.

25. Receipt to Lieutenant Jonathan A. Watson from Thomas Camp, assistant quartermaster general, Fort Jackson, July 15, 1814, Records of the Office of the Adjutant General, 1780s–1917 (E-19, Box 205), RG 94, NARA.

26. Lackey, *Frontier Claims*, 31.

27. Pickett, *History of Alabama*, 2:274, states that Daniel and James, brothers of Dixon Bailey, died in the Mims house. Also see Grant, *Letters, Journals and Writings*, 665–66.

28. According to Pickett, *History of Alabama*, 2:274, James and Daniel, brothers of Dixon Bailey, were killed in the Mims house. Also see Tarvin, "Muscogees or Creek Indians," 137; Lackey, *Frontier Claims*, 28, 51. James Bailey's "surviving wife, Nancy Fisher and two children, Betsy Bailey and Thomas Bailey" are mentioned in Bureau of Land Management, Special Acts, Treaty of Fort Jackson, Durant Certificate No. 12, File 12, 1814 (15W3/21/23/1, Box 3), RG 49, NARA (cited hereafter as Durant Certificate).

29. Notes taken from the lips of Dr Thos G. Holmes, Pickett Papers, ADAH. According to a deposition in Lackey, *Frontier Claims*, 50. Peggy Bailey was "at the taking of Fort Mims where her three brothers and family were killed."

30. Her identity is uncertain. She may have been an undocumented daughter of Benjamin Durant and Sophia McGillivray (as some sources suggest), although we think it doubtful because her marriage to Bailey would have violated the rule of clan exogamy; both belonged to the Wind clan. We suspect she was, instead, a daughter of one of Sophia's sons, probably Lachlan, making Nancy a member of another clan (her mother's). Pickett, *History of Alabama*, 2:127; "Sketch of Weatherford, or the Red Eagle," in Meek, *Romantic Passages*, 264; Claim of James Bailey's Heirs, December 11, 1818, testified before David Mitchell, in Durant Certificate; Tarvin, "Muscogees or Creek Indians," 137. Charles Brashear provided the Brashear family history, pers. comm., January 24, 2003. A deposition in Lackey, *Frontier Claims*, 51, lists "James Bailey, a half breed who with his wife and children was killed at Mims' fort."

31. According to Pickett, *History of Alabama*, 2:274, Ralph was carried out of the fort by Tom, an African slave owned by his father, Dixon Bailey, then carried back to the Redsticks and killed.

32. Pickett, *History of Alabama*, 2:274; Grant, *Letters, Journals and Writings*, 665–66; Lackey, *Frontier Claims*, 28. Patrick May described Dixon Bailey as "a half-breed Indian—In Stature he was about 5 feet 8 or 10 inches high, square built, inclined to corpulency, & would have weighed I suppose 175 or 180—had a dark complexion, was a man of intelligence and noble bearing and of unsurpass'd chivalry . . . & displayed undaunted bravery." Notes furnished by Gen Patrick May, Pickett Papers, ADAH. Frank imagined the names Dixon and Richard to refer to two distinct individuals and James and Daniel Bailey to be twins; neither supposition is correct. Frank, *Creeks and Southerners*, 75.

33. The identity of Dixon Bailey's wife is uncertain. A letter written by Benjamin Hawkins in 1798 mentions an affair between a son of Richard Bailey (Dixon?) and the wife of an Upper Creek beloved man, but we do not know if this liaison lasted long; Grant, *Letters, Journals and Writings*, 1:210n.3. Halbert and Ball thought Bailey's wife to be a white woman

from South Carolina, though they also found it credible that she was a daughter of Sophia Durant. However, the second possibility seems based on confusion between Dixon and his brother James; see note 30, above. Halbert and Ball, *Creek War,* 164; "Sketch of Weatherford," in Meek, *Romantic Passages,* 264; Tarvin, "Muscogees or Creek Indians," 137; Bryant, *Tensaw Country,* 216. Karl Davis says Dixon married "the daughter of a wealthy Anglo-American Tensaw planter John Randon," yet his references do not support that assertion; Davis, "'Much of the Indian Appears,'" 122. Although her identity remains a mystery, a postwar claim in Lackey, *Frontier Claims,* 51, documents her presence: "Dixon Bailey, who with his wife and children was killed in Mim's Fort."

34. Claim of James Bailey's Heirs, December 11, 1818, testified before David Mitchell, in Durant Certificate.

35. Lackey, *Frontier Claims,* 51.

36. Ibid., 49.

37. Halbert and Ball, *Creek War,* 160; 1810 Federal Census of Washington County, Mississippi Territory, *U.S. Decennial Census Publications, 1790–1970.*

38. Pickett, *History of Alabama,* 2:270; Katy McCaleb Headley, *Claiborne County, Mississippi: The Promised Land,* 343; Joseph Dunbar Shields, *Natchez: Its Early History,* 117. Beasley served in the Mississippi Territorial General Assembly in 1811–12, according to Rowland, *Encyclopedia of Mississippi History,* 2, "Territorial Legislature" entry. His name first appears in the Amelia County, Virginia, tax rolls in 1787 as a free white male, age twenty-one or older, suggesting that he was born around 1766; Deeds, Wills, Orders, Land Tax Lists, Personal Property Tax Lists, Amelia County, 1734–1811 (microfilm, Library of Virginia, Richmond). Martha W. McCartney provided me with this information in her October 2004 report on Daniel Beasley's life in Virginia, which is on file at the Center for Archaeological Studies, University of South Alabama, Mobile. Beasley was "about 5 feet ten inches high, dark eyes & hair with a very fine looking & determined countenance," according to Notes of Doctor Thomas G. Holmes, Pickett Papers, ADAH.

39. Lackey, *Frontier Claims,* 46.

40. Ibid., 32.

41. Ibid., 46. This may be the "negro boy named Bob" whom Josiah Fletcher purchased from Charles Wolf on February 26, 1805, Deed Book 1, Probate Court Records, Chatom, Washington County, Alabama.

42. Rowland, *Mississippi Territory in the War of 1812,* 176. Clanton, "Massacre," in Clanton Papers, ADAH; Halbert and Ball, *Creek War,* 160.

43. Clanton, "Massacre," ibid.; Halbert and Ball, ibid., 160.

44. Lackey, *Frontier Claims,* 46.

45. General Thomas Pinckney to Secretary of War, "Information Given to Genl. Floyd by a Negroe," Milledgeville, January 21, 1814, Letters Received by the Secretary of War, Registered Series, RG 107 (M221, roll 51, P332), NARA.

46. Halbert and Ball, *Creek War,* 117; Rowland, *Mississippi Territory in the War of 1812,* 176.

47. Halbert and Ball, ibid.; Rowland, ibid., 177.

48. "Jack Cato, a colored resident of Clarke county, in 1880, says he was a drummer in the war of 1812, was a drummer at New Orleans in 1815. He claims to have been at Fort Mims and gives a graphic account of scenes there"; Halbert and Ball, *Creek War,* 161. Wyche Cato

is listed in the 1813 tax rolls for Washington County; Strickland and Strickland, comps., *Washington County, Mississippi Territory, 1803–1816 Tax Rolls*.

49. Rowland, *Mississippi Territory in the War of 1812*, 177; Brigade of Louisiana and Mississippi Territory Volunteers and Staff and Commissioned Officers of the Regiment of Mississippi Territory Volunteers, August 12, 1813, in Claiborne, *Mississippi*, 1:320; Monette, *History*, 406; Notes taken from the lips of Dr Thos G. Holmes, Pickett Papers, ADAH; Pickett, *History of Alabama*, 2:275–78.

50. Lackey, *Frontier Claims*, 33.

51. Rowland, *Mississippi Territory in the War of 1812*, 177; Clanton, "Massacre," in Clanton Papers, ADAH; Halbert and Ball, *Creek War*, 160.

52. Stiggins, "Historical narration," 67. Stiggins implies that this man was an Alabama and not the Dog Warrior from Atasi, a Tallapoosa town.

53. Lackey, *Frontier Claims*, 31.

54. Woodward, *Reminiscences*, 86; Grant, *Letters, Journals and Writings*, 667; Hawkins, "Extract of a Letter." Henry Halbert described Cornells as "a man of strong athletic build, but with a face terribly disfigured by the yaws, his mouth being contracted into a very small pucker"; *Creek War Incidents*, 101.

55. "Mr. Fletcher Cox (one who escaped) tells me that the Indians were within thirty steps of the gate before they were seen"; Claiborne, *Life and Times of Gen. Sam. Dale*, 109.

56. Beasley to Claiborne, August 6, 14, 1813, in Letterbook F, J.F.H. Claiborne Collection, MDAH.

57. Grant, *Letters, Journals and Writings*, 664–65. This is probably the same "Cyrus, negro man, aged 50 years," whom Samuel Moniac claimed was taken by Redsticks from his plantation on the Alabama River before the battle at Fort Mims; Letter from the Secretary of the Treasury, in "An Act for the Relief of Samuel Manac," 8.

58. Rowland, *Mississippi Territory in the War of 1812*, 50, 177; Halbert and Ball, *Creek War*, 160. According to Peter A. Brannon, "Through the Years: Survivors of Fort Mims," "Rev. J. G. Jones, of Hazelhurst, Miss., told the Rev. Ball in 1894 that Pvt. Daniels, of Jefferson County, Miss., survived." Also see Halbert, Incidents of Fort Mimms, March 3, 1887, in Tecumseh Papers, Draper, WHS.

59. Halbert and Ball, *Creek War*, 174–75. This Dog Warrior has at times been confused with another Creek of the same name, also known as Davy Cornells, who was killed by Georgians in 1793; Woodward, *Reminiscences*, 50, 96–97.

60. Beasley to Claiborne, 6 August 1813, in Letterbook F, J.F.H. Claiborne Collection, MDAH. Bryant, *Tensaw Country*, 260, maintains that Thomas was son of Cornelius Dunn of South Carolina and Sarah, a Creek woman from Spanish West Florida. According to the Baptismal Records, Diocese of Mobile Catholic Sacramental Records, folio 30, number 132 (translated), Thomas Dunn was baptized at Samuel Mims' house, "born 29 November 1788, legitimate son of Cornelius Dunn and Sara Lucas, of the Protestant sect, residents of the Alabama River and natives of North America." His mother's name, Sara Lucas, raises a question about his presumed Creek ethnicity. However, Tatum referred to "Mrs. Dunn a half breed woman" when passing her Alabama River plantation in 1814; Major Howell Tatum, *Topographical Notes and Observations on the Alabama River, August, 1814*, 166. On the other hand, "Sarah Dunn" signed a petition to Congress requesting compensation for damages

suffered in the war by herself and fellow white Americans in the Tensaw; Carter, *Territorial Papers*, 6:752–53. Cornelius Dunn willed his possessions to his wife Sarah Dunn and his children Thomas Dunn ("my only son"), "my eldest daughter Margaret Weekly," and "my youngest Daughter, Hannah Ryena"; August 17, 1811, in Will Book A, Probate Court Records, Bay Minette, Baldwin County, Alabama, 155.

61. Benjamin Durant, a South Carolinian, resided in Tensaw by 1797 and was married to Sophia McGillivray, Alexander McGillivray's sister. Arturo O'Neill, Spanish governor of West Florida, thought he was "an Indian half-breed . . . whose father was French." See O'Neill to Ezpeleta, October 19, 1783, in Caughey, *McGillivray*, 62. Also see Pickett, *History of Alabama*, 2:126; Woodward, *Reminiscences*, 98. Benjamin Hawkins thought him "a man of good stature, dull and stupid, a little mixed with African blood"; Foster, *Collected Works*, 43 (quote), 231; Bryant, *Tensaw Country*, 261. He was "killed at Fort Mims," according to the Durant Certificate.

62. Grant, *Letters, Journals and Writings*, 665. Said by Hawkins to have been part of John Randon's family (though spelled "Randall"), so probably married to Viney Randon, who may have been "one of his [John's] daughters."

63. Lackey, *Frontier Claims*, 49; Thompson, *William Weatherford*, 356; Bryant, *Tensaw Country*, 262, 329.

64. Dyer was said to be thirty-seven years old at the time of the 1787 Spanish census of the Tensaw; Hall, *Databases*. See Bryant, *Tensaw Country*, 262, 329; Letters Received by the Secretary of War, "Report of Col Pearsons Expedition Against the Hostile Creeks on the Alabama . . . June 1st 1814," Enclosure in Pinckney to Secretary of War, RG 107, NARA.

65. Susan Stiggins to Andrew Jackson, Fort Montgomery, June 2, 1818, and Receipt from Samuel Edmonds to Rachel Jackson, October 28, 1818, Jackson Papers, Library of Congress.

66. According to Woodward, *Reminiscences*, 84, "the oldest and principal chief, the one looked upon as the General, was a Tuskegee, called Hopie Tustanugga, or Far-off-Warrior; he was killed at Fort Mims." He may have been a brother of Fusihatchee Mico; Foster, *Collected Works*, 273.

67. By December 1796, Elizabeth Fletcher was married to a white man; Foster, *Collected Works*, 40; also see Lackey, *Frontier Claims*, 61. Bryant, *Tensaw Country*, 217, erroneously equates Peggy Bailey with Elizabeth Bailey Fletcher.

68. Foster, *Collected Works*, 40; Notes taken from the lips of Dr Thos G. Holmes, Pickett Papers, ADAH; Pickett, *History of Alabama*, 2:275–76. According to Fletcher's postwar claim, reproduced in Lackey, *Frontier Claims*, 48, "I was in the fort at the time." Frank asserts incorrectly that Fletcher was killed at Fort Mims; *Creeks and Southerners*, 76.

69. Rowland, *Mississippi Territory in the War of 1812*, 179. The notation "Ensign Gibbs" appears next to a tent depicted on the Claiborne "Map of Fort Mims and Environs," Pickett Papers, ADAH.

70. Receipt to Lieutenant Jonathan A. Watson from Thomas Camp, RG 94, NARA.

71. Monette, *History*, 2:407n, "The official list of killed in the tragedy of Fort Mims," original manuscript now lost, from the "Manuscript papers of General Claiborne"; Rowland, *Mississippi Territory in the War of 1812*, 179 ("Gowen").

72. Monette, ibid.; Rowland, ibid., 179.

73. "Private Thomas Hammon" listed in Rowland, ibid., 180.

74. Halbert and Ball, *Creek War*, 157; Bryant, *Tensaw Country*, 361.

75. Ibid.; Will Book A (1809–1827), December 27, 1812, Probate Court Records, Bay Minette, Baldwin County, Alabama. Born in the Creek nation in December 1795; Deposition of Susan Sizemore given in Baldwin County, Ala. before Joel Clayton, Commissioner, March 11, 1847, Weatherford vs. Weatherford, Mobile County Chancery Court, University of South Alabama Archives, Mobile.

76. Notes of Doctor Thomas G. Holmes, Pickett Papers, ADAH; Pickett, *History of Alabama*, 2:274–76.

77. Receipt to Lieutenant Jonathan A. Watson from Thomas Camp, RG 94, NARA. Hodge signed as a witness to a county court sale of Joseph Wilson's property on April 22, 1811; Will Book A (1809–1827), Probate Court Records, Bay Minette, Baldwin County, Alabama. He married Polly Booth on September 17, 1808, in Oglethorpe County, Georgia, and was a lieutenant in the 8th Regiment (Baldwin County) of the Mississippi Territorial Militia, in 1810, according to Papers of the Mississippi Territory, Register of Appointments, 1805–1817, Roll #544, p. 72, MDAH.

78. Monette, *History*, 2:406; Rowland, *Mississippi Territory in the War of 1812*, 180.

79. Testimony of Gilbert C. Russell, February 15, 1855, File 222, Probate Court Records, Monroeville, Monroe County, Alabama. According to Baptismal Records, Diocese of Mobile Catholic Sacramental Records, folio 3, number 134 (translated), William was baptized in Samuel Mims' house on March 4, 1789, "about 7 years old, mestizo, son of Adam Hollinger and an Indian."

80. Notes of Doctor Thomas G. Holmes, Pickett Papers, ADAH; Pickett, *History of Alabama*, 2:274–76; Martin, *Sacred Revolt*, 203; Rowland, *Mississippi Territory in the War of 1812*, 180. According to Woodward, *Reminiscences*, 91–92, "George Galphin, an Irishmen . . . had two negroes, Mina, a woman, and Ketch, a man; they were brother and sister. He raised one daughter from Mina, and called her Barbary. She married an Irishman by the name of Holmes, and raised Dr. Thomas G. Holmes, whom Col. Pickett often alludes to in his *History of Alabama*, as having had conversations with him. At Galphin's death Mina was set free, and died at old Timothy Barnard's, on Flint river, Ga., many years back."

81. Pickett, *History of Alabama*, 2:275–76; Bryant, *Tensaw Country*, 292.

82. Ibid.

83. Notes taken from the lips of Dr Thos G. Holmes, Pickett Papers, ADAH; Pickett, *History of Alabama*, 2:275–76; Bryant, *Tensaw Country*, 292. John Hoven was born in (Spanish) Florida about 1792, enlisted in the Tensaw militia in February or March 1813, according to War of 1812, Claim of Widow for Pension, filed by Mary Hoven, December 27, 1887, RG 15, NARA.

84. Graham, *History*, 52–53.

85. Bryant, *Tensaw Country*, 292. According to the "Book of the Baptisms of the Americans of Tombicbee and adjacent parts who follow the Roman Catholic Religion under the spiritual Government of the Rht. Rvd. Lord Bishop of Baltimore, 1801," Diocese of Mobile Catholic Sacramental Records, Mobile, folio 3, number 5, William was born June 24, 1797, Robert on March 27, 1799, James on March 9, 1801, all to Benjamin Hoven from Virginia and Mary Dunn from Georgia; Baptismal Records, folio 46, number 208, lists John and Elizabeth baptized on June 30, 1794, children of Benjamin Hoven and Mary Dunn, "Protestants."

86. Receipt to Lieutenant Jonathan A. Watson from Thomas Camp, RG 94, NARA.

87. "Major Kerr late commandant of Fort Decatur will deliver over to James Walker of Jones County Georgia one of the heirs of Wiseman Walker, who together with his family is said to have been killed at Fort Mims, two Negro boys (Viz) one named Jack. about 10 or 13 years of age, another named Jim. about 8 or 10 years old said to have been the property of the said Wiseman Walker at the time of his dicease"; H. W. Connor, Orderly Book, June 26, 1814, Joseph Graham Papers, NCDCR.

88. Lackey, *Frontier Claims*, 46.

89. Ibid., 34.

90. A native of Virginia, Richard Inman died in Wilkinson County, Mississippi, in 1848, "one of the few men who escaped from Fort Mims"; Dunbar Rowland, *Biographical and Historical Memoirs of Mississippi* (Chicago: Goodspeed, 1891), 1: "Inman" entry. Rowland, *Mississippi Territory in the War of 1812*, 180.

91. William Jack was born March 19, 1786 in Adams County, Mississippi Territory; Grant, *Letters, Journals and Writings*, 667; Rowland, *Mississippi Territory in the War of 1812*, 180. "Captain Jack was killed about the close of the scene, having previously received two wounds"; Monette, *History*, 406 (quote). Henry Halbert elicited the following information from J. G. Jones of Hazelhurst, Mississippi: "I knew the brave and noble Captain Jack. He was quite a young man and had just taken an additional course in our country school house to complete his primary education. Early in the fight, his right arm had been shattered by a ball, and he took his sword—an old fashioned cleaver, in his left hand, and used it with bloody effect until by loss of blood and additional wounds he fell to rise no more." Halbert, Incidents of Fort Mimms, March 3, 1887, Tecumseh Papers, Draper, WHS.

92. Grant, *Letters, Journals and Writings*, 667.

93. Lackey, *Frontier Claims*, 46.

94. Ibid.

95. Receipt to Lieutenant Jonathan A. Watson from Thomas Camp, RG 94, NARA.

96. H. W. Connor, Orderly Book, June 26, 1814, Joseph Graham Papers, NCDCR; see note 87 above.

97. In December 1814, Jo or Joe was badly wounded fighting as a Redstick in a skirmish with federal troops on Santa Rosa Bay, and was captured by the Americans soon afterward in Pensacola. Grant, *Letters, Journals and Writings*, 665; Notes taken from the lips of Col Robert James and Notes taken from the lips of Dr Thos G. Holmes, Pickett Papers, ADAH.

98. Daughter of Lucy Cornells and niece of James Cornells; James traded her to William Samuel Jones in exchange for Betty Coulter, according to Woodward, *Reminiscences*, 224–25. Jackson to Willie Blount, Ft. Jackson, April 18, 1814, in Bassett, *Correspondence of Andrew Jackson*, 1:503. Her father died at Tensaw sometime before 1797; Foster, *Collected Works*, 36–37.

99. Bassett, *Correspondence of Andrew Jackson*, 1:503; Deed, December 28, 1836, and Marriage Contract between Polly Oliver and Martin James, February 22, 1834, Probate Court Records, Monroeville, Monroe County, Alabama; Jones family records provided by Ruth Newlan, pers. comm., January 20, 2003.

100. Bassett, *Correspondence of Andrew Jackson*, 1:503.

101. Ibid.

102. Notes taken from the lips of Dr Thos G. Holmes, Pickett Papers, ADAH; Pickett, *History of Alabama,* 2:275–76. A "brave man formerly a Soldier in the North Western Army under Wayne was wounded and one of the last who escaped"; Grant, *Letters, Journals and Writings,* 667.

103. Lackey, *Frontier Claims,* 46.

104. Rowland, *Mississippi Territory in the War of 1812,* 181. Judkins was born ca. 1782, in Iredell County, North Carolina, married Parthenia (Perthaney, Carthenia) Williams on June 26, 1806, in Jefferson County, Kentucky, filed for divorce in 1812 in Mississippi Territory, divorce petition was dismissed October 1814; all information from Kathi Judkins Abendroth, Judkins Family Association, pers. comm.

105. John Lee Williams, *The Territory of Florida,* 214; James F. Sunderman, ed., *Journey Into Wilderness: Journal of Jacob R. Motte,* 283.

106. Notes of Doctor Thomas G. Holmes, Pickett Papers, ADAH; Rowland, *Mississippi Territory in the War of 1812,* 181.

107. Monette, *History,* 2:406; Rowland, *Mississippi Territory in the War of 1812,* 181.

108. Receipt to Lieutenant Jonathan A. Watson from Thomas Camp, RG 94, NARA.

109. "Negroe man named Lisbon about 27 years old killed," in Lackey, *Frontier Claims,* 32. A "negro woman named Lesbon about 18 or 20 years old" was sold by John McAllister of Green County, Georgia, for $450 to Robert McConnell of Washington County on May 28, 1806; Deed Book 1, Probate Court Records, Chatom, Washington County, Alabama.

110. Halbert and Ball, *Creek War,* 157.

111. Monette, *History,* 2:406; Rowland, *Mississippi Territory in the War of 1812,* 182 ("Low").

112. Lackey, *Frontier Claims,* 32.

113. Ibid., 46. This is probably the "negro man named Marengo, lately brought from Africa," whom Josiah Fletcher purchased from William Ashley on June 12, 1805 for $400; Deed Book 1, Probate Court Records, Chatom, Washington County, Alabama.

114. "An Act for the Relief of Susan Marlow . . . only surviving child of James Marlow, a Creek Indian, who lost his life at the destruction of Fort Mimms," *Private Claims, 24th Cong., sess. 1* (Washington, D.C., 1836), Chap. 334, Statute 1, July 2, 1836, 678; ibid., *sess. 2* (1837), 689, Chap. 29, Statute 2, March 2, 1837.

115. Lackey, *Frontier Claims,* 46.

116. Pickett, *History of Alabama,* 2:275–76; Rowland, *Mississippi Territory in the War of 1812,* 182.

"There was a Sargent Mathews taken with violent chill, & struck like a man with a third day fever & ague and from his sweating the water ran from him as freely as though he had been deluged with water from a river. his teeth chatering together as though he was freezing This brave Mrs [Daniel] Baily urged him from time to time to get up & fight like a man and defend the women children that were in the fort—he refused to do so, she earnestly assured him that if he did not fight that she would certainly bayonett him which by the by she done some 15 or 20 time in his rump, all to no purpose for he lay like an ox. afterwards he made his escape and fled & reached Mount Vernon where Claiborne was in command and then reported to the Genl that he had killed 20 odd Indians. it so raised him in the estimation of the Genl & the officers that they one and all recommended him to a commission in the army which it was probably he would have gotten if Dr Holmes had not have prevented this unworthy man from succeeding by his false statements to the general. When Dr H charged him with lying, he persisted in it until the Dr proved by the marks on his posterior that Mrs Baily had bayonetted him." Notes of Doctor Thomas G. Holmes, Pickett Papers, ADAH.

117. Lackey, *Frontier Claims*, 25, 27, 32.

118. Claiborne to Colonel Carson, September 4, 1813, Mount Vernon, in Letterbook F, J.F.H. Claiborne Collection, MDAH; Carter, *Territorial Papers*, 6:255; Potter, *Passports of Southeastern Pioneers*, 283; Rowland, *Mississippi Territory in the War of 1812*, 182; Monette, *History*, 2:406.

119. Woodward, *Reminiscences*, 86; Halbert and Ball, *Creek War*, 156.

120. "Jim Boy succeeded in saving Mrs. McGirth and her daughters, but her only son, James, was killed"; Woodward, *Reminiscences*, 85–86, 97.

121. Pickett, *History of Alabama*, 2:280–81. Pickett maintained there were seven McGirth daughters. Woodward listed five, though just one, Sarah, by name; *Reminiscences*, 97. General Claiborne's official report, quoted by Monette, mentions one civilian's "wife and six children, who were probably burned to death," almost certainly an oblique reference to Zachariah McGirth's family. Since one child, James, was killed during the battle, there must have been five girls in the McGirth family; Monette, *History*, 406. Also see Southern BorderWar, Massacre at Tensaw, *The War* (October 19, 1813).

122. Ibid.

123. Pickett, *History of Alabama*, 2:280–82; Woodward, *Reminiscences*, 85–86; Foster, *Collected Works*, 36–37.

124. Grant, *Letters, Journals and Writings*, 667; Bryant, *Tensaw Country*, 310. The family name was also spelled "McGirt," as it is today by descendants among the Muscogee Nation in Oklahoma.

125. Rowland, *Mississippi Territory in the War of 1812*, 183; Jamie Kay Kemp-Taylor, *William Middleton's (1685–1769) Children*, 5. "Captain Middleton . . . distinguished himself, having received four or five wounds before he fell. He was active, and fought bravely from the commencement of the action until he died"; quote from Monette, *History*, 406.

126. Receipt to Lieutenant Jonathan A. Watson from Thomas Camp, RG 94, NARA; "Report of Col Pearsons Expedition Against the Hostile Creeks on the Alabama . . . June 1st 1814," Enclosure in Pinckney to Secretary of War, June 28, 1814, Letters Received by the Secretary of War (M221, roll, 65, P27), RG 107, NARA.

127. Receipt to Lieutenant Jonathan A. Watson from Thomas Camp, RG 94, NARA.

128. Notes taken from the lips of Dr Thos G. Holmes, Pickett Papers, ADAH. As recounted in Pickett's *History of Alabama*, 2:273, "The venerable David Mims, attempting to pass to the bastion, received a large ball in the neck; the blood gushed out; he exclaimed, "Oh God, I am a dead man!" and fell upon his face. A cruel warrior cut around his head, and waved his hoary scalp exultingly in the air." Bryant, *Tensaw Country*, 316–19, disputes the notion that Samuel's brother David was killed in the battle, referencing documentary evidence that David died in 1819. However, a claim submitted to Congress in November 1815 and witnessed by William Mims, David and Samuel's brother, on behalf of the heirs of "David Mims who was killed at the Fort called Fort Mims," supports Dr. Holmes' account;

Lackey, *Frontier Claims,* 25, 33 (quote). David, Samuel, and William were sons of Benjamin Mims and Judith Woodson; Mims, *Leaves from the Mims Family Tree,* 29.

129. "Sworn statements with accompanying exhibits of sundry inhabitants of the Mississippi Territory, September–November, 1815, praying for relief from Indian depredations," 14th Cong., 1st sess., January 2, 1816, Other Select Committees (HR 14A-F16.7), RG 233, NARA, quoted in Lackey, *Frontier Claims,* 31, also see 25, 27. Samuel's wife and most of their children happened to be in Mobile at the time of the battle; Halbert and Ball, *Creek War,* 171; Bryant, *Tensaw Country,* 320; Mims, *Leaves from the Mims Family Tree,* 31–33.

130. Pickett, *History of Alabama,* 2:275–77; Rowland, *Mississippi Territory in the War of 1812,* 183 ("John" or "Joseph"); Halbert and Ball, *Creek War,* 160. A. J. Morris "died at Heflin, Alabama, April 5, 1891, nearly one hundred years of age. He is supposed to have been the last survivor of the inmates of Fort Mims"; *Covington Times* (April 25, 1891).

131. Rowland, *Mississippi Territory in the War of 1812,* 183; Clanton, "Massacre," in Clanton Papers, ADAH; Halbert and Ball, *Creek War,* 160. John Mountjoy is listed in the 1820 Federal Census as living in Redwood Creek township, Feliciana Parish, Louisiana.

132. Stiggins, "Historical narration," 62–63.

133. Lackey, *Frontier Claims,* 32.

134. Ibid., 46.

135. Ibid., 50.

136. Ibid.

137. Ibid.

138. George Cornells to Secretary of War, Letters Received by the Secretary of War, Registered Series, 1801–1870 (M221, roll 56, P316), RG 107, NARA.

139. Ibid.

140. Ibid.

141. Ibid.

142. Ibid.

143. Ibid.

144. Beasley to Claiborne, August 30, 1813, in Letterbook F, J.F.H. Claiborne Collection, MDAH.

145. Ibid.

146. Lackey, *Frontier Claims,* 37–38.

147. Ibid.

148. Ibid., 47–48.

149. Ibid., 49.

150. Ibid.

151. Ibid.

152. Notes taken from the lips of Dr Thos G. Holmes, Pickett Papers, ADAH.

153. Lackey, *Frontier Claims,* 61.

154. Grant, *Letters, Journals and Writings,* 664–65.

155. Notes taken from the lips of Col Robert James, Pickett Papers, ADAH.

156. Lackey, *Frontier Claims,* 45.

157. Ibid., 61.

158. Ibid., 47.

159. Ibid., 45.

160. In a letter to the governor of Pensacola, "the old intepreter" stated that his son "heded an army and went against a garrison at tennisau" and "put the garrison in flames . . . my son commanded the army that defeted the fort and I was in battle   old man as I am I help to cut the fort down"; Josiah Francis, The Old King, Old Interpreter, and Mougceweihche to Governor González Manrique, [August 1813], Papeles procedentes de la Isla de Cuba (PKY microfilm reel 311). Of the known Redstick leaders at the battle of Fort Mims, only Paddy Walsh had a father living in the Creek nation who could have functioned as a translator. George Stiggins described James Walsh as "a South Carolinian who in the american revolution was a despisable Murdering Swamp Tory which caused him after the close of that contest to leave that country where he had perpetrated so many bad crimes and settle himself in the creek nation, where he became the father of Paddy who lost his father while he was very young"; "Historical narration," 82. He may have been the man known as James Welch who worked as a trader among the Cherokees in 1797; Potter, Passports of Southeastern Pioneers, 329.

For a brief discussion of another interpreter, James DuRouzeaux, apparently adopted by the Creeks, see Frank, Creeks and Southerners, 35.

161. Ibid., 25, 27, 33; Claiborne Map, CB-23, ADAH.

162. Born on December 14, 1784, to Adlai Osborn and Margaret Lloyd in Iredell County, North Carolina. His middle name is represented variously in period sources as McKay, McCay, and McCall, and his last name as Osborn, Osburn, Osborne, and Osbourne. Spruce was one of three graduates, in 1805, from the University of North Carolina, Chapel Hill, where he studied medicine. His brother, Adlai L. Osborne, also a Mississippi Territorial Volunteer during the Redstick War, graduated there in 1802. See John Hill Wheeler, Historical Sketches of North Carolina from 1584 to 1851, 216. His name appears in "A Roll of officers educated at West Point who have died or been Killed in Service of the United States," J. G. Swift to Secretary of War, New York, February 4, 1817, R1815, Letters Received by the Secretary of War, Unregistered Series (microform 222, roll 7), RG 107, NARA; "Spruce M. Osburn, Lt. Vol. Service Killed by the Indians at Fort Mims, M.T." A. L. Osborne to Claiborne, St. Stephens, September 9, 1813, in Interesting Papers . . . by Col John F. H. Claiborne, Pickett Papers, ADAH; Claiborne, Life and Times of Gen. Sam. Dale, 79; Rowland, Mississippi Territory in the War of 1812, 183.

According to General Claiborne's official report (quoted by Monette), Osborne, "after receiving two wounds, was taken into a house, but requested to die on the ground, that he might, as long as possible, see the men fight"; Monette, History, 406. "Dr. Osborne, the surgeon, was shot through the body, and carried into Patrick's loom-house, where he expired, in great agony"; quote from Pickett, History of Alabama, 2:272. Also see Peter A. Brannon, "Spruce McCall Osborne." Brannon's article reproduced in black and white a portrait of Osborne clipped from an unidentified published source. The clipping is located in VF Person 1, Box 40, Folder 50, ADAH.

163. Rowland, Mississippi Territory in the War of 1812, 183; Wills and Administrations, vol. 1, 1809–1820, file 145, and Orphans Court Records, vol. 6, p. 30, Probate Court, Liberty, Amite County, Mississippi. The Orphans Court record for August 8, 1814, lists "Cornelius

Van Houten adminstr estate of James Otis, killed at Fort Mims." Also see Albert E. Casey, *Amite County, Mississippi, 1699–1865*, 384, 407. Otis enlisted on March 31, 1813, as a musician in Captain Abraham M. Scot's Company of the 1st Regiment.

164. Born on January 18, 1785 in Duplin County, North Carolina, to Thomas Page and Mary Scott. He married Elizabeth Crane June 15, 1830, in Hinds County, Mississippi, moved to Angelina County, Texas in 1851, and died there December 10, 1863. Page's log cabin still exists in Angelina County, a short distance from where it originally stood. Family genealogical information provided by Patti White, pers. comm., 2003. According to his official service record, Page served in Captain William Henry's Troop of Volunteer Dragoons, 1st Regiment Mississippi Territorial Volunteers, except from March 2 to December 3, 1813, when he was considered absent on command at Fort Mims with Cornet Rankin; Records of Men Enlisted in the U.S. Army Prior to the Peace Establishment, May 17, 1815, Registers of Enlistments in the U.S. Army, 1798–1914 (M233, roll 10, P-R]), RG 94 , NARA; Halbert and Ball, *Creek War,* 166–67; Henry S. Halbert, "An Incident of Fort Mimms"; Rowland, *Mississippi Territory in the War of 1812,* 184.

165. Receipt to Lieutenant Jonathan A. Watson from Thomas Camp, RG 94, NARA.

166. Ibid.

167. Pickett, *History of Alabama*, 2:275–77; Halbert and Ball, *Creek War,* 160.

168. Receipt to Lieutenant Jonathan A. Watson from Thomas Camp, RG 94, NARA.

169. Tuesday, January 10, 1832, *Journal of the Senate of the United States of America, 1789–1873* (Washington, D.C.). Upon the death of Jeremiah's brother George in 1798, George's wife married Wiseman Walker.

170. Beasley to Claiborne, August 6, 1813, in Letterbook F, J.F.H. Claiborne Collection, MDAH.

171. Halbert and Ball, *Creek War,* 157; Bryant, *Tensaw Country,* 361.

172. Son of Peter Randon and "a Creek woman of the Cotchulgee" (Panther) clan; Foster, *Collected Works,* 263–64; also, Bryant, *Tensaw Country,* 332.

173. Foster, *Collected Works,* 263–64. "John Randon . . . a wealthy indian Country man, was killed in Fort Mims with most of his Family," in Notes furnished by Col Jeremiah Austill, Pickett Papers, ADAH. John is described as "a half breed Creek Indian, killed at Fort Mims," in Special Acts, Treaty of Fort Jackson 1814, RG 49, NARA. Also see Bryant, *Tensaw Country,* 331; Book of the Baptisms of the Americans of Tombicbee and adjacent parts . . . , Diocese of Mobile Catholic Sacramental Records, Mobile, folio 3, number 2.

174. Book of Baptisms, ibid.; Notes taken from the lips of Dr Thos G. Holmes, Pickett Papers, ADAH; Pickett, *History of Alabama,* 2:275–76; Lackey, *Frontier Claims,* 49; Beasley to Claiborne, August 14, 1813, in Letterbook F, J.F.H. Claiborne Collection, MDAH. According to David Crockett, the parents, four sisters, and four brothers of Peter Randon died in the fort, figures not confirmed by family genealogical information; Crockett, *Narrative,* 105. Peter Randon testified in 1815 that "my father & all the family but myself two younger brothers & a small sister were killed" at Fort Mims; Lackey, *Frontier Claims,* 49. In a statement written on March 24, 1848, Gilbert C. Russell claimed that only one daughter was killed. The one daughter known to have died at Fort Mims was Mary Louisa Randon Tate. See "John Crowell, Peter Randon," *U.S. Serials Set, 31st Cong., 2nd sess., House of Representatives, Report No. 16,* 2. (James Parker provided a copy of this tract.) Karl Davis maintains that Peter Ran-

don married a sister of Dixon Bailey. However, documentation on the three Bailey sisters shows otherwise, and Davis' references do not support his assertion; "'Much of the Indian Appears,'" 73.

175. Thompson, *William Weatherford*, 356; Bryant, *Tensaw Country*, 262, 329.

176. Grant, *Letters, Journals and Writings*, 665–66. Viney's identity is uncertain. Hawkins spelled her name "Randall" but mistakenly used that spelling in reference to John Randon in a previous enclosure and in other contexts. He also implied that Peter Durant was a member of John Randon's family, perhaps through marriage to Viney. One of John Randon's brothers, David or James, married a mulatto women and had five daughters, four of whom (including Viney?) were still single when Brother Burckhard visited their home near the Chattahoochee River in 1812. See Mauelshagen and Davis, "Partners in the Lord's Work," 71–72; Foster, *Collected Works*, 203, 264.

177. Crockett, *Narrative*, 105. Crockett claimed that four daughters died at Fort Mims, but Randon genealogical information does not support this. Apart from Mary Louisa Randon Tate, two other Randon daughters—Rosa Zuba, born 1798, and Martha, born ca. 1788, may have perished at Fort Mims. Baptismal Records, Diocese of Mobile Catholic Sacramental Records, Mobile, records of November 2, 1788, and November 11, 1801.

178. Born November 4, 1788, in Mason County, Kentucky. Family genealogy provided by Mike Rankin, pers. comm., 2003 and Michael Smith, pers. comm., 2004.

179. Born August 8, 1783, in Frederick County, Virginia, eldest son of Richard Robert Rankin and Margaret Kendall Berry. Mabel Van Dyke Baer, "Abstracts of Important Documents Found in Pension Applications of Soldiers of the Revolutionary War, War of 1812, War with Creek Indians," 126–27. F. L. Claiborne to Colonel Carson, September 4, 1813, Mount Vernon, in Letterbook F, J.F.H. Claiborne Collection, MDAH; Rowland, *Mississippi Territory in the War of 1812*, 184. According to Henry Halbert, "the frightened and screaming women implored Cornet Rankin to hoist a white flag and beg the Indians to allow a surrender. Rankin rushed to the gate with flag in hand, but the swarming warriors paid no attention to the token, and in an instant Rankin fell dead under a shower of bullets." Henry S. Halbert, Incidents of Fort Mims, February 22, 1886, in Tecumseh Papers, Draper WHS.

180. Lackey, *Frontier Claims*, 27, 37. Additional information provided by a descendant, Farron Tucker.

181. Ibid., 27, 38.

182. Presumed killed at Fort Mims, though not certain. Monte George, pers. comm., March 9, 2003.

183. Pickett, *History of Alabama*, 2:275–77; Halbert and Ball, *Creek War*, 160; Records of Men Enlisted in the U.S. Army Prior to the Peace Establishment, M233, roll 10, P-R, 244, RG 94, NARA; Monte George, pers. comm., March 9, 2003. Martin Rigdon is apparently the drummer referred to in Major Beasley's letter of August 7 to General Claiborne: "I have sent down for a return for a drum; it is to be used by one of the Militia who beats exceedingly well having been in the regular Service for five years"; in Letterbook F, J.F.H. Claiborne Collection, MDAH.

184. Enoch Rigdon wrote to the secretary of war from Jackson, Mississippi, on May 6, 1824, "I had a brother that did [died] in the servis of the United States and am intiteld to

his land also, but they wish me to proov my hereship, but in that I cannot wish I could rase the ded, for all the family was Kild in mimse post but him and myself." Other members of the Rigdon family present at Fort Mims may have included father Enoch Rigdon (age forty-four), mother Sophia Shittle Rigdon, and unnamed sisters. Monte George, pers. comm., March 9, 2003.

185. Grant, *Letters, Journals and Writings*, 665. On December 22, 1796, Hawkins visited the town of Hoithlewaulee and breakfasted at the house of "James Russel, a native of the United States; he has been 12 years in the nation, has a decent woman and one son"; Foster, *Collected Works*, 45–46. Abram Mordecai, who also traded at Hoithlewaulee, described James Russel as a Tory; Notes taken from the lips of Abram Mordecai, Pickett Papers, ADAH.

186. Pickett, *History of Alabama*, 2:281–82. There is considerable disagreement in the sources about the identity of Sanota/Jim Boy; Pickett maintained that Sanota was killed at Horseshoe Bend, but according to Woodward, *Reminiscences*, 85–86, "Jim Boy [who did not perish at Horseshoe Bend] succeeded in saving Mrs. McGirth and her daughters, but her only son, James, was killed." These two accounts seem irreconcilable.

187. Woodward thought Seekaboo was a Mequashake Shawnee from the town of Wapakoneta. The "Shawnee, Seekaboo, and some of the McGillivray negroes got behind some logs that were near the Fort, kindled a fire, and, by putting rags on their arrows and setting them on fire, would shoot them into the roof of Mims' smokehouse, which was an old building, and formed a part of one line of the Fort. It took fire and communicated it to the other buildings—and that is the way Fort Mims was destroyed"; Woodward, *Reminiscences*, 33, 86 (quote); Halbert and Ball, *Creek War*, 40.

188. Lackey, *Frontier Claims*, 61.

189. Monette, *History*, 2:406; Rowland, *Mississippi Territory in the War of 1812*, 185 ("Zacharias").

190. Lackey, *Frontier Claims*, 34.

191. Pickett, *History of Alabama*, 2:275–77; Woodward, *Reminiscences*, 97; Halbert and Ball, *Creek War*, 160. Samuel Smith was "a Native of the Creek nation & one Eighth Creek blood," according to Laughlin Durant, Durant Certificate.

192. Pickett, *History of Alabama*, 2:275–76

193. Notes taken from the lips of Dr Thos G. Holmes, Pickett Papers, ADAH. "There were 4 Spanish sailors that had been mutineers from a Spanish vessel at Mobile and had taken refuge in Fort Mimms. These knelt made the cross and quietly submitted their throats"; handwritten notes (by Henry S. Halbert) in file, "Reminiscences of Ft. Mims," Clanton Papers, ADAH.

194. Six unnamed daughters were reportedly killed; Bryant, *Tensaw Country*, 350–58.

195. Notes taken from the lips of Dr Thos G. Holmes, Pickett Papers, ADAH; Pickett, *History of Alabama*, 2:275–76; Tarvin, "Muscogees or Creek Indians," 143; Bryant, *Tensaw Country*, 350–58; Stidham Family Tree provided by David R. Stiddem, pers. comm. According to translated Baptismal Records, Diocese of Mobile Catholic Sacramental Records, folio 46, number ——, on July 1, 1794, Thomas and Edward were baptized, boys of Moses Steadham and Winifred Spinger, Americans, Protestants.

196. Bryant, *Tensaw Country*, 350–58.

197. Ibid., 350.

198. Benjamin Steadham married a Creek woman while a trader in Georgia; Foster, *Collected Works,* 245–46; also Bryant, *Tensaw Country,* 350–58.

199. Notes taken from the lips of Dr Thos G. Holmes, Pickett Papers, ADAH; Pickett, *History of Alabama,* 2:275–77; Halbert and Ball, *Creek War,* 160; Bryant, *Tensaw Country,* 350–58.

200. Ibid.

201. Lackey, *Frontier Claims,* 25, 27, 32; Bryant, *Tensaw Country,* 352; family history provided by Charlene Moore, personal comm., September 15, 2003.

202. Bryant, *Tensaw Country,* 350, and see note 195 above.

203. Benjamin Steadham married a Creek woman and fathered a son (John) and two daughters while a trader at Palachooclee town (Apalachicola, a Hitchiti-speaking community) in Georgia; Foster, *Collected Works,* 171, 245–46; also see Bryant, *Tensaw Country,* 350–58.

204. Monette, *History,* 2:406; Rowland, *Mississippi Territory in the War of 1812,* 186.

205. Clanton, "Massacre," Clanton Papers; Halbert and Ball, *Creek War,* 160.

206. Sarah Summerlin must have been related (mother or sister-in-law?) to Nancy Summerlin, a former wife of James Bailey, and to Peggy Summerlin, "a half breed of the Creek nation," who fled in 1813 "from the half breed settlement in the Creek territory on the Alabama, to Peirce's fort near Mim's fort"; Lackey, *Frontier Claims,* 26, 29, 62–63 (quote). According to Henry Halbert, from his interview of the son of Rev. John Brown who assisted with the interment of those killed at Fort Mims, she was the only person identified among the dead by the burial party: "Near the western side of the ruined stockade, one of the soldiers recognized Mrs Sarah Summerlin, wife of John Summerlin. She was lying flat upon her back, with her arms stretched out at full length. She had been pregnant with twins. The Indians had disembowelled her, taken out the twins, and placed them on each side of the mother, the head of each infant resting on an arm of its mother. A most cruel and lamentable sight." Henry S. Halbert, "The burial of the dead at Fort Mims, March 3, 1887," in Tecumseh Papers, Draper WHS. Kathryn E. Holland Braund kindly provided this source.

207. F. L. Claiborne to Colonel Carson, September 4, 1813, Mount Vernon, in Letterbook F, J.F.H. Claiborne Collection, MDAH; Rowland, *Mississippi Territory in the War of 1812,* 186; Monette, *History,* 2:406.

208. Bryant, *Tensaw Country,* 331; Tarvin, "Muscogees or Creek Indians," 139.

209. Monette, *History,* 2:406; Rowland, *Mississippi Territory in the War of 1812,* 187 ("Turney").

210. Lackey, *Frontier Claims,* 46.

211. Bailey's "negro man, Tom, [was] still living, at Sisemore's plantation,)" in 1847; Pickett, *History of Alabama,* 2:274; see also Tarvin, "Muscogees or Creek Indians," 142.

212. "Uncle Tony Morgan . . . was interviewed on Oct. 1, 1884 by Jim Thomas, another [former] slave and a record of the conversation held in the files of a family in old Mobile, Alabama. Uncle Tony was 105 years old then. The story is told by Thomas, former slave of the Diard family. Uncle Tony was the slave of Mobile Judge H. Toulmin, grandfather of the later Judge H. T. Toulmin, who was appointed a judge by President Jefferson. . . . Uncle Tony's memory of what occurred at Fort Mims was vivid, according to Jim Thomas. The older slave related that he was one of many Negroes in the fort at the time. He said the

defenders had been sleeping off a night of dissipation the morning William Weatherford's warriors attacked. Men, women and children were butchered in the ensuing slaughter and the buildings were fired. The massacre continued until noon, Uncle Tony said, when the Indians retreated with scalps and several Negro prisoners to their camping site, called the Holy Ground. Here, the half-starved Negroes lived in constant dread that they would be butchered by war-inflamed Creeks. Uncle Tony also recalled carrying the mail from Fort Stoddert, in Alabama, through the State and Mississippi. On several occasions he barely escaped being scalped by Indians, he said"; Francois L. Diard, "A Slave Interviews a Slave, April 20, 1937," WPA Slave Narrative Project, Alabama Narratives, Federal Writers Project, WPA, Library of Congress. Another, very similar, interview of Tony Morgan appeared in Anonymous, "An Old Man Tells His Tale of Long Ago," *Mobile Register* (September 28, 1884).

213. Monette, *History*, 2:406; Rowland, *Mississippi Territory in the War of 1812*, 187.

214. "Major Kerr late commandant of Fort Decatur will deliver over to James Walker of Jones County Georgia one of the heirs of Wiseman Walker, who together with his family is said to have been killed at Fort Mims two Negro boys (Viz) one named Jack. about 10 or 13 years of age, another named Jim. about 8 or 10 years old said to have been the property of the said Wiseman Walker at the time of his dicease on condition the said James Walker will pay into the said Majr. David Kerr what expence is incurred on said Negroes & give them a Receipt for them on certain affadavits the said Walker has showing the right to said Negroes is vested in him"; H. W. Connor, Orderly Book, June 26, 1814, Graham Papers, NCDCR. An affidavit of Susannah Davis, Jones County, Georgia, January 4, 1817, SPR295, ADAH, "saith that John Walker is the brother of Wise Man Walker that they say was kild at fort mims." His name was also spelled "Wyseman."

215. Ibid. This woman had been married to Jeremiah Phillips' brother George. After George Phillips died in 1798, she married Wiseman Walker.

216. Ibid.

217. Receipt to Lieutenant Jonathan A. Watson from Thomas Camp, RG 94, NARA.

218. Stiggins, "Historical narration," 60, 65–66, 82; Woodward, *Reminiscences*, 80. After initiating the Redstick attack on Georgia militia troops at Calebee Creek, Walsh went to the lower Alabama River swamps near Standing Peach Tree where he remained, recovering from his wounds and ambushing passing whites, killing several, until captured and hanged in 1814 or 1815.

219. Pickett, *History of Alabama*, 2:267–75. Robert James described him as "six feet high—well formed & weighted about 165 lbs. . . . He had a high forehead, keen black eyes, very heavy eye brows firm white teeth—remarkably genteel in his person, dressed like a white man"; Notes taken from the lips of Col Robert James, Pickett Papers, ADAH. According to a relative, Weatherford "was said to have been in form, a perfect man, with all the physical graces which nature can bestow, He was 6 feet and 2 inches in hight, and weighed about 175 lbs, with a form of perfect mould, with the bearing and air of a Knight of the olden times"; J. D. Dreisbach Letter to Lyman Draper, July 1874, Draper WHS. Some mid-nineteenth-century sources give his Muskogee name as Lamochattee (*Lvmhe Catē*), Red Eagle.

220. Weekley family genealogy by Mrs. Donald Jones, 33465 Highway 1019, Denham Springs, LA 70706; Rowland, *Mississippi Territory in the War of 1812*, 186 ("Beford Weekley").

221. Hawkins to Armstrong, October 11, 1813, *ASP, Indian Affairs,* 1:852.

222. Halbert and Ball, *Creek War,* 157.

223. "Benjn. Whitehead (who was killed in Mim's fort)," in Lackey, *Frontier Claims,* 28, 64 (quote). He was probably related to Guillermo (William) Whitehead, who was listed in the 1787 Spanish census of the Tensaw; Hall, *Databases.*

Appendix 2

1. Up-to-date topographic maps are now available in atlas format by state. For instance, see *Alabama Atlas & Gazetteer.*

2. Charles W. Copeland, ed., *Geology of the Alabama Coastal Plain,* 35–36. John C. Hall reminded me of the geological interest of the Spanish Fort vantage point.

3. Town of Blakely, *Washington Republican* [Washington, Mississippi Territory] (Wednesday, October 6, 1813):1.

4. Thompson, *William Weatherford,* 358.

5. For a fascinating portrayal of modern-day racial conflict in the Tensaw, see Paul Hemphill, *The Ballad of Little River: A Tale of Race and Unrest in the Rural South.*

6. I am grateful to Jacob Lowrey for his willingness to share with me his very detailed knowledge of the Federal Road and other early paths and trails of southern Alabama.

7. Lawrence S. Earley, *Looking for Longleaf: The Fall and Rise of an American Forest,* 208–10, 219–21, 242, 251–53.

8. Robert Leslie Smith recounts how most of the cane in the Mobile-Tensaw delta disappeared mysteriously "in the winter of 1906–1907. The reason was never known to my parents. They speculated that the 1906 storm (hurricane) brought enough salt water up into the delta to kill the cane. Later in the year 1907, a fire broke out in the dead, dry rubble. Mother said that the entire western sky, as viewed from the family home on what is now Alabama Highway 59, was firey red in the night sky, and the sound of exploding cane carried for miles. Some have suggested that sudden die-off of cane is not unusual—that perhaps it is cyclical"; Smith, *Gone to the Swamp,* 3.

9. Quote from Billy Collins, "Plight of the Troubadour," 5.

10. Monette, *History,* 2:351 (quote). On December 14–17, 1804, itinerant ministers Learner Blackman, Nathan Barnes, Lorenzo Dow, and Randal Gibson held the first Methodist camp meeting in the territory on the Washington Campground. "Here by Washington, we appointed a camp meeting: there is ground laid off for a college;" in Dow, *Dealings of God, Man, and the Devil,* 100. William T. Blain, *Education in the Old Southwest: A History of Jefferson College, Washington, Mississippi,* 1–32. Perhaps someone will take an interest in Cowles Mead's residence and restore the building before it falls into irretrievable ruin.

11. Sue Moore suggested many of these historic sites in and around Natchez with Redstick War connections. See Jack D. Elliott, Jr., "City and Empire."

Bibliography

Manuscripts

Alabama, State of

Bay Minette, Baldwin County. Will Book A (1809–1827), Probate Court Records.
Monroeville, Monroe County. Probate Court Records.
Chatom, Washington County. Deed Book 1, Probate Court Records.

Alabama Department of Archives and History, Montgomery

Austill, Margaret Ervin. "Memories of Journeying through Creek Country and Childhood in Clarke County, 1811–1814," SPR237.
Claiborne, Ferdinand Leigh. Papers.
    John Durant to Alickander [Sandy] Durant "at the Apperlachcola," n.d.
Clanton, Dr. A. B. Papers.
Davis, Susannah. Affidavit, Jones County, Georgia, January 4, 1817, SPR295.
Dreisbach, J. D. "A Short Addenda to the paper furnished by the writer on June the 28th, 1877, Baldwin County, Ala.," July 28, 1883.
Estate Case Files of David Tate, Lynn Magee, George Stiggins, Dixon Bailey, James Earle, John Randon, and James Bailey. Final Settlements of Red Stick Claims, Baldwin County Probate Case 381, 1829–1855.
Pickett, Albert J. Papers. Pickett Family Papers (1779–1904), LPR185.
    Claiborne, Ferdinand Leigh. "Map of Fort Mims and Environs" [1813], CB-23.
    Notes Furnished by Col Jeremiah Austill, Section 1, Notes.
    Notes furnished by Col G. W. Creagh, 1847, Section 2, Notes.
    Notes furnished by Gen Patrick May, Section 3, Notes.
    Notes of Doctor Thomas G. Holmes, 1847, Section 4, Notes.
    Interesting Papers . . . by Col John F. H. Claiborne, Section 7, Notes.
    Very curious old M.S. furnished me by Dr. Edward Hamrick, Section 8, No. 12, Notes.
    Notes taken from the lips of Col Robert James, 1848, Section 12, Notes.
    Notes taken from the lips of Mr. George S. Gaines, Section 14, Notes.
    Notes taken from the lips of Abram Mordecai, 1847, Section 15, Notes.

Notes obtained from a conversation with Major Reuben Chamberlain, Section 18, Notes.

Notes taken from the lips of Hiram Mounger . . . by Col J Austill, 1848, Section 19, Notes.

Mr Byrne's account of the Death of his father, Section 20, Notes.

Notes furnished by Doct Thos G. Holmes, Section 22, Notes.

Notes furnished A. J. Pickett by the Rev Lee Compere, Section 24, Notes.

Notes taken from the lips of Dr Thos G. Holmes, 1848, Section 25, Notes.

Neal Smith to James Smiley, St. Stephens, Mississippi Territory, January 8, 1813. Neal Smith Collection.

Harry Toulmin to Ferdinand L. Claiborne, Fort Stoddert, July 23, 1813, SPR234.

Archivo General de Indias, Seville, Spain

Pedro de Favrot, Noticia y Nombres de los Habitantes en General, de la Plaza y Jurisdicción de la Mobila; en 1.° de Enero de 1786 [Census of the Mobile District, Mobile, 1 Jan. 1786], legajo 2360, fol. 50, Papeles procedentes de la Isla de Cuba. Cited as Noticia y Nombres, 1786.

Pedro de Favrot, Total General de la Jurisdicción de la Mobila del Primero de Enero del Año de 1787 [Census of the Mobile District, Mobile, 1 Jan. 1787], legajo 206, Papeles procedentes de la Isla de Cuba. Cited as Total General, 1787.

Cathedral of the Immaculate Conception, Mobile, Alabama

Baptismal Records Book 2 (1781–1850), Diocese of Mobile Sacramental Records.

Book of the Baptisms of the Americans of Tombicbee and adjacent parts who follow the Roman Catholic Religion under the spiritual Government of the Rht. Rvd. Lord Bishop of Baltimore; which Begins the 6th day of June of the year of our Lord one Thousand height hundred and one 1801. Diocese of Mobile Sacramental Records. Cited as Book of the Baptisms of the Americans of Tombicbee . . . 1801.

Marriage Book 1 (1724–1832). Diocese of Mobile Sacramental Records.

Church of Jesus Christ of Latter Day Saints, Family History Center, Salt Lake City, Utah

Court Minutes, 1803–1835, Orphans Court, Washington, Adams County, Mississippi (microfilm).

Court Records, 1805–1826, Port Gibson, Claiborne County, Mississippi (microfilm).

Court Records, 1802–1813, Fayette, Jefferson County, Mississippi Territory (microfilm).

Superior Court, Book C, Washington County, Mississippi Territory (microfilm).

Duke University, Rare Book, Manuscript, and Special Collections Library, Durham, North Carolina

Deposition of June 14, 1799, Jesse Rountree Papers, Collection no. 4581.

Fryeburg Historical Society, Fryeburg, Maine

Genealogical Records of the Frye Family.

Haverford College Library, Haverford, Pennsylvania

Indian Committee Records, Philadelphia Society of Friends Yearly Meeting (AA46), Quaker Collection.

Library of Congress, Washington, D.C.

Federal Writers Project, U.S. Works Progress Administration. Francois L. Diard, "A Slave Interviews a Slave, April 20, 1937"; WPA Slave Narrative Project, Alabama Narratives, 1:286–88.
Jackson, Andrew. Papers. Presidential Papers (M25).

Library of Virginia, Richmond

Amelia County. Deeds, Wills, Orders, Land Tax Lists, Personal Property Tax Lists, 1734–1811 (microfilm).
Chesterfield County. Deed Books 1–9, 1749–1783 (microfilm); Will Book, vol. 5 (microfilm).

Mississippi, State of

Chancery Clerk's Office, Fayette, Jefferson County. Will Book A, 1800–1833.
Orphans Court, Washington, Adams County. Court Minutes, 1803–1835.
Probate Court, Liberty, Amite County. Orphans Court Records.
Probate Court, Port Gibson, Claiborne County. Court Records, 1805–1826.

Mississippi Department of Archives and History, Jackson

Claiborne, J.F.H. Collection. Letterbook F: Letters and Papers Relating to the Indian Wars, 1812–1816. Cited as Claiborne, Letterbook F.
Jefferson County, Mississippi Territory
    Deed Book B1, 1804–1813 (microfilm)
    Minutes, Orphans Court Records, 1804–1814 (microfilm)
Mississippi Territory, Papers of, RG 2
    Territorial Governors' Papers, including Series 491, Executive Journal of Governor David Holmes (1813–1814); Register of Appointments (1805–1817) (microfilm); Series 487, Military Papers (1807–1815); Series 496, Bonds, Licenses, & Oaths of Office (1802–1817).

National Anthropological Archives, Smithsonian Institution, Suitland, Maryland

Shackelford, Edmund, to Ann and Frances Shackelford, Camp Armstrong, Chatahoocha, December 11, 1813, typed transcript, Manuscript 4911.

National Archives and Records Administration, Washington, D.C., and Silver Springs, Maryland

RG 15
    Records of the Veterans Administration, War of 1812, Claims of Widows for Pensions.

RG 49

Bureau of Land Management, General Land Office Records, Private Land Claims, Patent No. 246341.

Dinsmoor, Silas, and Levin Wailes, "Journal and Field Notes on the Boundary lines Between The United States and The Chaktaw nation of Indians Surveyed Pursuant to a Treaty concluded at Mount Dexter on the 16th day of November 1805," manuscript dated 1809. Old Case File, Item 1.

Records of the Bureau of Land Management, Special Acts, Treaty of Fort Jackson 1814, File 12, Laughlin Durant, Certif. No. 12, issued October 5, 1826 (cited as Durant Certificate); Report of David Mitchell, Agent for Indian Affairs, December 10, 1818, Treaty of Fort Jackson.

RG 75

Records of the Bureau of Indian Affairs, Letters Received by the Office of the Secretary of War Relating to Indian Affairs, 1800–1823 (M271), including Petition of Laughlin Durant & other half-breeds, Relatives of Alexr. McGilvray, a Creek Chief, May 29, 1815, and Petition of Sundry Halfbreeds, enclosed in Hawkins to Secretary of War, January 19, 1816.

Records of the Office of Indian Trade, Records of the Creek Agency East, Correspondence and Other Records, 1794–1818, Part 7, Box 1, PI-163, Entry 1065.

Property Left in 1836 in Tallassee and Chehaw Towns, May 6, 1838 (M574, roll 61), Special File 207.

RG 94

Carsons Ferry, Bill, August 3, 1813, Records of the Office of Adjutant General, Box 220 (Z).

Mims Ferry, Bill, August 2, 1813, Records of the Office of Adjutant General, Box 219.

Receipt to Lieutenant Jonathan A. Watson from Thomas Camp, Assistant Quartermaster General, Fort Jackson, July 15, 1814, Records of the Office of the Adjutant General (E-19, Box 205).

Records of the Office of the Adjutant General (1780s–1917), Compiled Service Records of Volunteer Soldiers Who Served during the War of 1812 in Organizations from the Territory of Mississippi, *National Archives Microfilm Publication* 678 (1967).

Records of Men Enlisted in the U.S. Army Prior to the Peace Establishment, May 17, 1815, Registers of Enlistments in the U.S. Army, 1798–1914 (M233).

RG 107

Records of the Office of the Secretary of War, Letters Received by the Secretary of War, Registered Series (1801–1870) (M221, 317 rolls), including "Report of Col Pearsons Expedition Against the Hostile Creeks on the Alabama, 'Camp Ho-to-wa Ninety four miles from Fort Jackson, East bank of the Allabama and half a days journey below the mouth of Ka-ha-ba, June 1st 1814," enclosure in Pinckney to Secretary of War, June 28, 1814 (roll 65, P27). Cited as "Report of Col Pearsons Expedition."

Letters Received by the Secretary of War, Unregistered Series (1789–1861) (M222, 34 rolls).

RG 123

U.S. Court of Claims, The Eastern Cherokee vs. No. 23,214 The United States, "Creek File Testimony" Taken before Guion Miller, Special Commissioner, February 1908.

RG 233

Records of the U.S. House of Representatives, 14th Cong., 1st sess., Other Select Committees, "Sworn statements with accompanying exhibits of sundry inhabitants of the Mississippi Territory, September–November, 1815, praying for relief from Indian depredations, January 2, 1816" (HR 14A-F16.7).

North Carolina Department of Cultural Resources, Division of Archives and History, Raleigh

Graham, Joseph (1759–1836). Papers.

P. K. Yonge Library, University of Florida, Gainesville

Cochrane, Admiral Alexander Forrester Inglis. Papers. MS 2328, National Library of Scotland, Edinburgh (PKY microfilm reel 65M).

Governor González Manrique to Captain General Ruiz Apodaca, Pensacola, July 23, 1813, in Archivo General de Indias, Papeles procedentes de la Isla de Cuba, legajo 1794, 1417 (PKY microfilm reel 112).

Josiah Francis, the Old King, Old Interpreter, and Mougceweihche to Governor González Manrique [August 1813], Papeles procedentes de la Isla de Cuba, legajo 221B, 335–36v (PKY microfilm reel 311).

Manuel de Lanzos to Arturo Oneill, Mobile, March 21, 1793, in Archivo General de Indias, Papeles procedentes de la Isla de Cuba, legajo 64, doc. 50, 31 (PKY microfilm reel 440).

Rockefeller Library, Colonial Williamsburg Foundation, Williamsburg, Virginia

Virginia Land Office Patent Books, 1623–1762.

St. Stephens Historical Society, St. Stephens, Alabama

Washington County, Mississippi Territory. Lower Court Docket Book, 1807–1812.

University of Georgia Libraries, Athens

Wheaton, Joseph. Papers, MS 1124.

University of North Carolina, Chapel Hill, Library, Southern Historical Collection, Manuscripts Department

Austill, Margaret Ervin. Early Life of Margaret Ervin Austill. Jeremiah Austill Papers, #2214 (typescript).

Claiborne Letters (1815–1836). Magdalene H. Claiborne Collection.

Osborne, Edwin Augustus. Papers.

University of South Alabama Archives, Mobile

Weatherford vs. Weatherford, Case No. 1299 (1846), Mobile County Chancery Court Records.

University of South Alabama Library, Mobile

Papers of Panton Leslie, and Co., edited by William S. Coker (microfilm edition). Woodbridge, Conn.: Research Publications, 1986.

University of Texas at Austin, Center for American History, Natchez Trace Small Manuscript Collection

Frye, Samuel. Papers, Box 2E558.
Shaw, John. Papers, Box 2E574.

Virginia Historical Society, Richmond

Chesterfield County. Beasley vs. Beasley Legatees, March 1794, 1794-17, Box 6, Chancery Court Records; Personal Property Tax Lists, 1796–1803.
Nottoway County Land Tax Lists, 1789–1799, and Personal Property Tax Lists, 1790–1797; County Court Papers, 1790–1817.

W. S. Hoole Special Collections Library, University of Alabama, Tuscaloosa

Griffin, Jesse. Manuscript Letter.

Wisconsin Historical Society, Madison

Draper, Lyman. Manuscript Collection.
    Dreisbach, J. D. Papers.
    Dreisbach, J. D. Letter to Lyman C. Draper. July 1874, Georgia, Alabama, and South Carolina Papers, 1782–1878.
    Halbert, Henry S. Letters on Fort Mims, November 10, 1882, to March 3, 1887.
    Series YY: Tecumseh Papers (microfilm reel 119).
    Stiggins, George. "A Historical narration of the Genealogy traditions and downfall of the Ispocaga or Creek tribe of Indians, written by one of the tribe," in vol. 1, ser. 5, Georgia, Alabama, and South Carolina Papers.

Maps

Anonymous. "Land Granted and Surveyed on the River and Bay of Mobile, ca. 1775," Colonial Office 700, Florida 51, The National Archives. British Public Record Office, Kew, London.
Anonymous. "Settlements on the Tombeckby & Tensaw Rivers," Old Map File, Alabama 2, Records of the General Land Office, RG 49, NARA.
Eleazer Early. *Map of Georgia,* prepared by Daniel Sturges, 1818. University of Georgia Libraries, Athens.

John Melish. *Map of Alabama*, 1819. University of Alabama Library, Tuscaloosa.

David Taitt. "A Plan of part of the Rivers Tombecbe, Alabama, Tensa, Perdido, & Scambia In the Province of West Florida, ca. 1771," Geography & Map Collection, G3971.P53, 1771.T3 Vault, Library of Congress, Washington, D.C.

[Howell Tatum]. General Jackson's campaign against the Creek Indians, 1813 & 1814, Civil Works Map File, RG 77, NARA, Washington, D.C.

Newspapers

Columbian Sentinel, Boston, Massachusetts
Courrier de la Louisiane, New Orleans, Louisiana
Covington Times, Andalusia, Alabama
Georgia Gazette, Savannah, Georgia
Mississippi Messenger, Natchez, Mississippi Territory
Mississippi Republican, Natchez, Mississippi Territory
Mobile Register, Mobile, Alabama
National Intelligencer, Washington, D.C.
New-York Spectator, New York, New York
Pennsylvania Packet and Daily Advertiser, Philadelphia, Pennsylvania
Raymond Gazette, Hinds County, Mississippi
Richmond Enquirer, Richmond, Virginia
The War, New York, New York
Washington Republican, Washington, Mississippi Territory
Weekly Chronicle, Natchez, Mississippi Territory
Weekly Register, Baltimore, Maryland

Printed Sources

Abernethy, Thomas P. *The Formative Period in Alabama.* Montgomery: Brown Printing, 1922.

Adair, James. *The History of the American Indians.* Edited by Kathryn E. Holland Braund. Tuscaloosa: University of Alabama Press, 2005.

Akers, Frank H., Jr. "The Unexpected Challenge: The Creek War of 1813–1814." Ph.D. dissertation, Duke University, Department of History, 1975.

Alabama Atlas & Gazetteer. 2nd ed. Yarmouth, Maine: DeLorme, 2003.

Albanese, Catherine L. "Savage, Sinner, and Saved: Davy Crockett, Camp Meetings, and the Wild Frontier." *American Quarterly* 33 (Winter 1981):482–501.

Anderson, Virginia DeJohn. *Creatures of Empire: How Domestic Animals Transformed Early America.* Oxford, U.K.: Oxford University Press, 2004.

Anonymous. "Editorial Notes—Literature." *Putnam's Monthly* 31 (July 1855):657–58.

———. "Federal Acknowledgment of the Poarch Band of Creeks; Proposed Finding." *Federal Register* 49 (January 9, 1984):1141.

———. "Notes and Queries: Ensign Isaac W. Davis." *Gulf States Historical Magazine* 1 (June 1903):456.

——. "An Old Soldier." *Washington Republican* 1 (October 27, 1813):2.

——. "Indian Eloquence." *Washington Republican* 2 (June 8, 1814):1.

——. *A Narrative of the Life and Death of Lieut. Joseph Morgan Wilcox, Who was Massacred by the Creek Indians, on the Alabama River, (Miss. Ter.) on the 15th of January, 1814.* Marietta, Ohio: R. Prentiss, 1816.

——. "An Old Man Tells His Tale of Long Ago." *Mobile Register* (September 28, 1884).

Appleton, James Lamar, and Robert David Ward. "Albert James Pickett and the Case of the Secret Articles: Historians and the Treaty of New York of 1790." *Alabama Review* 51 (January 1998):3–36.

Arthur, T. S., and W. H. Carpenter. *The History of Georgia, from Its Earliest Settlement to the Present Time.* Philadelphia: Lippincott, Grambo, 1858.

Austill, Jeremiah. [Autobiography]. *Alabama Historical Quarterly* 6 (Spring 1944):84–86.

Austill, Margaret Ervin. "Life of Margaret Ervin Austill." *Alabama Historical Quarterly* 6 (Spring 1944):92–98.

Baer, Mabel Van Dyke. "Abstracts of Important Documents Found in Pension Applications of Soldiers of the Revolutionary War, War of 1812, War with Creek Indians." *Kentucky Genealogist* 3 (October–December 1961).

Bagwell, David A. "The Treaty of Mount Dexter of 1805 and the Old Indian Treaty Boundary Line of 1809." Manuscript on file, Center for Archaeological Studies, University of South Alabama, Mobile, n.d.

Ballard, Robert D., and Spencer Dunmore. *Exploring the Lusitania: Probing the Mysteries of the Sinking That Changed History.* New York: Warner Books, 1995.

Barber, Douglas. "Council Government and the Genesis of the Creek War." *Alabama Review* 38 (July 1985):163–74.

Barnard, Susan K., and Grace M. Schwartzman. "Tecumseh and the Creek Indian War of 1813–1814 in North Georgia." *Georgia Historical Quarterly* 82 (Fall 1998):489–506.

Bartram, William. *Travels through North & South Carolina, Georgia, East & West Florida, the Cherokee Country, the Extensive Territories of the Muscogulgees, or Creek Confederacy, and the Country of the Choctaws.* Philadelphia: James & Johnson, 1791.

Bassett, John Spencer, ed. *Correspondence of Andrew Jackson.* Vol. 1, to April 30, 1814. Vol. 2, May 1, 1814, to December 31, 1819. Carnegie Institution of Washington, Publication 371. Washington, D.C., 1926.

——, ed. "Major Howell Tatum's Journal." *Smith College Studies in History* 7 (1–3, 1922).

Batson, James L. *James Bowie and the Sandbar Fight: Birth of the James Bowie Legend & Bowie Knife.* Madison, Ala: the author, 1992.

Beidler, Philip D. "A. B. Meek's Great American Epic Poem of 1855; or, the Curious Career of the Red Eagle." *Mississippi Quarterly* 51 (2, Spring 1998):275–90.

——. *First Books: The Printed Word and Cultural Formation in Early Alabama.* Tuscaloosa: University of Alabama Press, 1999.

——. "Literature and the Art of Political Payback in an Early Alabama Classic." *Southern Literary Journal* 30 (Fall 1997):1–12.

Benn, Carl. *The War of 1812.* Oxford, U.K.: Osprey Publishing, 2002.

Bergh, Albert Ellery, ed. *The Writings of Thomas Jefferson.* Vol. 10. Washington, D.C.: Thomas Jefferson Memorial Association, 1903.

Berkhofer, Robert F., Jr. *Salvation and the Savage: An Analysis of Protestant Missions and American Indian Response, 1787–1862.* Lexington: University of Kentucky Press, 1965.

Berlin, Ira. *Generations of Captivity: A History of African-American Slaves.* Cambridge, Mass.: Belknap Press, 2003.

———. *Many Thousands Gone: The First Two Centuries of Slavery in North America.* Cambridge: Harvard University Press, 1998.

Black, Henry Campbell. *Black's Law Dictionary: Definitions of the Terms and Phrases of American and English Jurisprudence, Ancient and Modern.* 5th edition. St. Paul, Minn.: West Publishing, 1979.

Blain, William T. *Education in the Old Southwest: A History of Jefferson College, Washington, Mississippi.* Washington, Miss.: Friends of Jefferson College, 1976.

Blair, Emma H., ed. *The Indian Tribes of the Upper Mississippi Valley and Region of the Great Lakes.* 2 vols. Cleveland, Ohio: Arthur H. Clark Co., 1912.

Booker, Karen M., Charles M. Hudson, and Robert L. Rankin. "Place Name Identification and Multilingualism in the Sixteenth-Century Southeast." *Ethnohistory* 39 (Fall 1992):399–451.

Borneman, Walter R. *1812: The War that Forged a Nation.* New York: HarperCollins, 2004.

Bourne, Russell. *Gods of War, Gods of Peace: How the Meeting of Native and Colonial Religions Shaped Early America.* New York: Harcourt, 2002.

Boyd, Mark F. "Diego Peña's Expedition to Apalachee and Apalachicolo in 1716." *Florida Historical Quarterly* 28 (April 1949):1–27.

———. "Documents Describing the Second and Third Expeditions of Lieutenant Diego Peña to Apalachee and Apalachicolo in 1717 and 1718." *Florida Historical Quarterly* 31 (July 1952):109–39.

———. "The Expedition of Marcos Delgado from Apalache to the Upper Creek Country in 1686." *Florida Historical Quarterly* 16 (April 1937):2–32.

Brannon, Peter A. "Dueling in Alabama." *Alabama Historical Quarterly* 17 (Fall 1955): 97–104.

———. "Spruce McCall Osborne." *Alabama Historical Quarterly* 5 (Spring 1943):68–70.

———. "Through the Years: Survivors of Fort Mims." *Montgomery Advertiser* (clipping), n.d.

———, ed. "Journal of James A. Tait for the Year 1813." *Georgia Historical Quarterly* 8 (September 1924):229–39.

Brasseaux, Carl E. *France's Forgotten Legion: Service Records of French Military and Administrative Personnel Stationed in the Mississippi Valley and Gulf Coast Region, 1699–1769,* CD-ROM. Baton Rouge: Louisiana State University Press, 2000.

Braund, Kathryn E. Holland. "The Creek Indians, Blacks, and Slavery." *Journal of Southern History* 57 (November 1991):601–36.

———. "Guardians of Tradition and Handmaidens to Change: Women's Roles in Creek Economic and Social Life in the Eighteenth Century." *American Indian Quarterly* 14 (Summer 1990):239–58.

———. "'Like a Stone Wall Never to be Broke': The British-Indian Boundary Line with the Creek Indians, 1763–1773." In *Britain and the American South: Encounters and Ex-*

changes from Colonial Times to Rock and Roll, edited by Joseph P. Ward, 53–80. Oxford: University of Mississippi Press, 2003.

Brookes, Richard. *Brookes's General Gazetteer.* 9th ed. Philadelphia, 1808.

Brooms, McDonald. *Archaeological Investigations at the Kennedy Mill Site: 1Ba301 in Baldwin County, Alabama.* Troy, Ala.: Troy State University, Archaeological Research Center, 1996.

Bruce, Dickson D., Jr. *And They All Sang Hallelujah: Plain-Folk Camp-Meeting Religion, 1800–1845.* Knoxville: University of Tennessee Press, 1974.

———. *Violence and Culture in the Antebellum South.* Austin: University of Texas Press, 1979.

Bryant, Charles E. *Oh God, What Have I Done.* Panama City, Fla.: the author, 2002.

———. *The Tensaw Country North of the Ellicott Line, 1800–1860.* Bay Minette, Ala.: Lavender Press, 1998.

Buchanan, John. *Jackson's Way: Andrew Jackson and the People of the Western Waters.* New York: John Wiley & Sons, 2001.

Burstein, Andrew. *The Passions of Andrew Jackson.* New York: Alfred A. Knopf, 2003.

Byrd, Max. *Jackson: A Novel.* New York: Bantam, 1997.

Calhoun, Robert Dabney. "A History of Concordia Parish." *Louisiana Historical Quarterly* 15 (October 1932).

Calvit, Alexander. "Extract of a letter from Capt. Alexander Calvit, aid-de-camp to Gen. Claiborne, Cantonment, Mount Vernon, Sept. 23, 1813." *Supplement to the Washington Republican—Sept. 29, 1813* (September 30, 1813):1.

Canclini, Néstor García. *Hybrid Cultures: Strategies for Entering and Leaving Modernity.* Minneapolis: University of Minnesota Press, 1995.

Carey, Mathew. *Carey's General Atlas, Improved and Enlarged: Being a Collection of the Maps of the World and Quarters, Their Principal Empires, Kingdoms, &c.* Philadelphia: the author, 1814.

Carter, Clarence Edward, ed. *The Territorial Papers of the United States,* vols. 5–6, *The Territory of Mississippi, 1798–1817.* Washington, D.C.: Government Printing Office, 1937–38.

———, ed. *The Territorial Papers of the United States,* vol. 18, *The Territory of Alabama, 1817–1819.* Washington, D.C.: U.S. Department of State, 1939.

Casagrande, Joseph B., Stephen I. Thompson, and Philip D. Young. "Colonization as a Research Frontier: The Ecuadorian Case." In *Process and Pattern in Culture: Essays in Honor of Julian Steward,* edited by Robert A. Manners, 281–325. Chicago: Aldine, 1964.

Casender, Don Pedro [M. Smith?]. *The Lost Virgin of the South: An Historical Novel, Founded on Facts, Connected with the Indian War in the South, in 1812 to '15.* Tallahassee, Fla.: M. Smith, 1831, and Courtland, Ala.: M. Smith, 1832.

Casey, Albert E. *Amite County, Mississippi, 1699–1865.* Birmingham, Ala.: the author, 1948.

Cashin, Edward J. *The King's Ranger: Thomas Brown and the American Revolution on the Southern Frontier.* Athens: University of Georgia Press, 1989.

———. *Lachlan McGillivray, Indian Trader: The Shaping of the Southern Colonial Frontier.* Athens: University of Georgia Press, 1992.

Caughey, John Walton. *McGillivray of the Creeks.* Norman: University of Oklahoma Press, 1938.

Cave, Alfred A. "The Delaware Prophet Neolin: A Reappraisal." *Ethnohistory* 46 (1999): 265–90.

Chaudhuri, Jean, and Joyotpaul Chaudhuri. *A Sacred Path: The Way of the Muscogee Creeks.* Los Angeles: UCLA American Indian Studies Center, 2001.

Chaudhuri, Joyotpaul, "American Indian Policy: An Overview." In *American Indian Policy in the Twentieth Century,* edited by Vine Deloria, 15–33. Norman: University of Oklahoma Press, 1985.

Claiborne, Ferdinand L. "To the Editor of the Mississippi Republican." *Supplement to the Mississippi Republican* (March 25, 1814):1–2.

———. "Extract of a letter from Gen. Ferdinand L. Claiborne to Gen. Flournoy, commanding the 7th Military District, Cantonment, Mount Vernon, 3rd September, 1813." *Richmond Enquirer, Extra* (October 9, 1813).

———. "From the Mississippi Republican Extra, Mount Vernon, Sept. 21st. 1813." *Supplement to the Washington Republican—Sept. 29, 1813* (September 30, 1813):1.

Claiborne, J.F.H. *Life and Times of Gen. Sam. Dale, the Mississippi Partisan.* New York: Harper & Brothers, 1860.

———. *Mississippi, as a Province, Territory and State.* Jackson, Miss.: Power & Barksdale, 1880.

Claiborne, Nathaniel Herbert. *Notes on the War in the South.* Richmond, Va.: William Ramsay, 1819.

Clark, Thomas D., and John D. W. Guice. *The Old Southwest, 1795–1830: Frontiers in Conflict.* Norman: University of Oklahoma Press, 1996.

Coker, William S., and Thomas D. Watson. *Indian Traders of the Southeastern Spanish Borderlands: Panton, Leslie & Company and John Forbes & Company, 1783–1847.* Pensacola: University of West Florida Press, 1986.

Collins, Billy. "Plight of the Troubadour." *Sailing Along Around the Room.* New York: Random House, 2001.

Comings, L. J. Newcomb, and Martha M. Albers. *A Brief History of Baldwin County.* Fairhope, Ala.: Baldwin County Historical Society, 1928.

Conn, Steven. *History's Shadow: Native Americans and Historical Consciousness in the Nineteenth Century.* Chicago: University of Chicago Press, 2004.

Copeland, Charles W., ed. *Geology of the Alabama Coastal Plain.* Geological Survey of Alabama Circular 47. Tuscaloosa, 1968.

Corkran, David H. *The Creek Frontier, 1540–1783.* Norman: University of Oklahoma Press, 1967.

Cox, Isaac Joslin. *The West Florida Controversy, 1798–1813.* Baltimore: Johns Hopkins University Press, 1918.

Cox, William R. "Postscript, Mr. William R. Cox, (surgeon's Mate in Gen. Claiborne's brigade,) arrived in town last evening from the vicinity of Fort St. Stevens, by whom we have received the following: Extract of a letter from Judge Tolmin, to General Flournoy, dated Sept 1." *Washington Republican* (September 8, 1813):2.

Crisp, James E. *Sleuthing the Alamo: Davy Crockett's Last Stand and Other Mysteries of the Texas Revolution.* New York: Oxford University Press, 2005.

Crockett, David. *A Narrative of the Life of David Crockett of the State of Tennessee.* Anno-

tated and with an introduction by James A. Shackford and Stanley J. Folmsbee. Knoxville: University of Tennessee Press, 1973.

Davies, K. G., ed. *Documents of the American Revolution, 1770–1783 (Colonial Office Series).*
21 vols. Shannon: Irish University Press, 1972–81.

Davis, Karl. "'Much of the Indian Appears': Adaptation and Persistence in a Creek Community, 1783–1854." Ph.D. dissertation, Department of History, University of North
Carolina, Chapel Hill, 2003.

———. "'Remember Fort Mims': Reinterpreting the Origins of the Creek War." *Journal of
the Early Republic* 22 (Winter 2002):612–36.

Davis, William C. *Lone Star Rising: The Revolutionary Birth of the Texas Republic.* New
York: Free Press, 2004.

Dawson, Henry B. *Battles of the United States by Sea and Land,* 2 vols. New York: Johnson,
Fry & Company, 1858.

Dennstedt, Alberta Marjorie. "The Cheathan Family of Colonial Virginia." *Virginia Genealogist* 28 (April–June 1984):102–12.

Dickens, Roy S., Jr. *Archaeological Investigations at Horseshoe Bend, National Military Park,
Alabama.* Alabama Archaeological Society, Special Publication 3. Tuscaloosa: Alabama
Archaeological Society, 1979.

Dickins, Asbury, and James C. Allen, eds. *American State Papers, Public Lands.* Vol. 4,
Commencing December 1, 1823, and Ending March 3, 1827. Washington, D.C.: Gales &
Seaton, 1859.

Dickins, Asbury, and John W. Forney, eds. *American State Papers, Public Lands.* Vol. 5, *1827–
1829.* Washington, D.C.: Gales & Seaton, 1860.

Donovan, Kenneth. *Slaves in Cape Breton, 1713–1815.* Lincoln: University of Nebraska
Press, 2006.

Doolittle, William E. *Cultivated Landscapes of Native North America.* Oxford, U.K.: Oxford University Press, 2000.

Doster, James F. "Early Settlement on the Tombigbee and Tensaw Rivers." *Alabama Review* 12 (April 1959):83–94.

———, ed. "Letters Relating to the Tragedy of Fort Mims: August–September, 1813."
Alabama Review 14 (1961):269–85.

Dow, Lorenzo. *The Dealings of God, Man, and the Devil: As Experienced in the Life,
Experience, and Travels of Lorenzo Dow.* New York: Lamport, Blakeman & Law, 1853.

Dow, Peggy. *Vicissitudes in the Wilderness.* New York: Lamport, Blakeman & Law, 1853.

Dowd, Gregory Evans. "The American Revolution to the Mid-Nineteenth Century." In
Handbook of North American Indians, vol. 14, *Southeast,* edited by Raymond D. Fogelson, 139–51. Washington, D.C: Smithsonian Institution, 2004.

———. *A Spirited Resistance: The North American Indian Struggle for Unity, 1745–1815.*
Baltimore, Md.: Johns Hopkins University Press, 1992.

———. *War Under Heaven: Pontiac, the Indian Nations, and the British Empire.* Baltimore,
Md.: Johns Hopkins University Press, 2002.

Driesbach, J. D. "Weatherford—'The Red Eagle.'" *Alabama Historical Reporter* 2 (February
1884):n.p., 2 (March 1884):n.p., and 2 (April 1884):n.p.

Dunham, Ethel Morgan. *Echoes of Alabama*. Cleveland, Ohio: Pegasus Studios, 1939.

Earley, Lawrence S. *Looking for Longleaf: The Fall and Rise of an American Forest*. Chapel Hill: University of North Carolina Press, 2004.

Edmunds, R. David. *The Shawnee Prophet*. Lincoln: University of Nebraska Press, 1983.

———. *Tecumseh and the Quest for Indian Leadership*. Boston: Little, Brown and Co., 1984.

Eggleston, George Cary. *Red Eagle and the Wars with the Creek Indians of Alabama*. New York: Dodd, Mead & Co., 1878.

Elliott, Jack D., Jr. "City and Empire: The Spanish Origins of Natchez." *Journal of Mississippi History* 59 (Winter 1997):271–321.

———. "The Plymouth Fort and the Creek War: A Mystery Solved." *Journal of Mississippi History* 62 (Fall 2000):328–70.

Ethridge, Robbie. *Creek Country: The Creek Indians and Their World*. Chapel Hill: University of North Carolina Press, 2003.

Evarts, Jeremiah [William Penn, pseud.]. *Essays on the Present Crisis in the Condition of the American Indians*. Philadelphia: Thomas Kite, 1830.

Fabel, Robin F. A. *The Economy of British West Florida, 1763–1783*. Tuscaloosa: University of Alabama Press, 1988.

Fagan, Brian. *The Little Ice Age: How Climate Made History, 1300–1850*. New York: Basic Books, 2000.

Fairbanks, Charles H., "Excavations at Horseshoe Bend, Alabama." *Florida Anthropologist* 15 (1962):41–56.

Faragher, John Mack. *A Great and Noble Scheme: The Tragic Story of the Expulsion of the French Acadians from Their American Homeland*. New York: W. W. Norton, 2005.

Feiler, Seymour, trans. and ed. *Jean-Bernard Bossu's Travels in the Interior of North America, 1751–1762*. Norman: University of Oklahoma Press, 1962.

Feldman, Jay. *When the Mississippi Ran Backwards: Empire, Intrigue, Murder, and the New Madrid Earthquake*. New York: Free Press, 2005.

Fiorato, Veronica, Anthea Boylston, and Christopher Knüsel, eds. *Blood Red Roses: The Archaeology of a Mass Grave from the Battle of Towton, AD 1461*. Oxford, U.K.: Oxbow Books, 2000.

Fischer, David Hackett, and James C. Kelly. *Bound Away: Virginia and the Westward Movement*. Charlottesville: University Press of Virginia, 2000.

Fleming, Thomas. *Duel: Alexander Hamilton, Aaron Burr, and the Future of America*. New York: Basic Books, 2000.

Flores, Richard D. *Remembering the Alamo: Memory, Modernity, and the Master Symbol*. Austin: University of Texas Press, 2002.

Floyd, John. "Letters of John Floyd, 1813–1838." *Georgia Historical Quarterly* 33 (3, 1949): 228–69.

Foster, H. Thomas II, ed. *The Collected Works of Benjamin Hawkins, 1796–1810*. Tuscaloosa: University of Alabama Press, 2003.

Fox, Richard Allan, Jr. *Archaeology, History, and Custer's Last Battle: The Little Big Horn Reexamined*. Norman: University of Oklahoma Press, 1993.

Frank, Andrew K. *Creeks and Southerners: Biculturalism on the Early American Frontier.* Lincoln: University of Nebraska Press, 2005.

Freeman, Joanne B. *Affairs of Honor: National Politics in the New Republic.* New Haven, Conn.: Yale University Press, 2002.

———. "Dueling as Politics: Reinterpreting the Burr-Hamilton Duel." *William and Mary Quarterly* 53 (April 1996):289–318.

Gaff, Alan D. *Bayonets in the Wilderness: Anthony Wayne's Legion in the Old Northwest.* Norman: University of Oklahoma Press, 2004.

Gillis, Norman E., comp. *Early Inhabitants of the Natchez District.* Baton Rouge, La.: the compiler, 1963.

Giraud, Marcel. *Le Métis canadien: son rôle dans l'histoire des provinces de l'Ouest.* Paris: Institut d'ethnologie, 1945.

Gosden, Chris. *Archaeology and Colonialism: Cultural Contact from 5000 BC to the Present.* Cambridge, U.K.: Cambridge University Press, 2004.

Graham, John Simpson. *The History of Clarke County.* Birmingham, Ala.: Birmingham Print Co., 1923.

Grant, C. L., ed. *Letters, Journals and Writings of Benjamin Hawkins.* 2 vols. Savannah, Ga.: Beehive Press, 1980.

Green, Michael D. "The Expansion of European Colonization to the Mississippi Valley, 1780–1880." In *The Cambridge History of the Native Peoples of the Americas.* Vol. 1, *North America,* part 1, 461–538. Cambridge, U.K.: Cambridge University Press, 1996.

———. *The Politics of Indian Removal: Creek Government and Society in Crisis.* Lincoln: University of Nebraska Press, 1982.

Greene, Jerome A., and Douglas D. Scott. *Finding Sand Creek: History, Archeology, and the 1864 Massacre Site.* Norman: University of Oklahoma Press, 2004.

Greenslade, Marie Taylor. "William Panton." *Florida Historical Quarterly* 14 (October 1935):107–29.

Gremillion, Kristen J. "Comparative Paleoethnobotany of Three Native Southeastern Communities of the Historic Period." *Southeastern Archaeology* 14 (1, 1995):1–16.

Griffith, Benjamin W., Jr. *McIntosh and Weatherford, Creek Indian Leaders.* Tuscaloosa: University of Alabama Press, 1988.

Gruzinski, Serge. *La pensée métisse.* Paris: Librairie Arthème Fayard, 1999. Published in translation as *The Mestizo Mind: The Intellectual Dynamics of Colonization and Globalization.* New York: Routledge, 2002.

Hahn, Marilyn Davis. *Old St. Stephens' Land Office Records and American State Papers, Public Lands.* Vol. 1, *1768–1888.* Easley, S.C.: Southern Historical Press, 1983.

Hahn, Steven C. *The Invention of the Creek Nation, 1670–1763.* Lincoln: University of Nebraska Press, 2004.

Halaas, David Fridtjof, and Andrew E. Masich. *Halfbreed: The Remarkable True Story of George Bent Caught between the Worlds of the Indian and the White Man.* Cambridge, Mass.: Da Capo Press, 2004.

Halbert, Henry S. "Choctaw Indian Names in Alabama and Mississippi." *Alabama Historical Society Transactions, 1898–1899,* 3 (1899):64–77.

———. "The Creek Red Stick." *Alabama Historical Reporter* 2 (May 1884).

———. "Creek War Incidents." *Alabama Historical Society Transactions, 1897–1898,* 2 (1898):95–119.

———. "Ensign Isaac W. Davis and Hanson's Mill." *Gulf States Historical Magazine* 1 (September 1902):151.

———. "An Incident of Fort Mimms." *Alabama Historical Reporter* 2 (May 1884).

———. "Some Inaccuracies in Claiborne's History in Regard to Tecumseh." *Publications of the Mississippi Historical Society* 1 (1898):101–3.

Halbert, Henry S., and Timothy H. Ball. *The Creek War of 1813 and 1814.* Chicago: Donohue & Henneberry, 1895.

Hall, Arthur H. "The Red Stick War: Creek Indian Affairs During the War of 1812." *Chronicles of Oklahoma* 12 (3, 1934):264–93.

Hall, Gwendolyn Midlo, ed. *Databases for the Study of Afro-Louisiana History and Genealogy, 1699–1860: Computerized Information from Original Manuscript Sources.* CD edition. Baton Rouge: Louisiana State University Press, 2000.

Hamilton, Peter J. *Colonial Mobile: An Historical Study.* Rev. ed. Cambridge, Mass.: Riverside Press, 1910.

Hardin, Stephen L., and Gary S. Zaboly. *Texian Iliad: A Military History of the Texas Revolution, 1835–1836.* Austin: University of Texas Press, 1996.

Hassig, Ross. "Internal Conflict in the Creek War of 1813–1814." *Ethnohistory* 21 (Summer 1974):251–71.

Havard, Gilles. *Empire et métissages: Indiens et Français dans le Pays d'en Haut, 1660–1715.* Quebec: Septentrion, 2003.

Hawkins, Benjamin. "Extract of a Letter to John Floyd, Sept. 26, 1813." *New-York Spectator* (October 16, 1813):4.

Headley, Katy McCaleb. *Claiborne County, Mississippi: The Promised Land.* Port Gibson, Miss.: Port Gibson–Claiborne Historical Society, 1976.

Heidler, David S., and Jeanne T. Heidler, eds. *Encyclopedia of the War of 1812.* Santa Barbara, Calif.: ABC-CLIO, 1997.

Heitman, Francis B. *Historical Register and Dictionary of the United States Army.* Washington: Government Printing Office, 1903.

Hemphill, Paul. *The Ballad of Little River: A Tale of Race and Unrest in the Rural South.* Tuscaloosa: University of Alabama Press, 2001.

Henri, Florette. *The Southern Indians and Benjamin Hawkins, 1796–1816.* Norman: University of Oklahoma, 1986.

Hickey, Donald R. *The War of 1812.* Urbana: University of Illinois Press, 1989.

Holmes, Jack D. "Alabama's Forgotten Settlers: Notes on the Spanish Mobile District, 1780–1813." *Alabama Historical Quarterly* 33 (Summer 1971):87–97.

———, ed. "Fort Stoddard in 1799: Seven Letters of Captain Bartholomew Shaumburgh." *Alabama Historical Quarterly* 26 (Fall–Winter 1964):231–52.

Horsman, Reginald. *Expansion and American Indian Policy, 1783–1812.* Norman: University of Oklahoma Press, 1967.

———. "The Indian Policy of an 'Empire for Liberty.'" In *Native Americans and the Early Republic,* edited by Frederick E. Hoxie, Ronald Hoffman, and Peter J. Albert, 37–61.

Charlottesville: United States Capitol Historical Society by the University Press of Virginia, 1999.

Howard, Clinton N. *The British Development of West Florida, 1763–1769.* University of California Publications in History 34. Berkeley, 1947.

Howard, James H. *Shawnee! The Ceremonialism of a Native American Tribe and its Cultural Background.* Athens: Ohio University Press, 1981.

Hudson, Charles M. *The Southeastern Indians.* Knoxville: University of Tennessee Press, 1976.

Hunt, David C., and Marsha V. Gallagher, eds. *Karl Bodmer's America.* Lincoln: Joslyn Art Museum and University of Nebraska Press, 1984.

Hutchinson, J. R. *Reminiscences, Sketches and Addresses Selected from My Papers During a Ministry of Forty-five Years in Mississippi, Louisiana, and Texas.* Houston, Tex.: E. H. Cushing, 1874.

Innerarity, John. "A Prelude to the Creek War of 1813–1814, in a Letter of John Innerarity to James Innerarity." *Florida Historical Quarterly* 18 (April 1940):247–66.

Jackson, Andrew. "To Gov. Blount, With the Creek Indians, November 4, 1813." *Columbian Sentinel* (December 1, 1813):3.

James, D. Clayton. *Antebellum Natchez.* Baton Rouge: Louisiana State University Press, 1968.

Jones, Charles L. S. *American Lyrics; Comprising the Discovery, A Poem; Sapphic, Pindaric and Common Odes; Songs and Tales on American and Patriotic Subjects, and also Imitations from the Greek, Latin, French, and Spanish.* Mobile, Ala.: Pollard & Dale, 1834.

Jones, Jacqueline, Peter H. Wood, Thomas Borstelmann, Elaine Tyler May, and Vicki L. Ruiz. *Created Equal: A Social and Political History of the United States.* New York: Pearson Longman, 2005.

Jones, John Griffing. *A Complete History of Methodism as Connected with the Mississippi Conference of the Methodist Episcopal Church, South.* Nashville, Tenn.: Southern Methodist Publishing, 1887.

Juricek, John T., ed. *Early American Indian Documents: Treaties and Laws, 1607–1789.* Alden T. Vaughan, series editor. Vol. 12, *Georgia and Florida Treaties, 1763–1776.* Bethesda, Md.: University Publications of America, 2002.

Kappler, Charles J., comp. and ed. *Indian Affairs: Laws and Treaties.* Vol. 2, *Treaties.* Washington, D.C.: Government Printing Office, 1904.

Kelsey, Rayner W. *Friends and the Indians, 1655–1917.* Philadelphia: Associated Executive Committee of Friends on Indian Affairs, 1917.

Kemp-Taylor, Jamie Kay. *William Middleton's (1685–1769) Children.* Abernathy, Tex.: the author, 2001.

Kimball, Geoffrey D. *Koasati Dictionary.* Lincoln: University of Nebraska Press, 1994.

———. *Koasati Grammar.* Lincoln: University of Nebraska Press, 1991.

Kinnaird, Lawrence, ed. "Spain in the Mississippi Valley, 1765–1794; Part 2, Post War Decade, 1782–1791." *Annual Report of the American Historical Association for the Year 1945,* vol. 3. Washington, D.C.: Government Printing Office, 1946.

Kirkland, Thomas J., and Robert M. Kennedy. *Historic Camden.* Columbia, S.C.: State Company, 1905.

Knight, Vernon James, Jr. "Fort Leslie and Upper Creek Ceramics of the Early Nineteenth Century." *Journal of Alabama Archaeology* 43 (1, 1997):35–45.

Krauthamer, Barbara, Tiya Miles, Celia E. Naylor, Claudio Saunt, and Circe Sturm. "Rethinking Race and Culture in the Early South." *Ethnohistory* 53 (2, 2006): 399–405.

Lackey, Richard S., comp. *Frontier Claims in the Lower South: Records of Claims Filed by Citizens of the Alabama and Tombigbee River Settlements in the Mississippi Territory for Depredations by the Creek Indians During the War of 1812*. Introduction by John D. W. Guice. New Orleans: Polyanthos, 1977.

Ladurie, Emmanuel Le Roy. *Times of Feast, Times of Famine: A History of Climate Since the Year 1000*. Translated by Barbara Bray. Garden City, N.Y.: Doubleday & Co., 1971.

Ladurie, Emmanuel Le Roy, and Micheline Baulant. "Grape Harvests from the Fifteenth through the Nineteenth Centuries." In *Climate and History: Studies in Interdisciplinary History*, edited by Robert I. Rotberg and Theodore K. Rabb, 259–69. Princeton: Princeton University Press, 1981.

Lambert, Frank. *Inventing the 'Great Awakening.'* Princeton: Princeton University Press, 1999.

Landsberg, Helmut E. "Past Climates from Unexploited Written Sources." In *Climate and History: Studies in Interdisciplinary History*, edited by Robert I. Rotberg and Theodore K. Rabb, 51–62. Princeton: Princeton University Press, 1981.

Lankford, George E. "Red and White: Some Reflections on Southeastern Symbolism." *Southern Folklore* 50 (1, 1993):54–80.

Lee, Harper. "Romance and High Adventure." In *Clearings in the Thicket: An Alabama Humanities Reader*, edited by Jerry Elijah Brown, 13–20. Macon, Ga.: Mercer University Press, 1985.

Lewis, David Levering. *W. E. B. DuBois: Biography of a Race*. New York: Henry Holt, 1993.

Lewis, David, Jr., and Ann T. Jordan. *Creek Indian Medicine Ways: The Enduring Power of Muskoke Religion*. Albuquerque: University of New Mexico Press, 2002.

Lincecum, Gideon. *Pushmataha: A Choctaw Leader and His People*. Introduction by Greg O'Brien. Tuscaloosa: University of Alabama Press, 2004.

Linton, Ralph. "Nativistic Movements." *American Anthropologist* 45(2, 1943):230–40.

Liston, Maria A., and Brenda J. Baker. "Reconstructing the Massacre at Fort William Henry, New York." *International Journal of Osteoarchaeology* 6 (1996):28–41.

Lockey, Joseph B., trans. "The St. Augustine Census of 1786." *Florida Historical Quarterly* 18 (July 1939):11–31.

Logan, Mary T. *Mississippi-Louisiana Border Country: A History of Rodney, Miss., St. Joseph, La., and Environs*. Baton Rouge, La.: Claitor's Publishing, 1970.

Lossing, Benson J. *Our Country: A Household History for All Readers*. 8 vols. New York: Lossing History Co., 1905.

———. *The Pictorial Field-Book of the War of 1812*. New York: Harper & Brothers, 1869.

———. "Scenes in the War of 1812, War with the Creek Indians." *Harper's New Monthly Magazine* 28 (167, 1864):598–616.

Loughridge, R. M., and D. M. Hodge. *English and Muskokee Dictionary, Collected from Various Sources*. St. Louis, Mo.: J. T. Smith, 1890.

Lowery, Robert, and William H. McCardle. *A History of Mississippi.* Jackson, Miss.: R. H. Henry & Co., 1891.

Lowrie, Walter, ed. *American State Papers, Public Lands.* Vol. 3, *1789–1834.* Washington, D.C.: Duff Green, 1834.

Lowrie, Walter, and Matthew St. Clair Clarke, eds. *American State Papers, Indian Affairs.* 2 vols. Washington, D.C.: Gales and Seaton, 1832.

Lowrie, Walter, and Walter S. Franklin, eds. *American State Papers, Claims.* Washington, D.C.: Gales and Seaton, 1834.

Lowrie, Walter, and Walter S. Franklin, eds. *American State Papers, Miscellaneous, Commencing May 22, 1809 and ending March 3, 1823.* Washington, D.C.: Gales and Seaton, 1834.

MacLean, J. P. "Shaker Mission to the Shawnee Indians". *Ohio Archaeological and Historical Publications* 11 (Columbus, 1903):215–29.

Martin, Jack B., and Margaret McKane Mauldin. *A Dictionary of Creek/Muskogee, with Notes on the Florida and Oklahoma Seminole Dialects of Creek.* Lincoln: University of Nebraska Press, 2000.

Martin, Joel W. "Cultural Contact and Crises in the Early Republic: Native American Religious Renewal, Resistance, and Accommodation." In *Native Americans and the Early Republic,* edited by Frederick E. Hoxie, Ronald Hoffman, and Peter J. Albert, 226–58. Charlottesville: United States Capitol Historical Society by the University Press of Virginia, 1999.

———. *The Land Looks After Us: A History of Native American Religion.* Oxford, U.K.: Oxford University Press, 2001.

———. "'My Grandmother Was a Cherokee Princess': Representations of Indians in Southern History." In *Dressing in Feathers: The Construction of the Indian in American Popular Culture,* edited by S. Elizabeth Bird, 129–47. Boulder, Col.: Westview Press, 1996.

———. *Sacred Revolt: The Muskogees' Struggle for a New World.* Boston: Beacon Press, 1991.

Mason, David Pierce. *Five Dollars a Scalp: The Last Mighty War Whoop of the Creek Indians.* Huntsville, Ala.: Strode Publishers, 1975.

———. *Massacre at Fort Mims.* Mobile, Ala.: Greenberry Publishing, 1975.

Matte, Jacqueline Anderson. *The History of Washington County: First County in Alabama.* Chatom, Ala.: Washington County Historical Society, 1982.

Mauelshagen, Carl, and Gerald H. Davis, eds. *Partners in the Lord's Work: The Diary of Two Moravian Missionaries in the Creek Indian Country, 1807–1813.* Georgia State College, School of Arts and Sciences, Research Paper 21. Atlanta, 1969.

May, Stephanie A. "Alabama and Koasati." In *Handbook of North American Indians.* Vol. 14, *Southeast,* edited by Raymond D. Fogelson, 407–14. Washington, D.C.: Smithsonian Institution, 2004.

McBride, W. Stephen, Kim Arbogast McBride, and Greg Adamson. *Frontier Forts in West Virginia: Historical and Archaeological Explorations.* Charleston: West Virginia Division of Culture and History, 2003.

McCartney, Martha W. "Daniel Beasley." Manuscript on file, Center for Archaeological Studies, University of South Alabama, Mobile, 2004.

———. "The Hatcher-Cheathan Site (44CF259): A Middling Farmstead in Rural Chester-field." Manuscript. Harrisonburg, Va.: James Madison University, Department of Anthropology, 1988.

———. "Middling Farm Households in York County, Virginia." Manuscript. Yorktown, Va.: Yorktown Victory Center, 2000.

McKenney, Thomas L., and James Hall. *The Indian Tribes of North America.* 3 vols. Edinburgh, Scotland: John Grant, 1833–34.

———. *History of the Indian Tribes of North America.* 3 vols. Philadelphia: F. W. Greenough, 1838.

McLoughlin, William G. *Cherokees and Missionaries, 1789–1839.* New Haven, Conn.: Yale University Press, 1984.

———, ed. *The Cherokee Ghost Dance.* Macon, Ga.: Mercer University Press, 1984.

McNemar, Richard. *The Kentucky Revival.* New York: E. O. Jenkins, 1846.

Medina Rojas, F. de Borja. *Jose de Ezpeleta: Gobernador de la Mobila, 1780–1781.* Seville, Spain: Escuela de Estudios Hispano-Americanos de Sevilla, 1980.

Meek, Alexander Beaufort. *The Red Eagle: A Poem of the South.* New York: D. Appleton and Company, 1855; reprinted with an introduction by Will T. Sheehan and George N. Bayer, Montgomery, Ala.: Paragon Press, 1914.

———. *Romantic Passages in Southwestern History.* Mobile, Ala.: S. H. Goetzel, 1857.

———. *Songs and Poems of the South.* Mobile, Ala: S. H. Goetzel, 1857.

Melish, John. *Travels through the United States of America in the Years 1806 & 1807, and 1809, 1810, & 1811.* Philadelphia: Printed for the author, 1818.

Mereness, Newton D., ed. *Travels in the American Colonies.* New York: Macmillan Company, 1916.

Merritt, Jane T. "Dreaming of the Savior's Blood: Moravians and the Indian Great Awakening in Pennsylvania." *William and Mary Quarterly* 54 (October 1997):723–46.

Miles, Tiya. *Ties That Bind: The Story of an Afro-Cherokee Family in Slavery and Freedom.* Berkeley: University of California Press, 2005.

[Milfort, Jean-Antoine Leclerc-]. *Chef de Guerre, Chez les Creeks.* Edited by Christian Buchet. Paris: Éditions France-Empire, 1994.

Milfort, Louis LeClerc. *Memoirs or a Quick Glance at My Various Travels and My Sojourn in the Creek Nation* [1802]. Translated and edited by Ben C. McCary. Savannah, Ga.: Beehive Press, 1972.

Miller, David Harry, and Jerome O. Steffen, eds. *The Frontier: Comparative Studies.* Norman: University of Oklahoma Press, 1977.

Mims, Sam. *Leaves from the Mims Family Tree: A Genealogic History.* Minden, La.: mimeographed by the author, 1961.

Mitchell, Margaret. *Gone with the Wind.* New York: Macmillan, 1936.

Monette, John W. *History of the Discovery and Settlement of the Valley of the Mississippi.* 2 vols. New York: Harper & Brothers, 1846.

Montesano, B. R. *Redstick: Or, Scenes in the South.* Cincinnati, Ohio: U. P. James, 1856.

Montgomery, Andrew. "Extract of a letter from Lieut. Montgomery of the Mississippi Volunteer Regiment to his father, Samuel Montgomery, Esq. of this county, dated Mobile, Sept. 4, 1813." *Washington Republican* 1 (September 29, 1813):3.

Mooney, James. *The Ghost Dance Religion and the Siouan Outbreak of 1890*. Smithsonian Institution, Bureau of American Ethnology, Annual Report 14(2). Washington, D.C., 1896.

———. "Tenskwatawa." In *Handbook of the American Indians North of Mexico*, edited by Frederick W. Hodge. Smithsonian Institution, Bureau of American Ethnology, Bulletin 30 (pt. 2, 1910):729–30.

Moore, John H. "Mvskoke Personal Names." *Names* 43 (September 1995):187–212.

Moore, Sue Burns. "Time Line for Dr. John Shaw." *Mississippi River Routes: Vicksburg Genealogical Society Quarterly Journal* 10 (Fall 2002):7–8.

Moser, Harold D., and Sharon McPherson, eds. *The Papers of Andrew Jackson*. Vol. 2, *1804–1813*. Knoxville: University of Tennessee Press, 1984.

Mould, Tom. *Choctaw Prophecy: A Legacy of the Future*. Tuscaloosa: University of Alabama Press, 2003.

Mulder, Philip N. *A Controversial Spirit: Evangelical Awakenings in the South*. Oxford, U.K.: Oxford University Press, 2002.

Nuñez, Theron A., Jr., ed. "Creek Nativism and the Creek War of 1813–1814." *Ethnohistory* 5 (1, 1958):1–47; 5 (2, 1958):131–75; 5 (3, 1958):292–301.

Oatis, Steven J. *A Colonial Complex: South Carolina's Frontiers in the Era of the Yamasee War, 1680–1730*. Lincoln: University of Nebraska Press, 2004.

O'Brien, Michael. *Conjectures of Order: Intellectual Life and the American South, 1810–1860*. 2 vols. Chapel Hill: University of North Carolina Press, 2004.

O'Brien, Sean Michael. *In Bitterness and in Tears: Andrew Jackson's Destruction of the Creeks and Seminoles*. Westport, Conn.: Praeger, 2003.

Olmstead, Earl P. *Blackcoats among the Delaware: David Zeisberger on the Ohio Frontier*. Kent, Ohio: Kent State University Press, 1991.

O'Malley, Nancy. *'Stockading Up': A Study of Pioneer Stations in the Inner Bluegrass Region of Kentucky*. University of Kentucky, Program for Cultural Resource Assessment, Archaeological Report 127. Lexington, 1987.

One of the Volunteers. "To Gen. F. L. Claiborne, Mobile, May 2, 1814." *Washington Republican* (May 25, 1814):2–3.

Orr, William Gates. "Surrender of Weatherford." *Alabama Historical Society Transactions, 1897–1898* 2 (1898):57–59.

Owsley, Frank L., Jr. "Editor's Notes." In *The Creek War of 1813 and 1814* by H. S. Halbert and T. H. Ball, 339–40. Chicago: Donohue & Henneberry, 1895; new edition, Tuscaloosa: University of Alabama Press, 1995.

———. "The Fort Mims Massacre." *Alabama Review* 24 (July 1971):192–204.

———. "Prophet of War: Josiah Francis and the Creek War." *American Indian Quarterly* 9 (3, 1985):273–93.

———. *Struggle for the Gulf Borderlands: The Creek War and the Battle of New Orleans, 1812–1815*. Gainesville: University Presses of Florida, 1981.

Owsley, Frank Lawrence, Jr., and Gene A. Smith. *Filibusters and Expansionists: Jeffersonian Manifest Destiny, 1800–1821*. Tuscaloosa: University of Alabama Press, 1997.

Page, Jake, and Charles Officer. *The Big One: The Earthquake that Rocked Early America and Helped Create a Science*. Boston: Houghton Mifflin, 2004.

Palmer, T. H. *The Historical Register of the United States.* 4 vols. Washington, D.C.: the author, 1814–18.

Paredes, J. Anthony. "Anthropological Report on the Poarch Band of Creeks." Manuscript. Washington, D.C.: Bureau of Indian Affairs, 1981.

———. "Back from Disappearance: The Alabama Creek Indian Community." In *Southeastern Indians Since the Removal Era,* edited by Walter L. Williams, 123–41. Athens: University of Georgia Press, 1979.

———. "Kinship and Descent in the Ethnic Reservation of the Eastern Creek Indians." In *The Versatility of Kinship: Essays Presented to Harry W. Basehart,* edited by Linda S. Cordell and Stephen Beckerman, 165–94. New York: Academic Press, 1980.

Paredes, J. Anthony, and Kenneth J. Plante. "A Reëxamination of Creek Indian Population Trends: 1738–1832." *American Indian Culture and Research Journal* 6 (4, 1983):3–28.

Pasley, Jeffrey L. *'The Tyranny of Printers': Newspaper Politics in the Early American Republic.* Charlottesville: University of Virginia Press, 2001.

Pate, James Paul. "The Chickamaugas: A Forgotten Segment of Indian Resistance on the Southern Frontier." Ph.D. dissertation, Department of History, Mississippi State University, 1969.

———, ed. *The Reminiscences of George Strother Gaines, Pioneer and Statesman of Early Alabama and Mississippi, 1805–1843.* Tuscaloosa: University of Alabama Press, 1998.

Pavao-Zuckerman, Barnet. "Culture Contact and Subsistence Change at Fusihatchee (1EE191)." Ph.D. dissertation, Department of Anthropology, University of Georgia, 2001.

———. "Vertebrate Subsistence in the Mississippian-Historic Transition." *Southeastern Archaeology* 19 (2, 2000):135–44.

Penick, James Lal, Jr. *The New Madrid Earthquakes.* Rev. ed. Columbia: University of Missouri Press, 1981.

Perdue, Theda. *"Mixed Blood" Indians: Racial Construction in the Early South.* Athens: University of Georgia Press, 2003.

———. "Race and Culture: Writing the Ethnohistory of the Early South." *Ethnohistory* 51 (Fall 2004):702–21.

Peters, Richard, ed. *The Public Statutes at Large of the United States of America.* Vol. 6, *The Private Statutes at Large of the United States of America.* Boston: Charles C. Little and James Brown, 1846.

Peterson, Jacqueline, and Jennifer S. H. Brown, eds. *The New Peoples: Being and Becoming Métis in North America.* Winnipeg: University of Manitoba Press, 1985.

Phillips, Paul Chrisler. *The Fur Trade.* 2 vols. Norman: University of Oklahoma Press, 1961.

Pickett, Albert James. *History of Alabama, and Incidentally of Georgia and Mississippi, from the Earliest Period.* 2 vols. Charleston, S.C.: Walker and James, 1851.

———. "McGillivray and the Creeks." *Alabama Historical Quarterly* 1 (Summer 1930): 126–48.

Piker, Joshua. *Okfuskee: A Creek Indian Town in Colonial America.* Cambridge: Harvard University Press, 2004.

Pollard, Tony, and Neil Oliver. *Two Men in a Trench: Battlefield Archaeology—The Key to Unlocking the Past.* London: Penguin Books, 2002.

———. *Two Men in a Trench II: Uncovering the Secrets of British Battlefields.* London: Penguin Books, 2003.

Pope, John. *A Tour through the Southern and Western Territories of the United States of North-America.* Richmond, Va.: John Dixon, 1792.

Posey, Walter B. "The Advance of Methodism into the Lower Southwest." *Journal of Southern History* 2 (November 1936):439–52.

Potter, Dorothy Williams. *Passports of Southeastern Pioneers, 1770–1823.* Baltimore, Md.: Gateway Press, 1982.

Prucha, Francis Paul. *American Indian Policy in the Formative Years: The Indian Trade and Intercourse Acts, 1790–1834.* Cambridge: Harvard University Press, 1962.

———. "Andrew Jackson's Indian Policy: A Reassessment." *Journal of American History* 56 (December 1969):527–39.

Rea, Robert R. *Major Robert Farmar of Mobile.* Tuscaloosa: University of Alabama Press, 1990.

Read, William A. *Indian Place Names in Alabama.* Rev. ed. by James B. McMillan. Tuscaloosa: University of Alabama Press, 1984.

Reid, John, and John H. Eaton. *The Life of Andrew Jackson: The Original 1817 Edition,* edited with an introduction by Frank L. Owsley, Jr. Tuscaloosa: University of Alabama Press, 1974.

Remini, Robert V. *Andrew Jackson and the Course of American Empire, 1767–1821.* New York: Harper & Row, 1977.

———. *Andrew Jackson and His Indian Wars.* New York: Viking Penguin, 2001.

Richter, Daniel K. *Facing East from Indian Country: A Native History of Early America.* Cambridge: Harvard University Press, 2001.

Riley, Elizabeth d'Autrey. *The Evergreen Old Historical Cemetery in Evergreen, Alabama, Conecuh County.* Brewton, Ala.: Escambia Printing and Office Supplies, 1971.

Riley, Sandra. *Homeward Bound: A History of the Bahama Islands to 1850, with a Definitive Study of Abaco in the American Loyalist Period.* Miami, Fla.: Island Research, 1983.

Rogin, Michael Paul. *Fathers and Children: Andrew Jackson and the Subjugation of the American Indian.* New York: Vintage Books, 1975.

Romans, Bernard. *A Concise Natural History of East and West Florida.* Edited by Kathryn E. Holland Braund. Tuscaloosa: University of Alabama Press, 1999.

Rowland, Dunbar. *Biographical and Historical Memoirs of Mississippi.* Chicago: Goodspeed, 1891.

———. "Military History of Mississippi, 1803–1898." *The Official and Statistical Register of the State of Mississippi, 1908.* Jackson: MDAH.

———, ed. *Encyclopedia of Mississippi History.* 2 vols. Madison, Wis: S. A. Brant, 1907.

———, ed. *History of Mississippi: Heart of the South.* Chicago: S. J. Clarke, 1925.

———, ed. *Mississippi: Comprising Sketches of Counties, Towns, Events, Institutions, and Persons, Arranged in Cyclopedic Form.* 4 vols. Atlanta, Ga.: Southern Historical Publishing Association, 1907.

———, ed. *Official Letter Books of W.C.C. Claiborne, 1801–1816.* 6 vols. Jackson, Miss.: State Department of Archives and History, 1917.

———, ed. *Third Annual Report of the Director of the Department of Archives and History of the State of Mississippi from October 1, 1903 to October 1, 1904, with Accompanying Historical Documents Concerning the Aaron Burr Conspiracy.* Nashville, Tenn.: Brandon Printing Co., 1905.

Rowland, Mrs. Dunbar [Eron]. *Andrew Jackson's Campaign against the British or the Mississippi Territory in the War of 1812.* New York: Macmillan Company, 1926.

———. *Mississippi Territory in the War of 1812.* Publications of the Mississippi Historical Society, Centenary Series 4. Jackson, 1921.

Russell, J. *The History of the War between the United States and Great Britain.* Hartford, Conn.:: B. & J. Russell, 1815.

Sabine, Lorenzo. *Biographical Sketches of Loyalists of the American Revolution, with an Historical Essay.* Boston: Little, Brown, 1864.

Sahlins, Marshall. *Apologies to Thucydides: Understanding History as Culture and Vice Versa.* Chicago: University of Chicago Press, 2004.

———. "Preface to Outside Gods: History Making in the Pacific." *Ethnohistory* 52 (Winter 2005):3–6.

Salinger, Sharon V. *Taverns and Drinking in Early America.* Baltimore, Md.: Johns Hopkins University Press, 2002.

Samuels, Peggy, and Harold Samuels. *Remembering the Maine.* Washington, D.C.: Smithsonian Books, 1995.

Sanders, Daniel C. *A History of the Indian Wars.* Rochester, N.Y.: Edwin Scrantom, 1828.

Sangster, Dess L., and Tom Sangster. *Fort Mims and the Tensaw Settlement.* Bay Minette, Ala.: Lavender Publishing, 1993.

Saunt, Claudio. *Black, White, and Indian: Race and the Unmaking of an American Family.* Oxford, U.K.: Oxford University Press, 2005.

———. "The Graysons' Dilemma: A Creek Family Confronts the Science of Race." In *Powhatan's Mantle: Indians of the Colonial Southeast,* rev. ed., edited by Gregory A. Waselkov, Peter H. Wood, and Tom Hatley. Lincoln: University of Nebraska Press, 2006.

———. *A New Order of Things: Property, Power, and the Transformation of the Creek Indians, 1733–1816.* Cambridge: Cambridge University Press, 1999.

———. "Taking Account of Property: Stratification among the Creek Indians in the Early Nineteenth Century." *William and Mary Quarterly,* 3rd ser., 57 (October 2000):733–60.

Sayre, Gordon M. *The Indian Chief as Tragic Hero: Native Resistance and the Literatures of America, from Moctezuma to Tecumseh.* Chapel Hill: University of North Carolina Press, 2005.

[Schoolcraft, Henry Rowe]. *Alhalla, or the Lord of Talladega. A Tale of the Creek War.* New York: Wiley and Putnam, 1843.

Schwarze, Edmund. *History of the Moravian Missions among Southern Indian Tribes of the United States.* Bethlehem, Pa.: Times Publishing, 1923.

Sciulli, Paul W., and Richard M. Gramly. "Analysis of the Ft. Laurens, Ohio, Skeletal Sample." *American Journal of Physical Anthropology* 80 (1, 1989):11–24.

Scott, Douglas D., and Richard A. Fox, Jr. *Archaeological Insights into the Custer Battle: An Assessment of the 1984 Field Season.* Norman: University of Oklahoma Press, 1987.

Scott, Douglas D., P. Willey, and Melissa A. Connor. *They Died with Custer: Soldiers' Bones from the Battle of the Little Big Horn.* Norman: University of Oklahoma Press, 1998.

Scott, Douglas D., Richard A. Fox, Jr., Melissa A. Connor, and Dick Harmon. *Archaeological Perspectives on the Battle of the Little Big Horn.* Norman: University of Oklahoma Press, 1989.

Severens, Martha R., and Kathleen Staples. "Benjamin Hawkins and the Creek Indians: A Study in Jefferson's Assimilation Policy." *Journal of Early Southern Decorative Arts* 29 (Winter 2003):1–38.

[Sewall, Lewis]. *The Last Campaign of Sir John Falstaff the II; or, The Hero of the Burnt-Corn Battle, A Heroi-Comic Poem.* St. Stephens, Mississippi Territory, 1815.

———. *The Miscellaneous Poems of Lewis Sewall, Esq., Containing the Last Campaign of Col J. Caller—Alias Sir John Falstaff the Second—Alias the Hero of Burnt Corn Battle; The Birth Progress, and Probable End of G. F. Mynheer Van Slaverchap's Grandson—Alias Doctor Furnace; The Battle for the Cow and Calf; The Canoe Fight; And Other Miscellaneous Matters.* Mobile, Ala., 1833.

[Shaw, Dr. John]. "Extract from the New Military Dictionary." *Washington Republican* 1 (October 13, 1813):2.

Sheehan, Bernard W. *Seeds of Extinction: Jeffersonian Philanthropy and the American Indian.* New York: Norton, 1973.

Sheidley, Nathaniel J. "Unruly Men: Indians, Settlers, and the Ethos of Frontier Patriarchy in the Upper Tennessee Watershed, 1763–1815." Ph.D. dissertation, Department of History, Princeton University, 1999.

Sheldon, Craig T., Jr., John W. Cottier, and Gregory A. Waselkov. "A Preliminary Report on the Subsurface Testing of a Portion of the Creek Indian Property at Hickory Ground." Montgomery. Ala.: Auburn University at Montgomery, 1988. Ms. on file, Alabama Historical Commission, Montgomery.

Shepard, Odell, and Willard Shepard. *Holdfast Gaines.* New York: Macmillan, 1946.

Shields, Joseph Dunbar. *Natchez: Its Early History.* Louisville, Ky.: J. P. Morton & Co., 1930.

Shoemaker, Nancy. *A Strange Likeness: Becoming Red and White in Eighteenth-Century North America.* Oxford, U.K.: Oxford University Press, 2004.

Siebert, Wilbur Henry. *Loyalists in East Florida, 1774–1785.* 2 vols. Deland: Florida Historical Society, 1929.

Smith, Marvin T. *Archaeology of Aboriginal Culture Change in the Interior Southeast: Depopulation during the Early Historic Period.* Gainesville: University Presses of Florida, 1987.

———. *Coosa: The Rise and Fall of a Southeastern Mississippian Chiefdom.* Gainesville: University Press of Florida, 2000.

Smith, Neal. "Letter of Dr. N. Smith to the Rev. James Smylie." *Alabama Historical Reporter* 1 (July 1880):2–3.

Smith, Robert Leslie. *Gone to the Swamp.* Latham, Ala.: Whirlwind Publishing, 2004.

Southerland, Henry deLeon, Jr., and Jerry Elijah Brown. *The Federal Road through Georgia, the Creek Nation, and Alabama, 1806–1836.* Tuscaloosa: University of Alabama Press, 1989.

Speck, Frank G. *The Creek Indians of Taskigi Town.* Memoirs of the American Anthropological Association 2. Washington, D.C., 1907.

Starbuck, David R. *The Great Warpath: British Military Sites from Albany to Crown Point.* Hanover, N.H.: University Press of New England, 1999.

Stern, Theodore. "The Creeks." In *The Native Americans,* edited by R. F. S. Spencer and J. D. Jennings. New York: Harper and Row, 1977.

Strickland, Ben, and Jean Strickland, comps. *Washington County, Mississippi Territory, 1803–1816 Tax Rolls.* Milton, Fla.: the compilers, 1980.

Sugden, John. *Blue Jacket: Warrior of the Shawnees.* Lincoln: University of Nebraska Press, 2000.

———. "Early Pan-Indianism: Tecumseh's Tour of the Indian Country, 1811–1812." *American Indian Quarterly* 10 (Fall 1986):273–304.

———. *Tecumseh: A Life.* New York: Henry Holt, 1997.

Sunderman, James F., ed. *Journey Into Wilderness: Journal of Jacob R. Motte.* Gainesville: University of Florida Press, 1963.

Swan, Major Caleb. "Position and State of Manners and Arts in the Creek, or Muscogee Nation in 1791." In *Information Respecting the History, Condition and Prospects of the Indian Tribes of the United States,* 6 vols., edited by Henry R. Schoolcraft, 5:251–83. Philadelphia: Lippincott, 1855.

Swanton, John R. *Early History of the Creeks and Their Neighbors.* Bureau of American Ethnology, Bulletin 73. Washington, D.C.: Government Printing Office, 1922.

———. "Religious Beliefs and Medical Practices of the Creek Indians." In *Forty-second Annual Report of the Bureau of American Ethnology, 1924–1925,* 473–672. Washington, D.C.: Government Printing Office, 1928.

———. "Social Organization and Social Usages of the Indians of the Creek Confederacy." In *Forty-second Annual Report of the Bureau of American Ethnology, 1924–1925,* 23–472. Washington, D.C.: Government Printing Office, 1928.

Sylestine, Cora, Heather K. Hardy, and Timothy Montler. *Dictionary of the Alabama Language.* Austin: University of Texas Press, 1993.

Tacitus. "For the Washington Republican." *Washington Republican* (October 20, 1813):3.

———. ["T."]. "Questions, Answers, Remarks." *Washington Republican* (December 1, 1813):2.

Taitt, David. "Journal of David Taitt's Travels from Pensacola, West Florida, to and through the Country of the Upper and the Lower Creeks, 1772." In *Travels in the American Colonies,* edited by Newton D. Mereness, 493–565. New York: Macmillan, 1916.

———. "Journal to and through the Upper Creek Nation." In *Documents of the American Revolution, 1770–1783 (Colonial Office Series),* edited by K. G. Davies, 5:251–72. Shannon: Irish University Press, 1974.

Tanner, Helen Hornbeck. *Zéspedes in East Florida, 1784–1790.* Miami, Fla.: University of Miami Press, 1963.

Tarvin, Dr. Marion Elisha. "The Muscogees or Creek Indians, 1519 to 1893." *Alabama Historical Quarterly* 17 (Fall 1955):125–45.

Tate, David. "David Tate to Cadet David Moniac, Letter of 1822." *Alabama Historical Quarterly* 19 (Winter 1957):407–8.

Tatum, Major Howell. "Topographical Notes and Observations on the Alabama River, August, 1814." In *Transactions of the Alabama Historical Society,* vol. 2, *1897–1898,* edited by Peter J. Hamilton and Thomas M. Owen. 2 (1898):130–77.

Tebbel, John, and Keith Jennison. *The American Indian Wars.* London: Phoenix Books, 1960.

Thomas, Daniel H. *Fort Toulouse: The French Outpost at the Alabamas on the Coosa,* with a new introduction by Gregory A. Waselkov. Tuscaloosa: University of Alabama Press, 1989.

Thompson, Lynn Hastie. *William Weatherford: His Country and His People.* Bay Minette, Ala.: Lavender Publishing, 1991.

Tiger, Buffalo, and Harry A. Kersey, Jr. *Buffalo Tiger: A Life in the Everglades.* Lincoln: University of Nebraska Press, 2002.

Toulmin, Harry. *A Digest of the Laws of the State of Alabama.* Cahaba, Ala.: Ginn & Curtis, 1823.

———. "Indian Warfare, Mobile, September 7." *Weekly Register* 5 (October 16, 1813):105–7.

———. *Statutes of the Mississippi Territory.* Natchez, Mississippi Territory: Samuel Terrell, 1807.

Townsend, Richard F., ed. *Hero, Hawk, and Open Hand: American Indian Art of the Ancient Midwest and South.* Chicago: Art Institute of Chicago, 2004.

U.S. Decennial Census Publications, 1790–1970. Woodbridge, Conn.: Research Publications, 1975.

U.S. Government. "An Act for the Relief of Certain Creek Indians." *U.S. Serials Set 173, House Document 200, 20th Cong., 1st sess.* Washington, D.C.: Gales & Seaton, 1828.

———. "An Act for the Relief of Samuel Manac." *U.S. Serials Set 173, House Document 200, 20th Cong., 1st sess.* Washington, D.C.: Gales & Seaton, 1828.

———. "An Act for the Relief of Susan Marlow . . . only surviving child of James Marlow, a Creek Indian, who lost his life at the destruction of Fort Mimms." *Private Claims, 24th Cong., 1st sess.* Washington, D.C., 1836.

———. "Heirs of Joshua Kennedy." *U.S. Serials Set 524, House Report 155, 30th Cong., 1st sess.* Washington, D.C., February 3, 1848.

———. "John Crowell, Peter Randon." *U.S. Serials Set, 31st Cong., 2nd sess., House Report No. 16.* Washington, D.C., January 29, 1851.

———. "Memorial on Behalf of Sundry Individuals Belonging to the Creek Indians." *U.S. Serials Set 213, Senate Document 65, vol. 2, 22nd Cong., 1st sess.* Washington, D.C.: Gales & Seaton, 1832.

———. *Message from the President of the United States, Transmitting a Report of the Secretary of War Relative to Murders Committed by the Indians, in the State of Tennessee.* Washington, D.C.: Roger C. Weightman, 1813.

———. "Report of the Select Committee of the House of Representatives." *U.S. Serials Set 161, House Report 98, 19th Cong., 2nd sess.* Washington, D.C., 1827.

———. *U.S. Census of Population.* Washington, D.C., 1811.

———. "Zachariah McGirth and Samuel Bradford." *U.S. Serials Set 263, House Document*

540, 23rd Cong., 1st sess., June 24, 1834, and *House Bill 547, House Reports*, vol. 4. Washington, D.C.: Gales & Seaton, 1834

Waldo, Samuel P. *Memoirs of Andrew Jackson, Major General in the Army of the United States; and Commander in Chief of the Division of the South.* Hartford, Conn.: S. Andrus, 1819.

Walker, Willard B. "Creek Confederacy Before Removal." In *Handbook of North American Indians.* Vol. 14, *Southeast,* edited by Raymond D. Fogelson, 373–92. Washington, D.C.: Smithsonian Institution, 2004.

Wallace, Anthony F. C. *Jefferson and the Indians: The Tragic Fate of the First Americans.* Cambridge, Mass.: Belknap Press, 1999.

——. *Revitalization and Mazeways: Essays on Culture Change.* Vol. 1, edited by Robert S. Grumet. Lincoln: University of Nebraska Press, 2003.

——. "Revitalization Movements." *American Anthropologist* 58 (1956):264–81.

Waselkov, Gregory. "Changing Strategies of Indian Field Location in the Early Historic Southeast." In *People, Plants, and Landscapes: Studies in Paleoethnobotany,* edited by Kristen J. Gremillion, 179–94. Tuscaloosa: University of Alabama Press, 1997.

——. "The Eighteenth-Century Anglo-Indian Trade in Southeastern North America." In *New Faces of the Fur Trade: Selected Papers of the Seventh North American Fur Trade Conference,* edited by Jo-Anne Fiske, Susan Sleeper Smith, and William Wicken, 193–222. East Lansing: Michigan State University Press, 1998.

——. "Exchange and Interaction since 1500." In *Handbook of North American Indians.* Vol. 14, *Southeast,* edited Raymond D. Fogelson, 686–96. Washington, D.C.: Smithsonian Institution, 2004.

——. *Fort Toulouse Studies.* Auburn University Archaeological Monograph 9. Auburn, Ala., 1984.

——. "French Colonial Trade in the Upper Creek Country." In *Calumet and Fleur-de-Lys: Archaeology of Indian and French Contact in the Midcontinent,* edited by John A. Walthall and Thomas E. Emerson, 35–53. Washington, D.C.: Smithsonian Institution Press, 1992.

——. "Historic Creek Indian Responses to European Trade and the Rise of Political Factions." In *Ethnohistory and Archaeology: Approaches to Postcontact Change in the Americas,* edited by J. Daniel Rogers and Samuel M. Wilson, 123–31. New York: Plenum Press, 1993.

——. "Intensive Subsurface Archaeological Investigations at the I-85 Shorter-Milstead Interchange, Alabama." Manuscript report to the Alabama Highway Department. Auburn, Ala.: Auburn University, 1984.

——. "Introduction: Recent Archaeological and Historical Research." In *Fort Toulouse: The French Outpost at the Alabamas on the Coosa,* by Daniel H. Thomas, vii–xlii. Tuscaloosa: University of Alabama Press, 1989.

——. "A Reinterpretation of the Creek Indian Barricade at Horseshoe Bend." *Journal of Alabama Archaeology* 32 (1986):94–107.

——. "Seventeenth-Century Trade in the Colonial Southeast." *Southeastern Archaeology* 8 (1989):117–33.

——. "Zumwalt's Fort: An Archaeological Study of Frontier Process." *Missouri Archaeologist* 40 (1979):1–129.

——, ed. "Culture Change on the Creek Indian Frontier." Final Report to the National Science Foundation (BNS-8305437) by Auburn University. Auburn, Ala., 1985.

Waselkov, Gregory A., and Kathryn E. Holland Braund. *William Bartram on the Southeastern Indians.* Lincoln: University of Nebraska Press, 1995.

Waselkov, Gregory A., and John W. Cottier. "European Perceptions of Eastern Muskogean Ethnicity." In *Proceedings of the Tenth Meeting of the French Colonial Historical Society, April 12–14, 1984,* edited by Philip P. Boucher, 23–45. Lanham, Md.: University Press of America, 1985.

Waselkov, Gregory A., and Bonnie L. Gums. *Plantation Archaeology at Rivière aux Chiens, ca. 1725–1848.* University of South Alabama, Center for Archaeological Studies, Archaeological Monograph 7. Mobile, 2000.

Waselkov, Gregory A., and Robert Eli Paul. "Frontiers and Archaeology." *North American Archaeologist* 2 (4, 1981):309–29.

Waselkov, Gregory A., and Craig T. Sheldon, Jr. "Cataloguing and Documenting the Historic Creek Archaeological Collections of the Alabama Department of Archives and History." Final Report to the National Science Foundation (BNS-8507469) by Auburn University. Auburn, Ala., 1987.

Waselkov, Gregory A., and Marvin T. Smith. "Upper Creek Archaeology." In *Indians of the Greater Southeast: Historical Archaeology and Ethnohistory,* edited by Bonnie G. McEwan, 242–64. Gainesville: University Press of Florida, 2000.

Waselkov, Gregory A., and Brian M. Wood. "The Creek War of 1813–1814: Effects on Creek Society and Settlement Pattern." *Journal of Alabama Archaeology* 32 (June 1986):1–24.

Waselkov, Gregory A., John W. Cottier, and Craig T. Sheldon, Jr. "Archaeological Excavations at the Early Historic Creek Indian Town of Fusihatchee (Phase 1, 1988–1989)." Final Report to the National Science Foundation (BNS-8718934) by Auburn University. Auburn, Ala., 1990.

Waselkov, Gregory A., Bonnie L. Gums and James W. Parker. *Archaeology at Fort Mims: Excavation Contexts and Artifact Catalog.* University of South Alabama Archaeological Monograph 12. Mobile, 2006.

Waselkov, Gregory A., Brian M. Wood, and Joseph M. Herbert. *Colonization and Conquest: The 1980 Archaeological Excavations at Fort Toulouse and Fort Jackson, Alabama.* Auburn University Archaeological Monograph 4. Montgomery, Ala.: Auburn University at Montgomery, 1982.

Watkins, Col. John A. "The Mississippi Panic of 1813." *Publications of the Mississippi Historical Society* 4 (Oxford, 1901), 483–91.

Weber, David J. *The Spanish in North America.* New Haven: Yale University Press, 1992.

Wells, Peter S. *The Barbarians Speak: How the Conquered Peoples Shaped Roman Europe.* Princeton, N.J.: Princeton University Press, 1999.

Wesson, Cameron B. "Households and Hegemony: An Analysis of Historic Creek Culture Change." Ph.D. dissertation, Department of Anthropology, University of Illinois at Champaign-Urbana, 1997.

West, Rev. Anson. *A History of Methodism in Alabama*. Nashville, Tenn.: Methodist Episcopal Church, South, 1893.

West, Elizabeth H., ed. "A Prelude to the Creek War of 1813–1814 in a Letter of John Innerarity to James Innerarity." *Florida Historical Quarterly* 18 (April 1940):247–66.

Wheeler, John Hill. *Historical Sketches of North Carolina from 1584 to 1851*. Philadelphia: Lippincott, Grambo, 1851.

White, Richard. "Frederick Jackson Turner and Buffalo Bill." In *The Frontier in American Culture*, edited James R. Grossman, 7–65. Berkeley: University of California Press, 1994.

———. *The Middle Ground: Indians, Empires, and Republics in the Great Lakes Region, 1650–1815*. Cambridge, U.K.: Cambridge University Press, 1991.

Willey, P., and Douglas D. Scott. "'The Bullets Buzzed Like Bees': Gunshot Wounds in Skeletons from the Battle of the Little Bighorn." *International Journal of Osteoarchaeology* 6 (1996):15–27.

Williams, Jack K. *Dueling in the Old South: Vignettes of Social History*. College Station: Texas A&M University Press, 1984.

Williams, John Lee. *The Territory of Florida, or Sketches of the Topography, Civil and Natural History of the Country, the Climate, and the Indian Tribes from the First Discovery to the Present Time*. Gainesvile: University of Florida Press, 1962.

Wills, Garry. *"Negro President": Jefferson and the Slave Power*. Boston: Houghton Mifflin, 2003.

Wilson, Samuel, Jr., ed. *Southern Travels: Journal of John H. B. Latrobe, 1834*. New Orleans: Historic New Orleans Collection, 1986.

Wolf, Eric. *Europe and the People without History*. Berkeley: University of California Press, 1982.

Wood, Peter H. *Black Majority: Negroes in Colonial South Carolina from 1670 through the Stono Rebellion*. New York: W. W. Norton, 1974.

———. "The Changing Population of the Colonial South: An Overview by Race and Region, 1685–1790." In *Powhatan's Mantle: Indians in the Colonial Southeast*. Rev. ed., edited by Gregory A. Waselkov, Peter H. Wood, and Tom Hatley. Lincoln: University of Nebraska Press, 2006.

———. "George Washington, Dragging Canoe, and Southeastern Indian Resistance." In *George Washington's South*, edited by Tamara Harvey and Greg O'Brien, 259–77. Gainesville: University Presss of Florida, 2004.

Woodward, Thomas S. *Woodward's Reminiscences of the Creek, or Muscogee Indians, Contained in Letters to Friends in Georgia and Alabama*. Montgomery: Barrett and Wimbish, 1859.

Works Progress Administration. *Interesting Transcripts of the British, French, & Spanish Records of the City and District of Mobile, State of Alabama, found in Probate Court in two volumes in the City of Mobile, 1715–1812*. 2 vols. Mobile: Municipal and Courts Record Project, 1937.

———. Historical Record Survey, Community Service Programs. *Transcriptions of Manuscript Collections of Louisiana: No. 1, The Favrot Papers, vol. 3, 1781–1792*. New Orleans: Tulane University, 1941.

Worth, John E. "The Lower Creeks." In *Indians of the Greater Southeast: Historical Archae-*

ology and Ethnohistory, edited by Bonnie G. McEwan, 265–98. Gainesville: University Press of Florida, 2000.

Wright, Amos J., Jr. *The McGillivray and McIntosh Traders on the Old Southwest Frontier, 1716–1815.* Montgomery, Ala.: New South Books, 2001.

Wright, Anne Mims. *A Record of the Descendants of Isaac Ross and Jean Brown.* Jackson, Miss., 1911.

Wright, J. Leitch, Jr. *Creeks and Seminoles: Destruction and Regeneration of the Muscogulge People.* Lincoln: University of Nebraska Press, 1986.

———. *William Augustus Bowles, Director General of the Creek Nation.* Athens: University of Georgia Press, 1967.

Wyatt-Brown, Bertram. *Honor and Violence in the Old South.* New York: Oxford University Press, 1986.

Wyman, Walker D., and Clifton B. Kroeber, eds. *The Frontier in Perspective.* Madison: University of Wisconsin Press, 1957.

Yellow Bird, Michael. "What We Want to Be Called: Indigenous Peoples' Perspectives on Racial and Ethnic Identity Labels." *American Indian Quarterly* 23 (Spring 1999):1–21.

Index